CITIZEN STEINBECK

Contemporary American Literature
Series Editor: Bob Batchelor

Gatsby: The Cultural History of the Great American Novel, by Bob Batchelor, 2013.

Michael Chabon's America: Magical Words, Secret Worlds, and Sacred Spaces, edited by Jesse Kavadlo and Bob Batchelor, 2014.

Hypermasculinities in the Contemporary Novel: Cormac McCarthy, Toni Morrison, and James Baldwin, by Josef Benson, 2014.

Stephen King's Contemporary Classics: Reflections on the Modern Master of Horror, edited by Philip L. Simpson and Patrick McAleer, 2015.

Beyond Gatsby: How Fitzgerald, Hemingway, and Writers of the 1920s Shaped American Culture, by Robert McParland, 2015.

Aging Masculinity in the American Novel, by Alex Hobbs, 2016.

James Jones: The Limits of Eternity, by Tony J. Williams, 2016.

Citizen Steinbeck: Giving Voice to the People, by Robert McParland, 2016.

CITIZEN STEINBECK

Giving Voice to the People

Robert McParland

ROWMAN & LITTLEFIELD
Lanham • Boulder • New York • London

Published by Rowman & Littlefield
A wholly owned subsidiary of The Rowman & Littlefield Publishing Group, Inc.
4501 Forbes Boulevard, Suite 200, Lanham, Maryland 20706
www.rowman.com

Unit A, Whitacre Mews, 26-34 Stannary Street, London SE11 4AB

British Library Cataloguing in Publication Information Available

Library of Congress Cataloging-in-Publication Data

Names: McParland, Robert, author.
Title: Citizen Steinbeck : giving voice to the people / Robert McParland.
Description: Lanham, Maryland : Rowman & Littlefield, [2016] | Series: Contemporary American Literature | Includes bibliographical references and index.
Identifiers: LCCN 2016012052 (print) | LCCN 2016025457 (ebook) | ISBN 9781442268302 (hardback : alk. paper) | ISBN 9781442268319 (electronic)
Subjects: LCSH: Steinbeck, John, 1902–1968—Influence. | Steinbeck, John, 1902–1968—Criticism and interpretation.
Classification: LCC PS3537.T3234 Z7324 2016 (print) | LCC PS3537.T3234 (ebook) | DDC 813/.52—dc23
LC record available at https://lccn.loc.gov/2016012052

Printed in the United States of America

CONTENTS

Acknowledgments   vii

Introduction   ix

1 The Life of John Steinbeck   1

2 A Sense of Place: Steinbeck's Early Fiction   27

3 *In Dubious Battle*   43

4 *Of Mice and Men*   59

5 *The Grapes of Wrath*   75

6 *Sea of Cortez*   101

7 Steinbeck at War   117

8 The Shorter Novels   133

9 *East of Eden*   159

10 *America and Americans*: Steinbeck in the 1960s   173

Notes   199

Bibliography   239

Index   251

About the Author   259

ACKNOWLEDGMENTS

The goal of this book is to introduce readers to the extraordinary variety in the works of John Steinbeck and to his commitment of care for humanity and his care for the art of writing. This study of Steinbeck owes a considerable debt to the work of many Steinbeck scholars and teachers of Steinbeck's writings. I write with appreciation for the continuing work of the Steinbeck Center. I am thankful for access to collections of the J. Pierpont Morgan Library and the New York Public Library and to the Steinbeck collection at Ball State University in Muncie, Indiana. Among the Steinbeck scholars whose work informs these pages are Jackson J. Benson, Susan Shillinglaw, Barbara Heavilin, Robert DeMott, John Ditsky, Warren French, John Timmerman, Tetsumaro Hayashi, Mimi Gladstein, Louis Owens, Donald Coers, Jay Parini, Susan Beegel, Danica Cerce, Henry Veggian, Michael J. Meyer, Brian Railsback, Luchen Li, Roy S. Simmonds, and many others. I am particularly indebted to the late Stephen K. George for his suggestions concerning new directions in Steinbeck studies. My thanks go to Bob Batchelor and Stephen Ryan, who have expertly guided the Contemporary American Literature series. This book also owes a debt to all of the teachers who have taught Steinbeck's stories, the often unsung heroes who work daily to expand our thinking, to improve our reading, and to help us to realize our voices and thoughts in writing. This book is dedicated to these thoughtful tenders of the human spirit.

INTRODUCTION

We have not yet discovered a path into the future. I think we will find one, but its direction may be unthinkable to us now.[1]

In *America and Americans*, the last book John Steinbeck wrote during his lifetime, he expressed care and concern for our world's future: "We are living in two periods. Part of our existence has leaped ahead and a part has lagged behind."[2] The suggestion that he was making is that our moral nature or humaneness must keep pace with our technological advancement. One might read his words alongside Alvin Toffler's claim, which soon followed in the 1970s, that people were living in "future shock," as the pace of technology, invention, and media increased. Steinbeck's insight was that human character needs to keep up with these developments. He was a writer of conscience who believed in both self-reliance and cooperative community, exercising care over one's work, honesty, and moral character. "Literature for Steinbeck was the stimulus to caring," writes his chief biographer, Jackson J. Benson. Steinbeck once told his agents and his publisher: "My whole work drive has been aimed at making people understand each other."[3]

John Steinbeck is relevant for us today because of his humanism, his accessibility, and the empathy that his stories can evoke. Playwright Arthur Miller once said that no other American writer "with the possible exception of Mark Twain . . . so deeply penetrated the political life of the country."[4] More broadly, Steinbeck's empathy for our world's marginalized people is important for a twenty-first-century world marked by conflict. Steinbeck continues to come alive for our time because he wrote books that a reader can participate in, while "writing seriously about little things and issues of great import," as Susan Shillinglaw has observed.[5] Steinbeck gave voice to common folks and found extraordinary worth in their ordinary lives. "The echoes haven't faded," Richard Corliss wrote of *The Grapes of Wrath* in *Time* (January 24, 2015), as his article "We're the People: John Ford's *The Grapes of Wrath* at 75" marked the anniversary of the 1940 film adaptation of the novel.[6] Steinbeck is still very much with us. In film and on the page, the echoes of Steinbeck's stories continue to come to life generation after generation.

There were about twenty-five hundred people living in Salinas, California, when John Steinbeck was born there in 1902. When he published *The Grapes of Wrath* there were about seventy-six million people living in the United States. That is about one-quarter of the population of the United States today. Amid new generations of readers, forty years after Steinbeck's death, Robert Gottlieb, writing in the *New York Review of Books* (April 17, 2008), asked a reasonable question: "Why Steinbeck?"[7] After all, Steinbeck has not always been esteemed by literary critics. True, he won the Pulitzer Prize and a National Book Award for *The Grapes of Wrath* and later was awarded the Nobel Prize. However, he was often criticized in his time and he was modest about his accomplishments. He confided in a 1946 diary: "I am not a great writer, but I am a competent one and I am an experimental one."[8] Is considering his work in the second decade of the twenty-first century an exercise in nostalgia, recalling an author best known for writing period pieces of the 1930s? Or is there something universal in Steinbeck's fictional world that speaks to our contemporary society? In a complex global age of cultural convergence, in what respect is Steinbeck an international writer, a storyteller for all of us? Why read Steinbeck *now*?

Perhaps the answer is that his work is inescapable. Books like those of Steinbeck help us to make sense of our own times. In 2002, the centenary of Steinbeck's birth, a variety of articles about him appeared in the news media. Subsequently, Steinbeck was deemed highly relevant by some journalists who focused attention on *The Grapes of Wrath*, connecting the novel with the economic recession. Novels like *Of Mice and Men, East of Eden*, and *In Dubious Battle* touch upon universal human concerns and help us to interpret the contemporary world. They not only emerge from a specific time and place, but they illuminate the human condition and address fundamental themes of importance to us all. They prompt us to think critically and contextually about our sociocultural world and what we value.

Steinbeck lingers among us as one of those American authors that most everyone has read, or has been asked to read in a school setting, at one time or another. Virtually all of Steinbeck's published works remain in print. *The Grapes of Wrath* sells thousands of copies every year. *Of Mice and Men* had another run on the Broadway stage in 2014. The story remains a staple in schools; it is a short novel that fits nicely into the high school curriculum. *The Red Pony* still arouses sentiment and *The Pearl* provides a brief moral tale for classroom use, while stories like "The Chrysanthemums" are regularly anthologized in college texts. Steinbeck is a storyteller who is accessible. His language is not complex and his syntax is not involved. He tells the stories of ordinary people, characters whose lives are lived on the margin of the social mainstream. Steinbeck created stories he hoped that people would read. "If people don't read it, it isn't going to be literature," he wrote.[9]

To read John Steinbeck is to open a mixed bag of stories, journalism, and plays that also appear as short novels. It is to enter fiction that ranges from realism to fabulism, from naturalism to the folktale, and from grand accomplishments to lesser accomplishments. In Steinbeck's work we meet with the flawed greatness of a writer who experimented with fiction, drama, and nonfiction forms. He was not always powerful but he was often poignant. Steinbeck's authorized biographer Jackson J. Benson recognizes that "the quality of his fiction is very uneven."[10] However, the variety of stories, essays, and plays he produced remain valuable and often entertaining and provocative reading.

Steinbeck has been labeled a realist, a writer of naturalism, a creator of sentimentalism, and a proletarian writer of the people, and his work has been criticized for being too overt in its symbolism.[11] His naturalism has to be qualified because it is in many respects unlike that of Frank Norris or Theodore Dreiser; it mixes with mythology and archetypes and allegory. One cannot simply label Steinbeck a proletarian novelist because while *In Dubious Battle* and *The Grapes of Wrath* can be read as supportive of workers, those novels rise to a universal quality and his other work steers away from the proletarian concerns of the 1930s. One thing is for certain: Steinbeck, a writer whose work falls into the middle decades of the twentieth century, has almost always been popular with readers.

Steinbeck's chief biographer, Jackson J. Benson, presents Steinbeck as a consistently popular writer whose books sell every year in the hundreds of thousands. This is surely because *Of Mice and Men*, *The Pearl*, *The Red Pony*, and *The Grapes of Wrath* appear regularly on school reading lists. To this he adds that as he worked on his biography of Steinbeck he met many readers "from plumbers to librarians to electrical engineers" who told him of how they "enjoyed Steinbeck's work." He describes Steinbeck as a writer of the people, rather than one who "wrote to please the academy."[12] Thus, Steinbeck appears as the epitome of the popular author and one of considerable longevity. He is also often regarded as "the spokesman for the thirties."[13] However, he produced many works of merit after *The Grapes of Wrath* and there was no falling off after that work of his strengths as a novelist, as some critics have claimed.[14] That Steinbeck may survive "as a classic young adult author" as Walter Clemons suggests is advantageous, since his stories enter the imagination of young readers. Yet it is also a limitation. The clear style of much of his writing tends to hide a more complex pearl beneath.

It is the humanity in Steinbeck's characters and his themes that best translates to our own time. When political scientist Michael Sandel wrote in *Democracy's Discontent* (1996) that "we must not become storyless," he was addressing the health of the American polity with an age-old truth.[15] Our age needs storytellers who tell stories of people's dreams. We need ways to look at our present condition through the lens of the past. We need to tell our stories. Literature, including Steinbeck's stories and essays, revives memories; it unearths archetypes; it retells important stories. Such stories are the fabric of a society, the cultural memory of individuals, families, communities, and nations. They are shared in conversation. They are read in the privacy of homes. They are cast into drama on movie screens. Like the enduring tale of *The Odyssey* or the fables and myths of indigenous cultures, what is universal in stories, a repository of the past, is continually renewed in new forms. Stories entertain. They teach. They remember.

Steinbeck, the storyteller, can be reconceived in ways that point to our world today. The ghost of Tom Joad, who once said "I'll be everywhere in the dark," is indeed everywhere. For he is the human spirit. Whether we hear echoes of Henry Fonda playing Tom Joad, or listen to songs by Woody Guthrie ("Tom Joad," 1941) and Bruce Springsteen ("The Ghost of Tom Joad," 1995), that figure represents millions of dedicated human lives and a kind of spiritual vision that can carry us into the future. If *The Grapes of Wrath* returns to the screen in tribute to the filmmaking craft of director John Ford the struggles and hopes of its characters and setting will still echo in our own time. Steinbeck chose to tell the stories of a class of people who were outsiders: the striking workers of *In Dubious Battle*, the Mexican immigrants of *Tortilla Flat*, the workers of *Cannery Row*, and the misfits George and Lennie in *Of Mice and Men*. Each of these characters is in an uncertain position, has limited means, and has no privileged access to an American middle-class dream. Steinbeck is not engaged in polemics; he is focused upon revealing the humanity, hopes, and search for freedom in the lives of his characters.

Steinbeck seems destined to continue to have mixed critical responses from literary critics. It also appears that he will continue to have a loyal following of common readers. All of his major works remain in print and *The Grapes of Wrath* and *Of Mice and Men* sell thousands of copies every year. Steinbeck remains popular in Europe and has become assigned reading in middle school, high school, and college classes in England. He was a writer who wrote in diverse forms: fiction, journalism, travel narratives, science writing, plays, propaganda pieces, political speeches, wartime correspondence, and the newspaper column. Yet some critics have complained that such variety came with "uneven" results. Steinbeck has been read as a writer of defeated idealism and as a moral writer. Some have read him as if he was a modern prophet crying out for social justice. He has been approached as a political writer and as a critic of capitalism, who has been read through the lens of ideology. Other critics, noting that *Of Mice and Men*, *The Pearl*, and *The Red Pony* receive a lot of attention among young readers, wonder if Steinbeck might be an author that one reads when young and then gets over.

The gap between Steinbeck's popularity and his critical reception is curious. He stands across that divide between popular and literary fiction. He wrote for a middlebrow audience in much of his fiction: *East of Eden*, *Sweet Thursday*, *The Winter of Our Discontent*. However, he wrote these books intensely and with purpose, not simply to churn out entertainment. He wrote with social concern in novels like *In Dubious Battle*, *Cannery Row*, and *The Grapes of Wrath*. He wrote journalism on location in California and overseas in Europe during World War II. He also wrote plays: *Of Mice and Men*, *Burning Bright*. Supporting his work was his fierce dedication to writing as an art and a form of action. As Benson has pointed out, Steinbeck had more than a passing interest in biology, anthropology, and astronomy and an ecological world view.[16] Steinbeck was not a political writer, although books like *In Dubious Battle* and *The Grapes of Wrath* triggered much political discussion. Steinbeck's *The Grapes of Wrath* and *Of Mice and Men* faced censorship. He and his work were often criticized. However, as is often the case, the response of the critic often says more about the critic and the critic's reading than it does about the writer and his work. Steinbeck's work captured a vision of a place and time but also, in most of his writing, his vision transcends that place and time to provide a thoughtful and sometimes arresting look at our humanity.[17]

This book looks at the public value of Steinbeck's work and at what readers today may discover in his stories. It examines the care that he brought to his work and articulated in his writing and the care that teachers of his stories practice as they share them with their students. Steinbeck's work has been a focus for comments by reviewers and critics for some eighty-five years. He has been a subject for full-length biographies by Benson as well as Jay Parini and the anticipated biography by William Sander, whose working title, as of this writing, is *Mad at the World: John Steinbeck and the American Century*. That book is expected to appear in 2019, which will be the eightieth anniversary year for *The Grapes of Wrath*. The critical world of 2019 will not be the critical world of 1929–1968, the years during which Steinbeck penciled stories on legal pads or typed his work. This author wrote during the era in which the formalist close reading of the New Critics predominated. "Close reading," or "practical criticism," aimed at careful analytic interpretation and attentiveness to what was on the page. Such focused concern on the text was similar to the observation of the scientist upon the object of study. The aesthetic response to literature respected the organic unity of the poem, or the story, and inquired into its specifically literary features. What mattered was the text itself. The biography of an author mattered little and even if an author's intentions could be glimpsed they were not of concern in the interpretation of the text. The idiosyncratic and subjective responses of individual readers were not as relevant as the story or poem's presumed meaning. The text would reveal its qualities objectively to the discerning critic. It was assumed that the story was something like a solid object and that the meaning of the story could surely be found.

This approach has its merits and it continues to be a dominant approach in introductory English and language arts classrooms. It provides a pedagogical method. Teachers instruct students about figurative language: metaphors and similes, imagery, symbols, personification, and other devices. The traditional structures of poetry are presented: rhyme scheme, sonnet forms, couplets and quatrains, alliteration, assonance and consonance. Stories and poems are analyzed, dissected like Doc's frogs in *Cannery Row*. One investigates the writing's form, its tensions and paradoxes, the ways in which it works. A study of the qualities of language leads toward a grasp of meaning. Terry Eagleton has pointed out, for example, that F. R. Leavis would work toward a formal criticism of poetry and a "moral" criticism of fiction.[18] Literature could be seen to have a didactic purpose.

Even so, Steinbeck's fiction can be read in a variety of ways and questioned via many approaches. His experiments with fiction were often not appreciated by formalist critics who insisted upon aesthetic quality and applied formal criteria to his productions. Some critics have asserted that Steinbeck was a popular writer but not a great writer. However, popular readers often read differently than critical ones and people in different regions and times bring different experiences to their reading. Some readers—particularly those in Eastern Europe and Russia—interpreted his novels of the 1930s through a political lens. Steinbeck's social novels like *The Grapes of Wrath* were controversial among some groups of readers: some readers in California were appalled by what he had written in that novel. The earthy language of *The Grapes of Wrath*, or the language in the often-taught *Of Mice and Men*, remains controversial in some school systems. Even the Steinbeck critics who so much value his work do not always agree on the quality of the writing that they see. Warren French and Roy S. Simmonds, for example, have contended that there was a falling off in the strength of Steinbeck's work after *In Dubious Battle*, *Of Mice and Men*, and *The Grapes of Wrath*. Meanwhile, Robert DeMott, John Ditsky, and others have countered that he was an experimental writer anticipating postmodernism and that his style and topics changed across the years.[19]

In 2002, in one of his brief book introductions, Harold Bloom wrote that it would be good if in the age of George Bush "the liberal and humane Steinbeck achieved prominence as a fiction writer." In that centenary year of Steinbeck's birth Bloom's next sentence was like a sigh:

"Alas, rereading the best of his novels and stories is a very mixed experience." Steinbeck's *The Grapes of Wrath* is an important book that ought to be read, Bloom concluded. However, Steinbeck never knew Oklahoma any better than he knew Afghanistan. The rural poor are conveyed more sharply by Eudora Welty or Robert Penn Warren. William Faulkner's Bundren family is portrayed with more "aesthetic dignity" than Steinbeck's Joads. It is John Ford's film that makes Steinbeck's characters appear larger. Consequently, *The Grapes of Wrath* and its predecessor *In Dubious Battle* are "period pieces," says Bloom, and the rest of Steinbeck is a mixed bag.[20]

With Steinbeck scholars such as Robert DeMott, Susan Shillinglaw, Barbara Heavilin, Jackson J. Benson, and others, this book argues for a reappraisal. Literature must be transposed generation after generation. If it is to mean something to today's readers and to future generations its themes have to be brought to life again *now*. We are continually reinterpreting writers like Steinbeck because his stories address human concerns, experiences, and aspects of the human condition. History changes, but what is universal still speaks to us across the generations. Through new films, the efforts of classroom teachers, and paperback Penguin editions of Steinbeck novels, a new generation meets Steinbeck's stories.

This introduction to Steinbeck's work intends to show that Steinbeck was a writer of wide interests, a man intrigued by metaphysics, ecological science, notions of consciousness and collective behavior. His clear, journalistic surfaces work across a series of "levels," as Shillinglaw points out, referring to Steinbeck's comments on *Cannery Row* to Joseph Henry Jackson.[21] Threads of inquiry weave through his writings about "ancient wisdom" (*The Pastures of Heaven*), communal rituals (*The Grapes of Wrath*), and Biblical themes (*East of Eden*).[22] In addition, Steinbeck's work continues to be valuable to student readers and to their teachers. He continues to be a doorway to literary reading and social reflection.

In Steinbeck, California is everywhere. He sets several of his strongest works of fiction in California, placing his array of characters in a specific place and time. Yet in this specificity is universality: they are studies of human aspiration and struggle in microcosm. His stories of "underdogs" in *Tortilla Flat*, *In Dubious Battle*, and *Of Mice and Men* are essential reading in a world of socioeconomic strife and diversity. They are important for the ways in which they draw our attention to the human condition and to the quality of care that is necessary for humanity to survive and prosper.[23]

To expand the boundaries of our conversation about Steinbeck I follow Robert DeMott's approach in *Steinbeck's Typewriter* (1995), when he writes that his book is "not a traditional scholarly monograph (in the heroic sense of that term) with a clearly developed thesis and commensurately uniform presentation." Rather, this book, which argues that Steinbeck is a crucially important ethical writer for our time, provides a reappraisal of Steinbeck's writings. This study is designed as an introduction for readers who have read some of Steinbeck stories, or would like to read them. It is for those who have seen a film adaptation of a Steinbeck story and would like to learn more about the man and his work. To introduce Steinbeck and to reassess his value for us as a voice that is still relevant for us in the twenty-first century, Steinbeck's biography is coupled with an overview and analyses of his works and remarks from teachers who regularly engage people with his writings. As DeMott wrote in his introduction, what follows here may be much like an informal classroom lecture, an invitation to explore why Steinbeck is important for our lives.[24] This approach to the work of John Steinbeck is a weaving of critical discourses with a form of personal criticism that focuses upon literature and education.

One of the goals of the Contemporary American Literature series is to approach significant authors and works of literature within their cultural and historical context. That is the approach that is taken here: one of intertextual, dialogical criticism and new historicism—with DeMott's emphasis on returning "meaningful personal emphasis to critical writing." We each read uniquely and I would like to encourage you to read through the rich variety of Steinbeck's works. My readings may differ from yours. What I hope to do here is to let you know a little about how different critics have viewed aspects of Steinbeck's stories. I would also like to share some comments from teachers in the United States, Canada, and Great Britain who have taught *Of Mice and Men*, *The Red Pony*, *The Pearl*, *The Grapes of Wrath*, and others in their classrooms. Hopefully, this can help us all to read John Steinbeck's stories and nonfiction with greater facility.

Citizen Steinbeck: Giving Voice to the People offers a brief for the importance of reading books like *The Grapes of Wrath* and *Of Mice and Men* because these works provoke critical thinking, moral reflection, and the development of empathy. This gathering of reflections upon Steinbeck's achievement is a personal engagement with Steinbeck's novels, plays, and nonfiction that is informed by primary source material from archives and is firmly situated within Steinbeck criticism. This book is an introduction and a meditation, supported by criticism and interviews, upon what Steinbeck's *The Grapes of Wrath* and *Of Mice and Men*, among other Steinbeck works, hold for the education and future of America and for our world.

A QUALITY OF CARE: LITERATURE, ETHICS, AND EMPATHY

"My whole work drive has been aimed at making people understand each other," John Steinbeck wrote in a letter in 1938, criticizing himself for writing a story that he then discarded: "the aim of which is to cause hatred through partial understanding."[25] John Steinbeck was an ethical writer. He practiced a form of virtue ethics and an ethics of care. He was a writer of conscience with a sense of mission to try to gain what Warren French has called "a better understanding of the conflicting forces at war in human nature."[26] One may argue that his books contain vulgar language, scenes of quiet desperation, violence, and prostitutes and preachers whose sexual habits are a disgrace to the cloth. Yet he was a writer who urged responsibility and who was responsible in his writing. He was a writer of care for the word, the crafted story that speaks of human concern. Steinbeck once wrote that "one job of a writer is to set down his time as nearly as he can understand it."[27]

Steinbeck does not so much impose a moral design as present a fictional world for our view. He offers a variety of characters who are social underdogs, people with a fighting spirit, and as he draws our sympathy for these people he appears to call for mutual respect, reverence, and compassion. He writes of people who care—the Joads, the Wilsons, Mae the waitress and Al the cook in *The Grapes of Wrath*—and he writes of those who do not care: the camp enforcers in that novel, the tinker in "The Chrysanthemums." Steinbeck writes of how people face difficult circumstances. He deals with the Darwinian view that there is a relentless struggle in nature. Naturalism was based in scientific determinism: that our lives are determined by natural laws, natural forces, environment, and

heredity. Steinbeck took this quite seriously but he was not only a determinist. He believed in the capacity of human will. He also emphasized
the interconnection in nature and between human lives.

To say that John Steinbeck was a writer of ethical importance raises
some questions: What is meant when we say "ethical fiction" and what is
the value of reading Steinbeck as a writer of ethical fiction in the midst of
our postmodern condition? Can reading literature make one a better person? What kinds of literature might assist in this process? After all, don't
people read differently? What one person sees and "gets" from a story, a
poem, or a play may not be what another person gets from it. Oscar
Wilde, in response to a review of his *The Picture of Dorian Gray*, asserted: "The sphere of art and the sphere of ethics are absolutely distinct
and separate."[28] Are they? Of what value is literature in a postmodern age
of cultural relativism and does it have both an aesthetic and a social
role?[29]

Then there are questions that may arise in us that are more personal.
What responsibility do we take for the world? What meaning do we
construct when we are reading Steinbeck's stories and essays? Steinbeck
viewed life holistically and ecologically, as interrelation. He sought
understanding. He wrote within a cultural moment and the humanity and
sense of value in his stories transcended this time, place, and culture.
Steinbeck was continually interested in values and this corresponds to his
interest in King Arthur's knights. The chivalric code is based upon notions of honor, character, and duty. Individuals transform ethical principles into ethical character and action. If we are to speak of Steinbeck as
an ethical writer, we might consider an ethical tradition stemming from
Plato, who, echoing Socrates, speaks of the good life and says that the
good life and the good person are connected. Or we might turn to Aristotle's notion of the good that connects the individual and the *polis*, or
community. Steinbeck's writings interrogate the interactions of individuals and, probing the modern human community, appear to say something
about the quest for virtue.

We now read literature in a variety of ways: poststructuralism, decon-
struction, feminisms, Marxist analysis, and gender theory among them.
For Roland Barthes, for example, the creation of meaning depends upon
the reader and there is a radical indeterminacy of language. So, if meaning is not fixed, how can a text convey a moral message? Yet language
does communicate. Whatever its ambiguity or potential for misreading

we often do have some agreed-upon terms. We can dialogue about stories. If we acknowledge the plurality of interpretations we might identify some common responses. We may ask, why *these* responses?[30]

The author is a means, a path for meaning. The reader will construct meaning from what he or she reads. What has been produced textually and contextually and intertextually comes into the reader's world, just as this book has come to you. Steinbeck's books need us if they are to have any moral impact upon the twenty-first century. So, there is the hope that we may read Steinbeck with openness to various viewpoints and search for meaning beyond the play of signifiers on the page. To bring Steinbeck to a general audience in a new era calls for us to not give up on language, or on aesthetic quality, but, rather, to believe in a meaningful universe, or in our meaning-making capacities, and extend our reflections with theory, philosophy, and cultural reflection.

Today, at least in democratic nations, we are generally inclined to consider the rights of individuals, to prize acceptance of differences among people. These notions exist in the social and political currents of our time. An ethical sense, a sense of what we value, lies behind this. We may resist being told how to live life via moral guidance, observe Steve Brie and William T. Rossiter. Yet this generation is repeatedly being told how to live life "by fashion designers, by car manufacturers, by supermarkets, by gossip magazines, by computer programmers, by the blogosphere, by social networking sites."[31] Steinbeck's voice still warrants some attention amid the chatter.

Wayne Booth once called books "the company we keep" and he explored issues of meaning and the reception of literature. He encouraged the exploration of how a story affects an audience. What might be a writer's responsibility to the truth or to the people that he was writing about?[32] Even so, J. Hillis Miller points out: "Ethics, or even ethics in its literary dimension, is a dangerous and slippery field, since it so tempts those who enter it to generalized speculation or prescription."[33] While that is so, to approach Steinbeck as an ethical writer is natural. Stories like *The Grapes of Wrath* stake a moral claim.

In the meeting of minds that reading allows for, our values are engaged as we read a novel like *The Grapes of Wrath*. We may dialogue about the text, if and how it moves us, and the values we come to it with. Stories—in books, plays, films, and television dramas—do involve us in thought about ethical concerns. Stories are our moral teachers, Booth

observed. They "hook us into plots that are inseparable from that thinking."[34] Of course, the same story may have different effects on different
readers. We bring our lives and our past reading experiences to what we
read. It is undeniable that "we are at least partially constructed in our
most fundamental moral character by the stories we have heard, or read,
or viewed, or acted out in amateur theatricals, the stories we have really
listened to," Booth wrote.[35] Literature is diverse and Booth has argued for
a critical pluralism. Aesthetic quality, craft, and the search for beauty
need not be "sacrificed to preaching."[36]

John Steinbeck was concerned about clarity and freshness in the uses
of language as well as in social justice, democracy, and upholding human
dignity. In this respect, to practice the craft of writing and thinking was
for him fully allied with his concern with human understanding. We
might ask what becomes of language when we use abbreviations instead
of words? What happens when we coin clichés like "no-brainer," which
require no brains to repeat? What becomes of learning and human knowledge when one substitutes the click of a button for research and lengthy
reflection? It matters which words we use to express our lives, to tell our
stories and share our feelings. In his 1996 book *The Education of the
Heart*, Thomas Moore points out that some words are evocative and when
they "ring true" we know that they are close to the truth that we feel.
Some ideas that take form in words carry life. This is the soul of a text.

Steinbeck's stories invite us to participate with our imaginations and
our feelings: to laugh or cry, to feel sympathy and tenderness, or to burn
with indignation. At times Steinbeck practices biocentrism: an effort to
see ecological relationships from a nonhuman perspective. He shows us
the turtle on the road in *The Grapes of Wrath*. He welcomes us to hear the
frogs that Mack and the boys scout for as they make their excursion from
Cannery Row. We are brought on travels with Charley, Steinbeck's dog.
Steinbeck gives us interdependent groups of people, or "the group mind."
This perspective is somewhat like that of ecologist Aldo Leopold when
he writes: "A thing is right when it tends to preserve the integrity, stability, and beauty of the biotic community. It is wrong when it tends otherwise."[37]

When Stephen K. George gathered essays for *The Moral Philosophy
of John Steinbeck* (2005) he and his contributors identified a central moral core of John Steinbeck's work. Such an approach to Steinbeck recognizes that there is an ethical force to literature that has been addressed in

recent years by philosophers from Martha Nussbaum to Richard Rorty. Wayne Booth, in his book *The Company We Keep* (1988), argued for a re-centering of ethics in our contact with literature. Booth, who spoke of "friendship with books" and of "the exchange of gifts," proposed that we who are concerned with ethics are interested in any effect on the *ethos*: in this case, on that of a reader or listener. Powerful stories, he said, may contribute toward a conversation among us. Martha Nussbaum's *Poetic Justice: The Literary Imagination and Public Life* (1995) likewise made a case for an ethical fiction. Nussbaum evidently has notions about how a work of literature, like Dickens's *Hard Times*, should be read and readers may or may not read in the manner that Nussbaum anticipates they will. However, it is clear that reading can have consequences, as she suggests, including moral and political ones. Imaginative literature, like the novels and stories of John Steinbeck, conveys ideas, often with considerable power. Something happens when we keep company with literature. So we are led to ask, what happens as we read the works of John Steinbeck? With what quality do I accompany this author and these characters, plots, and scenes? Who am I as I read and with whom am I keeping company?

When the novelist John Gardner wrote *On Moral Fiction* (1978), he rested his argument upon a tradition of the book that has been important in Western culture: the belief that fiction can point to significant issues and can have a moral effect upon readers. However, much literary theory has not been comfortable with ethical criticism. According to Richard A. Posner, Helen Vendler, for example, has rejected "treating fictions as moral pep pills" because of "the complex psychological and moral motives of a work of art."[38] It has been argued by others that the value of art cannot be ethical: some art is good although its ethics are bad. Oscar Wilde once wrote: "There is no such thing as a moral or an immoral book. Books are well written or badly written."[39] So what can we say about literature's presumed salutary effects upon the reader?

Steinbeck's stories and essays recognize that people are relational. A sense of place, tenderness toward creatures, and assertions of the dignity of common people are frequently present in the stories. *The Log from the Sea of Cortez* underscores the ecological relationship between the human and nonhuman world but so too does much of the fiction. The individual's interaction with a group, the phalanx theory, is repeatedly explored in his work. Steinbeck presents a deep social web of interrelationship that calls for helping, nurturing, and mutual respect. To use Carol Gilligan's language, social progress in the Steinbeck novel or essay has to do with the "progress of affiliative relationship."[40]

There are some interesting correspondences between Steinbeck's work and what we now call the ethics of care. This is a normative ethical theory that emerged from feminists who placed an emphasis upon responsiveness, the interdependence of people, and the context of situations. An ethics of care holds that people who are especially vulnerable deserve our concern. This contrasts with the deontological ethics that arises from the philosophy of Immanuel Kant and from the utilitarianism that comes from Jeremy Bentham, James Mill, and John Stuart Mill. With *In a Different Voice* psychologist Gilligan ventured a thesis that contrasted with the position of her mentor Lawrence Kohlberg, who had proposed stages of moral development. Gilligan said that women, in general, tend toward empathy and compassion in ethical decision making, whereas men tend more toward concerns with justice, contract, and abstract duties. Kohlberg's model favored those latter male tendencies. Gilligan sought to readjust that picture of development. She noted that those differences may be based in gender differences. Of course, care is not only a matter of gender. Nel Noddings called the ethics of care a relational ethics, and Steinbeck's writings are very much about relations between characters. The dynamic of attentiveness, responsibility, competence, and responsiveness that a theorist like Joan Tronto speaks of is something that all human beings can practice.[41] We can see some Steinbeck characters that practice this well and others who do not. Jim Casy and Ma Joad, for example, appear to grow in attentiveness, responsibility, competence, and responsiveness. They practice an ethics of care. Meanwhile, Steinbeck clearly invokes a concern with justice in *The Grapes of Wrath* and *In Dubious Battle*. A great deal of his appeal also arises through feeling and sentiment. His stories move many readers toward sympathy.

Booth pointed out that there are several kinds of story. In satire, our attention is on the targets that are being attacked. Texts in which ideas are dramatized encourage thought. Then there are novels in which characters are caught in situations and actions.[42] We become engaged with characters we care about. There are other kinds of story as well. Virginia Woolf's novels, for example, do not fit into any of these categories. They engage, rather, in lyricism, character psychology, and stream of consciousness; they illustrate life but do not necessarily have a strong plot, and they participate in what Booth has called the "aesthetic feeling of life."[43] A novel can be witty, or fun, or an experiment in style—why need it be ethical?

Of course, novels do call for responses from readers. In Booth's view they "irresistibly demand the reader's judgment."[44] Literary evaluation can focus upon the aesthetics of a work. One can practice close reading with detachment and observation of how a text is put together and performs its work. However, that story may also have an ethical appeal that must also be reckoned with. Charles Altieri points out that an ethics of reading may "involve substantial risks of subordinating what may be distinctive within literary experience to those frameworks and mental economies that are attuned to modes of judgment shaped by non-textual, and (usually) less directly imaginary, worldly demands."[45] Our appreciation of the exercise of craft, structure, and the artistic formulation of language—the literary beauty of a work—ought not to be sacrificed to a search for or explication of a moral theme.

Yet novelist John Gardner once wrote: "Nothing could be more obvious, it seems to me, than that art should be moral and that the first business of criticism, at least some of the time, should be to judge works of literature (or painting, or even music) on the grounds of the production's moral worth."[46] A novel like *The Grapes of Wrath* evaluated on the basis of its moral worth would rate no doubt highly, although others might disparage it, as many have done, for any number of reasons. In *On Moral Fiction* Gardner wrote: "Structuralists, formalists, linguistic philosophers who tell us that works of art are like trees—simply objects of perception—all avoid on principle the humanistic question(s): who will this work of art help?"[47]

More than a few teachers of Steinbeck's novels believe that his novels can help their students: to read thoughtfully, to develop empathy, and to do something more than pass a Common Core test. The Russian novelist Leo Tolstoy once wrote: "The task for art to accomplish is to make that feeling of brotherhood and love for one's neighbor, now attained only by the best members of society, the customary feeling and instinct of all men [and women]."[48] Steinbeck appears to have worked toward this goal. His stories provoke a response from us because he wrote responsibly. Often, Steinbeck would think about his story, engaging in much mental preparation, before he wrote. "You believe in the perfectibility of man," he said, when accepting the Nobel Prize in Literature. "Man will never be perfect, but he has to strive for it."[49]

America is a nation of considerable diversity. Recognizing this, John Steinbeck began his final book during his lifetime, *America and Americans*, with an essay on race, ethnicity, and diversity in America. He wrote: "From the first we have treated our minorities abominably, the way old boys do the new kids in school."[50] While working with laborers at the Spreckels Sugar Plant while in high school, John Steinbeck developed relationships with immigrant workers. As a creative artist, he appears to have identified with people who lived outside of the dominant culture. Steinbeck looked at the lives of these people and he brought them imaginatively into his fiction. His stories repeatedly stand against bullies and for outcasts, notes Susan Shillinglaw. She points out that "one third of his work is set in Mexico, or treats Mexican subjects."[51] There are many examples of this. *Tortilla Flat* features the paisanos of Monterey. Steinbeck and Ed Ricketts journeyed to the Sea of Cortez along the coast of Mexico and heard there the tale that Steinbeck crafted into the story of a Mexican boy, Kino, in *The Pearl*. The figure of Emiliano Zapata appeared in Steinbeck's script for a film directed by Elia Kazan. There are Chinese American characters in his work also, like Lee Chong of *Cannery Row*, a local businessman, and the mysterious shadow figure of the old Chinaman who walks the beach in the twilight hours. Tularecito, an Indian, appears in *The Pastures of Heaven*, and Gitano appears in "The Great Mountains," providing a sense of ritual, a deep tradition other than that of the white settlers of California. It is perhaps difficult for a white, middle-class, California writer to configure the lives of an ethnic population. However, Steinbeck's imaginative renderings are compassionate.[52]

Much of Steinbeck's fiction is also about how we see. Doc, in *Cannery Row*, viewed the world often through a microscope. *Sweet Thursday* provides a telescope. *Of Mice and Men* shows up-close compassion but unfolds in a narrative voice of distance. Steinbeck's work is marked by the features of compassion and objectivity. For our time, he offers us ways to see through different perspectives. He could look with detachment and objectivity, while also being compassionate, observes Jackson Benson.[53] "He was not a disillusioned romantic like London, Crane, or Norris. Rather, he was a man who knew anthropology and biology, who recognized humanity as a species that was often noble and sometimes careless or greedy. He had 'little faith in progress.'"[54] He would not substitute a notion of material progress for humaneness. Moral develop-

ment and human kindness were more important than commercial, technological priorities.

Steinbeck's fiction encourages compassion, tolerance, and respect for
diversity in a world in which an appreciation of difference is crucial. One
of the marks of postcolonial criticism is to argue on behalf of the "other"
who has been subjugated by the hegemony of the powerful colonizer.
Similarly, Steinbeck's fiction argues for us to see the "other" as fully
human and to empathize with the plight of these persons. The tensions in
The Grapes of Wrath reflect the xenophobia and socioeconomic concerns
that are present throughout Europe and the United States today, with
immigration, transient labor, and shifts in demographics. "Distrust of
outsiders and hatred of those of a different race or class or style of living
are subjects touched on in nearly all of Steinbeck's work," observes Benson.[55] The cultural difficulties that postcolonial critics, gender critics, or
critics concerned with racial issues point to are often highly charged and
are important for us to consider. The concern that René Girard presented
in his analysis of scapegoating and C. G. Jung's observations on "the
shadow" are ever crucial insights for self-reflection. Our world struggles
with violence that stems from prejudices, transference, and projection,
from limits or distortions of perception. As Benson asks, might Steinbeck's fiction be "an antidote"?[56] Joseph Conrad once wrote that his goal
was to help people "to see." Might fiction serve the purpose of broaden-
ing and sharpening our vision?

Steinbeck, observed Warren French, "resisted . . . trends" and pursued
an "inward ethical passion."[57] After his first novels, *Cup of Gold* and *To a
God Unknown*, Steinbeck turned to the landscape and the consciousness
of characters in California with *The Pastures of Heaven* and the stories of
The Long Valley. As French points out, Steinbeck portrayed "individuals
not strong enough to overcome the reductivist force of an insensitive
society."[58] His stories represent "romantic dreamers," "victims," "the defeat of pastoral dreams by the barbarity of modern technological society."
Steinbeck gives his readers naïve idealists like Jim Nolan of *In Dubious
Battle*, doomed dreamers like George and Lennie in *Of Mice and Men*,
and lyric beauty that brings us into contact with a boy's disappointment in
The Red Pony.[59]

The 1930s in America was a period filled with disillusionment and
confrontation with stark realities. Ma Joad, a woman of considerable
tenacity and compassion, sums this up when she considers the disintegra-

tion of her family's fortunes. In John Ford's film, we hear her say: "The family's breaking apart, Tom. We ain't the family no more." Gradually, she begins to see how the human family is beset by difficulties and that the story of the Joads unfolds out into this broader community: "Used to be the fambly was fust. It ain't so now. It's anybody." Feeding the children at a camp on the slender broth she has available, "anyone" becomes the family for which Ma Joad becomes responsible. Rose of Sharon realizes this in her compassionate, nurturing response to a dying man at the end of the novel. Tom Joad has picked up this vision from Jim Casy, a self-sacrificing man who has sought to understand and change things. Inspired by Casy, Tom discovers a sense of purpose that suggests hope, however uncertain, as he heads back across the horizon alone.

Steinbeck created flawed heroes: Tom Joad with his impulsive hot temper, the marginal paisanos of *Tortilla Flat*, *Cannery Row*'s Doc, the idealistic Kino who finds a great pearl and is left with broken dreams. Pointing to the humaneness of Mayor Orden, the mayor of *The Moon Is Down*, who expressed the integrity of resistance against the Nazis, French writes of Steinbeck: "His problem became that of creating heroes who could be thought credible in a skeptical age."[60] Those ordinary/extraordinary heroes are among us. Ma Joad and Doc are out there. So are the folks who dream futile, wistful dreams like Lennie and George, the hopeful ones like Mack, and the tragic ones like Danny, the new homeowner in *Tortilla Flat*. Steinbeck was an author who cared about his writing and about people. He wrote with guts and passion, exploring the plight of workers, the fire of war, the tangles of relationships and man's inhumanity to man. He concluded his career with essays of concern, *America and Americans*, in which he focused upon America's future. Yet, more broadly, Steinbeck was a world citizen whose work encourages us to appreciate relationships—human and ecological. His fiction and his varied journalistic and theatrical creations argue for an art of care that is crucial for our present-day world and our future.

I

THE LIFE OF JOHN STEINBECK

John Steinbeck was born on February 27, 1902, in Salinas, California, a quiet town set amid rolling hills. Steinbeck lived in Salinas at 132 Central Avenue with his three sisters. His father, John Ernst Steinbeck, worked for a time as a bookkeeper for Spreckels Sugar Company. He also had a feed and grain store. He was a lifelong Mason and he acted for a time as Monterey County treasurer. John Steinbeck's mother, Olive Hamilton Steinbeck, was a member of the Eastern Star Masonic Club and the Wanderers Social Club, where local women discussed travel books. John Steinbeck had a red pony as a child and he later brought vivid memories of that animal to his well-known story "The Red Pony." There is a 1908 photo of John with his sister Mary and the pony. "The Red Pony" is a sentimental and lyrical story that crosses the boundary between fiction that children find entertaining and that adults also enjoy. He wrote to George Albee: "It is an attempt to make the reader create the boy's mind for himself. An interesting experiment if you see nothing else."[1]

The boy that John Steinbeck was has been described as a bit of a loner, tall, with long legs, broad shoulders, and a bit of a stubborn streak. Early on he took a deep interest in words. He and his sister Mary both took piano lessons. When John Steinbeck had pneumonia as a child in 1917, the Steinbeck's family doctor was Dr. Murphy, who owned Esalen near Big Sur, where the hot springs were valued by the Native American Indians. Throughout his life, Steinbeck was intrigued by the natural world. He and his sister Mary studied marine biology at Hopkins Marine Station in Pacific Grove during a couple of summers. He worked at the

Spreckels Sugar Company and got to know the Mexican American workers there. Steinbeck was not only good with words; he was good with his hands. He worked at a ranch, on a dredging crew, on a construction crew, and later as a lodge caretaker and handyman.

Steinbeck made two attempts at studies at Stanford University. He dropped out both times, determined to pursue writing as a career. On the first occasion, after taking some courses in 1919, he traveled to New York City. Frustrated in his attempt to publish his fiction, he returned home to California and made another attempt at college, on-again off-again until spring 1925. Two stories appeared in the *Stanford Spectator* in 1924. He studied writing with Edith Mirrielees and read some literature and on biology but he decided that college was not for him. He sailed again for New York, via the Panama Canal and the Caribbean. Once there, he became a laborer and he pushed a wheelbarrow with cement to assist the men who were building Madison Square Garden. Then he sought a job in journalism and gained a position as a reporter at the *American*, a William Randolph Hearst newspaper, through a relative's assistance. However, he preferred to stretch the news toward fiction rather than report on it as fact. He did not last long as a journalist. He went back to California and worked as a winter caretaker of homes around Lake Tahoe. There he wrote, attempting to revise and expand a story he had begun called "The Lady in Infra-red."

Steinbeck's first novel was on the historical subject of the pirate Henry Morgan. With *Cup of Gold*, he was caught between a romantic myth and a naturalistic style. *To a God Unknown* (1933), written earlier and based on a play by Toby Street and Joseph Campbell, brought together realism and symbolism. This was an ineffective match and the novel floundered. When *Cup of Gold* was published in 1929 it received a lukewarm reception. Steinbeck made a concerted effort to finish "Dissonant Symphony" at the end of 1929 and in early 1930. He also turned from that naturalistic story to continue work on *To a God Unknown*. Most significantly, he decided that he would marry Carol Henning, who had typed the manuscript of his first novel. She was also typing his rewrites of *To a God Unknown*. They married in Glendale, California, in the San Fernando Valley, on January 14, 1930. He had visited his friend Dook Sheffield and his wife at their home near Occidental College, where Sheffield was working. Sheffield suggested that now that Steinbeck had published a novel, it might be possible for him to work part-time at the college. Carol and John Steinbeck rented a house in the hills nearby. Rather than teaching at the college, Steinbeck wrote, surviving on money from his book and the twenty-five dollars his father regularly provided. They paid fifteen dollars a month in rent and brought into their household a puppy, a Belgian shepherd. Dogs had always been present in Steinbeck's youth and he had enjoyed his time with two Airedales during his solitary stay at Fallen Leaf Lake. Steinbeck stayed close to his desk for five hours a day working on *To a God Unknown* and also worked on "Dissonant Symphony."[2]

To a God Unknown was an allegory that continued to change shape even as he wrote the story. In it seems to be a seed for his later novel *The Grapes of Wrath*. For now the story was following the lives of a New England farming family that had moved to California and found only trouble. Steinbeck drew the idea from his own family's Irish and German immigrant backgrounds. The notion of developing a novel of interrelated short stories occurred to him. However, those stories veered off in different directions and lacked a unifying structure. He sketched out characters from his mother's family, the Irish side of his family. The story of the Hamiltons was well known to him from the storytelling of his mother and his aunts and uncles. However, he drew upon his grandfather Johann Adolph to enter the mysteries of creating a character thoroughly from imagination. He made up stories about his father's father. The characters in his story "Dissonant Symphony" would talk about him, much like characters onstage might talk about someone who is offstage. That meant that this individual would only appear as he did from the different perspectives of the characters who were involved in the action of the story. The Johann Adolph character would be the center that would link them all. For Steinbeck, it meant that the truth of a person's life has much to do with how different people see him. From this mix of perspectives and images inevitably arose a contradictory picture of that person.

In April 1930, Steinbeck sent the manuscript of *To a God Unknown* to Ted Miller of McBride Publishing in New York. Steinbeck's agreement with McBride gave the company the first look at the book and the right of first acceptance or refusal. He had hopes of an advance. McBride rejected the novel. Steinbeck was convinced that his novel was better than *Cup of Gold*, which the firm had published. Meanwhile, the puppy died and that just brought more sadness. The Great Depression had come to America in full force and the McBride Publishing Company could not support the new novel on its diminishing resources. How an unknown writer writing an allegorical story like *To a God Unknown* could get published in such circumstances was a mystery. *To a God Unknown* was better than *Cup of Gold*, more thoughtful and serious, if not also better written. Readers beset by the severity of the Depression sought escape through adventure stories, not serious literary fiction.

Farrar and Rinehart rejected Steinbeck's novel. Harper Brothers rejected it also. Steinbeck completed "Dissonant Symphony." He had shifted his central character from one based on his imagined sense of his grandfather to one based more upon his father. The story was a dark, psychological story and hardly a work aspiring toward the market for commercial popular fiction. He sent it out for consideration in a contest for *Scribner's Magazine*. If they did not want the story, he would set it aside. Yet he was hoping for some income from his stories. The Steinbecks were holding on by a thread financially. In July the landlord told them that he had decided to give the house to his daughter as a wedding present. Steinbeck soon discovered that the rents elsewhere nearby were more than they could afford. It was time to move back to Pacific Grove, to the Steinbeck family cottage: a place where they could live without the monthly issue of rent. Steinbeck's father, meanwhile, helped Carol to obtain a secretarial job with the Monterey Chamber of Commerce.

In August they moved into the Steinbeck house on 11th Street. Carol Steinbeck started a job with the Chamber of Commerce. John Steinbeck dove into work on another novel. Frustrated by rejections of *To a God Unknown* and "Dissonant Symphony," he tore the new novel to shreds after writing a few dozen pages. However, soon he was back at work, banging out a mystery novel he thought would be a commercial property. Nine or ten days later he sent "Murder at Full Moon" to Ted Miller in New York. He told him he was trying to make some money to resolve a debt and to "remember that when this manuscript makes you sick." If the story ever got published, he said he wanted it to be published under a pseudonym.[3]

Steinbeck was making no money. Carol was supporting them on her secretarial salary, which was added to the twenty-five dollars they received each month from Steinbeck's father. He had to repay Carol's father, who had loaned him money for a dental bill. Steinbeck had periodontal problems and that bill from the dentist would have remained unpaid if not for Carol's father. It was a matter of principle that he would find a way to pay him back. He hoped that the story would bring enough money for that—and maybe more. Meanwhile, a kind of serendipity entered Steinbeck's life while he was visiting the dentist. He met a man who would change his life, a man who would become his close friend and intellectual confidant: Ed Ricketts.[4]

Edward F. Ricketts was a marine biologist. He was from Chicago and now supervised a marine laboratory and biological supplies business. The bearded scientist could be seen regularly on the Monterey waterfront, collecting specimens of invertebrates or following up on orders at the warehouse. Steinbeck learned that Ed Ricketts was a man who was fascinated by evolutionary processes. He was also a familiar sight at Cannery Row, a man who seemed able to comfortably chat with anyone, whether a scientist or a dockworker, a cannery worker, or a California Tech professor. From his sojourns along the coast, he was able to supply high school biology labs with specimens and provide materials for medical research. He was a witty, adventurous man who talked a lot, drank a lot, and was constantly on the lookout for women despite his shyness. Steinbeck was drawn by Ricketts's personality and intellectual energy. He also knew a few things about biology, having studied it in school.

Steinbeck began to visit Ricketts at the Pacific Biological Laboratories. He observed him working and sometimes he provided him with assistance. Ricketts was quick-witted, precise in his science, affable, and gregarious in discussions. Steinbeck was perhaps more deliberate, in his conversation as well as in his writing. He pondered the world philosophically, introspectively. It was during his visits to Ricketts that Steinbeck became acquainted with Cannery Row.

The workers of Cannery Row, he observed, lived on a fundamentally material level. They packed fish into cans and worked for money and for the things they could obtain with it. Their world was focused upon those basic material things that Abraham Maslow has indicated at the bottom of his hierarchy of needs: food, shelter, sex. Their lives were a struggle for survival, an attempt to lift themselves up from poverty, a dream sometimes expressed in a desire for things or some local form of status. Ricketts urged Steinbeck to view them as characters for a novel. It was a Darwinian struggle on the level of animal life, he suggested. They remained only partially literate and their lives and minds were held captive in repetition.

Steinbeck continued to be fascinated with myth and allegory and sought ways to use this in his fiction. Ricketts advised Steinbeck to get rid of allegory and to move beyond attempts to make quick money with guesses at what kind of fiction might work commercially. Instead, Ricketts contended, he should bear down and find the themes that were important to him. He should write about real people, not fanciful would-be pirates, or allegorical symbols. Ricketts, the scientist, pointed Steinbeck toward investigation and seeking evidence. Darwin had developed an empirical biological record. Similarly, Steinbeck should build novels through studied attention to the human condition. Ricketts encouraged him to stop preaching with his art and to become a "scientist of the imagination." Steinbeck set to work with renewed determination.

In spring 1931, Steinbeck welcomed Ricketts to Salinas. He had begun to think about writing about his home: Monterey and the valley in which he had lived most of his life. He took his wife, Carol, and Ricketts to his aunt's ranch at Corral de Tierra and talked with them about the long valley. There was a family that had come to the valley back in the 1870s. Things turned sour for them quickly: their barn burned down, their cows became diseased. The people in the area began to wonder if they were cursed. Maybe they were the curse themselves. Before long, they found it necessary to leave the valley, but the shadow of their tribulations seemingly lingered. For problems broke out throughout the valley and many wondered if they had left their curse behind.

Ricketts told Steinbeck a few days later that he ought to work with that story of the curse. Science could be used to critique superstition and a story could question mythical belief systems or religion. Humanity was not adept at adapting to changing conditions, Ricketts asserted. They had to let go of primitive beliefs, like one in supernaturalism and curses. Why not write about this presumably "cursed" valley?

Steinbeck's writer friend Carl Wilhelmson paid him a visit. Wilhelmson had signed with a literary agent. Ted Miller had recently suggested to Steinbeck that he seek an agent rather than try to pitch manuscripts through his law office. However, with the recent rejections of his stories, Steinbeck did not believe that an agent would take him on. Wilhelmson recommended the firm of McIntosh and Otis. Mavis McIntosh was his own agent and Elizabeth Otis was a very competent agent, he said. He would write to them on Steinbeck's behalf. Steinbeck wrote to Ted Miller, asking him to send the stories to McIntosh and Otis.

To a God Unknown did not impress Mavis McIntosh. It was too disparate and disjointed, she said. She would take on Steinbeck as a client but she would not shop his novel to the publishers. "Murder at Full Moon" could be a commercial work. Had he written other stories like it? She suggested that he might write on life in California. She was not interested in philosophical musings. Readers wanted characters, places, tangible details of lives in a specific environment. Ed Ricketts had said something similar to him. He was by no means convinced that he should write any more tales like "Murder at Full Moon." The idea of writing about California, however, struck him as an authentic possibility.

To a God Unknown remained unpublished. The short stories that Steinbeck sent to Elizabeth Otis were not sold. Mavis McIntosh urged Steinbeck to rewrite his novel. Steinbeck sent back a note that she might look at "Dissonant Symphony," not so much to try to sell it but to see in it the style and form in which he was approaching his story about the valley. It was a series of interconnected stories he was calling *The Pastures of Heaven*. When he completed this he sent it to McIntosh. It did not impress her any more than the previous novel had. She would circulate it to publishers but believed it had little chance of attracting any interest.

Meanwhile, tensions developed at home. Carol Steinbeck's attempts to start an advertising business had proven unsuccessful. John Steinbeck depleted his energy trying to write his novel *The Pastures of Heaven*. The tone of their relationship dissolved into argumentativeness. Money was a constant problem. He was troubled that he could not provide for her. They began to pull apart from one another. Carol had a brief relationship with their neighbor, the mythologist Joseph Campbell.

The Pastures of Heaven failed to gain any traction in New York. William Morrow Publishing rejected the novel. Steinbeck's agents tried other avenues. They reached to London and finally could offer Steinbeck some positive news: Jonathan Cape and Harrison Smith would publish the novel. The editor Robert Ballou had not only accepted the novel; he saw great promise in Steinbeck's work and agreed to a deal for the writer's next two novels. The advance money was small but Steinbeck finally had found a home for *To a God Unknown* and the prospect of publication for his next effort.

Steinbeck continued to talk about the novel with Ed Ricketts, who insisted that he focus upon naturalistic phenomena. Darwin had given the world clear evidence that humanity was engaged in a struggle with the natural environment. Steinbeck's fiction should emphasize those factors, not religion or myth. Look to the people in California who have recently experienced a drought, he advised. See what that has done to them psychologically. The religious beliefs of his characters, the Waynes, did not carry as much weight as the obvious plight of people dealing with the wind, the drought, and the land. Listening to Ricketts, Steinbeck began to revise his work in the spring of 1932.

Cape and Smith, like other publishers, were confronted with the Depression. They delayed the contract with Steinbeck for *The Pastures of Heaven* and for the two books that were to follow it. The firm reorganized as Jonathan Cape and Robert Ballou Publishing. However, Ballou soon left the firm and joined Brewer, Warren, and Putnam. He brought Steinbeck's contract with him and Steinbeck eventually signed it in September. There was no money forthcoming. Publication of *The Pastures of Heaven* was delayed again. Carol Steinbeck began to work in the laboratory with Ed Ricketts for fifty dollars per month. Throughout 1932, Steinbeck resumed work on *To a God Unknown*. He would have it ready for Ballou by February 1933.

When *The Pastures of Heaven* (1932) was published the novel did not sell well and reviews of it were mixed. The novel never made much money. However, what Steinbeck did realize in writing those twelve linked stories was that California was his subject. Meanwhile, *To a God Unknown* lingered in abeyance, as the publishing firm of Brewer, Warren, and Putnam tried to deal with the economy of Depression America. Steinbeck began to ponder death, as he observed his mother, Olive Steinbeck, dealing with a stroke and hospitalization at Salinas Valley Hospital. During this difficult time, Steinbeck thought back over his life and he worked on short stories. There was one about a boy and a chestnut red pony that particularly intrigued him. A longer story was also beckoning: that grand tale about the valley and the people who called it home. He wrote letters to his friends Carl Wilhelmson and Dook Sheffield and jotted down his ideas for the story. His ideas were sociological, reflections upon how people act in groups. These groups appeared to develop their own collective identity. They were, he wrote, "as separate and distinct from the individual men that compose them as individual men are separate and distinct from the bodily cells of which they are composed."[5] He dwelled upon how people of the valley had a group memory.

The stories of the people he experienced in California were now what most interested him. The workers of Cannery Row and the paisanos of Tortilla Flat all had stories. The Mexican poor who lived in ramshackle conditions and were mostly illiterate were people of dignity who persisted and survived poverty and adversity. He began to gather his observations and the folktales he was hearing and creating into a novel that he would call *Tortilla Flat*.

Steinbeck finished "The Red Pony," a story of about ten thousand words, and mailed it off to Mavis McIntosh and Elizabeth Otis. Meanwhile, Robert Ballou had informed Steinbeck that Brewer, Warren, and Putnam would not be publishing *To a God Unknown*, but he had developed funds to publish it through his own firm. Of course, there still was no money. Across the past seven years he had made only about $870 with his writing. McIntosh, Otis, and Ballou were all suggesting that there would soon be income from his work.

Naturalism—a grasp of the tangible world in characters and setting—gripped his imagination now more than allegory and he set to work on a method for his next novel. He need not create a fantastic hero in his fiction: a dashing knight, a would-be pirate. There was much heroism in common people who found themselves in extraordinary situations.

The New Deal of the Roosevelt years brought a branch of the California Emergency Relief Administration to Monterey and Carol Steinbeck went to work for the agency. Steinbeck's father, clouded by depression, stayed in the Pacific Grove cottage with John Steinbeck and his wife. Steinbeck's mother was dying. As he worked on his new story material, Steinbeck received word that "The Red Pony" would be published in the *North American Review*. The publication in two successive issues of the magazine brought his characters, the boy Jody and his father, to a broader audience of readers. It was, some said, a classic American short story, indeed a universal one.

The linked stories of *Tortilla Flat* absorbed most of his attention that autumn. However, to respond to the new readership for his stories, he wrote a story called "The Murder." It was quite a different story than "The Red Pony." In it a man from California marries a Slavic girl and discovers the ethnic values of another culture. He is surprised to discover his wife in bed with her cousin and reacts by killing the cousin and beating up his wife. He is unable to come to terms with his actions and with the foreign culture and the sexual liaison that provoked his behavior.

The story was published in the *North American Review* in April 1934 and went on to win the year's O. Henry Award.

Steinbeck had brought his concerns with social justice and his sensitivity to the value of cultural differences to bear upon that story. Both John and Carol Steinbeck were witnessing the responses of the settled, mostly white community to ethnic people in Monterey. He was writing about Mexican immigrants of Tortilla Flat and Carol was working at the Emergency Relief Administration with managers who were condescending toward the immigrants who were among the families seeking unemployment relief. Steinbeck's story, while compassionate, may carry some distance from his subjects. He identified with the struggle of the immigrants but they remained "other" in terms of his experience. His approach was compassionate but it was also that of an observer of psychological and emotional turmoil in a culture he looked at from the outside. His story was an examination of difference and of a broader social violence than merely the incident of murder that occurs.

Working with the stories of the Mexicans of Tortilla Flat for months had sharpened his curiosity and his sympathy for them. Yet he also cast an empirical lens upon the organic continuities and patterns of that culture. He had become something of a literary anthropologist, or sociologist, one with Ed Ricketts's biological, Darwinian perspective lingering in his thoughts. *Tortilla Flat* arrived in the office of McIntosh and Otis in winter 1934. His mother died on February 19. Her long struggle with illness was over.

Steinbeck worked on "The Raid," a story about labor tensions in California. He focused the story upon a Communist organizer in a trade union and the worker he was mentoring. Ed Ricketts argued that the Communist organizers of such movements were trouble. They didn't care for the workers; they cared for their ideology, he said. The politics of a totalitarian Communism would be far more oppressive than the greed that caused suffering in their lives, he added. Steinbeck gave much thought to this. He wrote a story in which the organizer was creating a mob. His story carried a warning, suitable for his time and ours: A group engaged in civil protest must not be mindless if it is to foster a new society.

Tortilla Flat was forwarded to Robert Ballou, but he did not care much for the story. Neither did other publishers. Steinbeck's revisions did not make the novel any more palatable to them. He worked on another story, the one he would call *In Dubious Battle*. The novel about the

Mexican immigrants sat on desks and in office drawers. For a time it was uncertain whether the short novel would ever see the light of day. However, it was with *Tortilla Flat* (1935) that Steinbeck found his voice and characters, a tone of humor, and his popular reading audience. *Tortilla Flat* gave the struggling writer his first taste of commercial success.

Publishing and book selling is an enterprise in which thousands of individuals participate. Sometimes the connections and degrees of separation of these individuals are as unexpected as in a Dickens novel. In Steinbeck's case, a Chicago bookseller, Ben Abramson, began promoting Steinbeck's books. He had enjoyed "The Red Pony" in the *North American Review* and was convinced that this was a writer of talent who had a great deal to say. One day, he was pitching *The Pastures of Heaven* to Pascal Covici, a publisher who was passing through Chicago. He urged him to take the book on the train back to New York with him. Covici was greatly impressed by the novel. He contacted McIntosh and Otis, inquiring whether Steinbeck was under contractual obligations with any publishers. Acknowledging that *Tortilla Flat* had been refused, they told him that there were none. Covici made an offer for *Tortilla Flat*. He told Steinbeck that his publishing firm would also reissue his previous novels. With that offer, Pascal Covici became a key player in the career of John Steinbeck.

Steinbeck then made an abrupt turn with the seriousness of *In Dubious Battle* (1936), a powerful proletarian novel about an agricultural strike. In February 1935, Steinbeck sent his manuscript of *In Dubious Battle* to his agents, McIntosh and Otis. An objective narrative carries the story. Jim Nolan is the youthful and idealistic follower of a radical Communist organizer, Mac. The story reveals a phenomenon that repeated in many different places in the world throughout the twentieth century into the Cold War era. The capitalists resist change and seek to maintain their business and the status quo that supports its continuance. The Communists seek to force their ideology and a new order upon the people. Steinbeck tells his story clearly, with a kind of realism that makes the story's characters easily available to readers. Among the cast of people in the story is Dr. Burton, a character based upon Ed Ricketts, who was often called "Doc." Dr. Burton repeatedly tells the other characters that change is inevitable; things always change. The goals of the organizers are shallow and illusory and their ideology is as inflexible as that of the capitalists. This was a dubious battle. The lives of the people are what really mattered and change was going to happen whether they liked it or not.

Once *In Dubious Battle* was completed, Steinbeck turned back to his search for the big novel he felt was waiting to be written: the one about that group-mind of people who lived in the valley. In March, "The White Quail" was published in the *North American Review*. His own marriage was the story's likely source. In the story, a wife is concerned about the uneasiness she feels in a world that seems uncertain. She seeks security and begins to put emotional walls around herself to avoid anxiety and pain. She tends the garden and seeks to manage it to keep it orderly, perfect, and impregnable. Then a white quail lands in it. A cat prowls through the garden in quest of the quail. The wife's orderly little garden world has been disrupted and she asks her husband to shoot the cat. The man, accidentally, kills the quail instead: the beautiful white bird that represents his wife.

Steinbeck's beautiful novel, *In Dubious Battle*, was almost killed also when Pascal "Pat" Covici argued that he had misrepresented Communist ideology in the story. He requested a rewrite that Steinbeck refused to do. Elizabeth Otis concluded that the politics of the novel, correct or in error, might actually increase sales and she made this point to Covici. He agreed to publish the novel. To this point, Otis had handled Steinbeck's short fiction. She now became the principal agent for all of his work. While *In Dubious Battle* was being prepared for publication, John Steinbeck's father, John Ernst, died. *Tortilla Flat* appeared a few days later.

Tortilla Flat immediately began to climb up the best-seller list. The book was circulated actively to book critics who regarded the story as a social comment. It was illustrated with line drawings by Ruth Gannett, whose husband, Lewis Gannett, a critic, of course recommended it. People living through the conditions of Depression-period America responded to what they took to be social commentary. The story had a wide readership. When Pat Covici finally met Steinbeck face-to-face he delivered his royalty check. That meeting was also the beginning of a long friendship between them. To follow this with *In Dubious Battle* was unexpected. Steinbeck had entered one of his most versatile and prolific periods as a writer.

When *In Dubious Battle* appeared the book became controversial, as Elizabeth Otis expected it would. The 1930s was a decade in which American society was strained by economic issues. Franklin Delano

Roosevelt's administration put forth measures of New Deal democracy to respond. In intellectual circles, socialist theory was approached quite seriously. Steinbeck asserted that rigid political ideologies dehumanized people. His novel carried humanistic concern but was misread by both professional reviewers and common readers. However, it was indeed being read and it was selling well. Steinbeck's most recent novels were being considered for adaptation to other mediums. Broadway producer Herman Shumlin was able to obtain the dramatic rights and contemplated creating a stage play from the novel. The film rights for *Tortilla Flat* sold for four thousand dollars.

The popular writer John O'Hara was hired by Shumlin to adapt *In Dubious Battle* for the stage. Steinbeck read some of O'Hara's fiction while he was on vacation in Mexico with Carol. A new story was taking shape in Steinbeck's mind. He began to call it "Something That Happened." It featured two laborers, one of whom was mentally deprived. Following conversations with O'Hara, Steinbeck began to look at the story as a play. He would experiment with O'Hara's style of dialogue. Soon the story of George, the ranch hand, and his mentally deficient associate Lennie began to take new shape. *Of Mice and Men*, begun as a play, was published in February 1937. It was selected by the Book-of-the-Month Club and immediately rose up the best-seller list. About one hundred thousand copies had been sold by the end of the first month.

Of Mice and Men offers an entrée into Steinbeck's fiction for many students. The story was based in dialogue because Steinbeck at first thought of it as a play. At about thirty thousand words, it is a story that can be read and taught in classrooms. That the story has appeared in film and on stage enhances its accessibility. Today students may cite computer problems as a reason why their work—the best laid plans of mice and men—does not always result in timely submission of term papers for their classes. Steinbeck could sympathize with them by referring to the age-old excuse of students writing term papers that "my dog ate it." His dog chewed up the first part of his story and he had to rewrite it.

Of Mice and Men soon moved from print to the stage and then to the screen. A new edition of *The Red Pony* (1937), with its linked stories, and *The Long Valley* (1938), a short-story collection, followed. Then came the blockbuster *The Grapes of Wrath* (1939), published in March and remaining on the best-seller list into 1940.

John and Carol Steinbeck purchased a house in Los Gatos, a town that is about midway between San Francisco and Monterey. His concern about people in California now extended to the lives of the migrant farm workers who had moved there in search of work. The *San Francisco News* gave him a commission to write a series of articles on the migrant workers and the conditions in which they labored. Steinbeck went to the Gridley Migrant Camp near Sacramento. There he began to discover that the tensions he had written in fiction, with *In Dubious Battle*, were occurring in practice among farmers' associations, workers, and the agricultural industry. Left-wing organizers threatened strikes, and from the farmers' associations had sprung vigilante groups that attempted to suppress them.

Steinbeck moved on to Bakersfield, where he found a government camp colloquially called "Weedpatch." In contrast with the previous camps he had witnessed, this camp, run by the Federal Farm Security Administration, was in excellent condition. At Weedpatch lived many itinerant farmers from Oklahoma, Arkansas, and the Texas Panhandle who had sought refuge from the environmental havoc of the Dust Bowl. There Steinbeck met a government employee, Thomas Collins, who gave him a book on the psychology of mob behavior. Tom Collins's reports would become important resources for Steinbeck as he began writing about what he witnessed at the camps.

By August, the series of newspaper articles had been completed. They were the first of Steinbeck's many sociopolitical forays into journalism and nonfiction. The articles were written in an objective style. They focused sympathy on the struggle of the farm workers and critiqued the farmers' organizations and labor practices. Collins sought to create a book from the reports he had made to agency administrators in Washington. Pat Covici told Steinbeck that such a book would never have any commercial potential. The *San Francisco News* published Steinbeck's articles as "The Harvest Gypsies." He remained angered by the situation that he had seen in the migrant camps and resolved to work out his concerns in fiction.

Steinbeck began working in earnest on his project about the migrant workers. However, there were calls from New York, where George S. Kaufman was at work directing *Of Mice and Men* as a stage production. George S. Kaufman was one of America's foremost writers for the stage between the 1920s and the 1950s. He had recently moved to a house in

New Hope, Pennsylvania, where he invited Steinbeck to visit. With Carol, John Steinbeck sailed on a freighter via the Panama Canal for about two weeks to get to New York. He met with Kaufman and with his agents. He then traveled to Russia with Carol. Meanwhile, his agents sold the *Tortilla Flat* film rights and Pat Covici developed a gift edition of *The Red Pony*. Upon his return from Europe, Steinbeck added a third section, "The Promise," to the previously published sections "The Gift" and "The Great Mountains." In the third section, his character Jody moved beyond boyhood to manhood. This ten-dollar gift edition sold well. The follow-up, a collection of fifteen Steinbeck stories as *The Long Valley*, would be Covici's last publishing effort of Steinbeck's work with the firm Covici-Friede. The company, plagued by the Depression economy, would go bankrupt in 1938. As a well-regarded editor, Pat Covici took a job with the Viking Press in New York. He would bring all of Steinbeck's works with him and Viking would be Steinbeck's publisher for the rest of his lifetime.

During this time, Steinbeck was working on the story of the migrant workers, the new novel that would become *The Grapes of Wrath*. He was angry at the situation in which he saw the farm workers. His visits to their camps in the San Joaquin Valley brought grim and pathetic sights and stories. Meanwhile, his relationship with Carol at home was like grapes that had grown sour.

One of the distinctive features of *The Grapes of Wrath* is its interchapters. The novel begins by focusing on the land, the wind, the changing and darkening colors of the dust storm. No human life enters this wind-swept scene until well into the chapter and then, as people emerge, as if from the natural world itself, they are simply referred to as the men, the women, the children, and they are beset by the elements. The women and children, drawing figures in the dust, look to see whether the men will break. They see that they will not and they are reassured. That tenacity is repeatedly underscored in the story that follows. However, as soon as we have been introduced to the book's characters, to Tom Joad and the former preacher Jim Casy, we are suddenly given the first of the interchapters that break up the action of the story. These interchapters seem at first like poetic asides, but soon gather force as reports from the field and a satirical stream of consciousness. They bring together Steinbeck's themes and focus the issues and ideas he is developing.

Reform, Steinbeck suggests, is a concern for everyone. As the Joad family makes the journey outward, they begin to realize that their family is related to a broader community of families. Their world broadens from insularity into a consideration of the many other families whose experiences are much like their own. There is a call to compassion, a growing awareness of the necessity of interpersonal cooperation. The call is a rallying cry like "The Battle Hymn of the Republic," which Steinbeck insisted appear at the end of his book in its entirety.

Writing to Dook Sheffield in a letter, Steinbeck commented on *The Grapes of Wrath*: "I must make a new start. I have worked the novel as I know it as far as I can take it."[6] In saying this he was referring to his narrative method, a way of writing without any heroic finale or deus ex machina that would save the day. Ed Ricketts had referred to this as a non-teleological method. In ancient philosophy, Aristotle had asserted that life and nature moved purposefully toward an end point. This is known as teleology. His moral view of humanity in the *Nicomachean Ethics* called for moderation and balance and a movement toward this potential. Ricketts countered with a scientific view that centered on observable and verifiable data, rather than a view that is sometimes colloquially expressed as "everything happens for a reason." His disposition was inclined toward naturalism rather than metaphysics, detachment and observation rather than a scheme of value in which what ought to be was inevitably being worked out.

When *The Grapes of Wrath* was published in March 1939 Viking printed many copies of the first edition. The novel began to sell remarkably well and soon it was on the best-seller list. The book was not only referred to in book reviews but was also frequently cited in editorials and political commentary. *Of Mice and Men* was now being made into a movie by director Lewis Milestone. A screenplay for *The Grapes of Wrath* was in the process of being written by Nunnally Johnson and a 20th Century Fox film would be directed by John Ford.[7] John and Carol Steinbeck went to Hollywood for meetings. Following a spat between them, John Steinbeck went to stay at a friend's apartment. While he was there, back pain kept him confined to the bed for several days. Max Wagner brought around Gwyndolyn Conger, an aspiring actress who wanted to meet him. Steinbeck was much taken by her and began accompanying Max Wagner and Gwyn Conger in town.

When the Steinbecks returned to Los Gatos, the writer spent much time at Pacific Biological Laboratories with Ed Ricketts. This brought him back to observations of Cannery Row and the Monterey waterfront. It also apprised him of the financial situation of Ricketts's business, which was not good. He decided to support Ricketts's flagging business with his newfound income from the success of *The Grapes of Wrath* and *Of Mice and Men*. They also talked about making an exploratory trip down the Mexican coast to the Sea of Cortez. *The Grapes of Wrath* was presented to film viewers in December. The film *Of Mice and Men* followed the next month. Popular attention to the work of John Steinbeck swept America.

The Grapes of Wrath caused a sensation. Some readers, still caught in the Depression, felt moved to sympathy. Opponents of the book were aroused to hostility. Steinbeck received death threats as well as praise. Upon that novel winning the Pulitzer Prize and the release of the documentary film *The Forgotten Village*, Steinbeck went on the research expedition with Ed Ricketts that is documented in *The Sea of Cortez* (1941).

Europe had been plunged into war and France was occupied in the summer of 1940 by the German army. Britain was in peril and Churchill and other leaders were asking Franklin Roosevelt for American assistance. Steinbeck's voyage with Ed Ricketts along the Mexican coast of the Sea of Cortez was focused upon science and ways he might approach writing and literature in an objective and disinterested fashion. Upon returning from their trip, Steinbeck learned that he had been awarded the Pulitzer Prize for *The Grapes of Wrath*.

The Roosevelt administration was now focused upon the war in Europe. Eleanor Roosevelt, with her ardor for social causes, had visited the California migrant camps. She had read Steinbeck's novel, seen the John Ford film, and, upon seeing the camps firsthand, attested to the reality of the conditions Steinbeck had written about. Amid the vehement arguments against the novel by farmers' groups and business concerns, Steinbeck now had a clear ally in the nation's first lady. He sought to visit the Roosevelts during a trip to visit his uncle Joe Hamilton in Washington, D.C. To the president he proposed the idea of rallying the radio and film industries to resist any German propaganda and to oppose any German designs on making a strategic base of sites in Mexico. Roosevelt listened, likely because of his wife's admiration for Steinbeck's novel, but there was no further action on any of the writer's suggestions.

Steinbeck returned to Mexico to work on a documentary. He recommended his friend Max Wagner for the film's narrator but the producers
decided otherwise. Steinbeck now confided in Wagner about his interest
in Gwyn Conger. The affair proceeded like a courtly romance with secret
communications between them by phone and mail. Gwyn Conger seemed
so energetic and vivacious in comparison with his wife, Carol, who was
domestic, orderly, and seemed to want to hold him tightly in place. Little
did he realize that there were tendencies in Gwyn Conger that were similar, or that she would mask feelings by turning to alcohol. Steinbeck
made trips from Pacific Grove to Hollywood to see her. He worked on his
new book, *The Sea of Cortez*. He told his wife about the affair and asked
for a divorce. She, at first, held on to him and to the marriage. Steinbeck
hired Toby Street, a lawyer, to work out a deal for a divorce. It may be
that he wanted the adventure, newness, and change that Gwyn Conger
represented. He sought to marry her as soon as he was able to. The
attraction and relationship brought two sons into his life.

In summer 1941, he began to wonder what would happen if America
entered the war. He began to think about an invasion story in which the
Germans had created command posts in Mexico. His documentary set in
Mexico, *The Forgotten Village*, was running into problems with political
censors and he asked Eleanor Roosevelt's intervention to clear the way
for the film. He traveled with Gwyn Conger to New York, where the
gossip columnists got hold of news of their affair. They escaped to actor
Burgess Meredith's home in Rockland County, just across the Hudson
and north of the New Jersey border. Once all the publicity about Steinbeck's doomed marriage and his affair had died down, Henry Fonda
found lodging for Steinbeck and Gwyn Conger in a small hotel in New
York City. Steinbeck began writing his invasion story. He was not sure
whether it would best be worked as a play or a novel, however—perhaps
both. In it, a little town would be besieged by the Nazis who brought with
them only moral darkness. He called it *The Moon Is Down*.

For the film of *The Grapes of Wrath*, director John Ford and cinema-
tographer Gregg Toland created an extraordinary visual masterpiece of
the interplay of darkness and light. Early in the film, a match is struck
against the darkness and soon illumines the face of Muley Graves. Later,
flashlights are beamed obnoxiously into Tom Joad's face. There are head-
lights and there is moonlight. The images of lanterns appear throughout
the film and Tom Joad recognizes that Jim Casy, in his integrity, was

"like a lantern." With *The Moon Is Down*, Steinbeck asked what would become of the light of civilization. What would the future hold? When the Japanese attacked Pearl Harbor on December 7, 1941, that question was on everyone's mind.

The Moon Is Down had prospects as a play. Oscar Serlin obtained the rights after Herman Shumlin, who had taken an option on it, turned it down. Serlin hired Lee Strasberg of the Group Theater to direct the play. Steinbeck worked on the script in winter 1942 while Pat Covici prepared the novel for publication at Viking. Once published, the novel quickly attracted readers. It also began to be circulated among the resistance in Scandinavia, in Denmark, Holland, Belgium, and in the French underground.

America now rose to face wartime with sacrifice, industry, and patriotic propaganda. Steinbeck joined the Office of Information, part of the OSS (the Office of Strategic Services), a predecessor of the CIA. Wartime film could rally the spirit of the nation and Hollywood wanted Steinbeck again. He had always consented to have adaptations of his work made but he had not especially wanted to write screenplays. This time things were different: the air force wanted him to develop a propaganda film for public relations. They sought congressional appropriations for bombers and supplies. Steinbeck was hired as a consultant to write a script, "Bombs Away: The Story of a Bomber Team." Personally, what he really wanted to do was join military intelligence for the United States Air Force. Darryl F. Zanuck at 20th Century Fox had other ideas. He wanted Steinbeck to work on a screenplay that would support the Merchant Marines. The project would not only be a promotional piece; it would be a feature film directed by Alfred Hitchcock. In *Lifeboat*, the characters were in a world drifting toward uncertainty. The script was written in an objective mode, which was entirely suitable to Hitchcock's techniques. Steinbeck returned to New York, where he urged New York newspapers to send him to Europe as a war correspondent. The *Herald Tribune* took him up on this and made him an offer.

Steinbeck left his new wife, Gwyn, in New York, a move that obviously was no benefit to their marriage. While she stayed in New York, he arrived in London in July 1943 and began to write about the British role in the war. His sister Mary's husband, William Dekker, was now missing in action. The Fifth Army had invaded Sicily and Dekker was nowhere to be found. Steinbeck went on an assignment in North Africa in August and then went on to Italy, where he witnessed fierce fighting near Salerno. The combat at Salerno included a German mortar barrage and Steinbeck's hearing was disrupted by the thunderous pounding of artillery. When he returned home, he suffered from headaches and blackouts. He drank. Gwyn drank. It did nothing to help their relationship with each other.

In February and March of 1944, Steinbeck made a trip to Mexico to try to shake off his depression and heal from the headaches and back pain he was experiencing. He recalled a folktale he had heard about a boy who had found a great pearl. (Some have said that he heard the story earlier while on his excursion to the Sea of Cortez with Ed Ricketts.) The boy, who was from an Indian family of fishermen, did not conceal the news of his find. He went to sell the pearl and the potential buyers attempted to cheat him. The boy soon realized that the pearl he thought was such a great discovery of wealth would subject him to a worse life than he had known before. This folktale was one that Steinbeck would turn into his story *The Pearl* (1947). In this story he responded to his own success with *The Grapes of Wrath* with a parable of how sudden wealth can affect a person spiritually. In an introduction to the novel Linda Wagner-Martin recalls Steinbeck's earlier struggle and how he drew upon a Bible reference, Matthew 13:45–46, for the title of his novel.[8] Kino, a poor diver, seeks the pearl to save his son, Coyotito, who has been stung by a scorpion. He and his wife, Juana, need money to pay the doctor. The villagers attempt to trick him into giving up the pearl and try to steal it. Kino becomes obsessed with the pearl. He fights off someone who would steal it from him. When Juana, seeing his obsession, tries to take the pearl from him to get rid of it, he is abusive toward her. Coyotito is killed accidentally by a thief. Realizing that his life has changed because of his newfound wealth, Kino tosses the pearl back into the sea.

Steinbeck returned home from Mexico in April. Gwyn was pregnant with their first child. Thom Steinbeck was born August 2, 1944. He would eventually write some fiction as his father had done. His younger brother, John, would be born a few years later. Meanwhile, his mother and father moved again to California. Pat Covici had encouraged Steinbeck to write about Cannery Row and the book was nearly complete. John Steinbeck wanted to go back to Monterey once he finished work on his new novel. Gwyn Conger Steinbeck wanted to go back to her friends in Los Angeles.

Cannery Row is set in an area that John Steinbeck knew well: the fish cannery area near Ed Ricketts's business. The story features "Doc," a character that Steinbeck based upon his friend. In composing the story, he followed the method Ricketts had so long advocated. He remained objective, offering clear description of his uneducated working characters. The novel was "non-teleological." However, the story was quite human. The workers attempt to throw a party for Doc, who runs a biology lab. At various stages their efforts to do this are thwarted. So are their ambitions and their search for respectability. At one point it appears that Doc might be paying for his own party. The character Mac travels with his coworkers up the Carmel River to look for frogs they can sell to Doc to help pay for the festivities. They meet the Captain, who invites them to his house, where they have a little too much to drink. Since Doc doesn't come back from his marine expedition on time they decide to have the party anyway and virtually destroy his laboratory in the process.

Cannery Row was published early in 1945. Steinbeck traveled to Mexico in April to assist with a film of his story *The Pearl*. He spent time in Mexico City and Cuernavaca. Gwyn and Thom arrived later and remained there into July. During this time, Steinbeck received an offer from director Elia Kazan to participate in writing a film about the Mexican revolutionary Emiliano Zapata. He also began to write ideas for a story about a group of Mexicans traveling on a bus. That story began to develop into a novel, *The Wayward Bus*.

In December the Steinbecks left Monterey and they moved to New York City, settling in a brownstone on 78th Street. On June 12, 1946, a second son, John IV, was born. In the autumn, the children were left in a woman's care and Gwyn and John Steinbeck made a trip to Sweden and Denmark. While in Scandinavia, Steinbeck developed *The Wayward Bus*, changing the setting of the story from Mexico to California. The couple returned home in November. Steinbeck hesitated about having the new story published but Pat Covici insisted on it. *The Wayward Bus* appeared in February 1947 and began to attract very strong sales.

A visit to Russia was now on Steinbeck's mind. Unfortunately, he first had a trip on the balcony at his home. He fell into the courtyard, breaking his knee. While he was healing from the injury to his knee, there were also breaks in his marriage. Gwyn accompanied him on the journey to Russia but she returned home on her own and was soon involved in an extramarital affair. This soured the relationship between them in 1948.

Meanwhile, his *Herald Tribune* articles on the Russian visit were being compiled in a book, *A Russian Journal*, and the film of *The Pearl* had made its appearance on the movie screen. Steinbeck left Gwyn and the children in New York and headed west to California to do research in the Monterey area for his next novel. When he returned to New York the marriage was no better off; nor was his knee. A varicose vein condition inflamed it and this sent him back to the hospital. The knee was a minor setback compared with the tragedy that then occurred.

Loss is difficult for anyone and accidents are unexpected, unpredictable, seemingly random events that disrupt lives. John Steinbeck lost his best friend, Ed Ricketts, to such an occurrence. Ricketts's car became stuck at a railroad crossing and was struck by a Southern Pacific train in Monterey. Steinbeck's best friend, his scientific-philosophical mentor, was gone. He was devastated. The losses continued: He made a trip to Mexico in June for the film on Zapata and returned to New York to find that his wife, Gwyn, had taken the children to Los Angeles. Her lawyer sent a letter soon afterward, indicating that the next move would be a divorce and a settlement.

While the relationship with Gwyn brought two sons into John Steinbeck's life, it does not appear to have been a happy marriage. With his family life gone and Ed Ricketts gone, Steinbeck returned to California, to Pacific Grove, perhaps attempting to regain a bit of a sense of home and a new start. He visited the set for the filming of *The Red Pony* and he went on a trip to Mexico to explore filming locations with the Zapata project's director, Elia Kazan. During this time he heard of his election to the American Academy of Arts and Letters.

Steinbeck met his future wife, Elaine Anderson Scott, through her friend Ann Sothern, an actress. At thirty-four, Elaine Anderson Scott was, at this time, married to actor Zachary Scott. A blonde from Texas, she had met the actor at the University of Texas twelve years earlier and they had a daughter. That marriage was unraveling. Elaine Scott had been a stage manager for the Theatre Guild and knew many actors in New York. As her marriage concluded, she went back to New York with her daughter, Waverly. Steinbeck left California and moved into an apartment on East 52nd Street.

The 1950s began with John Steinbeck in New York, being pulled back toward the theater by Elaine's social connections. He wrote a piece that he based upon the early medieval poem "Everyman," and looked into purchasing a townhouse on East 72nd Street. As the new decade began he wrote another short novel that was also intended as a play: *Burning Bright* (1950). *Burning Bright* is the story of a vital but impotent man named Joe Saul. In 1949, when Elaine Steinbeck and John Steinbeck were bound for New York, John Steinbeck was interested in writing for the theater. *Burning Bright* is essentially a play that should have stayed in the theater, where it did not burn very brightly. The novel is brief and breezy, beginning with circus performers, then becoming a story of farmers, and then a ship's crew. In the story the characters have the same names and relationships, although their occupations and circumstances change. Joe is so deeply loved by Mordeen that she will have a child by another man, Victor, to help Joe to feel fulfilled. Friend Ed counsels and assists both Joe Saul and Mordeen. Victor the villain is ultimately the loser, pushed overboard at sea. As a novel it is a somewhat confusing experimental melodrama. Of course, Steinbeck, recognized as a novelist, was a commercial writer, and his editor, Pascal Covici, was a commercially minded man. So they published the story as a book. Steinbeck had initially written *Of Mice and Men* for the stage. *Burning Bright*, perhaps, could go both ways, like a reversible vest: one text was a play script, the other was a novel. His play *Burning Bright* received its trial run in Boston in October. Despite rewrites the play did not last long when it was presented onstage in New York.

Elaine's divorce was completed in December 1950. Elaine and John Steinbeck were married at the home of Viking publisher Harold Guinzburg soon afterward. Pat Covici was the best man at the wedding. Following a honeymoon in Bermuda, they settled into their house on East 72nd Street. *East of Eden*, one of Steinbeck's most ambitious novels, emerged during that time of renewal. From the rooms at East 72nd Street in Manhattan, Steinbeck began to pull together his thoughts about the Salinas Valley. For years he had had elements of this story in his thoughts. He began with the Hamilton family and his grandfather, Samuel Hamilton. The Irish family had arrived in California during the Civil War. He worked for five or six hours a day, writing on the right-hand pages of a ledger and commenting about his writing on the left-hand pages. By April, he had begun to create a second family story, the dark story of the Trasks.

During the summer of 1951, Elaine and John Steinbeck took their children to Nantucket. There Steinbeck continued working on his novel.

The time frame of the story had opened out from the Civil War period to after World War I. Back in New York, from September to November he wrote diligently to complete his first draft. The story was turning out to be the longest of his novels. The Viking Press responded to the draft with criticisms. The editors suggested cuts and revisions to tighten the book. Steinbeck responded that the breadth of his narrative was intrinsic to the book. The story required this complex series of movements across a lengthy span of time. He refused to cut any of it. He revised lightly, conscious that *East of Eden* was the big book he had long been intending to write.

In the autumn of 1952 Broadway musical writer Frank Loesser, who had suggested a stage adaptation of *Cannery Row*, began to work with Steinbeck. The book required a rewrite, more romance and a love relationship, if it was going to work on the stage. The process continued into spring 1953, but when the adaptation was not working Loesser dropped out. Steinbeck, planning a sequel to *Cannery Row*, was creating a new story-play he would call *Sweet Thursday*. During much of 1954, he and Elaine were in Europe. *Sweet Thursday* appeared as a book early that year. The work was taken up as a theater prospect by Rodgers and Hammerstein, who turned it into the short-lived musical *Pipe Dream*. The book and the subsequent play received little positive critical notice from reviewers.

A new residence awaited the return of Elaine and John Steinbeck to America. They were moving out on Long Island to Sag Harbor. Following a brief trip to the Caribbean they settled into their new home. There he could cross a sprawling lawn shaded by trees to a small gazebo-like structure where he could spend the day writing. From it, across the wide lawn he could see the water of the bay. Steinbeck was thinking about Europe and history, and he sat down to write a manuscript that would emerge as *The Short Reign of Pippin IV*. French stories, visits to Paris, and the desire to find a new form for his writing coalesced with his work on the political campaign of Adlai Stevenson, who was reconstituted in this novel as Pippin. Steinbeck would resume work on behalf of Stevenson in the senator's second run for the presidency. He would engage in convention coverage in Chicago and San Francisco during that summer. The novel appeared in 1957.

Steinbeck's fiction stayed in an early-medieval frame of mind. During the next few years he read widely on the Arthurian legends and stories of the Knights of the Round Table. Malory's *Le Morte d'Arthur* had often impressed him as being a novel-like work and he wished to write a modern version. Pascal Covici did not think that Steinbeck's interest in this would result in a commercial venture. Essentially, Steinbeck was trying to create something new to prompt a shift in his writing. It did not work well and he abandoned his effort.

With 1960, Steinbeck observed the American scene with an anticipation of change. He still held the darkly pessimistic view that the materialist drives of American society tended to corrupt even the most virtuous of men. However, some optimism also arose as John Fitzgerald Kennedy was elected president and the possibilities of a new era began to appear. Steinbeck wrote grimly, thinking of politics, working to affirm the future of America. He had to deal with his health as he wrote, for he had experienced a mild stroke. However, he traveled across America and he attended the inauguration of the new president at Kennedy's invitation. He spent much of his time in Washington alongside his friend John Kenneth Galbraith, the economist who had become significant amid what was perceived by many as a new transition for American democracy. Steinbeck's journey to the inaugural in Washington was part of a cross-country journey he made accompanied by his dog, Charley. The journal he wrote of his experiences would become his best-selling book about American life, *Travels with Charley*.

All was not happy in Steinbeck's vision of America, however. One critic, John Ditsky, has described *Travels with Charley* as darkly pessimistic. Clearly, Steinbeck had been shocked by the racism he observed in New Orleans, where a little black girl walking toward a school had been shouted at viciously by a group of prejudiced women he called the "cheerleaders." His meditations on American dreams of success and corruption appeared in his novel *The Winter of Our Discontent*, which was published in June 1961. This was to be Steinbeck's last novel. Elaine and John Steinbeck took in Steinbeck's children, Thom and John, who were now teenagers. Steinbeck completed *Travels with Charley* at Sag Harbor. Then, from September 1961 to June of the next year, Elaine and John Steinbeck took Thomas and John IV on a long journey that began in England and concluded in Greece.

After they returned home to Sag Harbor, they settled in with the boys. *Travels with Charley* was published. Then came the news in October 1962 that Steinbeck had been awarded the Nobel Prize in Literature. The award, announced in Sweden, made Steinbeck one of six Americans so recognized. He joined Sinclair Lewis, Eugene O'Neill, Pearl Buck, William Faulkner, and Ernest Hemingway as American recipients of the award.

As a Nobel laureate, Steinbeck ably took on the role of public intellectual, commenting upon American politics and society. Following the assassination of John F. Kennedy in November 1963, he closely followed the work of Lyndon Johnson and was invited several times to meet with the president. Elaine had been a classmate in college with Lady Bird Johnson and the family spent some time at the White House. Steinbeck was supportive of Johnson's domestic policies and he remained particularly interested in social reform in the United States. In 1967, he made a trip to Vietnam to write about the war for *Newsday*, the chief Long Island newspaper. While he supported the Johnson administration's efforts, his sons began to embrace the anti-war movement. Ultimately, Steinbeck decided that while the war was controversial, his full support would remain with the soldiers who were serving the nation.

There were no more stories. Steinbeck's back began aggravating him again during much of 1967. In November he had a back operation, which kept him mostly confined to bed until February 1968. He moved back into the Sag Harbor house with Elaine that spring. However, he experienced heart attacks that summer and could not be fully restored to health. He died on December 20, 1968, at sixty-six, leaving behind Elaine, his two sons, and an extraordinary literary legacy.

2

A SENSE OF PLACE

Steinbeck's Early Fiction

An attention to place and setting became a central feature of Steinbeck's work early in his career. The natural landscape of California is depicted with great care in each of his works following his first novel, *Cup of Gold* (1929), and we begin to see the writer finding his subject in the land and its people. In *Cup of Gold*, history, myth, melodrama, and romance intertwine in a novel of romantic, lyrical style in which his writing is less restrained than in his later work. In *To a God Unknown* (1933) myth and allegory begin to meet with realism as Joseph Wayne leaves Vermont for California in search of a new beginning. The story brings us to the land and to his quest to make it habitable and useful. Joseph and his brothers, who arrive in California, can be seen in close parallel with the Biblical story. The land is presented in close relationship with the people who interact with it: it is a trust, perhaps even a covenant. The inhabitants of the region are shapers of the land who have to deal with the vicissitudes of the natural world. Their lives unfold in connection with their environment, and Joseph Wayne's American dream becomes symbolic of commitment.

American dreams abound in Steinbeck's work. He appears to have begun his writing with his focus turned inward upon his problems with the writing itself and to have gradually become more concerned with social problems. There was a transition from his own depression and poverty during the early Depression years to his work of conscience and social concern. "America was not planned, it became," wrote John Steinbeck in his final book, *America and Americans*.[1] Like the story of Joseph Wayne and his brothers, America unfolded rather unexpectedly, across a wide and diverse landscape, and achieved a life of its own. So too Steinbeck's life seems unplanned: an American experiment. He experienced the rich countryside of California, decided that he would write, worked hard at it, and he followed where that led him. In *To a God Unknown*, Steinbeck showed his careful attention to natural detail: a quality that continues throughout the nearly thirty books he wrote in his lifetime. The Wayne brothers immediately exemplify a prevailing characteristic in his work: the group that encounters a new place and circumstances together. They are brothers, a family forging a new life in a new land. The story emphasizes the theme of commitment and sacrifice that would appear in later Steinbeck novels. Yet, even before this value emerges, the novel offers an ecological sense of interrelationship as it depicts the interaction of humanity and the earth.

John Steinbeck grew up in Salinas, a rich agricultural area, a place of rolling hills. He lived in town and he learned about farming from his father and his mother.[2] After writing his story of Henry Morgan in *Cup of Gold*, Steinbeck gradually moved toward his true subject: the rather real, while partially imagined, land and people of California. *The Pastures of Heaven*, *To a God Unknown*, *The Red Pony*, and *The Long Valley* show this development of Steinbeck's fiction. *To a God Unknown* is set in a valley surrounded by mountains. We read: "Two flanks of the coast range held the valley of Nuestra Senora close, on one side guarding it against the sea, and on the other against the blasting winds of the Salinas Valley."[3] While providing a realistic setting, Steinbeck remained interested in mythic elements and in allegory, and these features in his fiction extended into his realism. He soon recognized that he had to work on writing things that he knew, not fantasies like *Cup of Gold*. He observed phenomena and sought detail. He observed people in his surroundings and listened to their voices and their patterns of speech. The clear surface of his writing would have underlying layers of meaning. His California settings would suggest a broader landscape and investigations of the human condition.

CUP OF GOLD

John Steinbeck was a mythmaker. This was apparent in his first novel, *Cup of Gold*, a tale of alienation dressed in the garb of a disillusioned romantic pirate. The publishers to whom Steinbeck's attorney friend Ted Miller showed the story found it interesting. Henry Morgan's story may be compared with the tragedy of Jay Gatsby, as Warren French has suggested. Morgan, like F. Scott Fitzgerald's character, seeks wealth, but he is not as appealing as Gatsby. He is "ungenerous, self-centered and distant," says Steinbeck biographer Jackson J. Benson.[4] In contrast with Morgan, Gatsby dreams a dream of romance, even as he falls under its weight. The lusty outlaw of Steinbeck's first novel is a morally compromised individual who is pulled from adventure tales like Rafael Sabatini's *Captain Blood* (1922) and classics like Goethe's *Faust*. *Cup of Gold* critiques the quest for materialistic success as in the colonial tale of Joseph Conrad's *Nostromo*, in which characters greedily exploit a mine in Latin America. Henry Morgan's inner being collapses like that of Mr. Kurtz in *Heart of Darkness*. Whereas Kurtz ends up alienated in deranged megalomania, Morgan faces the bitter truth that he will end up disillusioned: "alone in your greatness and no friend anywhere."[5] With the demise of this character, Steinbeck critiques ambitious cutthroat individuals who pursue personal gain at the expense of others: a theme we see in his later work. Morgan will hang his former cronies and he asserts: "Civilization will split up a character, and he who refuses to split goes under."[6] Henry Morgan's execution of his former buccaneers may recall Henry V's execution of Bardolf in Shakespeare's play. It is the action of a leader concerned with respectability. However, Morgan's action in *Cup of Gold* could never be one of justice; rather, it expresses disloyalty and selfishness.

The problem with *Cup of Gold* is its affected style. It is descriptive, filled with figurative language and symbolism. It is a potboiler romance, like that of popular 1920s writer James Branch Cabell, set in an exotic place. One might, perhaps, consider the novel through the lens of Northrop Frye's *Anatomy of Criticism* as a story poised between romance and tragedy and examine its archetypal figures. The novel might provide the basis for a melodramatic movie like *Indiana Jones and the Temple of Doom*, which is based upon H. Rider Haggard's adventure novels. *Cup of Gold* is ambitious. However, this cynical historical romance does not contribute much to Steinbeck's reputation as a novelist. With *Cup of Gold*, he was caught between a myth and a naturalistic style.[7] A reader who picks up this novel after discovering Steinbeck's *The Grapes of Wrath*, *Of Mice and Men*, or *In Dubious Battle* may simply ask: "Is this the same writer?" This first novel lacks the straightforward colloquialism or the measured realism of his later novels. Aside from the moral interrogation of selfishness and piracy in *Cup of Gold*, the story seems unlike his subsequent work.

TO A GOD UNKNOWN

To a God Unknown struggled toward publication and Steinbeck rewrote his story several times.[8] In his novel, Steinbeck suggests an organic interconnection of nature and humanity in which Joseph Wayne's life is fundamentally connected with the cycles of the natural world. Drought has come to Jolon, under Big Sur, and Joseph Wayne, who has left Vermont to seek his new life in the West, has to deal with the thirsty land. In writing this novel, Steinbeck remained caught up in an interest in allegory and in metaphysical speculation. However, he also turned toward science to question the prejudices that might be fostered by closed belief systems, as Jackson J. Benson has pointed out. Steinbeck alludes to the Biblical figures of Joseph and his brothers as Joseph Wayne calls upon his brothers to join him in California. Yet Joseph's religious delusions are an ineffectual response to the inexorable reality he encounters. He struggles with the land like Steinbeck did with his novel. For five hours a day Steinbeck worked at the novel. Yet the early drafts of *To a God Unknown* seemed to barely hold together. "It is out of proportion because it was thought of as two books," Steinbeck told his agents.[9]

To a God Unknown (1933) brings together realism and symbolism. The novel displays Steinbeck's interest in myth and allegory, which persisted throughout his lifetime. It takes its title from a Vedic hymn and one can sometimes see behind it Ed Ricketts's early influence on Steinbeck. Nature is at the center of the novel: its inexplicable vicissitudes that lie beyond man's control. One may also see elements of James George Frazer's *The Golden Bough*, or Joseph Campbell's inquiries into mythology, as the story engages in reflection that one might find in Campbell's *The Hero with a Thousand Faces* (1949) or *The Power of Myth* (1988). From the perspective of Jungian psychology it was synchronicity that Steinbeck, a novelist working on myths, should meet Campbell, a mythologist who had begun living near Ricketts's house. Steinbeck's research, writing, and reflections upon science and the conversations that he had with these men likely contributed to his merger of ecological and mythological ideas.[10] Steinbeck's fiction had been fashioned in connection with mythological archetypes from the time of his first novel, *Cup of Gold*. Yet he had also digested some of the thought of Charles Darwin and Herbert Spencer and a mechanistic world view. At the time he was writing *To a God Unknown*, Ricketts was introducing Steinbeck to his non-teleological view of life: that what is simply "is" and there are no meaningful end points toward which life is moving. Campbell, Ed Ricketts's neighbor on 4th Street in Pacific Grove, was increasingly interested in the interconnectedness of all of life.[11] Religion and philosophy are woven throughout the novel. As Steinbeck critic Robert DeMott has shown, Steinbeck and Ricketts owned books on Zen Buddhism, including D. T. Suzuki's *Essays in Zen Buddhism* and Lao Tze's *Tao Te Ching*. These works express the notion of enlightenment, process, and overcoming dualism. However, Steinbeck's novel is set in a world of natural patterns with "no ultimate cause or design."[12]

The inquiry that is present in *To a God Unknown* subtly runs through many more of Steinbeck's stories.[13] Steinbeck's keen attention to myth and allegory can be found in his interest in the Arthurian tales of Sir Thomas Malory, his use of Biblical names and symbols, and his awareness of America's myths and figures. Joseph Wayne's dream of settlement and his care and commitment appear in various ways in the dreams and commitments of other characters throughout the Steinbeck canon. So too does his relative distance from other people. His less-than-appealing qualities reemerge in characters like the manipulative Mac of *In Dubious Battle* and Juan Chicoy of *The Wayward Bus*, as Benson has pointed out. Joseph Wayne is a dreamer. Steinbeck writes in *America and Americans* that these are dreams of "something real," dreams that have been driven deeply into the collective psyche of people. He writes: "The national dream of Americans is a whole pattern of thinking and feeling and may well be a historic memory surprisingly little distorted."[14] Looking back across the history of the American experiment Steinbeck recognizes that Americans have a strong connection with home that seems archetypal. They may feel the pull of a tradition of hunters, trackers, and woodsmen that underwrites possession of firearms as a right. Folktales of cowboys and Indian fighters and "moral tales" of outlaws wearing black and righteous lawmen wearing white are "deepset in us," he writes.[15] These figures live in memory as part of a national dream, one of "vague yearnings toward what we wish we were and hope we may be: wise, just, compassionate, and noble."[16] These heroic figures of our myths and stories offer us hope. Steinbeck muses about these collective impulses and suggests, "That we have this dream at all is perhaps an indication of its possibility."[17]

As a reader opens *To a God Unknown* it soon becomes clear that Joseph Wayne's hopes rely upon his growth toward commitment and sacrifice to save the land. Joseph dreams of starting a family dynasty in the Santa Lucia coastal range in California. He represents America's movement west as he sets up his home in the valley of Nuestra Senora and calls upon his brothers to join him. He recalls the Biblical Joseph, who went ahead of his people into Egypt. He attempts to tend the land and hires Juanito, who is of the ancestry of the local people, and he seeks a wife, a remarkable woman named Elizabeth. Dreams follow Elizabeth as they proceed on their trek into the valley. She tells Joseph of an extraordinary experience of oneness: "I thought I suddenly felt myself spreading and dissipating like a cloud, mixing with everything around me."[18] The scene underscores Steinbeck's insight that humanity and the natural world are interdependent and mutually related. Elizabeth's perception of connectedness with what "is" is an ontological awareness that there is not dualism or opposition but unity. Joseph soon will lose his wife, who falls from a rock, and the viability of his land will be compromised by drought.

To a God Unknown reminds us that people in this region of California have faced the conditions of drought before. The native Romas and Juanito have told Joseph Wayne of the familiar cycle of nature: that there always is a drought that comes and later goes away. Joseph refuses to accept this. "I don't like to think about it. It won't come again, surely," he says.[19] He tells his brother Thomas that he has heard of the dry years but he insists: "They won't ever come again."[20] Soon, Joseph's reckless brother is killed by Juanito, who recognizes an ethic that Joseph has every right to kill him in return. Joseph spares him. From some deep impulse, Joseph begins to honor a great oak tree, until his overzealous Christian fundamentalist brother, Burton, calls this idolatry and kills the tree. Burton leaves for a revival camp in Pacific Grove. Joseph and his brother Thomas travel across the western mountains, the Santa Lucias, toward the sea.

This ambitious novel struggles to hold together. In it an ecological perspective and scientific world view mixes with Judaeo-Christian elements and mythology. The novel establishes a sense of place and also suggests an indefinable mystical consciousness, as Christian and pagan religious symbols overlap. Nature appears indifferent and humanity appears unimportant in the scheme of the physical universe's unfolding. Yet the story emphasizes the necessity for human commitment, a central theme across Steinbeck's work.[21] Integrity and clear vision are central to the stability of a family, a community, and the nation. Joseph Wayne, a rather self-isolated character, appears to be committed to a dream and to a hope. He has a religious impulse but little self-awareness. He does not see things as they are. Joseph tries to influence the weather to get rid of the drought and he kills a calf, as if in sacrifice, to propitiate the gods. Juanito burns a candle and Father Angelo, at the mission of Our Lady, prays for rain. Facing drought, the bartender in town has vowed that he would "set a barrel of whiskey in the road, free, if the rain would come tomorrow."[22] In their hope for rain, each offers a supplication to the gods. Joseph seeks some belief or magic that will end the drought.

A sometimes gruff, good-hearted man appears in the public image of John Steinbeck, as Jackson Benson has pointed out. His thoughtful speculations about science and about history and society are sometimes overlooked. Concerns with the past overlap with reflections on the future as Steinbeck considers that fine line between history and story. He writes that as a child he discovered in the attic a treasure of boxes of *The Atlantic Monthly* from the 1870s and 1880s. The periodicals stirred his interest in the American Civil War. Leaders from each side wrote about their experiences and their descriptions varied. He wondered how he could ever know what really happened in history: "for if the men who had been there were confused, what chance had I, a child, or a historian, of finding out."[23] Steinbeck once told a diplomat who said he read only nonfiction that Dostoevsky, Tolstoy, and Turgenev offer access to Russian thinking. While history probes what happened, fiction seeks to understand why it happened, he concluded. So, both history and fiction "are required for any kind of understanding."[24] Steinbeck never engaged in writing historical narrative. However, as he moved away from allegory and applied realism and documentary method in his stories, he began to gain his voice and subject. He began what might be called a fictional "history" of the people.

THE PASTURES OF HEAVEN

The Pastures of Heaven and the stories of *The Long Valley* mark a surer development of John Steinbeck's fiction. With interconnected short-story cycles he would avoid the structural problems that had haunted his first novels. *The Pastures of Heaven* was the second Steinbeck novel published. The story absorbed his interest even as *To a God Unknown* was struggling for life and begging for revision. With *The Pastures of Heaven* Steinbeck found his way more surely to the people of California: the land and consciousness that would become his most enduring subject. In ten stories he explored the dreams and failures of a community of people. These stories offered imaginative variations on the lives of people that he had observed. Carol Steinbeck, his wife, had heard the stories of Beth Ingels, her colleague at the advertising agency where she worked. John Steinbeck drew upon the stories of the "happy valley," a relatively isolated territory west of Salinas, named Corral de Tierra. The harmony of this little corner of the world had been disrupted when a curious family moved into the area, he told his agents: "But about the Morans there was a flavor of evil. Everyone they came into contact with was injured. Every place they went dissension sprang up."[25] The stories conclude with a bus driver, looking back upon the valley, who remarks: "I always like to look down and think how quiet and easy a man could live on a little place."[26] However, that long glance back at the pleasant surfaces of this place does not take in the disappointments, conflicts, and troubles of the valley dwellers that readers have been exposed to in these twelve stories.

Connecting the stories is the residents' contact with the new family in the valley. The Morans have become the Munroes. Bert Munroe tells the shopkeeper, T. B. Allen, that he feels that he is "under a curse" and that so is his farm. The shopkeeper imagines the ripple effect that soon will occur: "Maybe there'll be a lot of baby curses crawling around the Pastures the first thing we know."[27] The people of the valley have created well-protected, insular lives but the insensitivity of the Munroes acts like a disease as they force their way into roles that affect the community.

Watch who you meet, Steinbeck's stories seem to say. Your encounter with any new person could change your life for good or ill. You certainly do not want to meet the Munroes. The Munroes are trouble and their presence changes everyone's life. Bert Munroe assumes that he has to visit every family in the valley and he pries into their business. Bert also insists upon getting onto the local school board, to be a big man in their small town. In the first three stories, Bert suddenly appears often where he doesn't belong: crossing that line that people keep to preserve their privacy. He confronts Mr. "Shark" Wicks, asserting that he will be arrested for threatening his son Jimmy, who has made overtures toward Wicks's daughter. Bert Munroe insists upon reprisals when he is attacked by the retarded Tularecito, who has objected to his filling in the hole that he was digging. Tularecito is sent away to an asylum. Bert brazenly barges into Mrs. Van Deventer's world and she has to get rid of her troubled daughter.

In the next three stories, Mrs. Munroe joins Bert Munroe in disrupting the neighborhood. She forces Junius Malby's son Robbie to put on new clothes for a drive to the city and forces the Malby family to realize how poor they are and how embarrassing this would be to "respectable" people. Bert suggests to a woman that one of the Lopez sisters might run off with her husband. Molly Morgan's life is changed when Bert mocks a hired hand who is always drunk; she suspects that the drunken man might be her long-lost father.

The Munroes are clearly unaware of the consequences of their remarks and their actions. Munroe discourages Ray Banks from attending executions at San Quentin prison, although Banks really does not have much else in the world to live for other than these solemn affairs of justice. Munroe's daughter's apparent interest in Pat Humbert's house brings him hope but those hopes are dashed when it becomes obvious that she is not really interested. John Whiteside hopes for a family with a legacy and a revered, permanent place in the valley. Unfortunately, his son marries Munroe's daughter, who insists upon moving into town so she can be around her friends. The story ends with Whiteside's house going up in flames.

In the view of Steinbeck critic Louis Owens "the central message here is that there are no Edens, for that is the most American and most dangerous illusion of all."[28] These people of the valley may have to face their illusions but Steinbeck here seems to be addressing a need for civility and respect for one's neighbors. We cannot know another person's concerns or what someone else is thinking, unless that person tells us. We do not know in advance how what we say will affect someone. However, we can practice respect and sensitivity for one another. The disrespect for people's feelings that is shown by the Munroes seems to carry a moral message. The stories may prompt us to despair at the ironies that arise from their actions. The insensitive ignorance of the Munroes is that of the unsolicited phone call, the driver who races up in the right lane and cuts you off on the highway, the nosy-body and the meddler, that offensive joker at the bar with his off-color jokes that you don't want to hear. Steinbeck suggests the merits of a culture of virtue and respect.

On the other hand, we might consider Joseph Fontenrose's view that modern men and women have at last come to the valley to break up rural illusions of placid contentment. This, he says, is "nothing more than the entry of twentieth century civilization into the valley." It is an "exposure to the contemporary world."[29] The question, of course, is: What kind of neighbors does one have in this modern world? How are we and they affected by this civilization? Do we recognize mutual respect and civility when we speak of civilization?

The reviews for *The Pastures of Heaven* (1932) were better than those for the first efforts, although the novel never made much money. Steinbeck told an interviewer: "The first three novels I published . . . didn't bring me in a thousand dollars altogether. The first didn't earn the $250 advance I'd been paid; the second earned about $400; the third didn't even earn its $200 advance."[30] What Steinbeck did realize in writing those twelve linked stories, however, was that California was his subject.

THE RED PONY

The four stories that comprise *The Red Pony* are set in the Santa Lucia Mountains, where Jody Tiflin learns about the mysteries of life and death. Our attention is drawn to his wonder at the life of the pony, which he names for the mountains, the Gabilans, which rise to the east of the valley. In "The Gift," the first of the stories, Jody begins to encounter the mystery of death in the world around him. Jody observes the struggle of the pony, which, in its last moments, moves from the barn toward the hills to die. He sits by a spring, looking at the cypress tree, realizing that something is now different: "The place was familiar, but curiously changed. It wasn't itself any more, but a frame for things that were happening."[31] When a buzzard comes for its prey, the dying pony, Jody tries to chase it away. His personal connection with the pony is of no consequence in the fierce and impersonal pattern of nature. The buzzard presides over death. We read that "the fearless eyes still looked at him, impersonal and unafraid and detached."[32] Jody has been introduced to the organic cycle of life and death, a mystery that does not reshape him, but prompts his sense of wonder and appreciation of the value of life. However, he is still a child who will ruin the swallows' little mud houses, tease "that good big dog," and kill a bird. He has not matured into any sense of responsibility for the natural world and for life itself.

In the second story, "The Great Mountains," Jody looks at the darkening sky over the "curious secret mountains." Wondering about the mountains, he begins to ask his father about them. He is told that they are dangerous. Carl Tiflin says, "There's more unexplored country in the mountains of Monterey County than any other place in the United States."[33] Jody is moved by the mystery of the mountains. "Jody knew something was there, something very wonderful because it wasn't known, something secret and mysterious."[34] Jody feels the impulse toward wonder and adventure. "It would be good to go," he says. Yet the mountains, for all their mystery, are as impersonal and remote from his spirit as was the predatory buzzard. We read that "their very imperturbability was a threat."[35] The Santa Lucia Mountains sparkle with life and the western mountains portend danger and death. Even so, Jody wishes to explore, to go beyond the known toward the unknown. His father prefers to not think about the danger of the mountains, while Jody meets Gitano, an elderly paisano, who faces the great mountains and their suggestion of death with courage. We read that "Gitano was mysterious like the mountains. . . . And Gitano was an old man, until you got to the dull dark eyes. And in behind them was some unknown thing."[36] Gitano will go to the mountains and Jody feels a "nameless sorrow" for all that goes with Gitano: Old Easter, his old horse, and a tradition of the people. Gitano is on a quest and he and the horse will likely die in the mountains.

"The Promise" begins with hopeful spring, a time of renewal. Jody is able to take the mare Nellie to be bred. He is promised that he will be able to raise the colt when it is born. However, Billy Buck, who will deliver the colt, realizes that he will have to kill Nellie in order to spare the colt.

Jody again experiences death in a personal way and is again learning that death is inevitable and that life and death are interrelated.

"The Leader of the People" appeared in the 1945 edition of the story and recalls Jody's grandfather's quest to travel west to California, to the sea. Jody's mother says: "If there'd been any farther west to go, he'd have gone. . . . He lives right by the ocean where he had to stop." Carl Tiflin says of Grandfather that he just "stares off west over the ocean."[37] Jody thinks, "Maybe I could lead the people someday." Grandfather insists that there are no more horizons to reach for: "No place to go, Jody. Every place is taken."[38] For him, the frontier and the impulse to push on toward a distant horizon are gone. Yet, for Jody, there may be a world to explore, a commitment to undertake, a quest of a new frontier.

STORIES OF *THE LONG VALLEY*

"The Chrysanthemums" is perhaps Steinbeck's most often anthologized short story. The story focuses our attention on Elisa, a woman who yearns for life, appreciation, sexuality, and maternal possibilities of procreation, yet is sadly limited by the sterile repetition of existence in a fog-filled valley set apart from the world. This well-made story enlists our sympathy for a frustrated woman whose vital impulses for life are repressed and channeled into her tender care for her flower garden. That her life is closed off becomes evident in the opening section of the story, where we learn that "the high gray-flannel fog of winter closed off the Salinas Valley from all the rest of the world."[39] In this "closed pot" of a valley, Elisa Allen cultivates her garden, while her husband, Henry, is distracted with business. The land waits for rain and Elisa waits for love. There is expectancy in Elisa, a hope that things will someday flourish in her barren world. Her chrysanthemums are her children, a precious displacement of her sexual and maternal inclinations.

When a tinker comes along, intent upon making a deal or to provide a service like banging the dents out of pots, Elisa shows him her treasured flowers. The tinker's unattached, rambling life appears romantic, and desire fills her encounter with him: a dream of the romance that is lacking in her life. "When the night is dark—why, the stars are sharp pointed, and there's quiet," says Elisa, in phrases that carry natural impulse, phallic imagery, and sexual implication. "Why you rise up and up! Every pointed star gets driven into your body. It's like that. Hot and sharp and—love-ly."[40] Elisa makes a gift of her flowers: an act of care and trust in the tinker. She then finds them thoughtlessly tossed on the roadside. The tinker only values utility. Elisa's sensitivity embraces nature and life, extending to people a trust that the tinker has violated. When her husband agrees to go with her to the fights, she asks, "Do the men hurt each other much?" Perhaps she wonders at the violence that men do to each other, the harshness within nature, the callousness with which the tinker has discarded the flowers that have been precious to her. Elisa has shown care in contrast with his carelessness. She seeks connection with a world sometimes ignorant and harsh where she can overcome her isolation and loneliness.

In "The White Quail," Mary Teller also has a garden, one she separates from "the world that wants to get in, all rough and tangled and unkempt."[41] Harry says to her, "You're like your own garden—fixed and just so."[42] The garden, Mary's space apart, is subject to intrusion by the world outside it, by a gray cat, or by Harry, who shoots the marvel that appears there: the white quail. An insensitive worldly realism tramples upon Mary's Edenic paradise. The incompleteness of her life is exposed as the quail is killed and wonderful innocence and beauty is destroyed.

"Flight" has often been regarded as an initiation story. Pepe Torres ventures into the mountains. Pepe and his family live on the edge of a cliff, which suggests the uncertainty of life.[43] Pepe's father has tripped over a stone and fallen on a rattlesnake. Pepe flees because he has killed a man during an argument in town. His flight is a venture toward manhood. The young man's flight toward the mountains is one toward an ominous place, where there are "the dark ones" and unknowable paths. His journey is in the direction of death. "He has a man's thing now to do," says Mama Torres. Rosy tells Emilio that Pepe has gone on a journey and will never come back. Emilio responds, "He is not dead . . . not yet."[44] We are told that as he journeys, Pepe's outline has become gray and misty. He wears a black coat and a black hat and he has a black knife. Pepe becomes increasingly black, like the watchers that his mother has warned him about. He is swallowed up in the mountains and from Mama Torres comes a keening wail, for she knows that he will die. The mountains are an arid place of shadow, a deathlike symbol, and the watchers are indeed what Steinbeck critic John Ditsky has referred to as the walking dead of folk myth.[45] The wounded Pepe will join them. We follow Pepe's struggle as he is enveloped by the mountains and becomes primitive, animal-ized, and absorbed into the darkness and the natural world, as Louis Owens points out in his discussion of the story.[46] Pepe is captured within the jagged "teeth" of the mountains to each side of him. Pepe has the courage to face death and when he dies the earth itself rumbles and falls to cover him. The story's naturalist symbolism, in this final image and others, conveys the idea that people and earth and "the all" are always related, as Owens has pointed out. He quotes John Ditsky's observation: "The earth, with deliberate action . . . reclaims its own."[47]

In "The Harness," Peter is unfulfilled, and life with Emma Randall, who is "sick most of the time," keeps him limited. Their house is de-scribed as being as restrained as its owners.[48] Peter is a good, ordinary farmer but he is overly governed by his wife. To escape, Peter goes to "fancy houses" in San Francisco. When his wife passes away he plants sweet peas throughout the farm. Despite her death he is unable to break free. He plans to return from San Francisco and put electric lights on at the farm because Emma always wanted electric lights. He is still dutiful, incomplete, and trapped in her world.

"Johnny Bear" is set in the Salinas Valley, where Emalin and Amy Hawkins live. The sisters are the town's "community conscience," its heritage and aristocracy. They live behind a high cypress hedge. Howev-er, fog comes in on the town from the swamp outside it. There is no "green barrier" to the fog as it sweeps in. Alex Hartnell recognizes that "there's something hanging over these people." He adds: "They can't do anything bad. It wouldn't be good for us."[49] He learns that something has happened to Amy. In her final despair the community's illusions are revealed. Johnny Bear is just a kind of recording device, the narrator says. He is much like Steinbeck in the 1930s, writing realistically and holding objectively a representation of events.

"The Murder," an O. Henry Prize Story for 1934, appears in *The Long Valley* as a violent story set in Canon del Castillo in the coastal moun-tains. The past meets with the present as the rocks take on the image of a tremendous stone castle. Through "a strange accident of time and water and erosion" they appear to suggest that this place and the story set in it emerge from the realm of myth or legend. In the modern frame, instinct and violence are, perhaps, an inheritance from this past. Jim Moore's code of ethics and chivalry include the belief that he ought not to beat his wife. He finds "no companionship in her."[50] Jelka, alienated from him, turns toward a relationship with her cousin. Jim Moore kills the cousin and later beats Jelka with a whip. Jelka, associated with animal imagery and with a foreign culture, is a problematic character who appears to be an "other" in this story.

"The Raid" presents Communist organizers who are affected by a raid. The story seems to be an incident that might have been included in *In Dubious Battle*, as Peter Lisca has suggested.[51] The character of Root parallels Jim Nolan, the new party member in *In Dubious Battle*. "The Vigilante" is the study of one man within the group or phalanx, an individual within the action of a mob. Mike has participated in a group that has lynched a black man. His emotions and his perceptions are affected. "Mike filled his eyes with the scene. He felt that he was dull. He wasn't seeing enough of it."[52] Apart from the mob he feels loneliness and joins with Welch, the bartender. His wife claims that he has been with a woman. However, Mike has not and he has felt isolated, even while with Welch. He gave himself to the crowd, the lynching mob, and now he feels alone, apart from that group energy that persuaded him to be involved in the deadly act. Like Jim Nolan in *In Dubious Battle*, Mike wanted to belong to something bigger than himself: a horrible thing, but an experience of human connection and energy he now misses.

"The Snake" brings us to the sea at Monterey. We encounter the fictional image of Ed Ricketts, as Dr. Phillips, the lonely individualist who will reappear in *Cannery Row* and *Sweet Thursday* as Doc. We meet Dr. Phillips in that liminal space of his laboratory, which is on land but extends toward the sea. It is a space of conscious rational fact, a space of the unconscious and the mythological. A woman wishes to purchase a rattlesnake: a symbol of evil or rebirth, as Louis Owens suggests with reference to a dictionary of symbols.[53] He notes Charles E. May's view that the woman, the snake, and the sea bring Dr. Phillips to ruminate on the unconscious. Owens suggests that Dr. Phillips's disconnection is reflected in the detachment of Doc Burton in *In Dubious Battle*.

These stories were written in the 1930s, just before the period that Steinbeck critic Tetsumaro Hayashi has called Steinbeck's "years of greatness."[54] In *The Long Valley*, themes of commitment emerged that would continue in various ways throughout his fiction. With *Tortilla Flat* (1935) Steinbeck further found his voice, a cast of paisano characters, a tone of humor, and his popular reading audience. "Three of my preceding novels did not make their advance and the advance was four hundred dollars," Steinbeck wrote. "The largest amount I had ever got for a short story was ninety dollars. This was for *The Red Pony* and the payment was only because the story was very long."[55] It is clear that Steinbeck struggled with his early novels and had to embrace the California setting realistically for his work to break through to a wider readership. He then made an abrupt turn with the seriousness of *In Dubious Battle* (1936), a powerful proletarian novel about an agricultural strike. *In Dubious Battle*, *Of Mice and Men*, and *The Grapes of Wrath* have sometimes earned the label of "realism" or "social realism." Yet a concern with myth runs throughout his work, from his earliest novel, *Cup of Gold*, across his writing career to *East of Eden* and beyond. We can see his interest in myth in his use of a folktale form for *The Pearl* and in his interest in revisiting Thomas Malory and the legends of King Arthur. Across the years critics have recognized the mythic patterns in Steinbeck's stories. The knights of the Arthurian round table reappear in *Tortilla Flat*. The Joad family seeks a promised land in California. *To a God Unknown* draws upon Biblical stories with the experiences of Joseph Wayne and his brothers. Figures from the Bible fill *East of Eden*, which recalls the story of Cain and Abel in the generations of the Trask family. The early fiction set the stage for all of the investigations of life, infused with mythical imagination and grounded in realism, that were to follow.

3

IN DUBIOUS BATTLE

In Dubious Battle is one of Steinbeck's strongest novels in traditional novel form. The novel presents the tense moments surrounding a strike and captures a moment of history in a specific place. It is the social history of everyday people based upon a composite of actual places and events. Yet it is more than merely a period piece of the 1930s. Steinbeck's novel is a timeless inquiry into "group man" and humanity's struggle for dignity and social justice. *In Dubious Battle* starts briskly, focusing upon the protagonist Jim Nolan as he meets with party organizer Harry Nilson. We hear Jim tell Harry about the struggles of his family, about his father, who fought physically and with determination. Jim wants to fight for something and joining with this group gives him new life and a sense of purpose. Crisp dialogue brings us into the story and Jim meets Mac, a man who is sometimes humanistic and sometimes manipulates men to advance his cause of strike and revolution. The novel drives forward dramatically: Jim and Mac hop a freight train and they enter the area around an apple orchard where they will stir worker sentiment to strike. The workers' obvious leader is London, whose daughter is about to have a baby. Mac delivers the baby, wins London's trust, and begins to make use of him to manipulate the men around him into strike mode. When the benevolent Al gives Mac and Jim a free meal, Mac begins to persuade Al to obtain his father's farm, so the workers will have a place to stay during their strike.

In Dubious Battle has a film adaptation by screenwriter Matt Rager, directed by James Franco. The film suggests that Steinbeck's novel is not merely a period piece, a bit of 1930s cultural memory. Rather, *In Dubious Battle* is quite relevant to our time, in which concerns have arisen about employment, fair business practices, and haves and have-nots. The film went into postproduction in 2015 as California was experiencing drought, the American economy was seeing the light after a tunnel of recession, and New York was promoting a higher minimum wage for all workers. Selena Gomez, as Lisa London, carried a baby on the film set. Nat Wolff portrayed Jim Nolan. A stellar cast with Vincent D'Onofrio, Ed Harris, Bryan Cranston, Robert Duvall, and others gives new life to Steinbeck's novel. Franco, who plays Mac McLeod, has been asserting the continuing relevance of Steinbeck with his Broadway role in *Of Mice and Men* and with this film project.

A PARABLE ON THE HUMAN CONDITION

In Dubious Battle has sometimes been called a novel of social realism. However, the story is not only one of realism. It is "a parable on the universal human condition," as Jackson J. Benson and Anne Loftis point out.[1] The strike becomes the battle on the plains of Heaven in Milton's *Paradise Lost*. *In Dubious Battle* shows Steinbeck reflecting upon what Benson has called "moral alternatives."[2] Steinbeck favored neither the workers nor the business owners and managers in this story. His story remains objective. "I have used a small strike in an orchard and valley as a symbol of man's eternal, bitter warfare with himself," Steinbeck wrote in a letter to George Albee.[3] *In Dubious Battle* connected with his perspective on group man, or his "Argument of Phalanx" from 1933, concerning a collective emotion and energy that develops within groups. We can see this group psychology of the phalanx at work throughout the novel. With *In Dubious Battle*, Steinbeck was writing a tragic story that investigates commitment and purpose. He wrote: "I'm not interested in [the] strike as a means of raising men's wages, and I'm not interested in ranting about justice and oppression, mere outcroppings which indicate the condition." He was concerned with the human condition as one of struggle: "man's eternal, bitter warfare with himself."[4]

For his novel, Steinbeck drew upon accounts of strikes throughout the region. He combined these, changed the geography, and imagined scenes without having participated in any workers' strike like the ones he portrayed. Throughout the novel he presents owners and growers and striking workers, never taking sides with any of them.[5] The novel provides a bildungsroman, the story of a character's growth and development, rather than a close analysis of a 1930s strike. Jim becomes a leader but his idealism leaves him vulnerable to exploitation and to becoming a victim. He is passionate and lacks caution. He moves from a lighted office to the dark fields.

Doc Burton appears quite different from Jim in his motivation. Doc comments to Mac that he doesn't believe in the cause, but that he believes in men.[6] Doc is a scientific observer, nonjudgmental and open to possibilities on both sides of the struggle. "I don't want to put on the blinders of good and bad and limit my vision," he says.[7] Doc Burton clearly sees the power of the collective consciousness of the group: "A man in a group isn't himself at all, he's a cell in an organism that isn't like him any more than the cells in your body are like you." Doc insists upon this point, comparing the strike to a wound: "Group men are always getting some kind of infection . . . I want to watch these group men, for they seem to me to be a new individual, not at all like single men."[8] Never truly part of the group, never making a commitment, Doc is lonely and isolated. He represents a non-teleological view in contrast with the teleological approach of strikers who believe that their actions will indeed show results and contribute to change and meaning. In his detachment, he is quite different from Mac, who is engaged in social action. He observes the action and later drifts off into the night.

Through Jim Nolan's story John Steinbeck shows how an American dream does not necessarily lead to prosperity but sometimes moves toward struggle. *In Dubious Battle* presents determined efforts, hopes, and naïve dreams. The story unfolds in a pattern that is episodic, structured in scenes. We can see Steinbeck following this method in *The Grapes of Wrath, Cannery Row, The Red Pony*, and the stories of *The Pastures of Heaven*. Some Steinbeck works, like *Of Mice and Men*, are built like plays, or sometimes read like scenes in plays, as in sections of *The Moon Is Down*. *In Dubious Battle* is a full-length novel in traditional form that holds together well structurally. The dubious battle refers to Satan's rebellion in Milton's *Paradise Lost*. This is the heroic Satan of romantic readings like those of William Blake and Percy Bysshe Shelley. It is clear that the power of Milton's Satan diminishes during the course of the twelve books of the epic poem. The strikers, like Milton's fallen angel, are doomed to fail against the action of the growers.

The seething tensions we encounter in *In Dubious Battle* are ones that were exacerbated by the Great Depression. They are part of the story of American business and labor. In *America and Americans*, in the 1960s, Steinbeck, writing in different times, describes the corporation quite straightforwardly as "one of the strongest organisms in the present world." He observes that such a business must be efficient, productive, and minimize cost and maximize profit to be successful in the marketplace. Historically, when labor began to organize into group action the business fought against such organization. A kind of "warfare" at times emerged with "loud and piercing charges": labor was being "treasonable to business" and "coldhearted" business was "exploiting the workingman."[9] Such issues lie at the center of the dispute in the apple orchards in *In Dubious Battle*.

THE TURBULENT THIRTIES

In Dubious Battle is a proletarian novel like no other. Like many of Steinbeck's works it unfolds within a web of myth. The title evokes a struggle between cosmic forces. The "group man" or collectivity that the migrant workers become recalls Steinbeck's emphasis on the Arthurian legends, as in *Tortilla Flat*: the quest of would-be knights. Doc Burton appears as Steinbeck's wisdom figure in a novel that is saturated with ideas from biology. The collective of migrant workers is an organism that we are observing. Indeed, Doc views the group as a collective biological organism, or group man: the phalanx. Steinbeck maintains an objective narrative point of view.

As a reader begins this novel he or she is drawn into concern for the individual destiny of Jim Nolan. Gradually, Jim is subsumed into the collectivity that is the "group man." Mac is a master manipulator who cunningly partners with the naïve and idealistic Jim. Mac responds to London's daughter's pregnancy and delivers her child, although he knows nothing about obstetrics. This act of heroism wins over the alpha leader of the migrant workers. Suddenly we find ourselves in the midst of this large group of workers. For this is a story of the crowd. They are the men we see under hats on the bread line in a grainy black-and-white photograph in *Time* magazine. They are the anonymous soldiers under helmets embarking for Europe who are described by Steinbeck later in one of his World War II dispatches. Steinbeck did not approach the phenomenon of the crowd in the same critical way as José Ortega y Gasset in *The Revolt of the Masses*. He wondered at the collective energy that could arise in groups, that collective unconscious that sociologist Emile Durkheim identified. The collective was a feature of the thirties, and Steinbeck, intrigued by the biological world, was fascinated with the phenomenon of the crowd.

Steinbeck's writings of the 1930s are among the most memorable of his works and they illustrate some of the social challenges of this turbulent decade. In *On Native Grounds* (1956), literary critic Alfred Kazin referred to the 1930s as a time of "national self-scrutiny."[10] John Steinbeck's novels of the thirties are key documents that participate in the testing of America's conscience during this time. With *In Dubious Battle*, *Of Mice and Men*, and *The Grapes of Wrath* Steinbeck was recording history. "I'm trying to write history while it is happening," he wrote in a letter.[11] Steinbeck was not writing a tract for proletarian politics. "I'm not interested in strike as a means of raising men's wages," he wrote, "and I'm not interested in ranting about justice and oppression . . . I wanted to be merely a recording consciousness, judging nothing."[12] Steinbeck wanted to see the plight of migrants and to set it down clearly in his stories. He sought to "do an honest day's work" as a writer, he said.[13] He was not, he thought, of the same stuff as great artists are made. His goal was to show the concrete, the immediate, the animal basis of human life and material necessity. Steinbeck makes an appeal to "moral sympathy."[14] As Morris Dickstein observes, Steinbeck sees people as essentially good, though often twisted and damaged by what they have lived through and by institutions that were meant to serve them.[15] These migrants seemed to have little means to shape their own futures. Yet they are portrayed as resilient, as "the people."

Steinbeck was a journalist among the people who, with clear prose, sharply transmitted the images and voices of a specific place and time. "His strength is not in general ideas but in the concrete, visceral evocation of things as they are," observes Dickstein.[16] Steinbeck often seems intent upon asking how we can create a more compassionate and just world. Yet he also appears to often chart out an inexorable process, a kind of Darwinian determinism in which characters find themselves amid relentless, impersonal forces. In the thirties he was a working writer who could easily identify with the people that he was writing about.

Steinbeck emerged professionally during the economically troubled time of the thirties, a time during which government was recast for the people. Looking back, Steinbeck called the thirties a time when "imperceptibly the American nation and its people had changed."[17] He recalled an energy that was reshaping the infrastructure of America. He writes of "reforesting the stripped hills" and that "painters were frescoing the walls of public buildings."[18] Steinbeck writes that for him the 1930s are "a library of personal memories."[19] The Great Depression was no life-changing shock for him. "I didn't have any money to lose," he writes.[20] He had been "practicing the Depression for a long time."[21] He was "writing books that no one would buy."[22] Steinbeck watched the changes wrought by the Stock Market Crash and the subsequent economic downslide. He recalls: "Then came the panic, and panic changed to dull shock. When the market fell, the factories, the mines, and steel works closed and then no one could buy anything, not even food."[23]

For a time, Steinbeck stayed rent-free at his father's three-room cottage in Pacific Grove. He writes: "People in the inland cities, in the closed and shuttered industrial cemeteries, had greater problems than I."[24] Steinbeck recognized that he could survive by fishing the coastline and making simple meals. He remained in contact with Ed Ricketts and with the workers of Cannery Row and he was thoroughly conscious of how people struggled and endured. He wrote about the paisanos in *Tortilla Flat*: men that he had worked with, whose lives he had observed. They were outsiders, social outcasts. To him they offered a fascinating alternative to conventional American lifestyles.

The thirties was a time when American films and popular imagery represented the virtues of the common man. The screwball comedy attempted to lighten the social burden with entertainment. Meanwhile, the Depression years instilled an ethic of hard work, pride, and tenacity. People learned how to conserve, how to be frugal and to make use of what was available. Steinbeck recalls that entertainment was based upon fundamentals: "the public library, endless talks, long walks, any number of games."[25] A time of national trial called for solutions. There was a rare urgency for reform to restore stability.

In the first years of the 1930s more than ten million Americans were unemployed. Only a quarter of these people were receiving relief. One consequence of this was vagrancy. There were hundreds of people wandering, looking for work, much like George and Lennie in *Of Mice and Men*. Apples were left in the orchards of California. The cotton fields of Oklahoma and Texas were not productive. Mayor Curley of Boston cautioned President Herbert Hoover that his policies were creating "a nation of beggars."[26] The literary critic Edmund Wilson suggested that the predictions of Karl Marx about capitalism were coming true: Capitalism was imploding because of its inherent contradictions. The unrest included strikes in the coal fields in 1931. A near-fatal riot erupted in Dearborn, Michigan, in March 1932. In Oregon, striking agitators were arrested and sent into incarceration in a lunatic asylum. *Harper's* carried a news story that it titled "Rebellion in the Cornbelt: American Farmers Beat Their Ploughshares into Swords." It was a turbulent time.

The presidential campaign of 1932 brought a call to mend the nation's wounds. Franklin Delano Roosevelt was a man of personality born into a political family, the younger cousin of Theodore Roosevelt. He projected qualities of leadership and he had sharp, well-honed political skills. Unlike Roosevelt, President Hoover was not a man inclined toward rousing exhortation or dramatic gestures. Hoover carried on with what one British journalist described as his "sour, puckered face of a bilious baby, his dreary monotone reading, interminably and for the most part inaudibly. . . without a single inflection of voice to relieve the tedium."[27] Roosevelt, in contrast, offered a unique charisma matured by his crippling bouts with polio. His theme song, "Happy Days Are Here Again," sounded over his 1932 campaign.

When Herbert Hoover left office in 1933 the economic devastation was apparent across America. More than ten thousand banks had failed. Thousands of businesses had gone under. There were more than twelve million Americans out of work. It was no longer possible to rely upon local resources alone. Government intervention in the economy was needed. Franklin Delano Roosevelt's election coincided with a congressional majority of Democrats and he determined with that majority to put America back to work through government programs.

March 4, 1933, was an overcast day and Roosevelt declared: "I shall ask Congress for . . . broad executive power to wage a war against the emergency as great as if we were . . . invaded by a foreign foe."[28] The New Deal began. The Works Progress Administration (WPA) created 2,500 hospitals, 5,900 schools, 84 airports, 13,000 playgrounds, and more than 650,000 miles of roads. This infrastructure would last for years after World War II. In New York City the Public Works Administration built the Lincoln Tunnel and the Triborough Bridge. In Florida they created the Key West causeway. They created the dam on the Columbia River and Colorado River and the vast Tennessee River Valley project.

The Great Depression was a worldwide crisis. Instability challenged the very fabric of Western democracy. In Britain, the number of unemployed reached 2.5 million in 1930. The British conservative government worked to gradually reduce unemployment without deficit spending or large social reforms. In contrast, Sweden practiced socialism to overcome joblessness with public works and social welfare programs. France was in turmoil: shifting amid changes of government. In Germany the consequences were catastrophic. On July 31 some fourteen million Germans went to the polls and 37 percent voted for the Nazi Party. In 1932, Germany had been dealing with economic misery for years. Rising inflation had brought suffering. Some 43 percent of Germany was unemployed. On November 6, 1932, Germany had a new election and voted for its Reichstag. Amid a collection of Socialist and Communist politicians arose the National Socialists as the largest single political party. They were duly elected to office and they brought with them their new chancellor, Adolf Hitler. The results are well known: a militarized state that emphasized nationalism and pride and promoted an ideology of strength, steel, and the ugly demon of racism.

Europe in the 1930s faced a time of struggle between Fascist and Communist ideologies for the soul of the people. Hitler was successful politically and Mussolini was "riding up on Italian poverty and confusion," observed Steinbeck.[29] In 1934, Stalin's purges had eliminated his rivals and decimated much of the country. For Americans like Steinbeck the events of Europe were far away but they formed a shadowy backdrop for contemplation on the struggle to rebuild democracy at home. Roads, jobs, income were all vitally important. Lives were at stake. The social conscience of Steinbeck was engaged by what he saw at home in America. The American concern of this era focused upon the common man, the "forgotten man" of F.D.R.'s 1932 speeches: men and women trying to make ends meet.

The Great Depression had taken its toll on American labor. Unions had dwindled in the early 1930s from a membership of about five million to about three million. The unions in America regained some standing during the 1930s with the initiatives of the New Deal. There was increased labor organization in the steel mining, automobile, and textile industries. The National Industrial Recovery Act provided for collective bargaining. The 1935 Wagner Act, the National Labor Relations Act, required businesses to bargain with any union representing a majority of their employees. Steinbeck's *In Dubious Battle* was published at a time when labor unions began to experience a surge of political support. Union membership grew to eight million by 1939. Organized labor then burgeoned to fourteen million across the war years. Steinbeck wrote of apple-picking migrants in California who were not represented by ambitious leaders. The Democratic Congress passed the National Labor Relations Act in 1935. In 1936, the year the novel appeared, the Committee for Industrial Organization was formed. In Flint, Michigan, there was a General Motors assembly plant strike. American workers heard the call to unionize in the steel, automotive, rubber, and electrical industries.

Steinbeck could reach working-class readers with his simple, concrete, uncluttered style. Morris Dickstein observes that "no protest writer had a greater impact on how Americans understood their country."[30] The Depression itself is not presented explicitly in most Steinbeck novels of the thirties. It is the often unspoken backdrop and setting. Steinbeck viewed his characters from the outside and he portrayed their world with clear immediacy. They were invariably rooted in the land. They were America's working men and women.

Steinbeck sought objectivity in his novel *In Dubious Battle*. Yet his sympathy is clearly with the exploited. He remains focused on the group rather than individualizing characters or exploring the psychology of his characters. The story does appear to enter the consciousness of Doc at times but generally the characters are depicted in an external fashion. We watch Mac and Jim as they politicize and radicalize the migrant farm workers. Mac enlists London and Dakin, leaders among the migrants that he can persuade toward the cause. Mac is willing to sacrifice people and even uses the public display of a dead body to rouse resentment. He is energetic and confident while devious and manipulative, and Jim, a truly tragic character, falls under his spell.

ECONOMIC PARALLELS IN OUR TIME

Writing in the 1960s, Steinbeck points out that eventually shares in corporations came to be held by a wide variety of people who represented a cross section of Americans. Corporations began spending enormous sums on public relations to maintain a positive public image. Individuals' lives were lived within the corporation and position was "keyed to performance of duties, activities, and even attitudes which make the corporation successful."[31] In such circumstances, disputes were fewer and less violent. The corporation, in its single-minded pursuit of money, became "much more efficient than any existing government."[32] Of course, unions developed frameworks for workers' rights also. There was legal arbitration and government regulation. There were still strikes by workers, organized by their representatives, but they generally did not devolve into bloody riots. *In Dubious Battle* characterizes a period during which labor and management struggles appeared often but it also suggests a persistent tension in the economics of our time.

During the 2016 presidential debates the candidates of both parties have repeatedly turned to discussion of economic issues. Concerns have been raised about American labor and the corporate outsourcing of jobs to other countries. Questions about immigration have fueled the Republican Party debates, and the Democratic Party candidates have contended with the issues of economic disparity between the very wealthy and the American middle class. The issues of Steinbeck's migrants can provide a reference point for reflection on these issues. When Steinbeck's *In Dubious Battle* appeared, Asian and Mexican migrants in California had been partly replaced by migrants like those represented in his novel. We see the workers exploited by the owners of the corporate farms and we watch as they are persuaded by Mac's rhetoric.

Soon after the novel appeared, Fred T. Marsh of the *New York Times* wrote that *In Dubious Battle* was "both dramatically and realistically, the best labor and strike novel to come out of our contemporary economic and social unrest."[33] That unrest was heightened by the Great Depression. "The bottom dropped out, and I could see that clearly too because I had been practicing for the Depression a long time. I wasn't involved with loss," Steinbeck wrote.[34] On October 24, 1929, Black Thursday, the stock market went into panicked selling of shares. Financiers gathered to quell the panic, bought shares, and stocks rallied. Some thirteen million shares had been traded. On Monday, October 28, there were ten million shares traded and the *New York Times* index dropped forty-nine points. On Tuesday, October 29, the stock market opened with hundreds of selling orders and a sharp drop in prices. More than a million Americans were directly affected by the losses. However, the worst was yet to come: the deep abyss of painful years as economic problems dragged on.

Workers' strikes were an inevitable response to a deeply felt need for work and just wages. In the cold winter of 1930–1931 businesses were closing, banks were shutting their doors, wages and shares and industrial output were plummeting. Unemployment was steadily increasing and as people entered the desperate vacuum of joblessness the bread lines grew longer and the middle class tasted vulnerability. On May 1, the lights flickered on in the Empire State Building, with its steel peak rising 1,250 feet over a city where people struggled. For all the human aspiration that might reach for the sky, there were signs of misery in the streets.

Businesses now had an array of issues to contend with to make any profit in a depressed economy. Those Americans who could work struggled with the impact of the Depression, working diligently and becoming increasingly frugal. Some argued for their rights: for good working conditions and a reasonable income for a job well done. In New York, Franklin Roosevelt, with his eyes on the White House, asserted in August 1931 that government could and should assist people who could not help themselves. In California and other areas of the country, the unions spoke loudly, sometimes militantly, and the workers in California organized.

Wages fell. Ten million people were unemployed and nearly thirty million Americans lacked income. More than two million of these people, like Lennie and George in *Of Mice and Men*, wandered from place to place in search of work. In Detroit, some two-thirds of the population was out of work, and in Chicago 1.6 million were unemployed, while others waited much longer than in the past for a paycheck. Under these conditions some people began talking of strikes and others of revolution. On June 16, 1931, the *New York Times* reported that President Hoover warned of the detrimental result of revolutions in other countries. The answer was courage and faith in the American system, not revolutionary change. A "timid people, black with despair, have lost faith in the American system," he said.[35]

Steinbeck was aware that workers were troubled and he was equally troubled that industries were resorting to coercive practices to maintain order. Police took a firm approach backed by authoritarian assertions of law and order. However, the pressure applied against striking workers in other areas came from private security gangs. In Dearborn, Michigan, Henry Ford responded to a riot in March 1932 by creating a private security force. Industrialists like Ford hired security to protect their interests and hoods beat up on protesters.

In the presidential election, Roosevelt received 22.8 million votes, overcoming his Republican rival Hoover, who got 15.75 million votes. Roosevelt entered office with a huge challenge: nearly a third of America's potential labor force, about fifteen million people, remained unemployed. Banks were failing as depositors withdrew their funds. Disgruntled workers were restless. On March 4, 1933, inauguration day, Roosevelt spoke under cloudy skies and asserted that the nation's primary task was to put people to work. This could be accomplished through "relief activities." So he would work through the system to achieve this. "I shall ask Congress for . . . broad executive power to wage a war against the emergency as great as if we were . . . invaded by a foreign foe," he said. Roosevelt reassured a troubled America that much could be accomplished with fortitude: "We have nothing to fear but fear itself."[36]

The New Deal was born but need and restlessness were not easily overcome. Roosevelt's "Fireside Chats," his radio talks, came into the living rooms of people across America with a rare intimacy. In his first Fireside Chat the president insisted, "We cannot fail." Nor would the dollar fail. Treasury Secretary Henry A. Wallace called for the symbol of a pyramid to be placed on the back of the dollar bill, suggesting strength and all the hope and faith of the mystical Masons. An alphabet soup of agency names was soon announced: the AAA (Agricultural Adjustment Administration, May 1933); FERA (Federal Emergency Relief Administration, June 1933); TVA (Tennessee Valley Authority, May 18, 1933); NRA (National Recovery Administration, June 1933, not to be confused with the National Rifle Association, for which those letters are familiar today. The National Recovery Act was struck down by the Supreme Court in 1935). There would be a PWA (Public Works Administration, a rearrangement of letters with the WPA), CCC (Civilian Conservation Corps) work camps, and even the president himself would be translated to the famous initials F.D.R.

FERA allocated five hundred million dollars for humanitarian aid. The TVA created a vast project to channel the waters of the Tennessee River with dams that formed a great waterway system and a series of lakes. The Public Works Administration, managed tightly by Harold Ickes, built roads, bridges, canals, airports, schools, hospitals, office buildings, power plants, and sewer systems. Job creation programs like this put Americans back to work. However, as the economic crisis continued, so did tensions between labor and management. Severe labor disputes were familiar news of the day. Compounding problems in the plains states was the ecological catastrophe of the Dust Bowl, thrashing those states in May 1934 with 350 million tons of dust blown across many miles. The drought, like the impoverished conditions of the Depression years, forced a grain of toughness into the fiber of Americans. Some faced the crisis like the pioneers: They practiced tenacious endurance, they gathered up with sturdy values, and they fought back.

In Dubious Battle shows how a group of workers fought back but became manipulated by agitators. It dramatizes the bitter and violent protest of pickers in California and the commitment of a naïve but courageous man. Some reviewers, like Marsh, explored the basis of realism in the novel. Harry Thornton Moore proposed that the fictional strike was focused upon Pajaro Valley, near Watsonville, California.[37] Tagus Ranch, off Highway 99 between Fresno and Tulare, has also been cited. Steinbeck has said that it was an imaginative composite. "I have usually avoided using actual places to avoid hurting feelings," he wrote.[38] Yet the novel drew upon actual incidents. The California Agricultural Strike of 1933 included more than eighteen thousand workers during the harvest in fruit and cotton fields of the San Joaquin Valley. Workers protested pay cuts, which were particularly severe because of the Great Depression. A cotton workers' strike drew about twelve thousand workers and lasted twenty-four days. Workers were evicted from company housing. Workers were given about fifteen cents an hour, or $1.50 a day, for their efforts at Tagus: an amount upon which one could barely live on food from the company store. In frustration they asked for thirty-five cents an hour. With mediation involved, Tagus eventually agreed to twenty-five cents an hour.

On October 18, 1933, the *New York Times* reported on problems in Pixley, in Tulare County, where workers died and eight were injured:

> Ranchers who heard of the proposed meeting acquired a caravan of about thirty automobiles, drove into Pixley and surrounded the meet-

ing. Suddenly there was a shot from the caravan, then a volley. Three men fell dead and many more were wounded . . . but bloodshed at Pixley did not break the strike.[39]

In the novel, when Joy dies Mac uses this as a means to build passion and incentive among the workers for the strike. This also occurred in Pixley, where the union made use of the funeral of the workers to place pressure on the growers. In the film of *The Grapes of Wrath* we hear of Pixley. A man named Spencer in a fancy white car pauses to speak with the Joad family, who are gathered alongside the road. "You folks looking for work?" he asks. The Joads are told that work is waiting a few miles up the road. "Tell them Spencer sent you." Ma lets forth a rejoicing squeal of hope as the car pulls away. However, the reality that awaits the Joads is hardly cause for rejoicing. They encounter a police action that suggests an attempt to quell protest and they enter a camp that Tom Joad recognizes as "none too prosperous."

Some readers have found a proletarian politics in scenes like this. However, Steinbeck was always principally focused upon creating a story. He was not a writer of political tracts. He was a writer with a message who closely observed life around him and wrote of the conflicting tensions in human nature with a humane vision of social justice.[40] *The Grapes of Wrath*, *East of Eden*, *Of Mice and Men*, *Tortilla Flat*, *Cannery Row*, and others are timeless works that explore the human condition and convey a sense of the universal. A novel like *In Dubious Battle*, which has been called by Harold Bloom a period piece of interest only to cultural historians, extends beyond its place and time in the noble intentions of Jim Nolan and the vitality of the story's other characters, such as Mac, the labor organizer, and Doc Burton. Whereas a social historian may read the novel for descriptions of labor strikes, another reader may appreciate *In Dubious Battle* as a story about dreams and ambitions in a difficult world.[41] *In Dubious Battle* takes place in California, in a specific place and time. Yet in this specificity is universality: the novel expresses struggle and human aspiration.

The novel compels us to reflect upon labor, business, and human activity within groups. Historically, Americans have created and joined organizations, as Alexis de Tocqueville observed in the 1830s. "We are a very strange people; we love organizations and hate them," wrote Steinbeck in the 1960s.[42] In politics Americans join parties. In work situations they unionize and join in groups for strength in bargaining. Steinbeck noted the tendency of Americans to align themselves with Elks clubs, Rotary, women's clubs. There are "scores of lodges, orders, encampments"—"Elks, Masons, Knight Templars"—that have "seemed to fulfill a need for grandeur against a background of commonness, for aristocracy in the midst of democracy."[43] However, it is disturbing when "screwball" leaders generate fear, setting cohorts "in noisy motion," or when "screwball organizations" arise "which teach hatred and revenge to the ignorant and fearful people, using race or religion as the enemy."[44]

One may wonder how Steinbeck would view recent calls to build a wall on the border of Mexico, or the call to prohibit Muslims from entering the United States. How might Steinbeck respond to the populist strain in current American politics? Certainly, large rallies and political conventions intrigued him. Steinbeck was fascinated by the phenomenon of a labor strike. He wondered at how an individual could be swept up by that collective energy and his character of Jim Nolan is a clear example of that. Toward the end of his career he wrote in *America and Americans* of "the totem" as a primitive survival of human group-mind. Democracy, in Steinbeck's view, is about individualism: freedom of creative thought. Democracy expresses a commitment to human rights. It disturbed him to see mass behavior like that of the "cheerleaders" outside a New Orleans school who protested the integration of that school with violent obscenities. Steinbeck was fascinated by group behavior but also appalled by prejudice and ideology. The group always presented a "mask" to the world. The Ku Klux Klan was an example, but others can be located in modern history. "It must be secret, exclusive, mysterious, cruel, afraid, dangerous, and monstrously ignorant," he wrote.[45] The tension underlying *In Dubious Battle* includes the pressure of that which "still exists as a memory of our savage past."[46]

Steinbeck's fundamental belief in democracy was expressed principally in his writing. He brought into view society's outcasts, people who otherwise might not have had a voice. He wrote that the 1930s introduced "the new concept that the Government is responsible for its citizens."[47] "There are whole libraries of books about the Thirties—millions of feet of films, still and moving," Steinbeck says. There is "a library of personal memories."[48] The 1930s was a time when Americans tolerated scarcity, whereas in the 1960s, he argues that Americans are absorbed in things. He says that for entertainment in the 1930s they went to the public library, engaged in endless talk, took long walks, had sex, and listened to music. People learned how to be frugal and to make use of what was available.[49] He asserts that Americans were sustained by grounding their conduct and action in an ethical code and that this is essential to the survival of nations: "Ethics, morals, codes of conduct are the stern rules which in the past we needed to survive—as individuals, as groups, and as nations."[50]

From the 1930s on Steinbeck was a passionate creative journalist. *In Dubious Battle* began in concern, in a liberal position of support for workers organizing. Personally, Steinbeck disliked Communism and remained opposed to it. "I remember one book that got trounced by the Communists as being capitalist and by the capitalists as being Communist," he wrote.[51] *The Grapes of Wrath* began like an ethnographic study by a participant-observer. Steinbeck went to live with the Oklahoma families at the government camp at Arvin, near Bakersfield. Seven articles, "The Harvest Gypsies," appeared in the *San Francisco News* in 1936 and were later reprinted as *Their Blood Is Strong* in 1938. Tom Collins, the camp supervisor, could verify all of it. *Life* magazine found "Starvation under the Orange Trees" too much for its audience and canceled it. So the incendiary piece appeared in the *Monterey Trader* instead. George West of the *San Francisco News* asked for a news story, Steinbeck writes: "I went to live with these migrant people . . . I liked these people. They had qualities of humor and courage and inventiveness and energy that appealed to me."[52]

4

OF MICE AND MEN

Of Mice and Men is a study of relationships. It is the story of two itinerant farm workers, George and Lennie, and how their dreams come into tragic contact with the people on a rural farm in California. *Of Mice and Men* is much like Steinbeck's early works like *The Pastures of Heaven* and *The Long Valley*: a study of the interactions of people in a rural environment. It is not a social-political novel like *In Dubious Battle* or *The Grapes of Wrath*. This short novel reminds us that Steinbeck was not primarily a political protest writer, although some have cast him in this guise. Rather, he was an ethical writer, one who looked squarely at the determining factors of animal life and human life. He was an earthy writer, who cast the world with immediacy in concrete language. His simple, accessible style in *Of Mice and Men* has made this novel widely available as an introduction to literature for many young readers.

Of Mice and Men displays Steinbeck's attention to the simple and often forgotten common man. The Nobel committee pointed out Steinbeck's capacity for showing "compassion," and this book, as much as any other in his oeuvre, reflects this. The story of George and Lennie is a simple portrait set in a small frame. The story is set firmly in a description of the land and proceeds to examine the quest for human dignity, hope, and survival. Steinbeck's modesty as a writer comes through in his recognition that his novel was a "little book." "Steinbeck leaves man's more sublime aspirations to writers of cosmic or tragic ambition," writes Morris Dickstein. Steinbeck welcomes being considered a minor writer. He is a man with a vision of humanity that is tied to the land, to basic needs for food and shelter and for belonging, companionship, and care. The basic needs of George and Lennie are faced with a competitive system that ignores them. Their dreams are never to be realized.

Reflecting upon the reception of his novel, Steinbeck wrote to George Albee: "As usual it is disliked by some and liked by some. It is always that way." In another letter to Albee, dated January 11, 1937, he wrote that he had no expectation of money from the book. "It's such a simple little thing." However, shortly after he sent this letter, the Book-of-the-Month selection of Steinbeck's novel catapulted the book onto the best-seller list.

The novel was both applauded and derided by critics. That like and dislike for the novel continues to this day. Jonathan Leaf in *Criterion* (December 2007) writes: "Even by Steinbeck's own modest standards, *Of Mice and Men* is melodramatic and contrived." "Both the dialogue and the narrative of the book are impressive," he says. Yet the characters are "crudely rendered and unbelievable." He notes that the early reception of the novel suggested a "left-right divide": Eleanor Roosevelt liked the book while conservative pundits derided it. The persistent presence of the novel in classrooms is also addressed: "Certainly some of its appeal to high school teachers is that it is so reductive: almost anyone can understand its lessons and its obvious symbolism after a helpful in-class discussion."

Of Mice and Men is one of the most often taught of Steinbeck stories. The short novel has become a steady part of the curriculum in the United States and Britain. It becomes new for each generation because Steinbeck's readers respond in new ways to his stories. *Of Mice and Men* is often one of the first Steinbeck stories that readers encounter. The sentences are crisp, the language simple, and the images clear. At the heart of the book the relationship of care and concern between George and Lennie often draws readers' sympathy. With *Of Mice and Men*, Steinbeck explored chance, vulnerability, violence, and innocence.

Of Mice and Men began as an idea for a play, a story for young people that Steinbeck called "Something That Happened." The plan evolved into the story of two farm workers who appear at a ranch after running away from another job. They dream of one day having a farm of their own. George wants to protect Lennie, a mentally limited individual of great strength who has no family. Lennie has a liking for small creatures like rabbits and mice, and he has a tendency toward violence. When they come into contact with Curley, the ranch owner's son, and with his wife, the stage is set for a tragic story. Lennie, who likes things that feel soft, unintentionally kills a mouse and then a puppy. When Curley's wife suggests that he touch her soft hair she also is killed. Curley vows revenge and summons a posse to hang Lennie. George steals a gun from a farmhand and uses it to kill Lennie before the mob can get to him. They speak of their dream to get a farm in the moments before George pulls the trigger, ending the dream. When it is over, Slim takes George up the trail for a drink. A compassionate character, Slim shows care in a world that, for George, is bleak and broken. The farmhand who owned the gun looks at them as they walk away, and says, "Now what the hell ya suppose is eatin' them two guys?"

George and Lennie are deeply flawed outcasts who will never achieve their dream of a farm. They reflect the lives of people for whom all the schemes of mice and men will come to nothing. Both are lonely and in need of the companionship that they find in each other. Lennie wishes for rabbits, for warmth and contact: "the inarticulate and powerful yearning of all men," Steinbeck calls it. The story affirms that people need this connection. Lennie is described as childlike and he is as committed to George as George is to him. "Sure, he's jes like a kid," says George of Lennie, who is strong, violent, and fundamentally dangerous. While the conclusion of the novel seems pessimistic, the way that George takes responsibility for Lennie shows a humane connection between them. [1]

Steinbeck viewed his initial effort with *Of Mice and Men* as a not-quite-successful attempt to meld theater and the novel form. The play-novelette had been an experiment. "I thoroughly intend to try it again," he wrote. [2] Plays may be difficult to read, he observed. They require visual imagination and some knowledge of dramatic symbols. Plays are meant to be acted for a live audience and that contact between people is one experience that a novel does not participate in. Group experiences like war, a community's religious experience, or a prizefight "cannot be understood in solitude." [3] The force of a play is what Steinbeck was after in writing *Of Mice and Men*. Revised and directed by theater and film professionals, the story has taken on new life. There have been three major film productions and several Broadway runs of the story.

A MORAL SENSIBILITY

Of Mice and Men remains a story that conveys a profound moral sensibility. Robert Coles, the noted child psychologist, recognizes this moral quality as "the central issue of our existence, the factor that defines the quality of our lives as human beings." Coles has written of people finding a source of inspiration in literature, an experience that literature teachers can also attest to. "Literature can be a moral catalyst," he observes, "because great writers explore a serious question: Why do people do what they do?"[4] Steinbeck presents this question in the story of George and Lennie. Their commitment to each other and to a dream persists despite their flaws and limitations. *Of Mice and Men* is like a simple bridge undergirded by Steinbeck's moral imagination, and this moral concern is a quality that persisted across his entire writing career.

Steinbeck and Coles were both present in New Orleans on November 14, 1960, when six-year-old Ruby Bridges was ushered past barricades and hostile protestors and became the first student to integrate a Louisiana school. Steinbeck was appalled by the jeering from an organized group of women he called "the cheerleaders." The incident struck the moral imaginations of both men. Coles visited Ruby Bridges and her family afterward and listened to her story. Coles's distinguished career in psychiatric fieldwork began with this experience. Steinbeck's career was coming to a close with *Travels with Charley* and *The Winter of Our Discontent*.

Coles writes: "Morality defines not only how we get along with the world and one another and the rules of life: it characterizes our very nature." He adds that morality has to do with human connection. "It has to do with the kind of connection that responds to others, and in turn earns the caring response of others."[5] Steinbeck appears to hope that something can be learned that will improve "the kind of connection that responds to others" in a fashion of respect. In his work and in that of Coles is a belief that literature can contribute to this connection. In *The Call of Stories: Teaching and the Moral Imagination*, Coles recalls the comments of a student who told him that the experiences of some characters in literature helped him to make choices: "They really speak to me," he said, "there's a lot of me in them, or vice-versa."[6]

The characters of George and Lennie in *Of Mice and Men* have spoken to many young readers who pick up Steinbeck's story in school settings.

They respond to it in personal terms. Of course, literary critics have had different views from those of common readers. Edmund Wilson called *Of Mice and Men* Steinbeck's "compact little drama." Peter Lisca called this story "the fallen world inhabited by sons of Cain, forever exiled from Eden, the little farm of which they dream." Warren French suggested that readers ought to consider the story "an expression of Steinbeck's outraged compassion for the victims of chaotic forces."[7]

Before the appearance of Steinbeck critics like Peter Lisca or Warren French, reviewers in the popular media often attempted to locate what was exceptional, or different, about Steinbeck's work. *Of Mice and Men* drew many such comments. When Lewis Gannett of the *New York Herald Tribune* reviewed *Of Mice and Men*, he asserted that John Steinbeck wrote differently from the writers who create "tough talk and snarl in books that have power without pity." Gannett perceptively observed: "The most significant things John Steinbeck has to say about his characters are never put into words; they are the overtones of which the reader is never wholly conscious—and that is art." Wilbur Needham of the *Los Angeles Times* on February 28, 1937, saw Steinbeck as an innovator. He experiments, Needham observed, but he "always has his feet on the ground and is rooted in the earth." Louis Paul of the *New York Herald Tribune* called this a "prose made of wind and soil and weather."[8] F. Scott Fitzgerald, on the other hand, in the years of his decline, charged Steinbeck with being a "cagey cribber," who had allegedly "cribbed" a section of *Of Mice and Men* from Frank Norris's *McTeague*. "His debt to *The Octopus* is also enormous," Fitzgerald wrote to Edmund Wilson.[9]

The responses of common readers—those who are not professional critics, editors, or professors of literature—may be even more interesting. In the *New York Times* (March 5, 2012), Winnie Ho reported on the difference in readings of Steinbeck's *Of Men and Men* that had recently taken place in eighth-grade classes in the upper-middle-class suburban town of Westfield, New Jersey, and the more urban Plainfield, New Jersey. Classes at both schools discussed chapter 4 in *Of Mice and Men*, in which Crooks, a black man, and Curley's wife appear. Students at Roosevelt Intermediate School in Westfield tended to focus their understanding on a wife trapped in a relationship, who taunted men to gain attention. The students in Plainfield responded to racism on the ranch and to Crooks's experience.[10]

Steinbeck did not write *Of Mice and Men* with classrooms in mind. The world was the classroom that mattered most to him. He once counseled his son, who asked how long he had to go to school. His reply of "about fifteen years" met with another question: "Do I have to?" The same tone may be heard in some homes or classrooms nationally when students are assigned to read *Of Mice and Men*, which is one of the mainstays of the English curriculum. The answer parents and teachers might offer is the same as Steinbeck's answer to his son: "I'm afraid so." However, as Steinbeck added, if you have the luck to have a good teacher you have "a wonderful thing."[11] (Several female teachers were significant in Steinbeck's life. His mother was a schoolteacher. Edith Brunoni taught him to play the piano and encouraged in him an appreciation for music. Ora M. Cupp encouraged his writing.)

Teaching Steinbeck's story can encourage reading as an act of discovery. Reading is a skill that we cannot afford to lose because it engages our thinking and our creativity. If a purpose of literature is "understanding and communication," as Steinbeck said in his Nobel Prize speech, that act of understanding begins in reading, with a reader. He once reminded his readers that some adults forget "how hard and dull and long school is." He wrote: "Learning to read is probably the most difficult and revolutionary thing that happens to the human brain." Then he referred his readers to observe the efforts of an illiterate adult trying to read. Steinbeck did not say much about how we read or about our interpretation of what we read in his brief comments on school and teachers. However, he did share his discussion with his son about his own teachers and what he had learned from them. What those teachers had in common, he said, was a love for what they were doing. They cared. They were committed. They confronted the truth, opened horizons, chased away students' fear or anxiety, and opened possibilities in which "the unknown became knowable."[12] However, one teacher that Steinbeck recalls would likely not have survived for long in our days of the Common Core. Emma Hawkins was let go from her teaching job because she did not "teach the fundamentals," Steinbeck says. While she lasted at that school, her class was noisy and vibrant and she aroused curiosity and a passion for learning; she created "a new attitude and a new hunger." He called himself the "unsigned manuscript of that high school teacher."[13]

In Steinbeck's view, it follows that a student is "lucky" when he or she has a good teacher who is able to take a book and make of it an engagement in discovery. He never expected that *Of Mice and Men*, *The Grapes of Wrath*, *The Pearl*, or *The Red Pony* would become classic classroom texts. Yet he clearly hoped that his work would have an impact that was didactic and enlightening as well as entertaining.

OF MICE AND MEN AND CENSORSHIP

One great hurdle for *Of Mice and Men* in school settings has been the objection to elements of the novel that some parents have found inappropriate for students who are assigned this book. Some school districts have challenged whether the novel should be taught at all. Among the many challenges to *Of Mice and Men* came one in 2008 from Appomattox, Virginia, that place of peace and reconciliation where the American Civil War was concluded. Efforts to remove *Of Mice and Men* from the Appomattox High School arose from a concerned parent who was troubled by the coarse language in the book. The high school principal, Dr. Gregory A. Wheeler, assembled a committee to study the matter. The National Coalition against Censorship opposed removing the book and observed that profane language is present in some of Shakespeare's plays and in novels by Ernest Hemingway, William Faulkner, Toni Morrison, and other writers.[14] In contrast to the dispute in Appomattox, the *Montana Standard* (September 25, 2014) reported that teachers at Butte Hills High School were encouraging their honors classes to read the book. That difference of opinion in different American communities is borne out in schools across the United States. Union Press High School in North Carolina (December 9, 2014) decided to set the stage for reading *Of Mice and Men* so that students would not be shocked by it. Parents in Cameron, North Carolina, in Moore County, might well have been alarmed by "vulgar and offensive language." A teacher introduced that language and the social and historical context to pave the way for an understanding of the novel. Principal Robin Lea told news media that the school had determined that the best solution was to teach and explain about American history at the time in which the novel is set.[15]

In May 2015, the quiet town of Coeur d'Alene, Idaho, challenged whether Steinbeck's *Of Mice and Men* should be read in its schools. A concerned parent noted "more than 100 unsuitable words" in the novel. In Britain, an article by Richard Lea in the *Guardian* quoted someone in

Coeur d'Alene as saying that the novel is "neither a quality story nor a page-turner."[16] The original source of this information appears to have been a report in the *Spokesman-Review*. A curriculum committee in Coeur d'Alene pondered for several months whether the novel ought to be read on a voluntary basis or on a small-group basis only. "Nobody's banning or burning books," school board trustee Dave Eubanks was quoted as saying. "There was just too much darn cussing." School board member Eugene Marano expressed concern that the story's plot is "too dark for ninth graders." Such were the thoughts of concerned parents and school board members, who are correct in saying that *Of Mice and Men* is "dark" and includes much "cussing." Librarian Bette Ammon is also correct when she says that the characters in the novel would have spoken that way. Kirsten Pomerantz, a teacher at Lake City High School, told the school board that the novel keeps her students engaged and that the novel is "relevant."[17] Following much discussion, the school board decided not to ban the book.

Coeur d'Alene is in northern Idaho, in that distinctive section on the map that looks a bit like an exclamation point pointing upward toward Canada. The town is about thirty miles east of Spokane, Washington, and has about 44,130 residents. It is a place of traditional family values and traditional religious values, according to school board members. The town is named after the response of French fur traders to a tribe of Native American Indians. In the Oregon Treaty, Britain ceded this area to the United States in 1846. Per the 2010 census, the town is described as 93.8 percent Caucasian, 1.2 percent Native American Indian/Alaka Native, and 0.4 percent African American. The Coeur d'Alene school district serves more than ten thousand students in two high schools, three middle schools, an alternative high school/middle school, and ten elementary schools.

Most school boards recognize that parents have every right to be concerned about what their children read and to ask if they are mature enough to read it. However, some might say that the town of Coeur d'Alene would be missing the forest for the trees by focusing on language use rather than upon context and meaning. *Of Mice and Men* is a novel about relationship, loneliness, dreams, and human struggle. One of the advantages of presenting this novel in a classroom is that it is short. It has only six chapters. However, *Of Mice and Men* is also taught for its sense of humanity, for empathy. The novel is characterized by clarity in the

writing, short sentences, and themes of relationship and social conscience. Whether it is suitable for ninth graders is another matter: one that
thoughtful people in Coeur d'Alene and other places that treasure whole-
some character, expletive-free language, and family values must discern.

It would be sad if young people who live in such a beautiful area as
Coeur d'Alene, a place surrounded by trees, verdant land, and lakes left
by the great glaciers, were not introduced to Steinbeck's ecological sensibility. The residents of Coeur d'Alene could also develop further sensitivity to their own town's past by reading Steinbeck's *In Dubious Battle.*
The Coeur d'Alene Mining District had two strikes in the 1890s. In 1892,
the cowboy-detective Charlie Siringo was sent there on behalf of the
Pinkerton Detective Agency to investigate the labor strike. Harry Orchard
attempted to assassinate the governor Frank Steunenberg over the labor
disputes in Idaho.[18]

Coeur d'Alene is not alone in its challenge to *Of Mice and Men.* Since
the novel is among the most often taught novels in the English or language arts curriculum, it frequently draws ire, or provokes worry. The
concern arises as to whether the works of John Steinbeck are too dark, too
depressing, or too vulgar for some children to read in school. Steinbeck
became quite accustomed to these challenges to his books during his
lifetime and he satirized the censors. There is usually someone who in-
itiates a campaign against the book, he said. "The odd thing is that this
March Hare mother need not have had children nor have read a book—
indeed often has done neither." He added: "In many cases it develops that
no one—supervisor, principal, teacher, student, or the Iron Mother herself—has ever read the books in question."[19] The result is that sales of the
book increase in the area in question, largely because of curiosity.

Steinbeck singles out the "curious woman" who insists upon censorship of his books in the public library as well as in the schools. Her
"victims are the teachers, the school board, and sometimes county or state
officials" who are sensitive to such criticism. However, a deeper concern
might be raised by another of his comments: "It does not occur to this
mother that the children are successful in resisting reading of any kind."[20]
In our world of cell phones, text messaging, television, and video games,
it sometimes is the task of a parent or teacher to cut through resistance to
get children to read at all.

Children are now a target group for advertising, as Steinbeck noted in
the mid-1960s. Yet they need to be allowed to have a childhood, as

Steinbeck points out in his essay "The Pursuit of Happiness" in *America and Americans*. "We do not permit them to be children and insist that they become adults," he writes.[21] Then, when they are approaching adulthood, we tend to treat them like children, he adds. Strain may be placed upon children by parents dissatisfied with their own lives, he says. One may hear behind each of these parents' desires to make their children stars on the Little League field or A students in academics the voice of Arthur Miller's Willy Loman and his dreams for his confused son Biff. Such children may be so active on the field and in sports camp that they neglect to take time to read and to learn. Others acquire As and headaches that send them to the child neurologist. Steinbeck, meanwhile, argues that little is done to teach teenagers responsibility for their actions "for this is supposed to come automatically on the stroke of twenty-one."[22]

TEACHING STEINBECK

Many students have found *Of Mice and Men* captivating and thought-provoking and many teachers regard the short novel as stimulating reading. Whether through personal interest or pedagogical necessity, they have created ambitious and innovative lesson plans. *Of Mice and Men* has been used for years to promote reading in the United Kingdom and in the United States and Canada. Teachers who assign the short novel recognize that reading is an empowering practice that ought never to be lost or diminished in a world in which people are increasingly inclined toward interaction with television and film media, Internet, and video games. Reading and thinking and writing are thoroughly connected and fundamental to learning and personal growth.

In Britain, *Of Mice and Men*, *The Crucible* by Arthur Miller, and *To Kill a Mockingbird* by Harper Lee have recently been removed from the GCSE, or General Certificate of Secondary Education, exams. In 2013 Michael Gove, Britain's education secretary, called for children to read more books: up to fifty a year. But the question arose as to which books ought to be read. The BBC reported in March 2011 that *Of Mice and Men* is taught in "over 90 percent of schools in Britain."[23] Gove, who reportedly dislikes *Of Mice and Men*, argued for more focus on British literature. While there is obviously much merit to Dickens, Hardy, Austen, Eliot, the Brontës, and other British literature and much value to learning

British literary traditions, the problem with this view is that literature in our world is not hermetically sealed into national cultures. Ought British children to be reading a novel about displaced American ranch workers that was published in 1937? The answer for many teachers and students is yes, because the novel, with its unique brevity and appeal to human sympathy, remains relevant.

One British educator, Marty Phillips, in an article in *The Steinbeck Review* in 2014, argued for the value of these American novels. "To understand the social, historical, and cultural context" is an important skill, noted Phillips. Steinbeck's *The Pearl*, *The Red Pony*, and *The Moon Is Down* are sometimes used in Key Stage 3 in the U.K., he pointed out. Phillips was so interested in the Steinbeck novel that he and his associate Tim Arnold visited Steinbeck scholar Susan Shillinglaw for an interview at San Jose State University. They filmed on location material and developed a study guide that includes material on the Great Depression, the Dust Bowl, the notion of the American dream, and other social and historical contexts. However, these innovative materials will no longer be introduced to British students if the curriculum focuses only on British classics. One professor at King's College has said that the education secretary's proposal has resulted in "a syllabus out of the 1940s."[24] To critics, Gove's perspective seems rather insular. British students may become better acquainted with some of the fine qualities of British literature, but they may then miss the important contributions of world literature to discussions of social issues, gender, class, ethics, and human capabilities.

The challenge for teachers is to bring Steinbeck's story alive for young readers. When a person *chooses* a novel he or she is usually favorably inclined to read. However, assigned reading for school may be perceived as a task. A teacher provides an introduction to the reading experience and the classroom becomes a field for shared interpretation and analysis. How can a teacher make this interesting? Literary critic Morris Dickstein expressed some gratitude that he did not have to read Steinbeck in the classroom: "Luckily I was never assigned one of his novels to read in high school or college: his more ambitious books were not ruined for me by bad teaching or premature exposure," he wrote.[25]

Yet an introduction to Steinbeck in a classroom need not be coupled with "bad teaching." Dozens of teachers who make use of Steinbeck's stories have found that they can stimulate reading interests in their students and that the experience can lead to curiosity, thought, feeling, and understanding. If we consider Dickstein's concern, we may ask how to offer these novels in a school setting and avoid ruining them. A survey of the practices of a few teachers may offer some clues.

Should *Of Mice and Men* be taught to high school teenagers? one blog asked of high school teachers. Those who responded to the query on eNotes.com said yes. Amy Lepore emphasized how the story promotes empathy. A teacher named Kiwi said that she was "always moved and astonished by the responses" that she has received from students and that she encourages parents to read the novel also. College teacher Susan Hurn commented that her students have usually focused on the friendship between George and Lennie rather than the marriage between Curley and his wife. However, "Crooks in his isolation draws their sympathy." She added that a novel like *The Grapes of Wrath* brings attention to segments of society that are often overlooked.

Debora Stonich, an English as a second language (ESL) teacher in Dallas, Texas, has been an English teacher, chair, and curriculum coordinator. When she taught her students *Of Mice and Men*, she encountered resistance from some of their parents who objected to the novel. One of them commented that there was no morality left in the world anyway and that novels like this "exacerbated the moral decay in our society." Read the novel, she encouraged them. Or she handed them a copy of *The Pearl*. She taught *Of Mice and Men* for more than ten years. In an article in *Steinbeck Studies*, she called teaching Steinbeck's fiction "one of the most enjoyable experiences a high school teacher can have during her teaching career." However, there were those concerned parents, some of whom "believed their children could be injured by reading the words."[26]

Just to get students to read *Of Mice and Men* is the difficulty for Jerry Heverly in San Leandro, California. He has posted online that about 50 percent of his students don't read at all and some 40 percent have read "some sort of facile teen literature" like *Harry Potter* or *Twilight*. Three years ago he began to perform dramatic readings of the novel in the classroom, walking around the room while reading Steinbeck's novel. The lack of reading by students in his classes suggests a form of mental impoverishment, he believes. Heverly clearly does his best to provide liveliness in the classroom, but perhaps media stimulation has created a predisposition in his students toward expecting entertainment and immediacy and has encouraged the passive reception of texts.

Dramatic reading of the novel is also the method of Vincent Gibbs of Robert E. Peary High School in Rockville, Maryland, who has recorded his readings of *Of Mice and Men*. He reads the novel aloud to his eleventh-grade students. He first heard the novel read aloud in 1972–1973 and was struck by the story. He has created MP3 recordings of his readings for educational purposes.

William Johnson, a special-education teacher in Brooklyn, has discussed his experience of teaching his students *Of Mice and Men* for the third consecutive year. He wrote for a Brooklyn schools publication, *First Person*, about this. "The students love it," he wrote. "Something about George and Lennie's plight resonates with them, even though a ranch in 1930s Salinas, Calif., seems a world away from a high school in New York City in 2012." In his essay he explored why his "city-smart students love reading about two Depression-era farm workers." Among his observations is that the students appear to recognize that George and Lennie deserve better. "My students know that they deserve better too," Johnson says.

"It is not easy for my students in suburban St. Louis to connect with the characters in John Steinbeck's *Of Mice and Men*," writes Debra Solomon Baker. "The novel is packed with gruff men. Middle aged, mostly friendless, they are struggling to eke out an income on a ranch somewhere in California." Yet this language arts teacher at Wydown Middle School writes in *Teaching Tolerance* (November 18, 2010) that Steinbeck offers valuable insights. "Yet, in a society where individualism is paramount, George does far more than put up with Lennie. He cares for this mentally challenged man." Baker provides her class with an inquiry into human responsibility, an ethics of care. She leads her students to think toward "the larger question" of what our responsibility to other people is. Do we have any particular moral obligations to people "who may be weaker, or isolated, or mistreated"? She asks her students if George's choices are heroic, or simply human.[27]

In Baltimore, high school English teacher Mark Miazga has turned to *The Grapes of Wrath* and "The Harvest Gypsies" in conjunction with the social studies department for a unit on the question of people's reactions during times of scarcity of resources. His class applies the seven articles in "The Harvest Gypsies" and "uses Baltimore as a tool for social change." Students read each article, look up the words, and underline key details. They then complete a Guided Notes handout. Miazga wrote in

2013 that he had learned much from being chosen as a participant in the Steinbeck Institute and he was disheartened that the National Endowment for the Humanities had not funded the project in 2014.[28] He continues to bring Steinbeck's novels to his classes.

The teacher who has created the ambitious website *Learning from My Mistakes: A Teacher's Blog* speaks of being "haunted" by teaching *Of Mice and Men*. The website indicates the many things that this teacher does to teach the novel and asks what other teachers do. The teacher works on textual analysis of the story's opening and ending and themes. Students write diary entries from one of the character's viewpoints. They also draw the bunkhouse where George and Lennie stay and analyze their conversations. This teacher uses props. Objects are pulled from a bag and students are asked to decide which prop fits with Crooks and which fits with Curley or George or Lennie. The teacher encourages students to design a stage set and cast a theatrical version of the story with reference to their favorite film actors and actresses. This teacher also introduces intertextuality by connecting Charles Dickens's *Oliver Twist*, the class's previous literary encounter, with *Of Mice and Men*.[29]

Aware that Steinbeck's novel is taught widely in high schools, the La Jolla High School English Department in California offers worksheets and lesson plans for the book on a website. The lessons include exploring characterization, setting, foreshadowing, and figurative language in the text.[30] Teachers of the novel will find other sites like this on the Internet, which generally call for a New Critical close reading of the text. One may explore other approaches to the novel through considerations of gender, race, class, psychology, and commitment. The Steinbeck Center supports a "Steinbeck in Schools" service to the educational community and provides some helpful suggestions. *Of Mice and Men* continues to be widely taught despite occasional resistance to its language, or its recent dismissal from British testing. Perhaps offering a reader the freedom to pick up the novel and read it without a test is a good thing. While it is valuable to introduce the novel to students, hopefully the opportunity for reflection it offers transcends mere testing. *Of Mice and Men*, in prose or in dramatic form, presents a story that may be read in a few sittings. It offers a story that will have resonance long after the novel is read.

FICTION AND EMPATHY

Steinbeck was able to bring his readers details of the lives of people like George and Lennie because he participated imaginatively in their plight. Steinbeck's experiences as a journalist sharpened his sense of his solidarity with the migrants. Morris Dickstein identifies Steinbeck's "shifting viewpoint" on migrant workers as a movement from seeing them as oppressed and exploited social victims to "identifying with them" and "seeing the world through their eyes."[31] *Of Mice and Men* is part of this movement toward personal identification. George and Lennie are an odd couple who express the human need for security and reassurance and to have a dream, a place in the world. They wander together, lonely drifters through a fateful world. George and Lennie pick up where Mac and Jim of *In Dubious Battle* left off. There is between them "another deep bond that culminates in rupture, sacrifice, and loss," as Dickstein points out.[32] They are Huck and Jim on the Mississippi, drifters in search of freedom. They place their hopes in an elusive American dream.

John Steinbeck's fiction is often linked with the notion that literature can promote empathy: the ability to "feel with" and stand in someone else's shoes. The philosopher and ethicist Martha Nussbaum claims that literature can contribute to one's social and political education by nurturing and developing empathy in readers. She points to novels like Dickens's *Hard Times* and Steinbeck's *The Grapes of Wrath* as social realist novels that can contribute to the development of empathy in readers. This appears to be premised on the view that an imaginative involvement in a character's situation will move a reader to empathy. Nussbaum claims that reading stories "exercises the muscles of the imagination, making people capable of inhabiting for a time the world of a different person."[33] This reading will "encourage the bonds of identification and sympathy."[34] It promotes perspective taking, the ability to comprehend another person's experience by imagining oneself in that character's situation. This prompts an extension of concern, an extension of empathy that is central to our political life and has a "vital political function."[35]

One might say that the power of the narrative in *Of Mice and Men* lies in its ability to prompt compassionate empathy, "feeling with" the characters. Steinbeck's own ethnographic approach, his visiting farm workers and living among them, led to his own sense of compassion and identification. Indeed, the term "empathy" is frequently used in discussions of

Steinbeck. *American National Biography Online* comments, "that association deepened his empathy for workers." The National Steinbeck Center writes, "Steinbeck's empathy for the workers is palpable." The website eNotes.com includes the remark: "Steinbeck is a master at getting his audience to empathize." Penguin's *Of Mice and Men: Teacher's Deluxe Edition* (2013) tells us that "Steinbeck's greatness lies in his empathy for common people." The Steinbeck Institute's "About John Steinbeck" notes that "he wrote with empathy, clarity."

Can reading Steinbeck's fiction increase our ability to "feel with" others? That is a question that is difficult to answer with any precision. Researchers at the New School in New York assert that they have evidence that reading literary fiction can increase a reader's ability to understand what other people are thinking and feeling. No study can say for sure whether this produces more sympathetic people, observes Lee Siegel in *The New Yorker* (November 6, 2013). Siegel points out that Americans who focus on "concrete results" may find reading fiction not purposeful. They might respond well to the notion that literature can contribute to the useful social quality of empathy. However, he asks, must literature have a "socially useful purpose?" There is nothing wrong with "idleness" and simply enjoying reading a novel for its own sake, he asserts. [36]

Even so, even when Steinbeck is entertaining us with apparently light fictions like *Tortilla Flat* or *Cannery Row* he also seems to have been deeply engaged with his characters. Likewise, with George and Lennie, he illustrated the ways in which their lives express challenges to a materialistic interpretation of the American dream. Steinbeck's novels are indeed involved in a kind of cultural work, affecting readers, moving them toward empathy for the Georges and Lennies of our world.

5

THE GRAPES OF WRATH

HISTORY AND CULTURE

The Grapes of Wrath, arguably Steinbeck's most memorable and influential work, begins in the dust of a land that has sustained generations. In an overture of apocalyptic tone that suggests Genesis inverted, we are introduced to the changing colors of the sky, the shadows of dust upon the land, and the life of animals and human beings who face the tumultuous transitions of the natural world. Not a single person is named in the first chapter of the novel. Humanity endures in a context of wind and aridity in which horses push their noses through the dust collecting in water troughs. The children draw with sticks in the dust and the women look to see if their men will break. These are tenacious, resourceful people who gaze at the sullen sky and endure. There is nothing sentimental in the first chapter of *The Grapes of Wrath*. Humanity is close to the earth, interdependent within an ecosystem that has been damaged. Like the graphic depictions of the Dust Bowl given to viewers by Ken Burns's documentary *The Dust Bowl*, or the struggle recalled in the songs of Woody Guthrie, Steinbeck's novel presents us with hard realism, a literary naturalism that emphasizes struggle for survival.

The Dust Bowl was one of the greatest environmental disasters in American history. It spread from its epicenter in western Oklahoma across the Great Plains. Coupled with the deprivations of the Great Depression, this ecological calamity caused adversity for people of Oklahoma, Arkansas, and the Texas Panhandle. Farmers who were affected directly or indirectly could no longer sustain a living on the land. Some set out on a migration west toward California. With this momentous upheaval begins the story of the Joad family of Steinbeck's novel.

The Joads were sharecroppers from Sallisaw in Sequoyah County. The town's name comes from a French word, *salaison*, which can be roughly translated as "salt provisions." This is a rural area in which the local economy was focused on cotton production. In the 1920s, development of lumber, oil, and natural gas industries had begun in the area. The *Sequoyah County Times* was their local newspaper. The news clipping that Ma Joad held in her hand, the one that said that Tom Joad was receiving a jail sentence, likely came from it. Today Ma Joad might have picked up her postcard of the Statue of Liberty from the post office at 111 McGee Drive. However, in John Ford's film we see a windblown mailbox. Sallisaw had recently witnessed the funeral of Pretty Boy Floyd. About forty thousand people came through town—some of them, perhaps, to make sure that he was dead.

Steinbeck's novel suggests that the Joad family was swept up and forced to move by the fierceness of the Dust Bowl drought and windstorms that descended upon Oklahoma. There is a bit of poetic license at work in this portrayal. There was an apocalyptic quality to this natural disaster. To place the Joad family squarely within the Dust Bowl's fury was to underscore this story's mythical character. Sallisaw was not part of the Dust Bowl but it was seriously impacted by it and deeply affected by land problems of its own. It suffered from issues of climate, land use, and repercussions from the Depression. Migration to rural and eastern Oklahoma began in the first part of the 1930s with the Great Depression. Some of the people who were displaced from the labor wage economy in urban centers, or oil and mining industries, attempted subsistence farming. Some of the residents from the semiarid region of the Dust Bowl who had lost their farms sought small tenant farms. The droughts and floods of the mid-1930s caused repeated crop failures across Oklahoma, including in the cotton region. Farmers had to produce enough crops to pay the landowners. Between 1935 and 1937 severe storms caused flooding and crop damage in Sequoyah County. Crop failures resulted in displaced tenant farmers. The small-acre tenant farmers became the largest group to head west. At mid-decade, sociologist Otis Durant Duncan reported that "an exodus from the State is proceeding rapidly." Most people did not leave Oklahoma, although some three hundred thousand did, between

1935 and 1940. At least one-third of these people headed west for California. [1]

The people who headed west were mostly small nuclear families like the Joads. A decade earlier many people had traveled from Oklahoma to California. In the mid- to late 1930s an even greater number were making that same migration. James Gregory, who studied this pattern, called it "a guided chain of migration." Gregory's evidence shows that several people who headed west followed the lead of family members and joined them in California. In *Factories in the Field*, Carey McWilliams observed migrants in California who hailed from the same Oklahoma counties banding together. One can see similar patterns in immigrant clusters in American cities. [2]

The troubles that compelled the Oklahoma families to pack their belongings and head west might remind one of the Irish potato famine of the 1840s. The plight of the Irish and the unsettling of German families in Europe lay deep in John Steinbeck's own ancestry. On his mother's side, which was Scots-Irish, the family had secured farmland in California. However, the situation for Oklahoma families was caused by an array of factors, as Robert McMillan has pointed out: "landlessness, small farms, poor soils, large families," and a reliance upon cotton and corn and a few farm animals. Tenant farmers were more than 68 percent of the farming population. [3]

It was a great modern odyssey and Steinbeck, like Homer, would write the epic tale of a journey, an archetypal American movement west to a destination with which he was familiar: the California where his fertile imagination blended with the stark realities of his observations, his angry drive for justice, and the deep roots of his human sympathy. The novel is framed by the Biblical story of the exodus. The Joad family sets out with great hopes of a promised land. [4]

The problems that began with the Great Depression were compounded by agricultural issues. In March 1935, Hugh Hammond Burnett, one of Franklin Roosevelt's advisors, testified before Congress about the need for improved soil conservation techniques. The issue was of dire concern to people in Oklahoma. "To the red country and part of the gray country of Oklahoma, the last rains came gently, and they did not cut the scarred earth," Steinbeck would begin his novel. Then came the wind, the dust, the blackening of the sky: "The dawn came, but no day." [5]

April 14, 1935, was Black Sunday, the day that a brutal dust storm darkened the skies and blew across the Great Plains. The National Weather Service office in Norman, Oklahoma, has described it as "a wall of blowing sand" that "blasted into the Oklahoma panhandle and far northwestern Oklahoma around 4 P.M."[6]

Robert Geiger of the Associated Press and his editor are said to have contributed the report and headline that coined the phrase "dust bowl." Geiger was at Boise City, Oklahoma, with photographer Harry G. Eisenhard when the dust storm came. His Associated Press report said: "Three little words . . . rule life in the dust bowl of the continent—'if it rains.'"[7]

There was drought and dust in Oklahoma on April 15, 1935, a day on which the House of Representatives met in Washington to discuss the Social Security bill, unemployment, and the right to work. The nation's legislative body reflected on the general welfare: an issue that had become paramount as F.D.R.'s New Deal attempted to respond to the pain of the Great Depression. The general welfare of Oklahomans was seriously affected by the Dust Bowl, as well as by the Great Depression. Drought alone did not cause the Dust Bowl. Agricultural mismanagement contributed to the loss of topsoil and to difficulties with the land. Attempts to expand farm acreage to maximize crop yields and loss of topsoil made the plains vulnerable to the blasts of dust storms. The Depression, coinciding with this, compounded problems for the people in Oklahoma.

In fact, the Joad family living in Sallisaw were not directly in the Dust Bowl. In *Nature's Economy*, historian Donald Worster chides Steinbeck for getting the geography wrong. Sallisaw, he writes, "was almost on the Arkansas border and hundreds of miles east of the dust center."[8] However, that perspective also takes the novel quite literally, rather than as a mythopoetic depiction of an event of Biblical proportions that displaced people and prompted their exodus. Worster, of course, knows well the history of the conditions in eastern Oklahoma but Steinbeck, possibly also aware of the geography, was more interested in mythmaking. Worster went on to say that Steinbeck "assumed too simply that people like the Joads were victims of a natural disaster that gave the banks and landlords an excuse to put them off the land, but in truth, their somber story was only peripherally connected with the drought on the plains."[9] However, this does not account for the fact that people who migrated to eastern Oklahoma and cotton farmers of the Sallisaw area left Oklahoma in large numbers for California in the mid- to late 1930s. Worster correctly indicates that the problem the Joads faced was a result of farming practices. That was true in eastern Oklahoma. Yet there is also evidence that Dust Bowl impacts were widespread.

The issues that the Joad family and others like them faced stemmed from the Great Depression. Problems arising from land use were exacerbated by the disastrous effects of dust storms and drought. In October 1929, when the stock market based on Wall Street was on the brink of collapse, the *M'Alester Guardian* appears to have been more concerned with local and state news than with the financial crisis that was about to erupt across America. On October 17, the paper carried news about a "Depositors Dividend about Xmas" and that "Only Five County Cases Do Not Involve Liquor Laws." October 24 brought the news that a developer could put a roof on a hotel at the present rate and that, under new laws, there would be exams for teacher certificates. There was an important story for the area's famers: "This County Selected as One of Two for Detailed Soil Surveys."

When the stock market crashed, the articles on the front page of the *M'Alester Guardian*, on Thursday, October 31 (like "Stop, Look, and Listen"), gave no indication of the devastation. "State Tax Board Gets Results Involving over Two Million Dollars in Tax Levies," one headline ran. An anthrax outbreak south of the city had been reported, presumably carrying the concern that this would affect cattle. An article titled "McAlester May Get Federal-State Man in Labor Program" was hopeful. The middle of the page proclaimed optimism: "National Bank Stock Almost Tax Free under High Court Ruling." On page 2, readers could learn that they could save money on groceries and animal feed at the Ross-Way Grocery. The ad chimed that "the Ross Way is the Right Way." A week later, on November 7, the newspaper reported: "House Bill No. 4 Knocked Out by Supreme Court: The People Still Rule in Oklahoma." The people may have still ruled but more ominous was a headline directly beneath this: "Measures Taken to Redeem Denuded Land in Oklahoma." A title like this one hints at problems concerning land use that would later develop in the cotton lands of eastern Oklahoma and the land to the west, which a few years later would be called the Dust Bowl. [10]

McAlester, Oklahoma, is the site of the state penitentiary where Tom Joad would have served his time of incarceration. It is in eastern Oklahoma, in Pittsburg County, and the town had a population of 17,783 at the turn of the twenty-first century. In the 1930s, its population varied from

11,804 in 1930 to 12,401 in 1940. Tom Joad would have had to have picked up his ride from the trucker in McAlester. To get home to Sallisaw, some 66.5 miles away, but closer to 88 miles by car, he would have had to head north on what is today Route 69 and then head east toward Fort Smith, which had historically been a post at the edge of Indian territory. Sallisaw is southeast of Muskogee, some twenty-two miles from Fort Smith.

J. J. McAlester, after whom the town is named, was a character in *True Grit*, a story that became a John Wayne film in 1969 and was remade in 2010. During the Civil War, McAlester, an officer in the Confederate Army, learned of coal deposits in Choctaw Indian territory. He knew that a railroad was planned to go through Indian land. He recognized that coal deposits north of Perryville could fuel the railroad. At Fort Smith he got maps and he started a general store/trading post in 1869. McAlester sought from the Choctaw Indians the rights for the land where the coal deposits were. Then the Union Pacific came through. New York businessmen had sought an extension through the Indian territory. The Katy Railroad of the Missouri-Kansas-Texas Railroad was now a reality and so was McAlester's good fortune.

In the mid-1930s, when the families of eastern Oklahoma packed up and headed west, they usually did not take the train lines. They put their belongings into vehicles like those that we see in John Ford's film of *The Grapes of Wrath* and they headed west out on the long road to California. In Steinbeck's novel the Joads undertake an archetypal journey. They represent human aspiration, the effort of thousands of pioneers who settled the American frontier. They are the people that Moses once led in search of a promised land. They are people who are representative of the hopeful, determined, and resilient spirit that Steinbeck saw in humanity.

ARRIVING IN CALIFORNIA

For all the richness of its beautiful landscapes, California was not the promised land for the Joads. For every admonition to "go west, young man," for every gold rush speculation, or tuneful "California, Here I Come" or "California Dreamin'," there were many disappointments for migrants. It has become almost a cliché of American fiction and film that for every starry-eyed quest of Hollywood there is the disillusion of "Do

You Know the Way to San Jose?" Hollywood is a place of dreams, of success and failure, a place where stars that never were park cars and pump gas. Nathanael West satirized the motley simulated environment of Hollywood in *The Day of the Locust*. Steinbeck depicted desert and sunshine, fruitful fields and agricultural business. He presented the hopefulness of the Joads as they crossed into California and the difficult conditions that they found there.

The California of *The Grapes of Wrath* is a land of contrasts. "Ain't she perty?" says little Ruthie as the Joads arrive at the California border in the Ford film and they look out across the fertile expanse of the landscape. "Sure don't look none too prosperous," says Tom, upon seeing the shabby migrant camp into which their vehicle is rolling. John Steinbeck rolled into those camps to have a look at them and to meet the people who lived there. One might call his journalistic experience and work there a kind of ethnography. "I lived, off and on, with those Okies for the last three years," Steinbeck told Tom Cameron of the *Los Angeles Times*. "Anyone who tries to refute me will just become ridiculous."[11] What he witnessed was deprivation and economic struggle.

Tom Collins, who set up the Arvin Camp called "Weedpatch," provided documentation on migrant camp life that supported Steinbeck's perspective. However, Steinbeck scholar Susan Shillinglaw shows that other people had a different view. Frank J. Taylor (1894–1972), a journalist who wrote for California-based publications, sought to show an alternative picture of the migrant workers. He wrote that Steinbeck had his facts wrong. Carey McWilliams produced those facts and further incited the ire of some people. Shillinglaw points out that at the end of August 1939, "five thousand persons heard speakers denounce recent books dealing with California's migrant problem, call for cessation of relief for transients, and praise efforts of individual farmers to better conditions for migratory workers."[12]

The novel suggests that greedy landowners in California cast aside humanity. However, a novel, even one backed by solid documentation, engages in some poetic license. Steinbeck was writing a story, not a political tract. The point, it seems, was to show a contrast between kindness and inhumanity, to recognize that a faceless force was affecting lives, at times willfully, but that the human spirit would not be defeated. The situation was complex in the San Joaquin Valley and the other areas of California that are the setting for the novel. The local economy there rested upon agriculture. California farm production relied upon seasonal labor but residents were stunned by the increasing population of migrant workers. Some of them were uneasy with the growing tax burden for schooling and health care that would come with the increase in population. Some California residents were uncomfortable with the poverty that they saw surrounding the Oklahoma families. Meanwhile, corporate farmers in California reacted to the possibilities of a migrant vote. The Associated Farmers conducted a campaign with the California Citizens Association to limit migration to the state and to get migrants to return home.[13]

In his article "The Merritt System," in 1938, Frank Taylor describes the Tagus Ranch, owned by the Merritt family, as having "brought to farming the restless search for efficiency." The elder Merritt had learned about this in the industrial world. This is phrased as resulting in a positive benefit: "and they have made Tagus Road a year-round producer." Nothing is said about how industrial production and the division of labor in assembly-line production dehumanized workers while proclaiming efficiency as the primary value.[14] Shillinglaw notes that Marshall V. Hartranft contrasted positive features of agricultural production in California with *The Grapes of Wrath*. Hartranft was a fruit grower near Los Angeles who sold oranges to the East Coast and produced a horticultural daily trade publication. He offered enthusiasm about the business of agricultural cultivation.[15]

Yet there were ongoing problems. Labor unrest was a concern in Kern County throughout the 1930s. Steinbeck's articles for the *San Francisco News* directed a searching light on the troubling migrant issues. His novel and the film that followed evoked human concern, found a wide audience, and provoked fury among some farm owners and other residents who felt slighted by the treatment of their homeland and businesses in the book. The *Bakersfield Californian* (June 11, 1939), on the front page, reported that the president "has recognized the disastrous effect of the industrial strife now prevalent in the country and the unsatisfactory operation of the national labor relations act." The article told readers that "a special committee had been appointed to study the entire problem."[16]

Almost as notorious as *The Grapes of Wrath* in California was the report by Carey McWilliams, in *Factories in the Field* (1939), which was reviled by many growers. McWilliams wrote: "This attempt to impose Fascism from the outside, so to speak, was not successful, but, by 1934, the large growers themselves recognized the necessity of organizing for the primary purpose of fighting labor organization."[17] This became the Associated Farmers of California. McWilliams is particularly critical of its methods. From the standpoint of California's growers, the implications of his language could be seen as inflammatory. He urges a closer look at the organization: "as it has many points of similarity with organizations of a like character in Nazi Germany, it warrants careful scrutiny."[18]

McWilliams writes that he has a stenographic report of the May 7, 1934, meeting at which it was formed, with S. Parker Frisselle presiding, in which Frisselle "stated that the finances for the organization would unquestionably have to come from the banks and the utility companies."[19] In 1933, the California Farm Bureau Federation and California State Chamber of Commerce proposed a study of farm labor conditions. In 1934, the farmers of Imperial Valley joined together and "pledged to help one another in case of emergency."[20] From the perspective of many growers this must have been an association intended to preserve stability and profits, not the sort of Fascist organization that McWilliams insists subsequently developed.

Farm labor tensions had increased. McWilliams says that in 1935 he inspected files in the San Francisco office and that they included a list of "dangerous radicals." He points to the Salinas strike and says that fifteen hundred men were deputized in a day.[21] McWilliams then notes that the *Nation* (August 29, 1934) reported lists of arrests and beatings of workers, which were also mentioned in the *San Jose Mercury-Herald* (July 20, 1934). He asserts that "workers were taken from their homes and beaten."[22] McWilliams continues to document what his book claims is a series of injustices.

Steinbeck's novel also suggested a series of injustices toward the migrants. When the Joad family seeks work, they find hope in the handbills that claim that there is work for pickers in California.[23] They dream of re-creating their farms in the West. California's agribusiness required a large and temporary workforce. That possibility for employment made the Joads hopeful. However, growers and cartels desired to increase their profit margins. So they limited payments for the transient laborers. Low wages made life difficult for the Joads and other migrant families. David N. Cassuto points to these practices and observes that people who once depended on the land for their sustenance sought shelter from the elements. Later they became part of an industrial machine, a factory farming process, and they were forced to adapt. "Class stratification depicted in *The Grapes of Wrath* arose from corporate control over the region's most precious resource": water.[24] The ecological historian Donald Worster commented on *The Grapes of Wrath* in his study *Rivers of Empire*.[25] In that book he pointed out the hydraulic issues in California. Worster asserted that in California, as in Oklahoma, "it is finally the apparatus and ideology of unrestricted environmental conquest which lies at the root of the Joads' affliction."[26]

From each of these perspectives we see complex ecological and economic issues that led to social strife. One has to look at this great influx of people from the perspective of the residents of central California in the 1930s. They were raising their families, working at their business, and suddenly their neighborhoods were filled with downtrodden folks from out of state who were performing temporary labor and who needed health care. Their own children were increasingly in contact with the children of Oklahoma migrant families who needed schooling. In the midst of the Depression years, tax bills were sure to go up and that would affect these residents. The population of Kern County grew by 63 percent from 1935 to 1940. Word of job opportunities brought many Oklahoma families and Arkansas families to central California's region of corporate farms. Established workers did not want Oklahoma and Arkansas families taking their jobs, or blighting their towns. However, in most cases those Oklahoma families were filled with hardworking, decent people, like the Joads, who had fallen on hard times. Poverty assailed them. Yet they had skills that the big farms needed. They could pick fruit and they knew how to pick cotton. California farms needed water and sometimes the migrants could build irrigation ditches. Not everyone was as hostile toward them as the film and novel might suggest. California farm industry had long made practical use of immigrant workers and now it was making use of the labor of the people who had been called Okies.

Oklahoma schools were funded by property taxes. In California, in the areas where landowners were in the minority, those landowners had little incentive to fund schools. Farmers who were without land often had less education and few had gone beyond elementary school. Such individuals did not always prize education for other people. Of course, some farmers are extremely well-read; they are practical, thoughtful, and diligent. The Jeffersonian ideal was one of the yeoman farmer who combined these characteristics with a vibrant sense of democracy. In California, Oklahoma families sought education for their children. In 1938, one-quarter of Kern County schoolchildren were originally from Oklahoma.[27]

One of the problems in some of these schools is a problem that we continue to face today: discrimination and bullying. There was also a form of segregation, or separation of Oklahoma migrant children from county resident children. In one case, in Vineland School, children had to sit on the floor in the back of the room.[28] In an effort to remedy the situation, a school was built for the migrant children: Sunset School.

In 1952, Steinbeck looked back on the troubled social context that had led him to write *The Grapes of Wrath*. In an interview with the Voice of America (February 11, 1952), Steinbeck stated that he had revised his view on the tension that existed in the region of California where the migrant work was done. "I had been filled naturally with a certain anger at people who were doing injustices to other people, or so I thought. I realize now that everyone was caught in the same trap."[29] He now saw that California residents of Kern County, San Joaquin, Fresno, and other areas were concerned about the Depression. They were concerned by the great influx of people into their areas and that there would be a tax burden for them. "When you become angry you fight what you are angry at," Steinbeck said. "They were angry at these newcomers." Eventually, that anger dissolved as time went on and the two sides got along. They "were able to get to know each other and they found they didn't dislike each other at all."[30]

THE GRAPES OF WRATH: THE NOVEL AND THE FILM

In *The Grapes of Wrath* stark realism meets with moments in the Joad family's journey that make a sentimental appeal. Tom Joad's return home, which begins his quest, and his reunion with Ma Joad and with his family initiate this sentimental strain in the novel. The struggle of the family, the deaths of the grandparents, and the pregnancy of Rose of Sharon all contribute to this appeal to the heart. John Ford's film extends the sentimental quality. Ma casts away her memorabilia to the tune of "Red River Valley" and later Tom dances with her as he sings that song. However, music and song in the novel are signifiers of something more tenacious. From fiddles, guitars, and harmonicas, song and communal dancing arises and creates community. The common struggle of the migrants is transformed into moments of hope, happiness, and solidarity.

This often-discussed Steinbeck novel brings us the collective journey of the Joad family and the development of Tom Joad, Jim Casy, and Ma Joad toward commitment and compassion. In contrast with the continuous action of John Ford's film, Steinbeck's novel interrupts the action with his interchapters. These are overviews of the situation, often poetic and descriptive, sometimes satiric—as in the voices we hear at a used-car dealer's lot. The interchapters of *The Grapes of Wrath* Steinbeck called intercalary, which means a day or a month inserted into the year to balance out the solar year, like a leap year. Screenwriter Nunnally Johnson drops the interchapters from his script but he maintains Steinbeck's focus on the people and human interconnection with the natural world and community as he develops the dramatic scenes from the novel. In his journal Steinbeck calls his characters his "people": "Yesterday it seemed to me that the people were coming to life."[31] The novel suggests a movement from the Joads' attention to their own needs to their recognition that they are connected with the human community.

We begin with Tom Joad, convicted for murder in self-defense, appearing as a lone man, released from jail, walking on a road under a vast sky. He is the individual on an epic journey of growth and learning. In Ford's film, he is placed at the "crossroads" of his life, outside a restaurant of that name, as big band jazz plays from a radio inside and he bums a ride from a hesitant trucker. The rough-edged quality of Tom emerges, as he censures the driver for nosiness: "Get off it buddy . . . you been going over me like a sheep in a vegetable patch." Dropped off near his destination, he exits with a declaration: "Bet you're about to bust a gut to know what I done. . . . Homicide!" With that, he slams the door, leaving the wide-eyed driver shaken. The film does not give us Steinbeck's ecological symbol of a turtle that Tom picks up from the side of the road. This creature of endurance, like the Joad family, has been respected by a woman who has driven her car carefully around it but the turtle has been tossed aside by a male trucker who has driven head-on at the turtle, clipping its shell and sending it sailing to the side of the road. The impersonal machine driven by an anonymous man has shown its force to denigrate nature. Tom appreciates the small, toppled creature and carries it with him for a time. The film excludes this incident and presents Tom Joad on a dusty road, a horizontal marked by vertical phone poles, upon which he soon meets Jim Casy, crouching low, singing of his savior in a world he "ain't so sure of anymore."

Jim Casy is a man bothered by doubt. The tune he sings by the roadside, "He's My Savior," seems like a simple child's song of faith that may be compared with "The Battle Hymn of the Republic," a song about a fierce Old Testament God who is "trampling out the vintage where the grapes of wrath are stored." Behind the title of the novel lie the lyrics by Julia Ward Howe and Steinbeck insisted that they be printed in their entirety. "The Battle Hymn" evokes a fierce quality that is present in this story that belies any notion of sentimentality. In the nineteenth century, these lyrics were set to a melody that was originally connected with words recalling "John Brown's Body." Some have called John Brown heroic and others have called him mad, but few have ever called him sentimental. There was a fierce quality to his abolitionist rebellion. John Seelye points out that the song lyric is about "quite a different Christ from the one found in sentimental literature" for this is "a militant savior."[32]

Jim Casy, whose initials are J.C., is a gentle but no less committed voice for social justice. Jim falls into a condition of doubt and agnosticism and a troubled, searching quest for faith. His loving everybody signals a man of great spirit but his reverence of women ("they's holy vessels") is tangled up with a sensuality that his evangelicalism will not abide. He is puzzled by the pain he sees around him and he has no theodicy to respond to the anguish of the people of the Dust Bowl. His theology, if he has one, is homegrown and simple: "Maybe there ain't no sin and there ain't no virtue. It's just what people does." In his doubt is an extraordinary faith in humanity. "I'd pray for people who don't know which way to turn," he says over Grandpa's grave. Jim's journey is one in which he becomes Christlike. He shields Tom from the law and, in self-sacrifice, allows himself to be arrested in his place. He embraces a social gospel of seeking justice as he assumes his role as a labor leader. He is crucified in the process, with the final words—"You don't know what you're doing. You're helping to starve kids"—reflecting the gospel words, "Father forgive them for they know not what they do." A sentimental approach to the figure of Jesus, or to the matter of belief or unbelief, is surely not what Steinbeck had in mind. Jim Casy may be likable, eccentric, and uncertain, but he is dedicated and determined, not sentimental.[33]

Nor is Ma Joad wholly a sentimental character. Ma Joad is the family center, the tenacious and compassionate force that holds them together. Tom's reunion with her is poignant. The Joads' departure from home is sentimentalized in the film, which shows Ma Joad discarding memorabilia into a fire as "Red River Valley" plays. She pauses over a news clipping about Tom Joad's imprisonment. A postcard from New York City and a tiny figurine recalling the anniversary of the Louisiana Purchase signal the history and reach of the American continent. A set of sparkling earrings recalls her youth. The scene also underscores displacement by the Dust Bowl and homelessness. It anticipates the letting go that Ma will soon have to do: the loss of home that is followed by the loss of her parents and the eventual departure of Tom, who will venture on the road to find out his mission in life.

The film concludes shortly after Tom's famed "I'll be there" speech. He chooses to steal away at night, gathers his things, kisses his sleeping father on the forehead, and pauses when his mother says, "Tommy, ain't you going to tell me goodbye?" The conversation that follows deeply focuses the film. The interaction between Ma Joad and Tom Joad is all the more poignant in retrospect when one thinks of all the young Americans who would leave home for war in Europe and the Pacific a year or so later, after December 1941.

Indeed, Steinbeck's novel (and Ford's film) recognizes the importance of motherhood. However, Steinbeck provides an earthy and gritty portrayal of Ma Joad as a tough individual, the backbone of the family whose principal qualities are care and endurance. Ma Joad is an archetype; she has a mythical quality of the sort that Steinbeck drew upon as far back as his first novel, *Cup of Gold*. Ma is family and tradition; she is a woman who is "a flow" that is closely connected with the natural world. Ma, never merely sentimental, is a fighter. Novel and film both show Ma as ever the strong and resourceful familial center. She moves "toward the center of power," as Seelye observes.[34] In her are represented the pioneer strengths of previous generations, an American spirit of endurance that is emphasized at the end of the Ford film: "They can't wipe us out . . . 'cause we're the people." The film ends on the first words of the U.S. Constitution, affirming the tenacity of the Joads and that of viewers of the film. *The Grapes of Wrath* joins other films of the 1930s and 1940s, like those of Frank Capra, that celebrate the people. As we see the final shot of a caravan of vehicles heading into the darkness, we are reminded again of how our attention in this story has been moved from a focus on the Joad family toward the procession of life in the human family.

The novel concludes not in sentiment but in Rose of Sharon's act of mercy and compassion in giving her breast milk to a starving man. With the silent nod that is exchanged between Ma Joad and Rose of Sharon there is a tacit recognition of how life can be sustained despite all odds. This, as Seelye points out, "elevates these two women to a salvational and central position."[35] The act is a recognition of the centrality of woman-hood in Steinbeck's novel. There is in it an ethics of care: a reference to the maternal, to biology and the creative life force in nature. This act of compassion recalls Ma's attempt to feed the children at the camp, a gesture that reflects the Biblical account of the miracle of the loaves and fishes. It suggests that the collective life of humanity will be sustained. Pat Covici told Steinbeck that editors wanted to cut the scene, or to have him provide some background for the character of the starving man. Steinbeck refused to alter his ending. The randomness and spontaneity of the act was the point, he said. There was nothing sentimental about it.

John Ford's film did not include the scene, partly because of potential censorship and because he and screenwriter Nunnally Johnson had another ending in mind. Steinbeck's novel offers the government camp episode as an interlude before the Joads' experience of the oppressive Keene Ranch. Johnson's screenplay reverses this, in the interest of moving toward a hopeful conclusion. The Ford film then sentimentalizes the relationship between Tom Joad and his mother, as they have one last dance that is underscored by the film's continuing theme song "Red River Valley." The government camp appears as a brief reprieve in the novel and as hopeful New Deal beneficence in the film. Steinbeck's vision does not flinch from the harsher reality. Steinbeck builds our sympathy for the Joad family. Gradually, they begin to see how many families are just like them, in the same predicament. The novel moves us toward the recognition that the entire community, the future of America, indeed the future of humanity is at stake.[36]

Casy, for Tom Joad, is a Virgilian figure who he recognizes is "like a lantern" for his journey toward the future. Through Casy's example, Tom has begun to realize that he must fight not only for his family's sake, but for everyone. In his memorable final speech to Ma Joad he echoes this sense of purpose and connection with humanity. Tom shares his sense that he is perhaps part of "one great soul" through which social justice can be advanced. Tom's poignant "I'll be there" speech still reverberates today; it echoes much like Martin Luther King's "I Have a Dream" speech from 1963. He will be there in the night when someone is hurting, hungry, and in need, or when people are in the houses they build with their own hands and are celebrating life. "I'll be all aroun' in the dark. I'll be ever-where, wherever you look," he says.[37] Ma simply says she doesn't understand it and Tom replies, "Me neither. It's just something I've been thinking about."

A story like this had to be tempered by a sense of justice and compassion and to not be merely motivated by anger. Early on in his process of composing a work that preceded the novel, Steinbeck wrote to Pat Covici: "My work drive has been aimed at making people understand each other and then I deliberately write this book, the aim of which is to cause hatred through partial understanding."[38] Steinbeck tossed aside that manuscript and began to focus on the story that would become *The Grapes of Wrath*. Nature and land appeared at the center of *The Grapes of Wrath*: land use, its cultivation, ownership, and loss. After Muley Graves and his family are dehumanized and turned to shadows on the earth after the tractor destroys their home, he becomes a broken, sympathetic everyman crouched beneath his hat close to the earth as he turns over the dirt in his hands. His ancestors settled the land and he asserts that what matters is "workin' on it, livin' on it and dyin' on it" and "not no piece of paper with writin' on it" that he cannot understand. The unlettered Muley cannot decipher the legal language that supports the claim of the Shawnee Land and Cattle Company and the bank in Tulsa to take his land away from him. He represents a pattern of settlement by his ancestors: the Americans generations before him who occupied and nurtured the land. Muley and his family have been uprooted by a depersonalizing mechanism.

The ecological sense of a land ethic is supported by scenes in John Ford's film. We see Tom Joad acting locally with ecologically responsible behavior as he shuts off a dripping water valve in the government camp. A tall gentleman at the dance removes a cigarette from the mouth of one of the thugs assigned to interrupt the festivities and he says, "We've got to keep the camp clean." This ecological awareness and responsibility also corresponds to the mutual care of persons for each other. Steinbeck's novel emphasizes relational interactions. An "I-it" instrumental rationality that is mechanistic and impersonal is represented by distant and anonymous managers and owners, or by bullying enforcers. The "I-Thou" of warm interpersonal relationships and community are present in the Joads' relationships and in the dance of a community at play.

Sympathy in readers and film viewers is moved by a narrative that repeatedly calls for responsibility, sensitivity, and understanding. The Joads on their journey encounter the desert and its images of death, an agricultural inspection on the border of Arizona, the uncomprehending response of white-uniformed gas station attendants. The Joads pause at the roadside and gaze at the panoramic view, which Pa, like Moses on the mountain, announces as "the land of milk and honey," California. From behind a fence, they see fertile fields in which they might labor: a richness that is surely owned by someone. However, the family has crossed a threshold. They have reached California amid another sacrifice: Grandma has died. "You say we got across?" Ma Joad says to Tom. A goal has been achieved. "Now Grandma can lay her head down where it's nice and green and 'perty'; she got to lay her head down in California after all."

The Grapes of Wrath raises a protest against insensitivity. In Ford's film, a worker declares that the men should ask to see the contract for work that has been proposed by a corpulent, arrogant potential employer who leans upon a car. The enforcement heavy in the back seat responds in a stereotypical Edward G. Robinson mobster tone: "Hey you, get in the cah." The worker runs and a gun is fired; the bullet hits an innocent woman, who falls to the ground. When the officials arrive, an elderly woman appeals to them, "This poor woman is bleeding to death." The response comes from a character that seems to have stepped right out of a John Ford western, who says callously: "What a mess them forty-fives make. Better get the Doc." Lack of care and concern is again accentuated.

The claims of human sensitivity and dignity confront ignorance throughout the film. Two station attendants dressed in untarnished white uniforms assert that they "got sense" although they cannot understand the migrants' situation. "Holy Moses," one of them says, underscoring for us the great Exodus journey. "What a hard looking outfit." While indifferently tossing gum wrappers across the pavement, the other attendant concludes that "them Okies ain't even human. No one would live the way that they do." These are men who represent the gap in understanding and sympathy. They are like those who could not quite understand the migrants who were arriving.

The Grapes of Wrath is filled with good people: the waitress at the diner who gives the Joad children candy for a reduced cost; the border police who do their work efficiently, including a compassionate official who offers advice about how to get Grandma to a hospital for health care. However, people in the novel are also caught in a web of indifference or misunderstanding. Families like the Joads have fallen on hard times. Rather than receiving support and encouragement, they are caught in the wheels of systemic injustice. The Joads want to work for their living, honorably and respectfully. However, they are beset by monster figures. Once the Joads get to the migrant camps, they encounter the guards that Jim Casy later calls "those tin shield fellas." They respond to the migrant family with the abuse of the bully. The harsh light of a flashlight is beamed into Henry Fonda's face and, as Tom Joad, he says, "You mean I can't even get out of here?" Liberty has been restricted by simian Neanderthals with billy clubs and clipboards. The coercive regimentation immediately feels dehumanizing and their clipboard accounting of people by number is reminiscent of the Nazis' perverse emphasis on meticulous record keeping. Indeed, John Ford's shot of the gate over the Keene Ranch reminds one of the hopeless gate of hell that begins the third canto of Dante's *Inferno*. The image of children clinging to the fence inside which they are imprisoned suggests entrapment—or worse, a chilling foreshadowing of the genocide that would begin occurring in Poland in 1940–1941. To read the film this way is perhaps anachronistic. However, the issue of the dehumanization and scapegoating of "unwanted" human beings, outsiders, or those considered "other" is a perennial one. Steinbeck, upholding the dignity of those made marginal, faced off against what Hannah Arendt has called "the banality of evil."[39]

Steinbeck suggests that America, like the government-sponsored camp of *The Grapes of Wrath*, can be more like a community insofar as it is inclusive and respectful. "How come there ain't more like it?" Tom Joad asks in the film. "I don't know. You find out. I can't," says the camp supervisor. A celebration of communal strength and hope appears in the dance scene at the government camp in John Ford's film of *The Grapes of Wrath*. However, this camaraderie would be shattered by the aggressive fraud of hired thugs who would deliberately break up the dance and cause a riot. Ma and Rose of Sharon stand innocently in the foreground as the men line up behind a fence, hats slung low over their shadowed faces. A passing gentleman removes a cigarette from one of them, insisting upon integrity: "We've got to keep the camp clean." The migrants are sturdy, resourceful, and responsible in how they deal with the trouble that has come their way.

Steinbeck leaves his conclusion to his novel open-ended, much as Dickens did with *Great Expectations*, or, as Warren French points out, with *Hard Times*.[40] We do not know what the future of Tom Joad or the Joad family will be any more than we know, at the end of Dickens's novels, what the future will hold for Pip and Estella, or for Louisa Gradgrind.

The ethical appeal of *The Grapes of Wrath*—its cry for social justice—is one of the novel's key features. As indifferent and remorseless as nature may be, courage and compassion do stand out. In the first essay in Stephen K. George's collection on Steinbeck, *The Moral Philosophy of John Steinbeck* (2005), Patrick Dooley of St. Bonaventure University points out that "unnoticed and ignored, forgettable and seemingly unexceptional common men and women populate his works." That is true of Steinbeck's works that address his encounters overseas also, he adds. He describes *The Grapes of Wrath* and *Of Mice and Men* as "gritty." He believes that Steinbeck's later works suggest a discontent among Americans with "ease" and with "things" and dissatisfaction with conspicuous consumption and "sometimes specious wants." Then he sets Steinbeck alongside Aristotle's *Nicomachean Ethics*, in which Aristotle asserts that a good person is a happy person and that moral goodness corresponds with happiness. "Conversely, a disordered society cannot facilitate happiness, goodness, or development."[41]

Turning to *The Grapes of Wrath*, Dooley points out the duty to share as a moral obligation. We read: "What you gonna eat, Muley?" He traps rabbits. "You sharin' with us, Muley Graves?" he is asked. "I got no choice in the matter," he says. When the Wilsons loan their shelter to Grandpa, he responds that the Joads are beholden to them. "'There's no beholden in a time of dying,' said Wilson, and Sairy echoed him, 'Never no beholden.'" The waitress at the diner likewise reflects this, particularly in the film. She is a bit resistant when Pa seeks a loaf of bread, concerned that they will run out of bread. Pa seeks a fair exchange. Al, the cook, tells Mae, the waitress, to "give them the bread." Mae responds compassionately to the Joad children, discounting the cost of candy. They offer an act of human kindness and are a bit of goodness in contrast with all the difficulty and hostility the Joads will later encounter.

Generosity also appears in the form of the border official, who recommends a hospital for Grandma. In this case, human responsiveness goes beyond the letter of the law or the rulebook. Generosity is passed along as Ma Joad feeds the children in the camp, sharing what little she has. "You want to eat, huh? . . . Didn't none of these here have no breakfast?" The children look forlornly at her and she ponders the situation. "I dunno what to do. I got to feed the fambly. What'm I gonna do with these here?" Uncle John is ready to set aside his plate: "I ain't hungry," he says. "Now you go in and eat that," Tom Joad says in the film. "I'd still see them inside the tent," Uncle John says.

Sharing what one has becomes an ethic of community. In chapter 17 of *The Grapes of Wrath*, families who have to camp together become a community. As Dooley points out, they have implicit rights and a duty not to eat in front of others who do not have food. The ethic is one of "respond to family needs first, and others if possible."[42] The Joads and the Wainwrights share like one family. Ma acknowledges this. "You been frien'ly," she said. "We thank you." "No need to thank. Ever'body's in the same wagon." Yes, Ma agrees. It used to be that the family was first. "It ain't so now. It's anybody."

Let us transpose *The Grapes of Wrath* to today, urges Joseph Allegretti. Steinbeck cannot answer the problems that "afflict business now" but a focus upon rural, itinerant workers is not irrelevant either. There is no direct advice from literature concerning what to do about a toxic dump site, an unsafe product, or an unethical business practice, Allegretti says. Literature alone will not provide a solution. However, in our contemporary world, amid a global economy, multinational corporations, and Internet commerce, literature can be of use in "strengthening moral reasoning about a problem."[43] Stories are important to life because "they help us to understand" in ways that our legal constructs, like codes and case law, cannot. Stories help us to explore "why a person does what she does, at what cost, and for what reasons."[44] He goes on to say that in most business ethics classes utilitarianism and deontology, or the "ought" posed by Immanuel Kant, are discussed. These views are then applied to business cases. However, a story gets to the heart of the matter more tellingly because a story involves us and provides contexts. The personal nature of a reader's response is all-important, Allegretti suggests: "When we experience great works of literature, our life story intersects with the story we are reading."[45] Steinbeck's work beyond *The Grapes of Wrath* is filled with moral concern, this critic points out. When we read *In Dubious Battle*, we may see that individual morality may be "submerged and lost within the group or institution."[46] A reader confronts the "defeating nature" in *Of Mice and Men* and may consider society's obligations to people who live on the margins of society.

PUBLIC RESPONSE TO *THE GRAPES OF WRATH*

The Grapes of Wrath has stirred emotions in many readers across the years and the novel has been controversial ever since it first appeared. It has been acclaimed, taught, criticized, and censored. Steinbeck received criticism in newspapers and death threats in letters. He shares with Salman Rushdie the dubious distinction of being an author who was targeted by death threats. "You may think you're safe 3,000 miles away, but we're coming for you," one of the letters to him said. He had previously been told at a picnic: "You'd better stop writing what you've been writing."[47] Some of the letters that Steinbeck received expressed concern with "the organized threat to commerce—particularly agriculture," as Susan Shillinglaw notes.[48] She points out that Frank J. Taylor wrote articles that supported the farm owner's position and contested Steinbeck's perspective. The fiction of Ruth Comfort Mitchell, a woman of the elite class, wrote alternative versions of California in her novel *Of Human Kindness* (1940).

After *The Grapes of Wrath* was published, Steinbeck often kept his distance from public activities. The *Los Angeles Times* reported that he had retreated to Los Gatos, where he was "inaccessible to friend and enemy alike."[49] He told Tom Cameron of the *Los Angeles Times* that the public persona that the critics of *The Grapes of Wrath* were attacking was a figure of their own imagining and construction: "He's a straw man and he bears my name. I don't like him, that straw man . . . [H]e's the Steinbeck the public created out of its own imagination and thinks ought to be me."[50] The undersheriff of Santa Clara County told Steinbeck not to go into any hotels alone. He said that "the boys got a rape case set up for you."[51] He was advised to keep a diary record of the people he saw and the times when he saw them, so that he would always have an alibi if he needed one. Meanwhile, his marriage to Carol Steinbeck was deteriorating. He wrote in a letter to his agent Elizabeth Otis: "The simple fact of the matter is that Carol doesn't like me."[52]

The Grapes of Wrath sold briskly. Film rights of seventy thousand dollars for *The Grapes of Wrath* made Steinbeck well-off financially. This amount would be about one million dollars today. With the success of *Of Mice and Men*, he considered giving three thousand immigrants two dollars each, but Pascal Covici "talked him out of it."[53] Steinbeck's book remained on the best-seller list throughout much of 1940. However, he knew of the public tensions surrounding his recent novel and the film. When Lewis Milestone visited Steinbeck and they rode across the California countryside, they did not stop at any ranches. When Milestone asked Steinbeck why, he said, "Because I'd get my ass full of rock salt."[54]

Far from Kern County, where the book was ritually burned by members of the Associated Farmers, discontent about the novel flared up across the country. *The Grapes of Wrath* was burned in East St. Louis. It was banned in Kansas City. It was prohibited from libraries in Trenton, San Francisco, and Detroit. Library scholar Christine Pawley states: "In Buffalo, New York, Kansas City, Missouri, and East St. Louis, Illinois, the book had been removed from library shelves; in other libraries, including Trenton, San Francisco, and Detroit, it was sequestered."[55] When the book was banned in Kern County, Gretchen Knief, the county librarian, called the reasons for this economic. Negative publicity from the book could have an impact upon the commerce that was the area's livelihood. Steinbeck later recalled that "when a town wanted to make a burnt offering of an offending book of mine" the book was not available and they had to order ten copies just to burn them.[56]

The Grapes of Wrath drew antagonism in Oklahoma where Congressman Lyle Boren called the novel "a lie, a black, infernal creation of a twisted, distorted mind." There were fabricated letters, ostensibly from Oklahomans who had come west, saying that what was shown in the novel did not exist. However, Dorothea Lange's photographs documented the conditions of the migrant workers. So did Tom Collins's reports and Carey McWilliams's book. Steinbeck had indeed lived with the migrant workers "off and on" as he prepared his articles and he had written his novel by imaginatively extrapolating from observation and experience. Meanwhile, Eleanor Roosevelt asserted, "I have never believed *The Grapes of Wrath* was exaggerated."[57]

Tulare County growers claimed that there was a more sympathetic response to the migrants than the scenes that were depicted in the novel. There were claims that the Tagus Ranch treated migrants well and that in Tulare County people were good to them. However, in Kern County, *The Grapes of Wrath* met with rejection. The president of the Associated Farmers of Kern County, W. B. Camp, declared the novel "obscene in the extreme." Camp, Clell Pruett, and L. C. Plymele ritually burned the book on August 24, 1939. There is a photograph of them putting the book into a garbage pail and their faces are unclear. Local librarian Knief attempted to convince the Board of Supervisors of the merits of the book. She sought to overturn the ban on *The Grapes of Wrath* because it set a bad precedent. The Kern County ban remained in place for two years. It was rescinded in 1941.

As *The Grapes of Wrath* later began to enter school curriculums, censorship doggedly followed the novel. Several oppositions to *The Grapes of Wrath* have arisen across the past three and a half decades. Kanawha High School in Kanawha, Iowa, looked askance at the novel in 1980. Richford, Utah, schools challenged the novel as required reading because of the language in the story and Jim Casy's taking advantage of women.[58] Morris in Manitoba, Canada, was the site of another challenge in 1982. During this same period several libraries opposed censorship. For example, in New Jersey, the Camden Public Library teamed with the municipality of Pennsauken in 1986 for a drive against book banning and censorship.[59] However, school boards in several other places in the United States continued to meet with distressed parents. Anniston, Alabama, placed Steinbeck's novel on restricted use. Cummings High School in Burlington, North Carolina, challenged the novel on a Christian basis for "filth." The Moore County School in Carthage, North Carolina, opposed it for its blasphemy of "god damn." Greenville, South Carolina, schools heard complaints about the novel's "vain and profane manner along with inappropriate sexual references." Union City, Tennessee, also expressed concern about the novel in 1993. The challenges to *The Grapes of Wrath* generally claim that the novel is unsuitable for school reading because of blasphemy, vulgar language, sexual references, or conflict with family values and moral codes.[60]

The Grapes of Wrath is not the only Steinbeck book to have suffered being restricted. Steinbeck's *The Moon Is Down* was censored and prohibited by National Socialist authorities in occupied countries during

World War II. That, of course, did not stop it from being widely distributed by the underground resistance. It is plausible that a rebellious teen in a school that has publicly suppressed *Of Mice and Men* or *The Grapes of Wrath* might seek out a copy of the book while wondering what the fuss is all about. The American Library Association has often expressed opposition to censorship. Perhaps John Milton's *Areopagitica* offers a guide. He asserted that it is important to allow for freedom and observed that inevitably the bad will diminish and fade away.

Steinbeck's novel and John Ford's film encourage us to recall the environmental disaster of the Dust Bowl and, more broadly, issues of displacement of people from their habitats. The story of the Joads is a catalyst for cultural memory. It turns our attention toward thinking about how people dealt with a difficult time in American history.[61] Such stories preserve historical memory. Cultural memory is one of the many reasons why these books are taught. Another is that we can look through Steinbeck at contemporary issues. For example, Chris McGreal, developing articles for the *Guardian*, took the Oklahoma family's route on Route 66 to California, documenting his trip in writing, photos, videos, and audio. Rachel Dry directly connected recent economic concerns with Steinbeck's fiction in her article "A Recession Only Steinbeck Could Love" in the *Washington Post* (March 22, 2009).[62] Today there is no mass migration from Oklahoma but America is increasingly mobile and people still lose their jobs or their homes, or are compelled by necessity to relocate. Simon Stow in *A Political Companion to John Steinbeck* points to the downturn of the U.S. economy, which he recognizes as being "prompted by unregulated lending practices of major financial institutions, decades of anti-labor policies, and rampant globalization." *The Grapes of Wrath* is brought into connection with the recent recession, he writes, "when that crisis has driven families from their homes." Stow points to Steinbeck's novel as opposing "a faceless economic system in which empathy, pity, and understanding were seen as market failures rather than the basis of decent human activity." He takes a position of considerable sympathy for people injured by economic failure. However, there is little analysis of the systemic causes of the economic downturn beyond calling globalization "rampant" and, as in Steinbeck, there are no remedies offered for responding to it. It would be interesting to know which labor policies Stow is calling into question as a factor that precipitated the recession. There is notable concern in his commentary, however, and his emphasis upon empathy, pity, understanding, and "decent human activity" corresponds with a sympathetic reading of Steinbeck's characters.[63]

THE GRAPES OF WRATH IN SCHOOLS

The Grapes of Wrath continues to be taught often in high schools and colleges. In 2000, Mary M. Brown's study indicated that less than 20 percent of the 150 university English programs she surveyed were teaching *The Grapes of Wrath*.[64] However, in 2016, many school classes are still being introduced to Steinbeck's novel. Indeed, the *New York Times* (August 10, 2010) noted that the recession has made *The Grapes of Wrath* "more relevant than ever."[65]

Daniel Reynolds at Northgate High School in Walnut Creek, California, teaches *The Grapes of Wrath* often. Proponents of the concept of multiple learning styles would be proud of his work. He creates a seventy-five-foot time line based on the book for visual learners. There are square-dance lessons for kinesthetic learners. He posts signs to get students to think about the book. There is an emphasis upon the theme of working together against great odds.

Fremont High School teacher Deborah Thorsen also teaches *The Grapes of Wrath*. "I tell my students that this is the kind of book that can change the way you look at the world," she says. "It tells them that they have a chance to change the world." Her students "come away from the novel with a sense of injustice, wanting to do something about it."[66]

The Grapes of Wrath also signals its usefulness to history and social studies teachers. Economics professor Stephen Ziliak of Roosevelt University in Chicago has found *The Grapes of Wrath* a valuable text to include in his Introduction to Microeconomics course. To include a novel invites dialogue, a plurality of voices and interpretation rather than a mere "banking approach" to education, he contends. An economic historian by training, Ziliak has set aside the monological approach of neoclassical economics, he says, in order to broaden inquiry. His own background as a welfare and food-stamp caseworker in Indianapolis contributed to his perspective as he began to present Steinbeck's novel to students who had not yet experienced a recession. *The Grapes of Wrath* raises pointed questions about utilitarian economics.[67]

The novel does not only provide a resource for exploring ongoing economic issues, it also trains our attention on the realities of migration in our world. In September 2015, as a new school year began, attention turned increasingly to the Syrian refugee crisis. Suggestions were made for teaching *The Grapes of Wrath* as a text that might prompt further discussion in classrooms.[68]

Other Steinbeck fiction remains popular in the nation's schools. In the *Christian Science Monitor* (March 26, 2002) a story appeared by Marjorie Coeyman about Peggy Stark's eighth-grade class in Saratoga, California: "Why Teachers Treasure Steinbeck's Tales." Stark had been teaching *The Pearl* for fifteen years. When Mike Sheridan retired from Saddle Brook High School in New Jersey, the school did a marathon reading of John Steinbeck's *East of Eden* to say farewell and celebrate the popular teacher. Sheridan had taught there for thirty-six years across a variety of subjects, from science, math, and industrial arts to English and social studies. Another high school English teacher, James Garvey, suggested the idea, and for eight hours students, teachers, and administrators took turns reading *East of Eden* aloud. Sheridan dedicated his life to teaching and he recalls that a vice principal at the high school once told him: "Don't ever look back on your life and regret this, because it is what you were born to do."[69]

6

SEA OF CORTEZ

Once Steinbeck had written *The Grapes of Wrath*, it seemed natural to many readers that he would again write a novel that addressed a pressing social problem. Instead, he changed direction and went on an expedition of scientific exploration down the Baja coast of California and on to the Sea of Cortez with his friend Ed Ricketts. "We made a trip to the Gulf; sometimes we dignified it by calling it an expedition," he writes.[1] The text that emerged from this expedition holds a key to Steinbeck's thought and writing, as Jackson J. Benson has pointed out. "We were curious," Steinbeck writes. "We wanted to see everything our eyes would accommodate, to think what we could, and, out of our seeing and thinking, to build some kind of structure in modeled imitation of the observed reality."[2] He pointed out that, though *Sea of Cortez* was nonfiction, the design and pattern of the book emerged from the perspectives of two men on a scientific fact-finding mission.

John Steinbeck's fascination with Mexico led to his excursion to the Sea of Cortez with Ed Ricketts and is captured in stories like "Flight" and *The Pearl* and in his screenplays for *The Forgotten Village* and *Viva Zapata!* He had made several trips to Mexico in the 1930s. Now Steinbeck and Ricketts made their sixty-five-hundred-kilometer voyage to explore the coast and observe the distribution of marine invertebrates. Their voyage was focused upon descriptive invertebrate taxonomy and biogeography. Steinbeck and Ricketts suggested that they were exploring a continuous, biologically rich ecosystem, one that Jacques Cousteau later called "the world's aquarium." They navigated down the coast alongside a harsh and inhospitable landscape. Some five million years ago the San Andreas Fault tore through the region to create a series of mountain ranges and the Sea of Cortez. "It is fierce and hostile and sullen," they wrote. "The stone mountains pile up to the sky and there is little fresh water."

"We had no urge toward adventure," Steinbeck says.[3] Yet the expedition was, in part, a romantic journey: a quest of wonder by errant knights following their curiosity. "Our curiosity was not limited but was as wide and horizonless as that of Darwin or Agassiz."[4] So down the coast they went, along "a long, narrow, and highly dangerous body of water" subject to intense storms.[5] On the seventy-six-foot charter, the *Western Flyer*, amid sun, waves, and salt air, Steinbeck thought about the storm that the war in Europe had created many miles away: "Hitler was invading Denmark and moving up towards Norway; there was no telling when the invasion of England might begin; our radio was full of static and the world was going to hell."[6] Steinbeck's narration invites us to imaginatively come on board the boat and we travel with him. Thoughts on American preparedness for war arise as the *Western Flyer* sails into the San Diego harbor where the American fleet is stationed. "All about us the war bustled, although we had no war," he writes.[7] His narrative shifts into a meditation on how the military mind has to focus upon objectives and how the human repercussions of bombing from a distance may be disturbing. A naval officer they meet is asked, "Have you thought what happens in a little street when one of your shells explodes, of the families torn to pieces, a thousand generations influenced when you signaled Fire?" He concludes that anyone performing this function has to not permit himself to think, so that he can maintain "the whole structure of his world."[8]

In *The Log from the Sea of Cortez* we see a John Steinbeck who is curious about biology and behavior but worries about the world. "We wonder whether in the present pattern the pieces are not straining to fall out of line; whether the paradoxes of our times are not finally mounting to a conclusion of ridiculousness that will make the whole structure collapse."[9] As these meditations come and go, he keeps us focused on the journey down the coast. He introduces us to the crew, including Tex Travis, engineer, and Sparky Enea and Tiny Colletto, the seamen, all "reluctant" and new to the gulf. His wife Carol is there also, but he never mentions her in the text. Steinbeck and Ricketts emphasize the group and

their contact with the sea, highlighting a sense of participation, interconnection, and experience. Steinbeck draws our attention to specifics, beginning with their provisions for the journey: cases of spaghetti, fruit,
tomatoes, Romano cheeses, canned milk, flour, and other items are stored
for eating. A small library consists of a wooden case, the front of which
comes down to form a desk, and there are twenty large volumes, "scientific reprints," and space for letters. Steinbeck gives us a list of specific
objects that sounds like inventory in a Staples or Office Max store. His
attention to detail provides the reader with a clear picture of this area of
the boat and suggests the importance of the implements of writing and
reading, research volumes on "the Panamic and Gulf fauna," and materials for collecting specimens: shovels, nets, fish-kits, barrels, jars, and
other containers.[10] Scientific method begins in specifics and precisely
identifies physical properties and organic life. Steinbeck's writing has
about it this physicality and careful delineation of the world.

The "honesty of a boat," its sturdiness and physicality, is set in connection with the human life and emotion of people on board. Wood, cedar
chests, ice buckets, and beds come into contact with human consciousness. "A man builds the best of himself onto a boat—builds many unconscious memories of his ancestors," Steinbeck writes. "How deep this
thing must be, the giver and the receiver again; the boat designed through
millenniums of trial and error by the human consciousness."[11] Travelogue intersects with realist description. Narrative is coupled with solid
facts and sensation. However, like a boat on a vast sea, it drifts amid
speculation, myth, and stories: "In the evening we came back restlessly to
the top of the deckhouse, and we discussed the Old Man of the Sea, who
might well be a myth, except that too many people have seen him."[12]

ECOLOGICAL SCIENCE

The Log from the Sea of Cortez becomes a space for musing about relationships between groups and presents a sense of ecology: "Our own
interest lay in relationships of animal to animal. If one observes in this
relational sense, it seems that species are only commas in a sentence."[13]
Sea of Cortez, like *The Grapes of Wrath*, reflects Steinbeck's awareness
of the interdependent relationship of humanity and the natural world. His
work anticipates the deep ecology of Arne Naess and the land use ethic of

Aldo Leopold. Steinbeck appears to imply that nature has its own rights, which are to be respected. He attempts to articulate this sense that all of life is relational: "And then not only the meaning but the feeling about species grows misty. One merges into another, groups melt into ecological groups."[14]

Steinbeck's ecological orientation may be connected with the concept of the "superorganism," observes James C. Kelley. This is an idea that Steinbeck learned about at Hopkins Marine Station and from Ricketts's thoughts on "group cooperation" among organisms, which were partly derived from studies with Warder Clyde Allee and studies of William Emerson Ritter. He refers to Ricketts's notion of "breaking through," science based upon ecological principles and visceral and transcendent thinking. Kelley points out that in Steinbeck and Ricketts, "empirical scientific understanding met with visceral understanding."[15] A reader may observe that Steinbeck has been engaged in scientific reflections throughout the journey: "Now if we admit for the moment the potency of this tidal effect, we have only to add the concept of inherited psychic pattern we call 'instinct' to get an inkling of the force of the lunar rhythm so deeply rooted in marine animals and even in higher animals and in man."[16] As chapter 21 concludes, these musings coalesce into thoughts on "the feeling we call religious." He suggests that this "is really the understanding and the attempt to say that man is related to the whole thing, related inextricably to all reality, known and unknowable."[17] This is "the profound feeling" within Jesus, St. Augustine, St. Francis, Roger Bacon, Charles Darwin, and Albert Einstein, he says. It is a sense of "astonishment" that all of life is connected, "that all things are one thing and that one thing is all things."[18] Steinbeck's narrative attests to his sense that pure science is motivated by wonder and curiosity and that this is deeply connected with this sense of relationship. He writes, "The true biologist deals with life, with teeming boisterous life, and learns something from it, learns that the first rule of life is living." Such vigorous inquirers must be distinguished from "the embalmers of the field" who from "their own crusted minds . . . create a world wrinkled with formaldehyde."[19] He and Ricketts sit on a crate of oranges and proclaim "what good men most biologists are, the tenors of the scientific world—temperamental, moody, loud-laughing and healthy."[20] They are inquisitive scientists who seek to understand a living world of relationships.

This sense of wonder about the natural world in Steinbeck's work may have had origins in the land and mountains that form the landscape of his youth. In 1923, John Steinbeck and his sister Mary spent days by the sea when they took a summer course at the Hopkins Marine Station. This experience brought them to investigate the tide pools on the coast near Monterey. Charles Vincent Taylor, their instructor, had been a student of Charles Kefoid, who had been deeply influenced by the work of William Emerson Ritter. Professor Ritter had taught the University of California marine biology summer course, beginning in 1892, for many years. Steinbeck's sense of the relationship of humanity to the earth was further brought into focus for him by his relationship with marine biologist Ed Ricketts. The friendship between Steinbeck and Ricketts may have developed, in part, "out of common interest in biology."[21] They met in a dentist's office in 1930, shortly after Ricketts had set up his laboratory on the Monterey coast. Ricketts pointed to the behavior of groups of animals and how the group modifies. This was something that Ricketts had studied with W. C. Allee of the University of Chicago. Steinbeck developed ideas of a "superorganism" that reflect what we today call an ecosystem. These ideas led toward Steinbeck's phalanx idea of "group man" that appears in his novel *In Dubious Battle* and later in *The Grapes of Wrath*. Such a collective may be considered as an ecosystem, an organism with an energy that goes beyond that of individuals. "Steinbeck's fiction in many ways demonstrates such a holistic system," observes Brian Railsback.[22] In *Sweet Thursday* we read: "Everything falls into place, irrelevancies relate, dissonance becomes harmony, and nonsense wears a crown of meaning . . . reaching the greatest mystery of the human mind" in Darwin, Newton, Einstein.[23]

MYTHOLOGY, MYSTICISM, AND MUSIC

Steinbeck's approach to observation and writing has often been described as much like that of a scientist observing group animal behavior. However, he also realized that the human species is not measurable only in scientific terms. Rather, he recognized that humans are communal and religious creatures engaged in forms of contact that include the rituals of life.[24] Joseph Fontenrose has claimed that Steinbeck does not have "a genuine theory of society," so in his novels "biology takes the place of history, mysticism takes the place of humanism."[25] This is debatable, in part because some might suggest that mysticism and humanism are not separate and others might insist upon biology and ecology as integral parts of history. It is doubtful that Steinbeck was more concerned with sociology than artistry, as Fontenrose suggests. He was a writer ever concerned with craft, with effectively drawing characters, with seeing clearly and experimenting with form. Those are not traits of a sociologist; they are aspects of literary art.

Mythologist Joseph Campbell may have been another influence. Campbell connected with Steinbeck's interest in mythology, symbol, and allegory. He lived near Ricketts on 4th Street in Pacific Grove and visited Ricketts's lab during 1932. When Campbell visited Ricketts's lab the three men would engage in lengthy discussions. Interconnection was also a central concept in Joseph Campbell's work. Campbell saw mythologies that were connected with archetypes, which psychologist Carl Jung theorized emerged from the collective unconscious of the human race. Steinbeck shared with Campbell a lively interest in myth. Campbell's inquiries into mythology also contributed to Steinbeck's merger of ecological and mythological ideas, observes James C. Kelley.[26] Steinbeck's fiction had been fashioned in connection with mythological archetypes from the time of his first novel, *Cup of Gold*. Campbell was increasingly interested in the interconnectedness of all of life.

A seldom-mentioned interest they both shared was their interest in music. Steinbeck weaves elements of music throughout his work. In "About Ed Ricketts," the preface to the 1951 printing of *The Log from the Sea of Cortez*, he writes of Ricketts's appreciation of Bach's *The Art of Fugue*: "He once told me that he thought the Art of the Fugue of Bach might be the greatest of all music up to our time. Always 'up to our time.' He never considered anything finished or completed, but always continuing, one thing growing on and out of another."[27] This suggests that Steinbeck and Ricketts perceived the connection of mathematics and music in Bach's precise counterpoint and structures, a recognition of correspondences and processes in nature as in art. Steinbeck would later bring the art of music to bear upon *Cannery Row* and *The Pearl* and he would make use of counterpoint in his novel *East of Eden*. Music and science likewise intersected in Charles Darwin's reflections on his method: "As in music, the person who understands every note will, if he also possesses proper taste, more thoroughly enjoy the whole, so he who examines each part of a fine view, may also thoroughly comprehend the full and combined effect."[28] Similarly, careful observation informed by something like a refined aesthetic understanding will enable one to appreciate the phenomena being studied.

As Steinbeck wrote *Sea of Cortez* he had in front of him Ed Ricketts's journal and his essay on "Non-teleological Thinking," which comprises chapter 14 of his book. The first publication of *Sea of Cortez* bore the names of both men, at Steinbeck's insistence. However, when we see Steinbeck and Ricketts mapping out a view of species in *Sea of Cortez* their ideas are not always the same. Whereas Ricketts rejects goal-oriented activity, Steinbeck "advocates a philosophy of action."[29] Ricketts is non-teleological always: that is to say that things are not improving toward an end point or goal. Steinbeck appears to advocate a kind of human purpose. Naturalism holds that human life is determined by natural laws and that social and economic laws build upon and within these contexts. In Steinbeck's stories people make choices. He holds a sense of free will alongside non-teleological thinking. Steinbeck focuses upon "what is." People are in given situations. Yet they can still make choices within these circumstances.[30]

Within his non-teleological perspective, Ricketts did not see any purposeful end point of the evolution of species. However, he did have a notion that there might be something like peak experience, a coalescence in which there was a "breaking through." In "About Ed Ricketts," Steinbeck writes:

> He was walled off a little, so that he worked at his philosophy of breaking through, of coming out through the back of the mirror into some kind of reality which would make the world seem dreamlike.[31]

DARWIN AND THE *ORIGIN OF SPECIES*

Like Ed Ricketts, Charles Darwin did not associate natural selection with progress. Darwin has a ghostly presence throughout Steinbeck's recollections of his journey with Ricketts. "Steinbeck patterned his attitude and approach to the Sea of Cortez adventure on Darwin's *Beagle* voyage," observes Brian Railsback.[32] To this day, naturalists base their explorations in Darwinian theory and so did Steinbeck and Ricketts. Railsback reminds us of Steinbeck's emphasis on showing "what actually is," "the human place" in nature, viewing the human as a species, as a biological creature.[33] Railsback provides an interesting analysis of how Darwin's natural selection plays out in *The Wayward Bus* and in other Steinbeck stories. We read in *Sweet Thursday*: "Charles Darwin and his *Origin of Species* flashed complete in one second and he spent the rest of his life backing it up."[34] Darwin never claimed this. He did, however, back it up with a great deal of observation and experimental evidence. He revised *Origin of Species* six times during his lifetime. Steinbeck takes some liberties to drive home the point of inspiration or realization in an intense moment of "breaking through."

The Log from the Sea of Cortez brings readers on a voyage that is rendered in crisp imagery. We stand on deck with Steinbeck and Ricketts as evening comes and we ride over tall waves, eating snacks, putting on heavier coats. We read that "the sharp, painful stars were out and bright enough to make the few whitecaps gleam against the dark surrounding water."[35] We are among these men: the mustached old pilot, Tiny and Sparky, who "loved to catch every manner of fish"—sardines, bonito, a fish of the mackerel family—but would never touch a porpoise, for as Sparky said: "They cry so, when they are hurt, they cry to break your heart."[36] Steinbeck adds: "The nature of the animal may parallel certain traits in ourselves—the outrageous boastfulness of porpoises, their love of play, their joy in speed."[37]

Throughout the text Steinbeck's observations are careful and caring. "The pattern of a book, or a day, of a trip, becomes a characteristic design," he writes.[38] The design that he gives us brings us to Mexico, to the Indians who, he says, have a different "time world . . . from ours." The encounter seems "to trail an expanding universe, or perhaps to lead it."[39] He thinks about how we observe the world and how our teleologies affect our observation. If a reader can drift with these waves of reflection, he or she joins Steinbeck's thoughts on human communication: "We had many discussions at the galley table and there had been many honest attempts to understand each other's thinking."[40] Steinbeck asserted that reception and understanding is possible between people and whether we can absorb another person's ideas and feelings is important: "When I have understood what you are saying, only then will I subject it to my scrutiny and my own criticism."[41]

THE FORGOTTEN VILLAGE

The Log from the Sea of Cortez begins to suggest the possibilities of cross-cultural communication. It brings into contact the culture of white Americans from California with that of the natives of Mexico and it suggests a dialogue between the human and the natural worlds. Mexico becomes a place where a primal world of indigenous people meets the world of contemporary technology. Mexico steadily drew Steinbeck's interest and he created a script, *The Forgotten Village* (1941), about a Mexican community affected by an epidemic that it could not curtail by using traditional folk remedies. The villagers have to be convinced by a teacher that bacteria in the water is causing problems and that doctors from Mexico City have to be summoned to bring medical science to the village. Juan Diego has lost his brother to the epidemic and he ventures to Mexico City to bring back doctors with a modern cure. Ed Ricketts saw the character of Juan Diego as "so imbued with the spirit of modern medical progress that he leaves the traditional way of his people to associate himself with the new thing." His teleological view appears to have prevailed. Neither *The Forgotten Village* nor *The Grapes of Wrath* ought to be taken as a paean to progress, however. In spite of human acts of courage, sacrifice, and love, Steinbeck recognizes a biologically deterministic environment. [42]

The clash of herbal remedies and the holistic methods of traditional healers with the approaches of Western medicine continues in some parts of our world and debate about the merits of traditional remedies lives on in "new age" reflections. Postcolonial theorists persist in rejecting any imposition of modern Western categories and lifestyles upon indigenous people. In Mexico today, electric power lines and modern technologies dot the landscape but travelers are advised to not drink the water. Mexico is filled with diverse species but has suffered environmental impacts of industrialization. Despite structural adjustments in connection with the World Bank and the International Monetary Fund, issues of poverty and public health remain present concerns in Mexico and goals of efficiency need to be balanced with social justice.

Mexico's gross national product is about sixteenth in the world. It is the world's sixth largest oil producer, producing some 2.7 million barrels a day. Yet there is a disparity between those who are well-off and people who live in poverty. There is also a legacy of social stratification that

Steinbeck saw in his own time. One-half of the people of Mexico are mestizos: a mixture of Spanish and Indian blood. Steinbeck once wrote: "The Indian was not even a citizen. He was a native animal."[43] Indians were a lower class of society. In *The Pearl*, Kino knows that if he has accidentally killed a man in a fight he must leave town. "We do know we are cheated from birth to the overcharge on our coffins," says his brother.

Ed Ricketts could not agree with Steinbeck's approach in his thirty-six-page script. However, censors were more of a problem for Steinbeck than his friend's objections. They descended upon the film of *The Forgotten Village* for its inclusion of a scene of childbirth. Steinbeck had to rely upon his newfound acquaintance with Eleanor Roosevelt, who had much liked *The Grapes of Wrath*, to change the minds of the censors. However, even the good word of the first lady could not save the film. For in December the United States was embroiled in the global conflict of World War II. *The Forgotten Village* was quickly forgotten. Steinbeck's fascination with Mexico and his attention to the world south of the border was only beginning. He would make several more trips to Mexico, experiencing its folk culture, making the film *Viva Zapata!* with Elia Kazan, and writing memorable stories based upon anecdotes he had heard in Mexico, like *The Pearl*.

VIVA ZAPATA!

Elia Kazan had been thinking of creating a film on the Mexican revolutionary Emiliano Zapata "since 1938," following a trip to Mexico. He made notes for such a film in 1944. Steinbeck writes that the idea for the project came his way from another source. "I was approached the other day by an outfit that calls itself Pan-American Films with the proposition that I do a film on the life of Emiliano Zapata. There is no other story I would rather do. But there are certain things that are in the way." Some men were still in power in Mexico "who helped to trick and murder Zapata." He made a 1948 research trip to Mexico. He wrote to a friend about the project: "It will be unbearably hard work and that will be a good thing." He had to condense several stories into a narrative. "I will go to work on it with great energy." He wrote, "The churning joy in the guts that to me is the physical symptom of creation is there again."[44]

Steinbeck's *Viva Zapata!* sought to emphasize Western democracy and support for the dispossessed. The film's producer, Darryl F. Zanuck, did not so much want historical accuracy. He wanted an exciting film that would sell and he cast Marlon Brando in the lead role. *Viva Zapata!* was never intended to be an accurate account of the Mexican Revolution. Steinbeck completed his draft of the screenplay. Jules Buck was assigned by Zanuck to develop the script. Buck further dramatized the action but was never credited. The opening credits feature Steinbeck's name. Steinbeck accounted for some forty-five sequences for the film. He insisted that Mexico's history was more than the stereotypical concept many American had of "a series of banditries and small revolutions and revolts led by venal and self-interested men." He wrote a lengthy introductory statement, the script, and commentary.

Steinbeck once wrote a short piece in which he said that he too was "a revolutionary." His "revolt," he said, was the assertion of individuality and democracy. In the "savagely applied system" of Marxism, he said, the individual is the victim. "Herein is my revolt," he wrote. "I believe in and will fight for the right of the individual to function as an individual without pressure from any direction. I am unalterably opposed to any interference with the creative mind."[45] He asserted the right of playwright Arthur Miller to his "private morality" during the HUAC inquiry by the U.S. Congress. He wrote: "In their attempts to save the nation from attack, they could well undermine the deep personal morality which is the nation's final defense. The Congress is truly on trial along with Arthur Miller."[46]

The film industry in 1952 was faced with the scrutiny of the House Un-American Activities Committee (HUAC), which targeted directors and actors it believed had Communist sympathies. Elia Kazan's *Pinky* (1949) was banned and this ruling was upheld by the U.S. Court of Criminal Appeals. From Rome, on a honeymoon with Elaine Scott, Steinbeck wrote to screenwriter Jules Buck that Kazan "has taken a terrible beating. But he'll come through it. He is a great guy. And he will do better work than he has ever done."[47] That future work would include another film project that would involve Steinbeck: the screen adaptation of his novel *East of Eden.*

ECOLOGY AND EMPATHY

If it is possible that reading Steinbeck's stories can promote empathy, the stories of his Mexican characters are valuable to us, for they often carry a moral message. *Viva Zapata!* suggests the need for a revolution for liberty. Kino's experience in *The Pearl* points to the reality that all that glitters is not gold and that the material gain of a great pearl may lead to unforeseen problems. *The Forgotten Village* points out the impact of modernization and addresses the need for modern science and medicine so that a community locked in superstition does not succumb to disease. Yet the stories also may suggest the impoverishment of people, such as the native Indians, and the decimation of the land. Mexico today has several environmental issues. Changes in the environment of the Sea of Cortez have been documented by scientists who have repeated the Steinbeck-Ricketts excursion and have compared their records with their own recent findings.[48] The rough and intriguing seascape called for investigation and raised curiosity in these biologists, the sense of wonder that leads to scientific inquiry.

The scientific pursuit by Steinbeck and Ricketts was an exercise in wonder. To Steinbeck and Ricketts the Sea of Cortez was a continuous ecosystem. Their science not only was masculine, rational, and objective but also integrated the human sense of awe and curiosity and a perception of connection and relationship. This is a science that Evelyn Fox Keller, writing on scientist Barbara McClintock, has given the title *A Feeling for the Organism*.[49] It is careful observation of that "superorganism" that was practiced by Steinbeck and Ricketts as participants in a drama of biological inquiry. These same qualities carry over in Steinbeck's fiction and his essays. He approaches human lives in specific environments in ways that are contextual, pluralistic, inclusive, holistic, compassionate, relational, and respectful of diversity. Steinbeck shows that people and other living creatures are related to their environments. His non-dualistic approach is one that includes an appreciation of the non-instrumental value of nature. Steinbeck is attentive to the patterns of life along the California coast and to the simple value of his dog Charley curling up on a rug beside the fireplace at his home on Long Island.

Steinbeck's journey with Ed Ricketts to the Sea of Cortez and his ongoing interest in Mexico point to a crucial aspect of Steinbeck's art: his writing and his interest in science converge in an ethic of care and in a proto-ecological perspective. This interest in marine biology, in animals, and in the pattern of ecosystems, or what he and Ricketts referred to as superorganism, extended from his summer studies of the coast near Monterey through his relationship with Ed Ricketts and his Pacific Biological Laboratories to his "voracious" reading of science and history.[50] The most thorough account of this passionate lifelong inclination toward what we would today call ecological science appears in *Steinbeck and the Environment*, a book of essays edited by Susan Beegel, Susan Shillinglaw, and Wesley Tiffney Jr.[51]

Steinbeck's observation of nature is evident to any reader who picks up his novels. Many of his stories immediately bring the reader to a description of the landscape and provide a sense of place. He anchors us in this sense of place in his essays also. For example, while living in Sag Harbor, Long Island, he wrote "My War with the Ospreys" as a reflection upon observing and being troubled by the ospreys. Before he gives us his anecdote of that encounter, Steinbeck sets the scene by telling us that he settled in a residence by the bay, "on a beautiful little point of land on the inland waters, a place called Bluff Point."[52] He describes this place as "shaded by oak trees" and says that he planted "a thousand Japanese black pines."[53] He then recalls that he began "to learn the names of trees and bushes, of berries and flowers." This is Steinbeck the naturalist, the observer. With a telescope given to him by his wife Elaine he "watched muskrats and a pair of otters swimming in our bay."[54] He attempted to identify migrating ducks and geese. From his vegetable garden and from his house's sun porch he looked out on the bird feeder he had placed outside and tried to identify the birds that arrived by checking an Audubon guidebook. Throughout this essay, we see an individual with an appreciative eye for natural phenomena who is intent upon observing details and identifying and cataloging wildlife.

This keen observation anchors us in a sense of place. His work announces that it is about "seeing." In the Sea of Cortez "seeing fully is set out as his primary task," observe Jackson Benson and Susan Shillinglaw.[55] They remark that Steinbeck was also a moralist and an idealist, a man seeking "the meanings or patterns behind what he observed."[56] When Steinbeck gives us the region of Monterey he always offers us the inner life of this place: the lives of characters who are intimately tied to their environment. Steinbeck interpreted American life from the perspective that all things—human and natural—were ultimately connected. This holism "brings together the human heart and the land," as Barry Lopez has said.[57]

Steinbeck connects the human mind with physical life and the exterior world in a movement that overcomes the Cartesian split of mind and world. René Descartes, back in the early 1600s, claimed that reality consists of minds and bodies. The mind included all thinking, or consciousness. For Descartes, the physical world was mechanistic and thus lacked moral standing. Only consciousness could have moral standing. Steinbeck challenges this by suggesting that human consciousness is alive in interaction with an animated natural world and that creatures, like his dog Charley, are quite conscious and sensitively aware beings.

Aldo Leopold has spoken of a holism of relationship of organisms, and Steinbeck and Ricketts point to this relationship of organic life in their text of their Sea of Cortez journey. J. Baird Callicott writes of Leopold's land ethic: "A species is what it is because it has adapted to a niche in the ecosystem. The whole, the system itself, thus, literally and quite straightforwardly, shapes and forms its component parts."[58] Steinbeck and Ricketts did not use the term "ecosystem" but they did recognize an organic connectedness within the natural patterns of life in the Sea of Cortez. Steinbeck writes that Ed Ricketts always saw biological life in process: "He never considered anything finished or completed but always continuing, one thing growing on and out of another. It is probable that his critical method was the outgrowth of his biological training and observation."[59] It is equally likely that Steinbeck's writing was informed by this sense of writing as process and life as a process. When he writes of his friend Ed Ricketts, at times it seems as if he could be writing about himself also. "His scientific interest was essentially ecological and holistic," Steinbeck writes of his friend.[60]

"Our trip to the Gulf of Lower California was a marvel of bumbling efficiency," Steinbeck recalls.[61] They speculated that the Pacific coast was one continuous system and thought of next going to Alaska to the Aleutians. The war made that impossible. Yet the romantic spirit of discovery, the knight's quest of wonder, remained. It appears that Steinbeck and Ricketts were working out a world view that was not strictly human-centered. Theirs was a perspective that acknowledged the human as animal and the intrinsic value of nonhuman life. The Sea of Cortez was a system of biological richness and diversity through which maritime life and solar and chemical energy flowed. The processes and relations of the system—chemical and biological—were necessary for the life of the individual organisms, but the individuals only were alive because of the energy in the ecological system. Steinbeck was fascinated by how individuals relate to their surroundings. In this universal energy flow the individual was not separate and isolated but was ever drawn into the flow and pattern of life. This view had implications for his ideas about "group man," or the collective action of humans in social groups.

Steinbeck's essays can contribute to reasoned dialogue on human and environmental issues. In *America and Americans*, Steinbeck criticizes an American orientation toward consumerism and getting lost in "things." This is connected with his environmental concerns. He writes: "Our towns are girdled with wreckage and debris."[62] The polluters are not bad people, he decides. They have just become "heirs to the early conviction that sky and water are unowned and that they are limitless."[63] He criticizes "irresponsibility" and he integrates reflections on American history into his claim that Americans need to reverse this legacy of environmental destruction. He points to the nineteenth century, in which settlers "abandoned their knowledge of kindness to the land in order to maintain its usefulness."[64] More problematic, perhaps, was the destructive path cut through the countryside. He writes: "The merciless nineteenth century was like a hostile expedition for loot that seemed limitless."[65] He concludes, "Conservation came to us slowly, and much of it hasn't arrived yet."[66] Steinbeck suggests that "awe and humility" are an appropriate response to nature's wonders and that this was his own response to the California redwoods that he saw as a child.

Arne Naess, the deep ecologist, has characterized the opposition to pollution and resource depletion as a "shallow environmental perspective."[67] One must probe for the underlying causes and take a "relational, total field" perspective, one that goes beyond the human, or the anthropocentric. This explanation turns on the view that a radical change in our perspective is necessary to transform our current relationship with the natural world so that the future will be sustainable. One may ask if Steinbeck's ecological consciousness in *America and Americans* was participating in a critique of the dominant Western world view, which some eco-critics view as responsible for environmental destruction. Steinbeck never offered specific policy recommendations. However, there is throughout his writings an implicit concern with human responsibility for the earth and for the life of future generations.

One of the problems with Steinbeck's essay is that it treats U.S. history in broad generalizations. Not all humans—in the nineteenth century or now—are equally at fault for environmental problems. Certainly, the characters of *Tortilla Flat* and *Cannery Row* were not participants in the same world view. They were more like people in underdeveloped countries: poor and oppressed. They were not socioeconomic elites and they were not conventional Americans. George and Lennie in *Of Mice and Men* are also outsiders. Steinbeck begins *Of Mice and Men* with the land. He then unfolds a story of care and commitment between George and Lennie. There is a correlation between this committed bond between them and the human-nature relationship. This is not an ethics of abstract rules and principles, rights, and duties but a contextualized ethics focused on relationship.

Steinbeck was specifically concerned with the renewal of America through the everyday actions of people. The change would come through cooperation and relationship. Steinbeck seems to echo ecological writer Murray Bookchin's view: "The very notion of the domination of nature by man stems from the very real domination of human by human."[68] Steinbeck's historical essay in *America and Americans* is principally a call for social justice. He calls for the moral responsibility each of us has to preserve human rights and our environment and for the commitment to transform our relationships with each other and with the natural world.

7

STEINBECK AT WAR

THE MOON IS DOWN

When war erupted in Europe in 1939 America held to its neutrality. President Roosevelt offered moral exhortation but Congress maintained a policy of isolationism. "We watched the approach of war as a bird helplessly watches an approaching rattlesnake," Steinbeck wrote.[1] In *The Moon Is Down* (1942), John Steinbeck addressed World War II. A year before the attack at Pearl Harbor, he had begun to wonder what would happen if an invading army occupied American territory. In his original conception of the novel, he imagined that a small American community was subdued by a foreign force. This was a variation on the invasion scare novel that H. G. Wells had produced when he wrote *The War of the Worlds*, which had more recently been aired as a radio drama by Orson Welles in 1938. Steinbeck's publishers did not like the idea. They felt that it would trouble Americans and diminish their morale. Steinbeck rewrote the story, setting the action in an unnamed occupied country in Europe, one that appeared to reflect the situation in Norway. He wrote some of the novel while in Suffern, New York, and at Snedens Landing, in 1941.[2]

The book became popular in Europe, where copies were circulated by members of underground resistance movements. The Norwegians, in particular, saw an image of their own struggles in the novel. The military force that had subdued them may have been technologically superior but the resistance fighters were tenacious, savvy, and devoted to the cause of their freedom. They recognized the vulnerability of their foes. Stein-

beck's character Mayor Orden is a man of integrity, a hero. His opposite
is Colonel Lanser, leader of the invading force that has swept in upon the
town. Lanser is an educated man who knows the classics but he is also a
military man who has to carry out his duty.

The film of *The Moon Is Down*, with Nunnally Johnson's screenplay,
begins by giving us a map of Norway and a hysterical voice speaking in
German that any viewer would immediately associate with Adolf Hitler.
This opening is then contrasted with the sounds of children playing in an
idyllic village filled with waltzing background music. We see smiling
faces and hear bright, cordial conversation. "Have a good time!" someone
calls, bidding friends farewell. Suddenly, the Luftwaffe is sighted and a
nurse points at the sky and exclaims, "Look!" "Parachutes," someone
says. "Get to the woods, quick!" German soldiers march into town to
military drumbeats and the occupiers set up a brass band to convey
friendship. An announcement blares across a loudspeaker: "Under the
protection of the German army you have nothing to fear." However,
Colonel Lanser, who occupies Mayor Orden's house, soon makes it clear
that if the citizens do not comply with the goal to procure iron from the
mines there will be violence. Colonel Lanser is told, "We have lived in
peace so long that we don't believe in war."

The distribution and impact of Steinbeck's novel has been closely
examined by Donald V. Coers, in a manner that anticipated some of the
methods of book history.[3] Coers traces the reprinting, exchange, and
reception of the text in Norway, Denmark, France, and other areas of
Europe. He begins his study by recalling *The Moon Is Down* as a source
of debate in the United States. Steinbeck, he says, sought to celebrate "the
durability of democracy." Some American readers thought that he was
too soft on the enemy. Steinbeck drew portraits of his German characters
that suggested that while they were misled, they were also fully human.
The Moon Is Down presented the enemy as people with lives, just as it
presented the people of the occupied village as heroic. Clifton Fadiman,
who said he liked much of Steinbeck's work, could not find much to
interest him in Steinbeck's *The Moon Is Down*, and James Thurber's
review of it was harsh.[4] Despite this, the book sold well in the United
States and it became a resource, an encouragement to the fighting spirit in
Europe. Members of the resistance later wrote letters to Steinbeck about
the novel, which was smuggled, translated, and distributed in their coun-

tries. Coers's study includes interviews with people who lived through that difficult chapter in history.

The short novel had a mixed reception in America. When critics complained that the invaders, obviously Nazis, were not portrayed more negatively as the enemy, Steinbeck responded that he was writing a novel, not wartime propaganda. *The Moon Is Down*, although sometimes classified as propaganda, is certainly more a story of moral integrity than a propaganda piece. The novel continues the emphasis of *The Grapes of Wrath* on a community that is beset by power seekers and bullies, like the camp guards and California vigilantes. The novel opposes those who use violence to gain power over others. The occupation soldiers are less than complete men. Major Hunter is "a haunted little man of figures, a little man." He sets his men in rows, diminishing their humanity. There is in him no humor, music, or mysticism of mathematics; he is an arithmetician that counts men like beans. Captain Bentick is "a family man" who imitates the English and has no ambition and is too old. He is a man of pipes and sticks, a patriarch for the Freudian-minded reader. Captain Loft is his opposite: too young and overly ambitious. Loft is a sycophant. "He knew every kind of military courtesy and insisted on using it all."[5] He clicks his heels, in fine military deportment, and believes that women fall in love with a man in a uniform. He imagines, says the narrator, that if there is a God he is an old man in a sharp uniform putting wreaths on the graves of valiant soldiers.

The satire continues with a description of the lieutenants, Prackle and Tonder, whose very names convey ridicule. They are "snot-noses" who submit to ideology. They are "trained in the politics of the day, believing the great new system."[6] These emotional young men have been indoctrinated to hate "degenerate art," like the modernist creations so reviled by Hitler. Prackle draws pencil sketches and spends his time seducing Tonder's sister. Tonder is "a bitter poet," "a dark romantic." He dreams of honor by death on the battlefield and mythological glories "lighted by the setting sun": Valkyries, big-breasted women, "Wagnerian thunder."[7] These men follow the orders of Colonel Lanser, playing war as if it were a children's game of "Run, Sheep, Run."[8] Steinbeck portrays the colonel as a man who is not so deluded about the course of war. Lanser has fought in World War I and seen its horror: "treachery and hatred, the muddling of incompetent generals, the torture and killing and sickness and tiredness, until at last it is over and nothing has changed."[9] He tries to convince himself that this war will be different.

The humanity of these men is brought into focus, as much as their vulgarity. The second chapter of the novel introduces them with sharp satire but gradually begins to round out their characters with the quality of a play, portraying them as they take over and settle into the mayor's "little palace." The narrator suggests that their minds have been fogged by parades and crowds and triumphal nationalism. This celebration of military vitality brings a "gray dream" in which "real things become unreal." Tension and excitement, weariness, movement all merge in "one great gray dream" and one forgets how one has killed and ordered men to be killed.[10] The conquerors are men a long way from home, bound up in a situation, caught up in a nightmare.

The novel presents a variation on "the phalanx theory," or group mind. This group mind, Steinbeck noted in a letter, "has emotions of which the unit man is incapable."[11] Steinbeck's interest in this phenomenon carries over from his work on *Tortilla Flat*, *In Dubious Battle*, *The Grapes of Wrath*, and other works. One may claim that *The Moon Is Down* was weakened by his return to the phalanx theory, as does Warren French.[12] However, Steinbeck was onto something quite serious in this case. The group psychology of "ordinary men" was examined by Christopher Browning in his inquiry into "police" actions and exterminations of the Jewish population in Poland in 1940. The dissociative mental fogging and "splitting" of conscious and unconscious minds of National Socialists during the Holocaust has been examined by Robert Lifton and other psychologists.[13]

When we turn to the resistance fighters of *The Moon Is Down*, the question becomes whether people who love freedom and are willing to fight for their homeland can become a group, or phalanx, also. Mayor Orden certainly becomes a hero and a martyr to the cause. He is not a victim, in the manner of Jim Nolan in *In Dubious Battle*, as French points out, because he knows exactly what he stands for and knows the consequences of his commitments. Facing execution, Mayor Orden sets the case before Dr. Winter by recalling his reference to Socrates in *The Apology* during a graduation speech forty-six years before. He says: "A man who is good for anything ought not to calculate the chance for living or dying; he ought only to consider whether he is doing right or wrong." The town's resistance forces have been told that the mayor will die if they persist in their actions. Mayor Orden stands firm, telling Colonel Lanser that he and his men will be "driven out": "The people don't like to be conquered, sir, and so they will not be." [14]

Donald Coers's publication-reception history of *The Moon Is Down* supports the notion that the written word has power. A book can and does have an impact upon human consciousness and action. Coers places *The Moon Is Down* within social and political context and indicates how the book was printed, distributed, and utilized. Coers's study is indeed much like a history of the book: an analysis of the circulation of *The Moon Is Down* in Nazi-occupied Europe. Late in 1942 the book was printed in Sweden and circulated in the underground in Norway. Most of the books that were circulated in Norway were then reprinted in Norway. The book had an impact and "they believed it was about Norway," observes Coers. [15] The story does suggest an occupied Norway. Norway and Denmark were attacked by the Germans April 9, 1940. A resistance movement and the rejection of a quisling (or accommodating collaborator) are found in the novel. The British play version says that the action occurs in a small mining town in Norway.

Some readers in Norway were already familiar with Steinbeck's fiction. *Tortilla Flat* was published in Norway in 1938 and *Of Mice and Men* appeared there in 1939. *The Grapes of Wrath* reached Norway early in 1940 but no translations of Steinbeck's novels were published in Norway during wartime. *The Moon Is Down* clearly provided encouragement. American soldier Frank G. Nelson, who was seven months a prisoner of war in Norway, said that *The Moon Is Down* was "the truest picture I have yet found of both Germans and Norwegians under the occupation of Norway." [16] Following the war, Steinbeck was honored with a medal by the king of Norway. The king of Norway decorated Steinbeck for the contribution his novel had made to the resistance to Nazi occupation in Norway.

The Moon Is Down has not been regarded highly among Steinbeck's novels. However, the story does have the advantage of being relatively short. It is filled with material for ethical reflection. Mark D. Bradbury describes *The Moon Is Down* as "a compelling fictionalized case study of public service ethics and leadership, and the perseverance of free men." [17] The novel is recommended for students because of its relative brevity and the way it raises many points for discussion. The novel can be read in a few hours.

BOMBS AWAY

Bombs Away (1942), a recruiting text for the United States Air Force, clearly is propaganda and an extension of Steinbeck's concern with the U.S. war effort. In 1940, Steinbeck urged President Roosevelt to consider enemy surveillance from south of the U.S. border in Mexico. In a brief meeting on June 26, Steinbeck encouraged Roosevelt to maintain a watchful eye on the southern border of the United States. James Rowe Jr. commented to Roosevelt that Steinbeck probably had "no better information than any other sensitive and intelligent layman who has spent time in Mexico" about potential enemy military bases and surveillance posts.[18] Steinbeck also dreamed up a plan to flood the economy of the enemy power with thousands of bills that would inflate its economy, but the idea was considered impractical by U.S. Treasurer Henry Morgenthau and Lord Halifax in Britain. Steinbeck and his friend Ed Ricketts did have data on the Mexican coast that might have been useful, notes Coers. They had access to zoological surveys conducted by Japanese scientists among the Pacific Islands.[19] Steinbeck's suggestions indicate the level of urgency he felt to defend America and to be prepared in the event that the European war expanded further to affect American interests.

Once American participation in the war began, Steinbeck was anxious to contribute further. He sought to be a war correspondent overseas. He was drawn into a network of the foreign information services, which was connected with the OSS, the Office of Strategic Services, an organization that was later transformed into the CIA. In the Office of War Information he assisted with propaganda that was intended to encourage the will to fight for home, nation, and liberty and justice. He later commented on his experience: "I wrote everything: speeches, essays, stories, plays, broadcasts, a whole volume about the training of bomber crews, everything I could devise or that was suggested to me and there were dozens of writers doing the same thing."[20]

Steinbeck did not want to write *Bombs Away: The Story of a Bomber Team*, but he was persuaded to write this heroic portrayal of the training of a bomber crew. Its "flat" characters are like those drawn for a comic book; they are "a company of brave men," observes Warren French.[21] The crew is idealized, like the cartoon superheroes of Marvel comics. As was the case with King Arthur's Knights of the Round Table, there is a noble kinship among the men. Steinbeck's narrative asserts: "It is the greatest team in the world."[22] It was not Steinbeck's greatest book. However, he donated all of the proceeds to the Air Force Society Trust Fund.

Bombs Away, published on November 27, 1942, ought not to be evaluated as literature. It was a service to America and to the government, as Mimi R. Gladstein and other Steinbeck critics have pointed out.[23] John Ditsky is correct in calling this Steinbeck's weakest book.[24] However, as Rodney Rice has pointed out, it is unfair to evaluate *Bombs Away* in artistic terms. It is a public relations and recruiting piece written on assignment that was intended to show the development of a bomber squad. One must take each work by Steinbeck for what it is. In 1942, *Bombs Away* was a product of Steinbeck's role as a consultant to the secretary of war assigned to Army Air Force Headquarters. General Henry "Hap" Arnold had traced out the plan for the book, and Steinbeck's friend, the actor Burgess Meredith, had supported the idea. The author states that his purpose is to "set down the nature and mission of a bomber crew and the technique and training of each member of it."[25] Steinbeck was hesitant to engage in the project because he did not want the enthusiasm and patriotism aroused in young men reading this text to lead to their deaths in combat. However, it is possible that it attracted men to bomber squads who bravely fulfilled necessary missions, since this was the volume's purpose.

This volume is an expression of Steinbeck's phalanx theory, or group-man theory. A democratic team effort is presented. Steinbeck does not discuss the pilot first but, rather, places the pilot within the context of the group, where "he is no longer individually the most important man in the Air Force." This is a unit in which "each member is individually important."[26] When Rice examines Steinbeck's "recruiting text" and World War II military aviation, he begins with emphasis upon the devastation of Japanese cities by wartime bombing and recites statistics that show the loss of life among aviators. United States bombers dropped 2,790,000 tons of bombs on their targets.[27] The U.S. Eighth Air Force lost 8 percent and mathematically no one would survive to complete the standard twenty-five tours.[28] The United States experienced a total loss of 79,625 servicemen and Britain lost 79,281. According to historian Stephen Ambrose, some 6,537 B-17s and B-24s were shot down.[29]

Rice immediately points to what he calls a "paradox" between the "brute statistics" he has offered and the "lofty conceptions voiced in *Bombs Away*." However, Steinbeck writes: "It is a strange, almost mystical thing that happens to flying men." They remain part of a brotherhood in a way that is "something like a religion," in a mutual understanding "until some force outside himself drags him down from the sky."[30] While the "brute statistics" are striking, the experience of a brotherhood and that "mystical thing that happens to flying men" may be quite a real experience: one that is not merely rhetoric or propaganda. A religion suggests a commitment that binds together in a community. For Rice, the "dreamy vision of mystical brotherhood and spiritualism" are set against "the bleak backdrop of indifferent killing and indiscriminate destruction."[31] This experience of the men is dismissed as mere romance in contrast with reality. However, it may very well be a reality—not some airy notion. Comradeship was a reality. Spiritual experience for these individuals may have been a reality also.

Steinbeck asserts the importance of teamwork and intelligence in this democracy of men on a mission.[32] Steinbeck identifies the men as primarily midwestern or western in background.[33] Bill, the bombardier, is the son of a railroad engineer from Idaho. Al, the gunner, is like a frontiersman with a machine gun. Abner, the aerial engineer, is a "restless, intelligent man" from California. Allan, the navigator, is from Indiana and he exhibits controlled thinking and exactness, while Joe, the pilot from California, has qualities of alertness, strength, and fine coordination.[34] In *Bombs Away* Steinbeck repeats a familiar theme: the common man as heroic. There is confidence and faith in the action and valor of ordinary men who face the forces of war and modern technology. Photographs join the text and unify the information and message. Steinbeck shows that heroism in a group phalanx can uphold the principles of democracy with integrity in the midst of war.

The book was written quickly, with Steinbeck writing about four thousand words per day. Newspaper reviews of the book acknowledged it while voicing support for the new war effort. The *New Republic* recognized that the book had the same relationship to literature as recruiting posters did to art.[35] Clifton Fadiman, who had criticized *The Moon Is Down*, called *Bombs Away* an "extraordinary fine job of recruiting propaganda."[36]

LIFEBOAT

Next, Steinbeck was enlisted in writing the script for *Lifeboat* (1943), an Alfred Hitchcock film that bears Steinbeck's name in the credits but ultimately was predominantly the work of the director. The offer came from 20th Century Fox, which had produced John Ford's film of *The Grapes of Wrath*. Seven individuals are together in a lifeboat after a German U-boat has torpedoed their ship. Steinbeck had begun the story in 1941, viewing the situation of these characters much like an existentialist might. They are eight people in a cosmos adrift.[37] They rescue a German and drift toward a ship that flies the American flag but is being guided through the sea by men in German uniforms. Hitchcock's screenwriters deleted much of Steinbeck's dialogue and changed the script almost beyond recognition. Steinbeck was unsuccessful in his effort to have his name removed from the screen credits.

The story for *Lifeboat* began as a novelette. Again, as in much of Steinbeck's previous fiction, it brought together a group of people—a phalanx—tangled in a difficult situation. The story treatment was revised by screenwriters assigned by Hitchcock and Darryl Zanuck and, as is the case with many films, it was turned into a film that was at odds with Steinbeck's intentions. *Lifeboat* was produced to provide a strong sense of purpose to its viewers: to arouse them to patriotism, to win the war. Steinbeck's eighty-six-page script, however, had no heroes. It was dark and cynical, and it was as full of cosmic musings as an Ingmar Bergman film. *Lifeboat*, by Hitchcock and Zanuck, redrafted and filmed with commercial interests, was Hitchcock-eerie: fog and valor and victory at sea.

The general form of Steinbeck's original story remains in *Lifeboat*. A viewer encounters the phalanx theory again at work in the eight survivors of the sunken freighter and the U-boat commander who has joined them. However, the adaptation by screenwriter Jo Swerling and director Hitchcock rewrites the dialogue. Swerling, who rewrote most of *Lifeboat* for Hitchcock, was a screenwriter for Frank Capra films, and he was one of the writers on Gary Cooper's portrayal of the Lou Gehrig story, *The Pride of the Yankees*, and the Gary Cooper film *The Westerner*. In this film, Swerling makes the U-boat commander a significant figure. In the lifeboat is Connie Porter, played by Tallulah Bankhead: a wealthy, snotty reporter. Rittenhouse (Henry Hull) is a millionaire. Gus (William Bendix), one of the freighter's sailors, has injured his leg. Kovac (John Hodiak) is the sunken ship's oiler. Stanley Garrett (Hume Cronyn) is a British radio operator. Alice MacKenzie (Mary Anderson) is a nurse with the American Red Cross. Charcoal (Canada Lee) is a black steward. An Englishwoman has lost her baby. The Nazi (Walter Slezak) uses his skills to hold the boat upright, amputates Gus's injured leg, and assumes a position of leadership, although he is the enemy. Robert E. Morsberger points out in his introduction to the screenplay that in Steinbeck's original script, the Nazi commander does not have these attributes.

STEINBECK IN WORLD WAR II EUROPE

Finally, John Steinbeck gained the opportunity to report on the war in Europe. He bid his new wife Gwyn Conger Steinbeck farewell, packed his bag, and traveled for England. In 1943, Steinbeck posted eighty-five articles from Europe, where he was a wartime correspondent. Between June 21 and December 10 these pieces appeared in newspapers. They were later collected by editor Pascal Covici in a volume titled *Once There Was a War* (1958). Steinbeck was not writing like most war correspondents, that "hard-bitten bunch" as he called them. He was writing what we would today call feature stories. They were sketches, travel observations, myths, and stories of war offered to the public by a civilian traveling with the troops. He started with pieces that show the depersonalized movement of troops by ship and daily reports of their transport across perilous waters patrolled by German U-boats. While in London, he sent reports from a bomber base that are vignettes, or brief stories: "A Plane's Name," about designating names for planes, was followed by "Superstition," in which the tail gunner on a bomber has lost his "medallion," or good luck charm. He next underscores English valor in their fight against the Axis powers but suddenly turns to a fanciful essay about "The Alcoholic Goat." Mascot for the fighters, the goat has become a symbol of good luck. "In every way he is a military figure. He is magnificent on parade."[38]

Steinbeck provided portraits of dynamic individuals. Private Big Train Mulligan appears on July 25 and is the subject of articles on August 4 and 12. He drives the officers to important rendezvous in a brown Ford. He is an enlisted man who rejects promotion to the ranks of officer. "I don't want to tell a bunch of men what to do," he says.[39] In the August 12 piece, Mulligan tells a story, one of his famous "lies," about a gambler who believes he can always win on Sundays—but what day is it if one crosses the international timeline in Greenwich?

Arriving on the continent in Italy, via North Africa, Steinbeck participated in a military action led by actor Douglas Fairbanks Jr. He observed, "You can't see much of a battle."[40] However, he could focus on the people and incidents he saw around him. One character he gives his readers is "Bugs," who has found a mirror that was spared from a bombing raid in Sicily. He takes it with him from place to place as the war rages around him. Finally, when he is about to hang the mirror up in a house the nail falls out and the mirror falls and splinters into "a million pieces."[41] In "Capri" the soldiers gather to toast the liberation of Italy with tea and scones with a woman who has been stuck there by the war.[42] In "The Worried Bartender," they try to rescue the bartender's pregnant daughter from the town toward which the Germans are marching.[43] The story is sheer melodrama, like out of a Douglas Fairbanks film.

Steinbeck's dispatches during his four and a half months overseas were published in the *Herald Tribune* (June 21–December 15, 1943). Twenty-three of these pieces appeared in the London *Daily Express*. They were syndicated to other newspapers. His method tends to be one of objectivity. He is a keen observer, selecting details and drawing characters as he would in his fiction. While he is a participant on Red Beach in Italy, he writes with detachment. He is like the lens of Robert Capa's camera, providing a series of images and stories that we can look through.

Steinbeck presents experiences on site, in the midst of war in Europe. His wartime missives are about individuals and groups of people fighting for a cause, to make a difference in the world. Later, he wrote to Joseph Bryan III, as he helped to prepare the articles for publication: "There are many things in them I didn't know I was writing—among others a hatred for war. Hell, I thought I was building the war up."[44] Some accounts of Steinbeck's life suggest that he returned from his experience of the war shattered, troubled, and cranky. It is plausible that he may have been experiencing post-traumatic stress disorder, although this was never diagnosed. Gwyn Conger's comments suggest that he was difficult to live with. They had bought two adjacent brownstones in New York City at East 78th Street. However, their marriage was beginning to unravel.

In 1944, American voters soon were told that once a nation is engaged in a great war it ought to support its president and not suddenly shift gears to elect someone new. Franklin Roosevelt would be running for a fourth term as the nation's chief executive and commander in chief of the armed forces. John Steinbeck was enlisted to write for his presidential campaign. It was the first in a series of such political efforts to which Steinbeck would lend his talents. He would write in support of two presidential campaigns for Adlai Stevenson and would later write on behalf of Lyndon Johnson. The Steinbeck contributions to Roosevelt's fourth presidential election campaign in 1944 have been studied by Cliff Lewis. Steinbeck wrote a document in the form of a letter that the president's speech writers used as a "Letter" to Robert E. Hannegan, the Democratic Party chairman, published on July 11, 1944. Steinbeck listed "eleven principles" in another document that provided the background for the speech with which F.D.R. would address the Democratic National Convention on July 20, 1944. The president's speech writers modified Steinbeck's comments and "absorbed only part of the poetry into their dreary prose," Lewis says.[45]

POSTWAR

A Bill Mauldin cartoon on April 8, 1946, shows a man in military uniform seated on a box at the side of a road. His son sits on the fender of an old car that is piled high with furniture and which recalls the Joad family vehicle. The caption reads: "Don't bother Daddy. He's writing a sequel to 'Grapes of Wrath.'"[46] Steinbeck, of course, would not write such a sequel. Upon completing *Cannery Row* (1945), he worked on *The Wayward Bus* (1947) and on *The Pearl* (1947). He visited Russia with photographer Robert Capa, completing *A Russian Journal* (1948). The trip to Russia was rich with observations and amply illustrated by Capa's photography. However, not knowing the Russian language limited both of them. Steinbeck could develop a travelogue but he could not converse well with the people he met. He and Capa were guided through Moscow, plied with vodka, and steered away from attention to dreary factories and long lines of people dealing with food shortages. Steinbeck and Capa also visited Kiev, Stalingrad, and Georgia. In his published journal, he did not write about Russian politics. He wrote about the Russian people and what he saw around him. Then he took on film projects and he returned to work on his "long novel," which would become *East of Eden* (1952).

Steinbeck remained politically involved after World War II. He claimed that he did some work on behalf of Harry S. Truman, although little has been written about any work Steinbeck may have done for that president's administration in the immediate postwar years. When Adlai Stevenson sought the presidency, John Steinbeck was in his camp. He wrote on behalf of Stevenson's campaigns and he attended nominating conventions. As Stevenson considered another run for the presidency in 1960, William McCormick Blair Jr. reached for the assistance of Stanley Frankel, who was the brother-in-law of Stevenson's law partner, Newton Minow. Frankel provided an eight-page memo in which he indicated that public relations clichés would not work against Richard Nixon's media and public relations team. Frankel proposed a novel about Nixon that would be election propaganda and cast a negative image of Nixon. Steinbeck was proposed as a potential writer of such a piece. However, Steinbeck responded that it would not work. Jonathan Swift had never won an election with his satire, he said. Steinbeck recognized that a novel would hardly have any effect on the outcome of a presidential election. It was a moot point. Stevenson had to get past John Fitzgerald Kennedy and he did not. Kennedy won the Democratic nomination. When Nixon secured the Republican Party nomination it was not books but speeches and television that had an impact on the 1960 presidential election. A book of Adlai Stevenson's speeches appeared with an introduction by John Steinbeck. He would have made a very good president in Steinbeck's view. "I love the clean, clear writing," he said. "As a man, I like his intelligent, humorous, logical, civilized mind."[47]

In contrast, Steinbeck did not like the politics of Dwight Eisenhower or Vice-President Richard Nixon. Although he was at first supportive of Eisenhower, he came to see him as an inarticulate war hero who, he claimed, was unable to formulate a good sentence in English. Steinbeck believed that there was in America a gradual movement toward "the theory of government by the common man." Americans were caught in a paradox: distrusting privilege and inherited position, property, and money, and having eliminated titles and aristocracy, there was only money and possessions to admire, he later wrote.[48] The qualities that Americans sought in a president were also paradoxical. In a president, he wrote, "we want a common candidate but an uncommon office holder."[49] Such a president is one of us, while also an extraordinary individual in office.

During those years, when the Cold War occupied all Americans who thought about international relations, Steinbeck's works were quite popular in Eastern Europe and Russia. In 1948 he published *A Russian Journal* and his novels *In Dubious Battle* and *The Grapes of Wrath* continued to circulate in Russia and East Europe. Danica Cerce has observed the complexities of this reception.[50] Popular reception of Steinbeck in Eastern Europe and in Russia has rested largely on his strong novels that feature the struggle of workers. Cerce writes: "His fortunes suffered from the fact that, despite the prodigious and startlingly diverse output of his career, he was known primarily for the social and political characteristics of such works as *In Dubious Battle* (1936) and *The Grapes of Wrath* (1939)."[51] There is little appreciation of his turn away from proletarian themes toward other kinds of writing. Rather, ideological forces have shaped his reception. Some readers appreciated his social and economic critique, as if he were writing a political tract rather than a novel. Steinbeck experimented with his fiction, as will any creative artist, but for many readers in Eastern Europe, says Cerce, "he ceased to be regarded as an individual and became a political tool, a 'sympathetic' advocate of the worker's cause."[52]

The first Czech translation of *The Grapes of Wrath* appeared in 1941. It was followed by a Slovene version in 1943. Critics there saw in him an "objective social chronicler," Cerce indicates.[53] Steinbeck was criticized when he veered away from what was considered to be social realism and he was applauded when he appeared to criticize capitalism or presented a "utopian model of social improvement." There were some seventeen translations of Steinbeck books to the Czech language by the early 1960s. Petr Kopecky, in *Steinbeck Studies*, wrote of the ideological burden that was placed upon Steinbeck's texts during this time.[54]

Twice he visited Russia: first with photographer Robert Capa shortly after the war in 1946 and later with his wife Elaine in 1963. The experience of his first trip to the Soviet Union has been recorded in his *Russian Journal*, illustrated with Capa's photographs. The second visit was part of a European trip with his wife. He met Elaine Steinbeck shortly after that first trip and by 1950 he was going to New York City with her. She was a woman who enjoyed the theater and she had been the Broadway stage's first female stage manager, for the musical *Oklahoma!* He wanted to write a play and so he set to work on one. *Burning Bright* quickly closed after thirteen shows. In 1954, *Sweet Thursday* was transformed into the

Rodgers and Hammerstein musical *Pipe Dream* but even with a musical score from that notable team it did not fare any better. *Of Mice and Men* was effective on the stage and continues to be performed, most recently in 2014. However, little else that Steinbeck wrote for the stage has been successful.[55]

Steinbeck seemed to fit into New York City well with Elaine. He had visited New York as a young man and had lived there with Gwyn for a time during their marriage. Yet he suggests that he only gradually became a New York resident after World War II. His first impression of New York City in 1925 had been one of being overwhelmed and "horrified." "There was something monstrous about it—the tall buildings looming to the sky and the light shining through the falling snow," he wrote. He lived in a room in Fort Greene Place, Brooklyn, while he rolled wheelbarrows of cement for the workers building Madison Square Garden. He got a job on the New York *American* and on assignments to Queens and Brooklyn he got lost. He didn't last at that job and he returned to California. Years later, he was back in New York. He says that, on that occasion, gradually he got to know people at the shops in the neighborhood, "the butcher and the news dealer and the liquor man," as individuals. Steinbeck writes about his experience of realization that he had become a New Yorker as something like an epiphany. On 3rd Avenue this awakening comes as "a kind of light, a kind of feeling."[56]

Director Elia Kazan wrote that he didn't think John Steinbeck should have been living in New York, or writing plays. "He was a prose writer, at home in the West."[57] Kazan and Steinbeck worked together on *Viva Zapata!* However, when they attempted to adapt *East of Eden*, Kazan commented to Steinbeck that neither of them was a screenwriter. Steinbeck critic Warren French believes that "Steinbeck's stature as an artist might have been greater had he concentrated on film."[58] Steinbeck's script for *Viva Zapata!* and his reworking of *The Red Pony* for the screen showed a remarkable talent for the film medium. However, Steinbeck gave up on Hollywood and on independent film and he became involved with a variety of other projects, such as travelogues and theater. He did not return to screenwriting after his attempt at it with Kazan on *East of Eden*.

8

THE SHORTER NOVELS

TORTILLA FLAT

To read *Tortilla Flat* is to be immediately struck by the energy of its humorous characters. In the first pages we meet Danny, a war veteran who has inherited two houses and does not want the responsibility of them. He vents his anger by breaking windows, gets hauled off to jail, and returns to have a relationship with Mrs. Morales. He "rents" one of his houses to his friend Pilon, whom he knows cannot pay him fifteen dollars in rent. Pilon enlists Pablo to pay the rent, so if he cannot pay it to Danny he can always blame Pablo. They, in turn, pass along the responsibility to Jesus Maria Corcoran, whose wine they imbibe. Jesus Maria wishes to get a pink brassiere for Arabella, "one of those wrap around things," and Pilon and Pablo try to discourage him so that they can get two dollars from him for wine. When a candle is lit in the "rented" house it seems to them a holy thing that has "aimed its spear toward heaven, like an artist who consumes himself to become divine."[1] We read that the candle was blessed and belonged to St. Francis. The tipped-over candle results in a fire that destroys the house. Pilon is thankful that he no longer has to think about paying rent and Danny is glad to be relieved of half his burden.[2] The friends "drink for friendship's sake" and join to live together in the remaining house.

This romp of misfits and mishaps has a serious edge, for Steinbeck himself identified with outsiders. His own work, as a writer, was not in a mainstream occupation and he interacted with individuals who were much like those he portrayed in many of his stories. With *Tortilla Flat* he created a group of paisanos who are entertaining and socially marginal— at least with respect to mainstream American society. One may argue that Steinbeck was a writer of the dominant culture who portrayed paisanos, people of mixed Indian, Mexican, and white background, as different or exotic, "mystical, untutored and spontaneous primitives," observes Susan Shillinglaw.[3] However, she points out that the characters that he created are almost inextricable parts of the settings in which they appear; they live in their environment and embody their environment. These marginal people have accepted life, accepted "what is," and this acceptance is presented in Steinbeck's non-teleological view.[4] Steinbeck's own background was also close enough to the immigrant roots of his German and Scots-Irish ancestry to recognize the struggle of those groups and their gradual assimilation into American society: a topic he discusses in his essay "E Pluribus Unum" in *America and Americans* (1966). As for Danny and his friends, they reflected people whom Steinbeck had contact with in and around Monterey. In *Tortilla Flat*, observes Shillinglaw, Steinbeck focuses on "questions of identity," codes of comradeship, and "the study of group man . . . the 'history' of a subculture."[5] *Tortilla Flat* is a story of a community in a culture of instability. It is a story of humorous, otherwise homeless characters who find a home in each other and express loyalty and interpersonal connection. On the first page, we read: "This is the story of Danny and of Danny's friends and of Danny's house. It is a story of how these three became one thing."[6]

Tortilla Flat shows the variety of individuals who gather in Danny's house, who become this "one thing." At first it seems that the common bond that fuses them together is a love of wine, a propensity for drinking, and a free-spirited rejection of responsibility. However, they exercise a care for each other. Considering them, Joseph Fontenrose recognizes that Steinbeck's fiction reveals the lives of simple people, suggesting that their values are "more healthy and viable" than "the values of a competitive society."[7] Nicholas Coles points out that Steinbeck likely knew that his attention to the paisanos of Monterey was "going against the grain" of the literature of the time. The literary critics of the 1930s were not trained in a "literature of women, of black, of ethnic, and working-class writers."[8] Steinbeck appears to be asserting that there is an overlooked quality of connection between these people that may be lacking in some respects in the society at large.

The ethnic working-class heroes of *Tortilla Flat* are fascinating in their uniqueness. They are something more than mock-heroic figures. They are a class of people living outside cultural norms who, in their countercultural lifestyles and difference, remind us that the possibilities for quest and the potential for heroism appear in unexpected places. "For Danny's house was not unlike the Round Table and Danny's friends were not unlike the knights of it."[9] Obviously, the men in *Tortilla Flat* are not knights. They are amusing. Danny, Pilon, and the troublesome Joe Portagee are wayward ne'er-do-wells who become sympathetic characters. The treatment that Steinbeck provides is not mock-heroic but sympathetic. He notes that he wanted to take the characters around Monterey and to "cast them into a kind of folklore."[10] This sympathy embraces these individualistic characters as an alternative to the mainstream of American life. They do not subscribe to an ethos of steady work and productivity, capitalism, and technology. They are not materialistic; they don't need things and they don't believe in progress. Perhaps Steinbeck is suggesting that mainstream life is not always reasonable. These characters live outside of norms and cultural expectations in ways that might seem incomprehensible to the man with the briefcase taking the train to his business office. Indeed, to anyone with an ingrained work ethic they may even seem a bit rambunctious, inept, or lazy. Danny's house is a place for uncommon spirits that bring life to this story.[11]

Pilon will not hesitate to trick and persuade Jesus Maria Corcoran to give up his wine, his money, or the pink bra intended for Arabella. When the burly Pirate, with his black and bushy beard, comes into view followed closely by his five dogs, Pilon is convinced that he will do him a favor by taking the money he hides away. He tells himself that after his daily rounds of pushing a wheelbarrow of kindling for sale Pirate should be spending his money on some warm clothes and good food. Behind Pilon's good intentions is his tendency to spend the money he acquires, by any means, on a jug of wine. The friends suggest that Pirate might move out of the abandoned chicken house he has been staying in and join them in Danny's house, with a special area set off for the dogs. Pirate tells Pilon that he has been saving his money to buy a candlestick for St. Francis. Soon Big Joe Portagee is introduced: a man who during World War I spent more time in jail than out of it.[12] He swung down into Monterey from the train, traded his military overcoat for a gallon of wine, and began to enjoy the ministration of harpies of the pit.[13] For we read that Joe Portagee liked the dissolute life. On St. Andrew's Eve the adventures of this gang begin: a quest for buried treasure that lies in the ground.[14]

Steinbeck, during his adolescent years, worked with paisanos at the Spreckels Sugar plant, and he had contact with them in his adult years in Monterey. It appears that his objective was simply to write a story and to draw upon the liveliness he saw in these people. Steinbeck was being playful with *Tortilla Flat* and he was entertaining his readers with a humorous cast of characters, while making a point about loyalty and dedication. At no point did he ever intend to be disparaging toward paisanos by giving his characters a tendency toward drunkenness. He was affirming, not mocking, their spontaneity. Certainly, he was conscious of his cultural difference from these people, but Steinbeck's approach to race and ethnicity is always one of sympathy and appreciation and his focus is always on people, whatever their background, and the respect and justice that is due to them. As William Rose Benét wrote in his response to the novel in the *Saturday Review*: "These silly bravos are always about to do something nice for each other, their hearts are soft and easily touched; and yet almost absentmindedly they live with atrocious disregard for scruple. To have presented them and made their story sometimes hysterically funny is no slight achievement."[15]

Thirty years later, Steinbeck began *America and Americans* with the essay "E Pluribus Unum," an account of the strengths and variety of the immigrant groups that have comprised America. He began the essay by indicating the tensions between these groups and discussing the process by which such a diversity of people became America. "Two racial groups did not follow this pattern of arrival, prejudice, acceptance, and absorption," he writes.[16] These were the American Indians, for whom he has a respectful admiration, particularly of their mysticism and relationship to nature and the land, and the African Americans, who did not choose to be in America but were brought to America's shores through slavery. The Native American Indians offer an example of myth, ritual, and reverence that is conveyed well in an anecdote Steinbeck tells about an individual named Jimmy.[17] The issue of slavery is given a chapter in *America and Americans*: "Created Equal." In his brief history of slave labor, Steinbeck recognizes that the methods of maintaining order among the slave population included teaching them from childhood of their supposed inferiority, punishing rebellion "mercilessly," breaking up families, and preventing education and the "questioning and communication" that can arise from it.[18] It was not kindness that kept slavery out of the northern states but economy, he asserts.[19] He turns to a Darwinian position in assessing the strengths of the African American population: "the fact that this strong, resistant breed had been developed by selection never occurred to the Southern whites."[20]

Tortilla Flat calls upon America to reexamine its national identity and character, including the many ethnicities of which the nation is comprised. It questions American notions of material progress and the work ethic, the relocating of native people to a lower class of work in support of financiers, agribusiness, or the railroads. Danny and his friends, unable to secure gainful employment, or forced to work in dull jobs, decide not to work at all. They are primarily agrarian, not industrial, in their orientation and they do not seek to acquire property. They want to participate: Danny, Pilon, and Joe Portagee all have volunteered for military service but they never serve in a combat zone. The paisanos of *Tortilla Flat* lack education, which is one of the answers to improvement of human conditions that Steinbeck offered in his mid-1960s essay. He recalls his Great Aunt Carrie, who started a school for African American children but was beset by the Ku Klux Klan. He writes of the rising economic importance and impact of Negro leaders, who are "educated, literate, thoughtful and experienced men."[21]

Steinbeck asserted that "any attempt to describe the America of today must take into account the issue of racial equality."[22] He was working toward that position in fiction in the 1930s. Ethnic prejudices and tensions are mentioned early on in the story, in Danny's grumbling against Italians on Alvarado Street. His inclination toward fighting and violence inflames his attitude toward Torelli. Yet this story is not an examination of race or ethnicity per se. It is a celebration of the paisanos of *Tortilla Flat*, who, perhaps, did not want education or change. One might wonder how formal American education might have changed them. Likely there would have been an insistence upon economics and responsibility rather than on creativity, spontaneity, and immediacy. Perhaps Pilon and Danny could have benefitted from a good ethics class to adjust their moral compass. However, adjustment to mainstream society might have dampened their vigor and natural aplomb. They are a resilient group of people, whose exuberance and difference testifies to the vitality of the human spirit and challenges the norms of American life.

The characters of *Tortilla Flat* are also people whose simplicity suggests an earthy spirituality. The imagery of *Tortilla Flat* offers us a group of characters that operate in a rather "Catholic" novel, some critics have claimed. One might see in their communal life a hint of a Franciscan brotherhood. There are many references to rituals, St. Francis, relics, holy objects, and masses. They become a brotherhood, caring for each other, drinking for friendship's sake, as if in a sacred rite of communion. Of course, the California setting itself may suggest the impact of Franciscan missions.[23] However, the violence in Danny's spirit is contrary to Franciscan emphasis on peace, and Pilon's stealing contradicts Christian ethics. Jesus Maria Corcoran, whose name evokes a religious sensibility, is perhaps an example of charity: "Together with his capacity for doing good Jesus Maria had a gift for coming in contact with situations where good wanted doing."[24] Steinbeck's evident concern for this motley group of paisanos anticipates a "preferential option for the poor" and Catholic social justice teachings that emerged from Vatican II in the early 1960s. The novel, like subsequent pastoral letters of the U.S. bishops, calls for the recognition of marginalized individuals. Even so, Danny has no clear faith. He is a character who welcomes community and expresses gallantry but is often troubled. He is a personality that draws this group of outsiders around him.

The novel was popular and sold well. "I am scared to death of popularity," Steinbeck wrote after *Tortilla Flat*. "It has ruined everybody I know."[25] The popularity of *Tortilla Flat* emerged, in part, because of the novel's entertaining characters. This is a relatively short novel that is accessible and easy to read. It offered readers in the mid-1930s the novelty of experiencing a subculture of genuinely interesting people who were as down on their luck as some of them were. Steinbeck created sympathy for Danny and his cohort. Readers who were beset by the Depression could find in them the image of the resourcefulness that they too needed to survive on very little and a spiritedness that made them laugh.

CANNERY ROW

Cannery Row (1945) appeared in the final year of the war. Steinbeck wrote a comedy about the adventures of a group of friends who want to have a party for their friend Doc. Once again Steinbeck was creating a group portrait. There is an unmistakable connection between these characters. *Cannery Row* was a nostalgic recollection of life on the coast of Monterey, where the sardine canning industry extended up to Pacific Grove. The novel received strong popular sales and a variety of reviews and is among the most accessible and most teachable of Steinbeck's works. Of course, on a secondary-school level there may be some criticisms of coarse language or Doc's appreciation of women who live in a brothel. Even so, Mack and Doc and the others are compelling characters and the novel can be read and enjoyed in a few sittings.

Cannery Row brings us immediately into Lee Chong's grocery and to the Palace Flophouse, into which Mack, Hazel, Eddie, Hughie, and Jones move. Lee Chong is their landlord who generally leaves them alone. In the nearby lot, Mr. and Mrs. Sam Malloy have moved into the rusted boiler, and Sam Malloy, a cagey entrepreneur, begins renting out space in the pipes. Mrs. Malloy wants to decorate with curtains. Doc's Western Biological Laboratory, clearly modeled after Ed Ricketts's laboratory, is another central setting. In it is a library or music room, where he listens to classical music, or plays it for his romantic dinners with women. He is unmarried but hardly celibate. ("What's celebrate?" asks Eddie. "That's when you can't get no dame," says Mack.)[26] His companions are usually "Dora's girls," the prostitutes who are managed by Dora, who has flaming orange hair and wears green dresses. Doc can often be found collecting marine specimens in the Great Tide Pool at the tip of the peninsula. Hazel, who has lived with a name that could be interpreted as a female one, accompanies Doc on an expedition and is puzzled by his claim that stinkbugs may be praying. Mack rallies the men at the flophouse. They want to give Doc a party. But they need money for it. They impose upon Lee Chong and ask to borrow his Model T truck. They are going to go on a quest to capture frogs. Their goal is to sell the frogs to Doc, whose payment to them will pay for his own party.

Cannery Row brought America some lighthearted laughter in 1945, the final year of World War II, when it was much needed. Steinbeck recognized that while *Cannery Row* was popular it also had its critics. He noted that the views of different critics tended to cancel each other out and that the critics of the New Criticism wrote in obscure jargon.[27] He was bothered by flattering reviews when the critic appeared to not understand his purpose.[28] As for the critical reviews, sometimes he recognized that he simply was not writing the book the critic appeared to want. He knew that he wrote short novels like *Cannery Row*, almost as "exercises," in between the long ones.[29] Soldiers had asked him to write something funny that wasn't about the war and he produced *Cannery Row*. The critics then said that he should be writing more seriously during such a serious time.[30]

Cannery Row features a group of characters who work in the sardine canning businesses along the pier in Monterey. Sardine canning began in San Francisco in 1889 at the Golden Gate Packing Company. The equipment was sold in 1893 to the Southern California Fish Company in San Diego. They canned sardines in mustard, oil, tomato sauce, and spices. Monterey fishing industry growth created the canning business. Frank Booth arranged to have the first cannery built: a salmon cannery near Fisherman's Wharf. Cannery Row developed farther from town near Ocean View Avenue. The first installation there, the Pacific Fish Company building, appeared in 1908. There were two sardine canneries in business along the pier in Monterey by 1915: the Booth plant and the Monterey Fishing and Packaging Company.[31] Another cannery opened in San Francisco. A demand for canned sardines emerged during World War I. By then a row of canneries had appeared to supply the growing trade. During World War I the sardine trade became the largest West Coast fishing industry. The output of the canneries leaped from 75,000 cases in 1915 to 1,400,000 in 1918.[32] The plants remained active through World War II but the industry went into decline afterward.

The cannery workers were mostly immigrants. The business concerns where they worked had factory whistles that blew in the morning to begin the workday. Boats went out to sea from the coast. In the morning, the night's catch was calculated and canned. Each evening the day's catch was completed. Imagine a cold, smelly factory floor, where the scent of fish overtakes the scent of sweat and the sea outside. Canneries took in fish that were dropped off on the pier that went out along the coast. The fish were hauled up in metal baskets, sliced up by workers, placed on wooden slats, and sent through boiling peanut oil and moved along conveyor belts. They were then drained and packed into cans. The cans were soldered closed, labeled, and boxed. Conveyor belts transported cans bayside to the street. In 1936, W. L. Scofield reported on California's commercial fish catch: "Last fishing season (1935–36) we caught sardines at a rate of more than 1500 tons a day for every day of the year or 65 tons per hour. This is more than a ton a minute for every minute of the 365 days." The catch included tuna and mackerel and other fish but the sardine catch was the largest: double the amount of all of the other fish that were caught.[33]

Much of this work on Cannery Row appears to have proceeded without much input from Mack and the boys, Steinbeck's characters. The canning factories form the backdrop of the lives of Cannery Row's female characters: women in a local brothel. Steinbeck's female characters were often from lower classes, as were many of his men. Indeed, the women in many of his stories are domestic. "Their spheres are the home and the brothel," Mimi Reisel Gladstein points out.[34] There is truth in that observation but the argument seems to imply that home is as distasteful and limited as the brothel. During the time that Steinbeck wrote, most women in society were in the domestic sphere rather than in the public and commercial spheres. That women in *Cannery Row* are in Dora's brothel is a comment on the socioeconomic limitation imposed upon them by the society. The argument cannot be solely an ad hominem one against Steinbeck's vision of women. This text may well carry an indictment of the society, as did George Bernard Shaw's *Mrs. Warren's Profession*.

Roughly at the midpoint of his novel, in chapter 14, Steinbeck writes: "It is the hour of the pearl—the interval between day and night when time stops and examines itself."[35] This brief interval is reminiscent of one of the interchapters of *The Grapes of Wrath*. The chapter begins with "Early morning": "In the gray time after the light has come and before the sun has risen, the Row seems to hang suspended out of time in a silvery light."[36] Time does indeed pass on Cannery Row and this chapter itself is suspended between the novel's scenes of action. As an old Chinaman passes by each day, one can almost keep time to his appearance and his shadow receding across the beach. Two soldiers and their girlfriends walk along the street at dusk. Steinbeck includes a mention of the Hopkins Marine Station. As Virginia Woolf once gave us "Time Passes," the midsection of *To the Lighthouse*, where the entirety of World War I drifts by in a few pages, Steinbeck, writing at the end of World War II, provides this interlude in which two passing soldiers with their lovers on their arms walk by into the sunset.

The story returns to the great frog hunt and moves toward preparations for the party. Doc, looking from his window, sees "Mack and the boys" in front of the Palace Flophouse and he comments: "Look at them. There are your true philosophers, I think."[37] They survive well in the world, better than others, he concludes. "In a time where people tear themselves to pieces with ambition and nervousness and covetousness, they are relaxed."[38] Doc continues musing and asserts that "everywhere in the world there are Mack and the boys": "maybe they are limited and maybe they mess up, but their intentions are good; . . . they wanted to give me a party."[39] However, in a story that has been mostly humorous, Doc ventures a serious critical observation:

> "It has always seemed strange to me," said Doc. "The things we admire in men, kindness and generosity, openness, honesty, understanding and feeling are the concomitants of failure in our system. And those traits we detest, sharpness, greed, acquisitiveness, meanness, egotism and self-interest, are the traits of success. And while men admire the quality of the first they love to produce the second."[40]

Mack and the boys will not sell their souls to gain the whole world, Doc says. Nor will many others like them all across the world. After this thoughtful aside we are returned to the action and life of Cannery Row and finally we are brought to Doc's laboratory, to his music and to a book in which is a final meditative prose poem. It speaks of wise men and of the sea, of cypress, roses, and mountains, and of savoring the fullness and the "hot taste of life."[41] Steinbeck leaves us with the idea that Mack and the boys represent a valuable source of generosity in humanity. Steinbeck has likewise been generous in writing *Cannery Row*. His goal seems to have been to tell a humorous and entertaining story and humor and entertainment is what the novel achieves.

Cannery Row is polyphonic in the sense that Russian critic Mikhail Bakhtin observed in the variety of voices in the novels of Dostoevsky and other writers. The characters of *Cannery Row* are from an underclass and their multiple voices, which Bakhtin would refer to as heteroglossia, offer an array of personal expression. Indeed, one might include the voices of the frogs that they go on their excursion to catch. The novel is also enriched by references to music. Doc often listens to music in his laboratory, where "a great phonograph stands against the wall with hundreds of records lined up beside it."[42] This may turn our attention toward the auditory aspects of this novel: dialogue, the rhythm of sentences, and musical references. As the novel begins, there is an alternation between chapters full of sound and chapters that are quieter. The first chapter, filled with the voices and sounds of Lee Chong's grocery, slips into the brief, reflective chapter 2, which consists of two long paragraphs: the first on Lee Chong and the second a description of Mack and the boys, "spinning in their orbits" as "the Virtues, the Graces, the Beauties" of this place. In their reverent irreverence they contrast with a world of men competing like "tigers" and scavengers, men who are rushing around getting ulcers from stress, who call them "no-goods . . . rascals, bums."[43] The quiet Chinaman of chapter 4 walks like a silent specter across the beach in contrast with the description of Doc's laboratory in chapter 5.

It is not clear that musical form operates structurally in *Cannery Row*. However, a kind of background music becomes evident in chapter 5, where we learn that Doc works amid reproductions of artworks that range widely across different periods and styles, from Daumier and Graham to Titian, and from da Vinci to Picasso and Grosz. Presumably his record collection is just as eclectic, as critic Michael J. Meyer has suggested. Dora's girls heard Gregorian chant there for the first time.[44] In chapter 10 we are introduced to Frankie, who is young, helpful to Doc, and awkward. In Western Biological this boy, neglected at home, sometime sleeps in an excelsior crate. He is excited about a party: "He could hear the chatter and the music from the great phonograph."[45] Frankie opens a door: "The music and talk roared around him." He carries a tray in and stumbles and the tray and beer fall into a woman's lap. He is stunned, then he runs and people in the room hear his footsteps running away down to the cellar. "They heard a low scrabbling sound and then silence."[46] He has hidden and Doc can hear him "whimpering."

When Doc discovers a body washed in on the reef, his throat tightens and his heart pounds and he has to sit down. The prosaic world has been shaken by this encounter with death: a chilling, transcendent moment of the sublime. He shivers in wonder and is taken up by the rhythm of the sea: "Music sounded in Doc's ears, a high thin piercingly sweet flute, and against this a pounding surf-like woodwind section. The flute went into regions beyond the hearing range."[47] Music, for Doc, appears to suggest a heightening of experience, an intimation of immortality, or to evoke some spiritual awareness. In this instance, the flute is sweet and beautiful but the experience of sea and body sends a shiver of terror through him.[48]

The aural quality of this novel sweeps into its final movement in Doc's laboratory. At a gathering of the friends Benny Goodman trios play and the music shifts to *Ardo* and *Amor* from Monteverdi, which turns the company's gaze inward. This is followed by Doc's reading from Sanskrit verse. The polyphony of the novel shifts as Doc goes back to his laboratory with his cold beer. He hears music in his head: "Violins and cellos, he thought."[49] Finally he puts a Pater Noster and Agnus Dei on the turntable and listens to voices that are "angelic, disembodied."[50] He begins to read aloud from a book and he becomes a solo voice.

THE WAYWARD BUS

Steinbeck made several unexpected turns after World War II. He wrote *Cannery Row* and he visited Mexico again and wrote *The Pearl*. Mexico was on his mind as he began a story about American travelers that would become *The Wayward Bus*. Initially he planned to set the story in Mexico but then he shifted the scene to Southern California where some members of a group of travelers are thinking about going to Mexico. *The Wayward Bus*, a story rich in symbolism and potent in critique, appeared in 1947. Its characters may suggest a cross section of America but they are paper thin. With *In Dubious Battle* and *The Grapes of Wrath*, Steinbeck created full-blooded, well-rounded, believable characters. With *The Wayward Bus* he creates caricatures, or types, to support a sociological analysis tinged with satire. This is a story that sometimes lacks momentum but includes the interesting technique of interior monologue. We are brought into the thoughts and stream of consciousness of several of these characters. While the plot is somewhat thin, there is a psychological exploration of their lives and motives.

Juan Chicoy, a bus driver, brings his white bus passengers across the San Ysidro Valley but the bus breaks down. When they are stranded by his deliberately grounding the bus in the mud, he ostensibly goes for help but really seeks to escape and run away. Juan's curious ancestry is Mexican-Irish. There is little at all in the novel to support the interpretation that he may be a Christ figure. He shares initials with Jesus Christ but not much else. Jim Casy in *The Grapes of Wrath* struggles with his loss of faith and feels unworthy of his vocation; he gradually recognizes his new vocation as a labor organizer and enacts a social gospel. Juan Chicoy attempts to run away from an alcoholic wife and to ignore his responsibility to the passengers in his charge. Only after a good time with Mildred in the hay in an abandoned barn does he resume his responsibilities and try to dig the bus out of the mud. If he is plagued by any sense of conscience it is attributed to his Mexican traditions: a totemic and superstitious sense that he is ever under the disapproving gaze of his Lady of Guadalupe statue that he keeps on the dashboard of his bus. At best he is a distant cousin of St. John of the Cross, toward whose city, San Juan de la Cruz, the bus travels: for he does not believe in the Lady of Guadalupe with his mind but with his sense.[51] This religious figure is more like a Mexican tradition, a childhood memory, and a good luck charm. Her presence forces conscience upon him. We read that "he couldn't run away without sanction. He had to have the approval of the Virgin."[52] If this figure can serve as a divine reference point, she is perhaps Hagia Sophia: a female sense of divine presence. However, Juan's actions are those of a fallible and troubled man and he does not even remotely resemble a Christ figure of faith, one who would be willing to teach and nurture others and to face death. In the end, perhaps, he "saves" the people on the bus. However, for much of the novel, if the J.C. of his name calls him to responsibility it is a call that he resists.

For the first eight chapters of *The Wayward Bus*, Juan's bus sits in the garage and the characters that will travel on it begin to appear. Pimples is a naïve, young apprentice mechanic who eats too much candy, has terrible acne, and has a raging sex drive. Juan, learning that Pimples's given name is Ed Carson, consents to call him Kit Carson. It is a gesture that builds the young mechanic's self-esteem. Norma is a naïve waitress who daydreams of Hollywood and Clark Gable. She has been employed by Juan and his wife, Alice, but has been criticized and scolded by Alice, a bitter and troubled woman, and she wants to get away. Sympathy for Norma is developed early on because she is so obviously good-hearted. Alice is irascible and Juan responds to appease her and manage her volatile temperament. She stays behind in the restaurant/garage getting drunk on whisky and beer, ostensibly to cure a toothache, and she swats at annoying flies that are always getting into the pies. In chapter 11 Alice has a conversation with herself and her self-talk and thoughts pass through pride, hope, self-recrimination, and memories until she attempts to swat a fly and falls down over a row of boxes. Earlier on, Steinbeck gave us a few moments in the consciousness of a fly. This is certainly odd and unique. Annoyances like flies or broken machine parts buzz on the surface of things. Tensions arise between the story's characters. Yet it is in the unveiling of each character's thoughts that this novel performs best.

Among the passengers are Camille Oaks, a stripper who is going to Los Angeles, and Mr. and Mrs. Pritchard and their daughter Mildred, who are going to Mexico. Camille, with her dyed blonde hair and curvaceous figure, attracts relentless male attention and she uses Norma as a shield to turn away advances from the men. She invents her name from a Camel cigarettes poster and the trees she sees around Juan Chicoy's establishment: a restaurant that doubles as a garage and a bus depot. To Norma, she provides some coaching on how to apply makeup, and Norma believes that she may have found a new roommate for when she reaches L.A. Mildred sees through Camille's persona as easily as she can read through her mother's pretenses. She is a feisty girl who wants to break free from her parents' control and way of life. In Mildred, there is something of a rebel and a new woman in the making.

Mr. Elliott Pritchard is a hypocrite. He is a consummate conformist who lives for "business," which becomes his excuse for every failing and flaw he has. He is troubled by the diversity of the group that he is traveling with and he hates foreign countries because he can find no other Mr. Pritchards there. He does not want to go to Mexico but he travels to please his wife, whom he infantilizes by always calling her "little girl." He is resigned to his wife's frigidity and he pampers her while containing her in a world of house and home and hypochondria: "Little girls better keep their noses out of what doesn't concern them," he says.[53] She will use headaches to get her way but she will never interrupt anything Mr. Pritchard calls business: "Business was her husband's magic circle. She had no right to go near him when it was business."[54] If Mrs. Pritchard had a Facebook account she would be always on it. She writes little letters to "friends" in her mind and she is ever concerned about her social reputation and oblivious to her own pretentiousness. In the bus with them is Ernest Horton, a World War II veteran who has become a salesman and whose entire world has become one of selling trinkets and gadgets. Van Brunt is a misanthropic complainer, a doomsayer who is certain the bridge is going to go out in a flood.

In these characters we meet a group that encounters a predicament, which is one of the typical features of many Steinbeck stories. The "group man" and their predicament is featured in *Tortilla Flat*, *In Dubious Battle*, *The Grapes of Wrath*, *Lifeboat*, *Cannery Row*, and *The Wayward Bus*. Once again we have a relatively short novel that is readily adaptable for film. The 1957 film provides a vehicle for Dan Dailey, Joan Collins, and

Jayne Mansfield. There are dramatic tensions between the characters. If this is a cross section of America they are a group with difficulties, perhaps suggesting a range of difficulties experienced by individuals in postwar America.

One of the striking aspects of this novel appears in how poorly the women are treated by some of the men. When Juan's gaze falls on Mildred she is perceived more as an object of desire than as a person, and his Indian blood stirs: "he could take this girl and twist her and outrage her if he wanted to."[55] Mildred has athletic stature and wears black-framed glasses that "give her a student look."[56] She dances well but a little too precisely, plays sports, and is tall, blunt, and analytical, and she is keenly aware of Juan's interest in her. The frustrated Mr. Pritchard reveals his misogyny. He assumes a guise of unassailable propriety but he lusts after Camille, whom he knows that he has seen at a business convention swirling in undress. He likes his wife's good housekeeping and spotless clothes.[57] He refers to women in disparaging terms and ultimately abuses his wife sexually. Pimples lusts after Camille also but ends up transferring his hormonal compulsions toward Norma, who responds sympathetically to him but then has to fight him off. Camille adopts her cunning disguise to ward off men like Alice swats away flies. The cosmetic industry has assisted her in this illusion. Beside her, Norma is simple and full of dreams. While she is coached in the art of makeup by Camille, it is clear that she may be devoured by Hollywood.

We encounter in this story a critique of postwar America as a land of advertisements, consumer products, and artifice. The travelers have different dreams and different world views. Norma's starstruck wonder at Clark Gable contrasts with the letters that Mrs. Pritchard writes in her head. Norma asks Ernest Horton if he can deliver a letter to Mr. Gable on the lot in Hollywood and she claims to be Clark Gable's cousin. Juan Chicoy's restaurant features posters of "bright, improbable girls with pumped up breasts and no hips." Faded underneath the designation of the bus "Sweetheart" is "el Gran Poder de Jesus." The figure of the Virgin of Guadalupe looks out from above the dashboard. Perhaps religious vision has faded, or perhaps the miraculous lies just underneath the surface of things.

Bus travel is a democratic mode of transportation, as Cathryn Halverson points out in her essay on the novel. There are no reserved seats, no boundaries, and there is one communal bathroom that is not built for balance or comfort. One waits for buses and sometimes endures long bus rides, looking out at cities or countryside. As Halverson observes, it is "the travel mode of the underprivileged," a method of transportation that "evokes the mundane and the extraordinary."[58] She points out that Steinbeck shows bus travel as "instructive." The bus is an adventure and "a new way of seeing is fostered on the bus."[59] This is similarly evident in Paul Simon's song "America," in which Simon and Garfunkel sing about the moments the narrator and Kathy experience along a cross-country journey. The tune evokes a forlorn spirit of disenchantment and longing, but perhaps a new way of seeing America through the eyes of a traveler is encouraged by Simon's song. From the window of a bus one can see cities, miles of fields, majestic mountains: a promising landscape. Perhaps Steinbeck found postwar America morally mired and stuck in the mud and so we have this wayward bus and its passengers—a story that presents social and psychological analysis.

SWEET THURSDAY

In the prologue to *Sweet Thursday*, we see a novel commenting upon itself, in a manner that anticipates postmodernism. Mack immediately sets up an intertextual relationship between this book and its predecessor, *Cannery Row*: "I ain't never been satisfied with that book *Cannery Row*." *Sweet Thursday* announces itself as a sequel, as Mack says: "If I ever come across the guy who wrote that book I could tell him a few things."[60] Mack would like to see chapter titles or descriptions. Then Mack expresses his own criteria for what makes a good book for him as a reader: "I like a lot of talk in a book, and I don't like having nobody tell me what a guy that's talking looks like."[61] Mack likes to be able to see objects, to know their color, how they look and smell and what a character feels about it— "but not too much of that." Yes, Mack is a critic, Whitey No. 2 agrees, and Eddie asks: "Mack, if the guy that wrote *Cannery Row* comes in, you going to tell him all that?"[62] The dialogue is playfully self-referential. Mack is clearly a reader who wants to get to the point. If a writer is going to "hooptedoodle," he or she had better just put that all up in the front of the book, so that he can skip over it. Mack is impatient with the craft and beauty of expression in literature that some readers admire: "Spin up some pretty words maybe, or sing a little song with language. That's nice. But I wish it was set aside so I don't have to read it."[63]

Mack's discourse highlights how we all read differently. He also signals a self-conscious shift in Steinbeck's writing. There is in Steinbeck "a postwar change of aesthetic sensibility," as Steinbeck scholar Robert De-Mott has observed.[64] There is a shift in fictive invention toward an overt presentation of fiction as something that is constructed. Steinbeck was engaging in experimentalism. He had largely let go of the mode of critical realism. Those unities of well-made fiction that New Critics esteemed— mimesis, narrative distance, a beginning, a middle, and an end—did not easily fit into the new textual strategies he was exploring. The play of his fiction was attempting new ways to "break through." Steinbeck was reinventing himself.

In 1948, Steinbeck's friend Ed Ricketts died and his marriage to Gwyn Conger Steinbeck collapsed. He had recently published *The Pearl* and *The Wayward Bus* (1947) and he appears to have then been as adrift as his characters in his 1954 story *Sweet Thursday*. He had made a trip to Russia with photographer Robert Capa. There were attempts at plays, rewrites of *Viva Zapata!* and the exhausting project of *East of Eden*. He met Elaine Steinbeck in May 1949 and was married again in December 1950. He turned toward the theater with *Burning Bright* and the play closed after thirteen performances. He now needed to recall Cannery Row and Ed Ricketts. Robert DeMott points out that as Steinbeck wrote of Doc trying to write his research paper, in his own effort he "turned out to be narrating nothing less than the symbolic story of his own emotional rescue and artistic refashioning."[65]

The keynote of *Sweet Thursday* is the recognition of change: "Yes, the war got into everybody." We read, "Change was everywhere" and "The street that once roared with trucks was quiet and empty."[66] Lee Chong is gone. Dora has passed away. Henri has left town. Even Doc is a little bit different. "Everything's changed, Doc, everything," says Mack. "I'm afraid I've changed," says Doc.[67] Steinbeck too has changed; he has undertaken a new style and approach to his fiction. His story suggests that he perceives a postwar shift in America as fostering something different than the atmosphere that preceded the war.

Change is more noticeable in retrospect: "Looking back, you can usually find the moment of the birth of a new era; when it happened, it was one day hooked on to the tail of another."[68] The history of any given day may be special, or seemingly ordinary. Perhaps "Sweet Thursday" was not so momentous as D-Day or December 7, 1941, "a date that will live in infamy," or as consequential as Sarajevo, Stalingrad, or Valley Forge, but Sweet Thursday was significant to everyone on Cannery Row. The sequence of chapters 19, 20, and 21 concludes on the caption to chapter 21: "Sweet Thursday was a hell of a day." It was a magical day, a day in which the boys had the energy and enthusiasm of plutonium." Yes, "forces were in motion on that Thursday in Cannery Row."[69]

Doc underscores the ethical tone of the first section of *Sweet Thursday* when he points out to a character named Joseph and Mary that it is not possible to cheat in the game of chess, or in mathematics. Doc asserts that there is a truth, that some things are grounded in a reality that is objective and not merely relative. A constable, Joe Blaikey, represents kindness, vigilance, and moral order. He knows what goes on in the town and assists Suzy, the girl who has come to town to work with Fauna, who is the new madam. There are new characters in a changing environment in which Doc asserts that principles and values remain a constant.

The mischievous playfulness of the gang at Cannery Row has shifted across the years. Men have been affected by the war, or have dispersed to new locations. The tone and rhythm of Cannery Row itself has changed. Doc continues his experiments in marine biology and he is trying to write a paper on his studies. However, a nameless discontent has emerged within him. "Where does discontent start? You are warm enough but you shiver. You are fed, yet hunger gnaws at you."[70] There is a creeping existential dread to this condition. Doc considers how his light is spent, as Milton once put it. He looks at time passing and dwells upon what he has not done, what he has not given to humanity. "Have I worked enough? Have I eaten enough? Have I loved enough?" The questions that rankle his spirit are profound existential ones: "What has my life meant so far, and what can it mean in the time left to me?"[71]

Doc is committed to his work but he doesn't so much want to work. His eye catches the movement of Suzy, waking by on the sidewalk below, and he watches her, musing about how people walk uniquely, wondering who she might be. A suggestion lingers that Suzy is going to play a role in Doc's future story. When he forces himself back to his desk the discontent returns with a poignant sense of his lonesomeness. "Looking for yourself in the water—searching, little man, among the hydroids of your soul . . ." Doc is described as "healer of the wounded soul and the cut finger."[72] Yet there is a gnawing ache within him as he stares down at the yellow legal pad on his desk and at the pencils lined up beside it.

Mack and Fauna and the others are concerned by Doc's malaise. They ponder this while telling Hazel that his horoscope says that he will become the next president of the United States. Maybe they should send some women Doc's way. He is never going to finish that paper, Mack concludes. Writing the paper is just a substitute for something, an "excuse to cover up something else—and maybe he don't even know it himself."[73]

One might imagine Steinbeck sitting by a window, like his character Doc, with his pencils and yellow legal pad, thinking back to Cannery Row and his friend Ed Ricketts. He gives us an image of Doc, who walks on the beach and wants "to go back to his old life."[74] Perhaps Steinbeck is likewise nostalgic for a time that has gone. Waves break steadily upon the shore in a pattern that forever seems the same but is ever new. Once upon the shores of the Aegean, Sophocles heard these sounds, as Matthew Arnold once wrote in his lyric poem "Dover Beach." Where now is the sea of faith? There is continuity and change.

Doc is alone on the beach, wanting to be alone, when a Whitman-like wanderer comes up behind him, a man in a straw hat who calls himself a seer. Perhaps Krishnamurti and the new age has auspiciously descended upon California, or a holy man has come in the form of this unwanted visitor. "Doc found himself wondering if some of the saints had not looked like this."[75] The man claims that he sees visions. He does not put these visions in scientific terms that describe reality, as Doc would. The seer expresses hospitality and he invites Doc to a dinner of food from the sea. The man is one of Steinbeck's Jesus figures. Doc tells him not to gather any disciples: "They'd have you on a cross in no time."[76] Doc sees the stranger's unique detachment: "The doctrine of our time is that man can't get along without a whole lot of stuff." This man has very little. In a world focused upon material acquisition, Doc tells him, "you're living treason." He says, "It is one of the symptoms of our time to find danger in men like you who don't worry and rush about."[77]

These moments on the shore are subtly graced with mystery. The man claims to have seen a mermaid. "What is it you want?" the stranger asks Doc. When Doc says he wishes to gather up the life he has seen, thought, and learned to find something of meaning, the stranger, pausing in the sound of the surf, tells him: "There are some things a man can't do alone." He would not take on anything as big as the search for meaning without love. There is a pause before he delivers those last two words and his comment is punctuated by the beam of a yellow light: "a clot of gold." "I have to go to the sun now," the man says, for he has grown to believe that the sun needs him. When Doc says, "I'll see you again," the man replies that he has a deep restlessness in him and he will probably soon be gone. Watching him walk away, Doc is much like T. S. Eliot's J. Alfred Prufrock, who concludes by saying that although he has seen mermaids, "I do not think that they will sing to me."

The scene may seem out of place in a comic novel. The mysterious Bodhisattva on the shore seems more appropriate to a work by Hermann Hesse. Yet Doc's encounter with the stranger conveys the spiritual dilemma of Doc quite well. Such serendipitous encounters may come unbidden. There is an aimless mobility to Doc's movement. Hazel wanders too, as he has since he wandered into the army years ago. Mack once pursued radium with a Geiger counter, hoping to capitalize on the need of the new atomic age. His journey took him in a circle, on an improbably round trip on which he ended up back in Monterey. In the wasteland by the sea Hazel has felt the shiver of an earthquake. He has watched a bird wander into the sea and drown. The antics of the tanned young men doing handstands for the ladies no longer hold his attention. Hazel is concerned about Doc and he insists that Mack not give up on him. "You said he can't write his paper," says Hazel, challenging Mack to a fight. Soon Mack is raising a toast: "Let us here resolve to get Doc's ass out of the sling of despond." Eddie recalls how they once messed up terribly in trying to give Doc a party. Mack responds: "We were younger then."[78] With that their plotting begins. They are going to think up another plan to help Doc.

Sweet Thursday attracted critical antagonism upon its publication in 1954. The book sold briskly. Some critics wondered if Steinbeck had produced a comic sequel to *Cannery Row* to capitalize on that book's popularity. Robert DeMott has asserted that Steinbeck was genuinely interested in experimentation. With *Sweet Thursday* he had written "a novel about the writing of a novel."[79] However, he also recalls that critics responded harshly. On *The Author Meets the Critics*, in August 1954, Joseph Bennett called the novel "dull, repetitive, and phony." Lewis Gannett defended it as "delightful" in its wit and humor.[80] For Bennett, Steinbeck was a commercially successful author who had produced a couple of good novels when he was angry—*In Dubious Battle* and *The Grapes of Wrath*. DeMott points out that Bennett's "rigorous intellectualism" and editor Pat Covici's commercialism both express "passionate positions."[81] However, DeMott suggests that we have to broaden our view by recognizing that Steinbeck was a full-time writer supporting his family with his writing. DeMott suggests that Bennett may have missed the self-reflexivity of the novel. *Sweet Thursday* is a playful story of "fabular dimensions."[82] People have read *Sweet Thursday* in diverse ways. The popular response to *Sweet Thursday* was marked by vigorous sales. The critical response was, as Roy S. Simmonds has said, "unfavorable and at best lukewarm." Often the novel has been overlooked critically, or only minimally acknowledged, or it has been roundly criticized.[83]

Sweet Thursday is about the creative process and the search for language. The novel participates in the tradition of "low comedy" that dates back to the plays of Aristophanes. It does contain the occasional broad satiric thrusts that Milton Rugoff of the *Herald Tribune* saw in the book.[84] This is a book that calls attention to itself as a construction, a writing in which DeMott has seen an "incipient postmodernism." Mack the common reader has critiqued the critics: "Some of them don't listen while they read, I guess," because they would rather use words and phrases to dismiss it than try to understand it.[85] The novel does not always make use of traditional representation. This Steinbeck story is experimental. Just as Doc is tinkering in his lab, trying to write a paper, the book's author is tinkering with the play of possibilities.

This is a story set in a wasteland of postwar life seeking revival, with men and women who are trying to gain a foothold on life again. Change has affected the psyche of Cannery Row, as well as its rhythms and patterns. As DeMott has recognized, there is a "postwar depletion that affected all levels of the Row's socio-economic, philosophical, aesthetic, personal, and linguistic existence."[86] This book is about change and the transformation of places, people, and style. As DeMott has pointed out, as Steinbeck wrote of Doc trying to write his paper, in his effort he "turned out to be narrating nothing less than the symbolic story of his own emotional rescue and artistic refashioning."[87] In *Sweet Thursday*, Steinbeck gives us the process of writing. He jests and invents scenarios. If he creates comic raucousness and caricatures it is because he wants to do this, to create "a comic strip." As DeMott says, "That, I suggest, was his desire; far from being proof of his decline."[88] If Steinbeck were alive

today he might play with the graphic novel, or with the Marvel comic
television series. He took on "exaggerated scenarios" to offer "a hilarious
picture of our ridiculous selves."[89]

These years found Steinbeck experimenting. He had written journalism and propaganda during the war. Then he had backed away from those
subjects and written something totally unrelated to wartime concerns. He
had returned imaginatively to Monterey with *Cannery Row* (1945). In
1947, *The Wayward Bus* was published. *The Pearl* was also published: a
moral parable that has been taught in schools often ever since. Yet, in
Commonweal, reviewer Frank O'Malley was dissatisfied and he asked,
"Why do so many of our serious American novelists deteriorate?"[90]
Steinbeck was not deteriorating. He was no longer writing the social
justice novels, such as *In Dubious Battle* and *The Grapes of Wrath*, that a
publication like *Commonweal* liked.

THE PEARL

The Pearl has often been read as a moral tale about how greed for wealth
and material possession is detrimental. An aesthetic approach to this story
may, instead, focus on structure and the musicalization of fiction. Song
appears early in the story with the Song of the Family: an ancestral song
that lives behind the personal songs of the characters. Kino's people "had
once been great makers of song so that everything they saw or thought or
did became a song."[91] The song in Kino's mind is the Song of the Family.
Juana, his wife, sings "an ancient song that had only three notes and yet
endless variety of interval."[92]

When Roger Caswell examines the music in *The Pearl*, he notes that
the story has 125 references to music. Michael J. Meyer analyzes the
contrast and alternation between dissonance and our expectations of harmony. Any expectation that the Song of the Family will be one of con-
cord is disrupted in Juana's song, which is "an aching chord that is caught
in the throat, saying that this is safety, this is warmth, this is the
Whole."[93] This sentence itself begins with discord—a harsh wail caught
in the throat—but concludes in the parallel of three smooth phrases landing on the words "safety," "warmth," and "Whole." Ultimately, dissonance itself can be brought to wholeness. This reflects the pattern of a
story in which Kino's discovery of the pearl causes considerable disso-

nance, bringing conflict, violence, and trouble and raising moral questions, a tension that is then resolved upon Kino's tossing it back into the sea.

The story may reflect an ecological position as well: the pearl belongs to the sea and has been extracted from it. Taken from its natural setting it is transferred into an economic sphere where it is highly valued for its material worth. Kino and his people have always been closely aligned with the land, the sea, and earth's creatures and this material discovery disrupts that alignment. Kino faces a disturbing song, "The Song of Evil," represented by the scorpion: "a savage, secret melody." It will "roar in his ears."[94] The ancestral and communal song contrasts with this: "Kino's people had sung of everything that happened or existed."[95] The people have sung to the elements themselves. There is a beautiful rhythm and balance to Steinbeck's sentence: "They had made songs to the fishes, to the sea in anger and the sea in calm, to the light and the dark and the sun and the moon and the songs were all in Kino and in his people—every song that had ever been made, even the ones forgotten."[96] One might hear echoes of Hemingway's use of the conjunction "and" or the rare balance of song in the canticle attributed to St. Francis of Assisi about "brother sun and sister moon." The passage evokes an ancestry of human song and story that recalls Homer and the telling of myths, as well as the songs, legends, and tales of an indigenous Indian community.

The ancestral song that Kino senses suggests a close connection between the human and the natural world:

> The song was in Kino and the beat of the song was his pounding heart
> as it ate the oxygen from his held breath and the melody of the song
> was the gray green water and the little scuttling animals and the clouds
> of fish that flitted and were gone.[97]

This "secret, little inner song, hardly perceptible," is one of relationship and connection. It is the song of the Undersea: a metaphysical ground of life. The "howl" of Kino upon his discovery of the pearl and the "shrill" sense of the pearl not only indicate a dissonant counter to the ancestral song but also portend a disruption of a way of existence. The music of morning goes out of Kino's head and is replaced by "the music of evil" weakly sounding.[98] Kino anticipates that the natural order will be disrupted. He does not recognize that he is involved in this break or transition.

Kino perceives the pearl with hope. "So lovely it was, so soft, and its own music came from it—the music of promise and delight, its guarantee of the future, of comfort, of security. . . . It closed the door on hunger."[99] However, "the circling of wolves and the hovering of vultures" soon begin. The pearl buyers try to swindle Kino with their appraisal that the gem is worthless. Tension arises between Kino and his wife, Juana. Jealousy and avarice bring "darkness . . . closing in on his family."[100] His boat is wrecked, his house burned. Trackers seek to eliminate his family, to take away his "treasure." Kino resolves to plot their deaths and to kill them and is transformed from loving father and husband into potentially an evil killer. Tragedy awaits him with the realization that his son Coyotito is far more precious a pearl in his life than the gem he has pulled from the ocean.

BURNING BRIGHT

In 1950, Steinbeck again explored the line between fiction and drama, as he had done with *Of Mice and Men*. *Burning Bright* reads like a play set in prose form with four characters: Joe Saul, Friend Ed, Mordeen, and Victor. The action moves across three "acts": the first set in a circus, the second at a farm, and the third onboard a ship. The characters are clowns or circus performers, then farmers, then voyagers upon the sea. The three different settings offer different angles on the relationships between the characters.

Joe Saul and Mordeen are in love, but Joe is unaware that he is sterile. Mordeen has a brief affair with Victor, which results, intentionally, in a pregnancy, so that she can claim that the child is Joe's. Then she insists that she is in love with Joe Saul and that Victor should go away. Joe Saul rejoices that he is going to have a child with Mordeen. However, when he goes for a medical checkup in order to be fully healthy for his child, he learns the harsh truth. The novel does not examine the pain of this crisis for Joe Saul. We are given little interiority because this work is chiefly intended as a play.

From early on in the novel, there is an undercurrent of tension between Victor and Mordeen and between Victor and Joe Saul. *Burning Bright* enlists our sympathy for Joe Saul and for Mordeen and tends to portray Victor as rather despicable and Ed as a judicious "friend" who calls Joe

Saul and Mordeen to reason. However, that Mordeen has used Victor to become pregnant on behalf of her love for Joe Saul raises some ethical questions. So does the elimination of Victor, however bothersome his character may be. Friend Ed is always the kind mediator, the man who is the voice of truth and compassion, who tells Joe Saul to look at what he has got in life and to stop being self-pitying. However, Friend Ed also intervenes in a way that is morally questionable.

Burning Bright is essentially a play and perhaps it should have remained one. The story is presented mostly in dialogue and it is easy to picture it on a stage. At times Joe Saul is given some eloquent and even mystical lines. As fiction, *Burning Bright* appears to be an experiment. If a reader can move through the oblique method of presentation, that reader will find enough drama to carry the story along. However, the shifting of settings and abstract approach in this short novel may be disconcerting to some readers. *Burning Bright* did not burn very brightly on the stage. In its theater run it burned out quickly. The story of Joe Saul and Mordeen is indeed unconventional: a three-act story of passion. Yet as a novel it mostly comes across as a curiosity. Steinbeck did not include it in his collection *The Short Novels of John Steinbeck*.

While *Burning Bright* has often been called the weakest of Steinbeck's novels its minimalism, clipped dialogue, and theatrical frame indicate that it was surely an experiment. Steinbeck wrote such varied work in style, approach, and quality that each work has to be taken for what it is. Steinbeck wrote in his rebuttal to his critics:

> If a writer likes to write he will find satisfaction in endless experiment with his medium. He will improvise techniques, arrangements of scenes, rhythms of words, and rhythms of thought. He will constantly investigate and try combinations new to him. [101]

In this respect, *Burning Bright* is a sign of creativity: an unsuccessful experiment that keeps the fire of the artist's soul alive.

9

EAST OF EDEN

"Nearly everything I have is in it," wrote Steinbeck of *East of Eden*.[1] The novel is sprawling and ambitious, bringing together a variety of Steinbeck's themes and memories of California, autobiographical elements and family history, Biblical references and symbols. The significance of the environment is immediately emphasized as the novel begins with a description of the Salinas Valley. The story of the Trask family and the Hamilton family that follows encompasses American history and the American experience. The novel weaves these family experiences in counterpoint and underscores them with the Eden myth, revealing the hopes and failings of people in a new world.[2] On the eastern hills the Hamiltons have established their family dynasty, and Samuel Hamilton, a realist, has no illusions. In the valley, Adam Trask also attempts to build a new world. His brother Charles is a dark character who brings conflict. When Cathy Ames Trask, Adam's wife, appears, she is a disturbing and monstrous figure, an evil individual often described in animal imagery.[3] In the final section of the novel, Adam's son Cal is contrasted with his brother Aron, a tragic figure of goodness. Steinbeck wrote to Pat Covici: "Cal is everyman. He is the battleground between good and evil." Cal emerges as a character who grows toward some depth and responsibility. Steinbeck told Covici that he had been thinking about "how long it is since a book about morality has been written."[4] The novel underscores the idea that people have free will and may choose good or evil.[5]

This story set in the Salinas Valley had been germinating for a long time. It required more space and more revisions than had *The Grapes of*

Wrath, which Steinbeck had written quickly, furiously across about seven months. While Steinbeck was working on *East of Eden* in 1951 he kept notes on his process and sent letters to his editor Pat Covici. His reflections appear in *Journal of a Novel*, published posthumously in 1969. Much of *East of Eden* was written at East 72nd Street in Manhattan. In the summer he took the project with him to Nantucket. He completed his drafts for *East of Eden* in November. A trip overseas with Elaine followed and they went to Morocco, Algeria, Spain, France, Switzerland, Italy, England, Scotland, and Ireland. The novel was published in September 1952 to mixed reviews.

With *East of Eden* a new aesthetic appears in Steinbeck's work in the form of a historical romance and family saga. The novel incorporates autobiography in Steinbeck's recollections of California and his younger self. However, the novel also projects a new vision and inquiry. *East of Eden* does not so much join the tradition of the novel as insist upon being itself, observes Henry Veggian, who asks: "Then why do so many continue reading it, as earlier critics did, as a naïve work or a sentimental and didactic family biography passing as a historical romance?"[6] We may ask why Steinbeck's reputation is associated with anti-intellectualism when there is so much thought and so many suggestions of wide reading in his work. There are always levels beneath Steinbeck's deceptive surface of simplicity. *East of Eden* begins "a glimpse of the postmodern" that includes "the confusion and wonder that belies the mixing of materials," observes Veggian, who suggests that from the outside it looks like "a quaint farmhouse" but that it is, rather, "a precarious, urbane world much like our own."[7]

East of Eden is an intermedial text that brings together verbal expression and musical structures. It combines elements of history, ethics, and Biblical features in an inquiry into perennial problems of good and evil. In the 1950s, the novel was criticized for its tendencies toward fable rather than consistent realism. It was disparaged for its apparent lack of unity in splitting the story between the Hamiltons and the Trasks. Critics objected to Steinbeck's obvious uses of the Bible story of Cain and Abel, his difficult-to-follow story line, and the story's intrusive narrator. Even Steinbeck's friend Elia Kazan, who directed the film *East of Eden*, admitted that in his view the novel *East of Eden* was not one of Steinbeck's best.[8] One would think that Steinbeck failed in his effort to make this story a capstone of his distinguished career. However, in this sprawling text Steinbeck gathers many ideas, employs innovative methods and varied materials, and does indeed offer "a glimpse of the postmodern." With *East of Eden*, he also wrote a popular novel: one that became a film with popular teen idol James Dean. *East of Eden* had a resurgence of popularity in 2004, when Oprah Winfrey made it her book club's featured choice.

On the screen, *East of Eden* was director Elia Kazan's first widescreen color film. Steinbeck and Kazan wrote a treatment, attempting to trim the lengthy novel to manageable proportions. They had recently worked together on the 1952 film *Viva Zapata!* with Marlon Brando starring as the Mexican revolutionary Emiliano Zapata. Steinbeck accounted for some forty-five sequences for the film. He insisted that Mexico's history was more than the stereotypical concept many Americans had of "a series of banditries and small revolutions and revolts led by venal and self-interested men." He wrote a lengthy introductory statement, the script, and commentary. However, adapting *East of Eden* soon became a more difficult project. In a letter to Steinbeck, May 18, 1953, Kazan recognized that the script was "still too diffuse"; it needed "continuity" and should be handed over to a "specialist" like Bob Ardrey or Paul Osborn. "These guys aren't up to your ankles as writers or artists," he wrote. However, screenwriting is a specific field, he explained, and neither he nor Steinbeck had expertise in writing screenplays.[9] Paul Osborn was hired to write the screenplay and he suggested omitting the first two-thirds of the novel. Kazan was able to have director's cut of *East of Eden*. That is, bringing the film in on budget, he had complete artistic freedom in completing the film.

In 2004, Imagine Entertainment obtained the rights to *East of Eden* in a deal with the Steinbeck estate. However, no film was ever made. In 2013, media sources announced that actress Jennifer Lawrence would play the role of Cathy Ames Trask in a film directed by Brian Ross. After all, Cathy Trask is a fascinating character who is called a monster and appears to typify evil and resistance to social norms. However, both Lawrence and Ross had other commitments, including a possible sequel to the successful *Hunger Games* film. Later, Ross offered the idea that two films might be made from Steinbeck's novel. The classic film of the 1950s with James Dean and Richard Davalos that was directed by Elia Kazan made use of only the final section of Steinbeck's novel.[10] There is a great deal more to Steinbeck's novel than appears in that film and Brian Ross appears interested in making effective use of this material.

COUNTERPOINT: HAMILTON AND TRASK

In his novel, Steinbeck sets up a counterpoint between the Hamiltons and the Trasks. The challenges of genealogy and uncovering family history become clear as the story's narrator begins to describe Samuel Hamilton in chapter 2. We are told of the Hamiltons: "They were not eminent and there are few records concerning them." This is the case for the Irish family records like those of the Hamiltons, which must be searched for in parish records. The Hamiltons could be located in birth, marriage, land ownership, or death records. However, in some cases in Ireland and North Ireland such records are missing, or there are gaps in the records. To find the voice of common individuals who never had social prominence one must locate diaries or letters, or rely upon family stories that have been passed down across generations. Samuel Hamilton, who traveled to the Salinas Valley, is a craftsman, a man good with his hands, a carpenter and blacksmith. He has never made much money or possessed much financial sense, but he was able to build his own house and tend the land; he has sturdy values, is a self-educated reader, and he raises a large family. The narrator mentions that he possesses Samuel's great black book of medical remedies, from which he can derive the family's medical history. Liza Hamilton, his wife, wears her brown hair in a tight bun and her attitude toward gregarious and playful people is similarly bound up and constricted. She cooks plain meals and casts harsh judgments against card playing and idleness. We are told that she is suspicious of dancing and even of laughter.

The narrator raises the question of why anyone would come to this territory in California. He arrives at an answer to this that underwrites the tenacious spirit of pioneers. The suggestion has been offered that a just moral God secured the faith of the farmers who came to this land. However, the narrator says he believes that "they believed in themselves" and that "they knew that they were valuable potentially moral units."[11] The key word "moral" immediately leads us into our introduction to the story of the Trask family and the Cain and Abel allusion that will begin to appear in the problematic childhood relationship between the Trask brothers.

Adam Trask is set in contrast to the Hamiltons. With Adam begins the Trask family story, which seems more compelling, or at least to hold more dramatic tension than that of the Hamiltons. Adam has come from

Connecticut with his wild father, Cyrus, whose leg was irreparably injured in the Civil War. Mrs. Trask is described as withdrawn, a woman who uses religion as a remedy for all ills. As Cyrus becomes increasingly military-minded, Adam and his brother Charles are forced to deal with their father's military drills. Adam retreats from violence to an inner sanctuary. He retires into "secretness" and "vagueness." Charles, his half brother, absorbs the family's atmosphere of violence. He is an athlete who will use lies to protect Adam and himself from their father's harshness. However, before long he will turn his aggression toward Adam. In the story of the Trasks we begin to see the roots of a dysfunctional family in which each member has taken on a role and methods of self-defense. Adam admires Charles, who at times seems like "a bright being, another species."[12] However, Charles is "dangerous, even at fifteen."[13] The violence within him seems like a genetic predisposition. Meanwhile, in a rather Freudian twist in characterization, Adam is intrigued with Alice, who is not his birth mother. We read that Adam had long felt a lack of maternal affection and that "he ached toward her with a longing he did not understand." We read of "twisted light" and shadows that "warped his seeing," perhaps suggesting Oedipus's inability to see.[14] Alice is a consumptive and will not survive long but she has some impact upon Adam Trask's life and development.

The Cain and Abel motif soon becomes obvious. One day, Charles, feeling insulted that Adam is besting him in a game, becomes violent and strikes him.[15] We read that Adam then began to choose not win, or else he would have to kill his brother. Cyrus counsels his son Adam, telling him that he can learn, whereas Charles is afraid of nothing and cannot be taught courage.[16] Adam will be prepared to become a soldier. Cyrus reflects upon how we turn people toward war and violence.[17] He tells Adam, "The soldier is the most holy because he is the most tested."[18] However, military training, he says, is designed to make one like the rest. One's dangerous difference will not do. The whole machine is devoted to the destruction of difference.[19] Honor and fortitude are gained by going down and rising from this.

Charles is isolated and looks on from a distance. He wants to know about the conversation Adam has had with his father. The parallel with the Cain and Abel story is obvious. Charles feels that their father has favored Adam. In response, he directs verbal abuse at Adam and he tells him that his mother drowned because of him. He again turns to physical violence to beat up Adam. Why did he do it? his father asks Adam. "He doesn't think you love him," Adam says. Perceptions are askew. Their stepmother, Alice, thinks that Charles has been leaving the gifts that Adam has been leaving for her.

Adam is soon sent to be in the cavalry and to go to Indian country.[20] He trades the conflict at home for the field of battle. Adam becomes a marksman and does not like the fighting. Adopting a position of nonviolence, he intentionally misses the enemy whenever he shoots. Charles, who stays home, bears the loneliness of the farm and receives the mark of Cain on his forehead in an accident. We learn that Adam has been discharged from the army, in 1885, and he wanders and puts off returning home. He reenlists and is directed to go to Washington, where he meets his father, Cyrus, who is now in an official government position and has become indistinguishable from his role. Charles, mostly alone at the farm, mistreating women, awaits Adam's return while Adam serves another five years in the army. We are brought into Adam's experiences, witness Charles being informed by letter of his father's death, and see Adam's return and the tensions in the conversation between the brothers upon their reunion. Given a legacy of a good deal of money and Cyrus's discharge papers, they begin to ask questions about their father's background. Their dispute over the love of their father persists and Adam, rather naïvely, insists that his father could not have stolen the money. The brothers' inheritance is perhaps morally questionable. As this moral quandary appears, Cathy Ames is introduced in chapter 8, which begins with the words: "I believe there are monsters in the world."[21]

Of course, this is just the beginning of a long novel: one that marks a shift in Steinbeck's writing and has been both popular and criticized. *East of Eden* was at first met with New Critical expectations and perceptions. In particular, as previously mentioned, several critics found the autobiographical elements and intrusive narrator a problem in the novel. However, in *East of Eden*, Steinbeck was reaching in new directions, with new techniques in composition. He had shifted away from his earlier realism and the communal hopes of *In Dubious Battle* and *The Grapes of Wrath* to a style that began to anticipate postmodernism and to the humanism and liberalism of the early Cold War. *East of Eden* was created in a context of society and culture that was different from the context of the American 1930s. To assess this novel we need to look for connections with the postwar culture in which this novel was produced. The novel became part of the creation of that society and culture.

In *Journal of a Novel*, which is written as a series of letters to his friend and editor Pat Covici, Steinbeck tells Covici that there will be a shift in pacing as the story moves from the Trasks to the Hamiltons. The Trasks are represented by aggressive energy and the Hamiltons are calmer and more deliberate.[22] The Trasks are "dark and dour" and "the next Hamilton chapter is light and gay."[23] In *East of Eden*, Steinbeck shifts out of chronology and "harsh prose" alternates with the poetic, as Michael J. Meyer has pointed out.[24] *East of Eden* also makes use of another Steinbeck stylistic move: he interjects "little blades of social criticism."[25]

Steinbeck specifically refers to the character of Samuel Hamilton meriting a "recapitulation with full orchestra." He writes: "Then I would like a little melody with one flute" starting as a memory and extending into the future. "Tomorrow I will take up this little flute melody, the continuous thing that bridges lives and ties the whole thing together, and I will end with a huge chord if I can do it."[26] He writes of counterpoint and considers the use of repetition and a refrain. "Refrain is one of the most valuable form methods," he writes. "Refrain is the return to the known before one flies again upward. It is a consolation to the reader, a reassurance that the book has not left his understanding."[27]

Some Steinbeck critics, like Howard Levant, have suggested that structural issues were responsible for his later works not gaining more critical approval. However, as Michael J. Meyer recognizes, Steinbeck brought an attention to structure that engaged the alternations and counterpoint suggested by music.[28] *Journal of a Novel* makes it clear that Steinbeck planned the dissonance in the Trask chapters and the movement of the Hamilton scenes to achieve a kind of harmonic pattern and compositional balance. Meyer points to a June 26 entry in which Steinbeck says "the tempo of the book [changes] just as the tempo of the times changed."[29] *East of Eden* is a postwar 1950s novel that participates in a different milieu than Steinbeck's novels of the 1930s, or his war correspondence. The novel draws upon family history and recalls California while also extending the societal critique present in *The Wayward Bus* and the "musical" techniques of *The Pearl*.

MORAL INQUIRY AND CATHY AMES TRASK

The figure of Cathy Ames Trask raises moral questions. Clearly, a person who entices boys into sexual experimentation, pushes a Latin teacher to suicide, sets her family house on fire, and runs off to work for a brothel owner is not a figure of probity. Nor is one who later shoots her husband and runs off from her two sons. However, the narrator complicates this characterization: "It is my belief that Cathy Ames was born with the tendencies, or lack of them, which drove and forced her all her life. Some balance wheel was misweighted, some gear out of ratio. She was not like other people, never was from birth."[30]

Imaging techniques and brain studies in recent years have indicated that the cerebral cortex is involved in modifying aggressive behavior and that the amygdala plays a role in aggression. Cognitive science has left us with questions as to what extent an individual with the enlarged amygdala or other issues of brain physiology is fully responsible for his or her behavior. A moral agent can make an autonomous choice when the conditions of independence from external constraints and inner compulsions can be met. Autonomy in moral decision making requires competency: that one is capable of rational deliberation and understands the consequences. The individual has to be able to evaluate the aims and values on the basis of which he or she makes a choice.

Cathy's behavior will strike most readers as immoral and reprehensible. One may ask if she is capable of free will. She represents the dangerous difference that Cyrus Trask referred to earlier in the novel. She has a shifting name: Cathy is Kate. She is a variation from the accepted norm, one "set apart."[31] She is subject to masculine control, as Carol L. Hansen has pointed out.[32] She is controlled by her father, beaten by Mr. Edwards, and she turns to Adam Trask for protection. There is a quest for freedom in her assertion, yet she is a sociopath who appears to be without conscience. Her children Cal and Aron are born into a troubling world in which *timshol*, a moral code, offers hope. In one respect, the narrative appears to uphold the value of Cathy's difference and nonconformity. In another, we read that her lies were never innocent and that she was a consummate manipulator.

The narrative tells us that she was running from something and "we can't know whether she escaped," and "It is easy to say she was bad, but there is little meaning unless we know why."[33] "Do you think I want to be human?" Cathy declares to Adam. "I'd rather be a dog than a human! But I'm not a dog. I'm smarter than humans. Nobody can hurt me." In the terms of Aristotle, who posits "rational man" and preaches the development of virtue based in balance and moderation, Cathy may appear subhuman and excessive. She appears to make a claim to stand outside the moral order like the Nietzschean superman, or a figure like Dostoevsky's Raskolnikov, who believes he can surpass morality. From another perspective, Cathy declares her difference, often through disturbing acts.[34]

The portrait of Olive Hamilton that is provided in chapter 14, in contrast, draws our attention to a young woman who can affirm difference and be a benefit to society. Olive Hamilton becomes a teacher in a community that favors farm duties over formal education. Olive, we are told, practices tact, and her elementary-school teaching involves her in diverse studies: she had to "teach everything . . . to all ages." She has the tenacity to endure, whereas other teachers "rarely lasted in the country schools."[35] She faces a situation in which her students and their parents do not see the efficacy of education. "There was a wall against learning. A man wanted his children to read, to figure, and that was enough."[36] The parents want their children to be practical, not "flighty," and too much education might coax a person to leave home for work in the city. "Learning was for doctors, lawyers, and teachers, a class set off and not considered related to other people."[37] What was valued was the ability to dig a well, shoe a horse, or operate a threshing machine, as Samuel Hamilton was able to do. A man like Samuel Hamilton was tolerated. We learn that Olive, an intuitive woman of courage, eventually married, and soon the narrator recalls (or Steinbeck himself interjects) a memory of Olive coming to his aid when he had pneumonia. Olive may have once dreamed of being "metropolitan" but she was not particularly cosmopolitan: "Her thinking was not international. Her first boundary was the geography of her family."[38] The anecdotes that follow tell us that "she brought ferocity to her work" during World War I and she was bold and flew in the cockpit of a flimsy plane that circled over the Spreckels Sugar factory performing aerial stunts.[39]

We return to the Trask family and we meet Lee, the Chinese cook who wears pigtails, a man with dark brown eyes that Cathy cannot read into. As keen as Cathy is in detecting men's desires, she finds Lee inscrutable. Adam sends Lee as a messenger to Samuel to request that he visit to discuss boring wells on his property. Samuel immediately decides that

Lee's pidgin Chinese is inauthentic: the man knows how to speak English well enough. Lee responds that he uses this manner of speech both as protection and "to be understood at all."[40] He has learned to recognize the prejudices that people approach him with, he tells Samuel. "You are one of the rare people who can separate your observation from your precon-ception," he says. "You see what is, where most people see what they expect."[41]

"A CANDLE OF TRUTH"

Steinbeck's attention to what "is" comes into play in an affirmation of his characters' common humanity. Samuel recognizes that there is "a candle of truth" in what Lee has said. This is an example of intercultural conver-sation in which there is a movement toward understanding. It is the kind of objective and open encounter that can most benefit us in our interac-tions in a pluralistic society and a culturally convergent world. When Lee is asked why he is content to be a servant he responds that service is noble. "I don't know where being a servant came into disrepute," he says, for "properly carried out, it is a position of power, of love."[42] He thinks of someday going to San Francisco to start a business. Would that be a laundry or a grocery store? Samuel asks. No, there are too many Chinese laundries and restaurants, Lee says. Maybe he will start a bookstore. (Of course that was in the days before online booksellers and mega shopping malls.) Then again, maybe he will just remain where he is: "A servant loses his initiative."[43]

Will Hamilton drives a shiny new Ford: one of the cars he dislikes that build his fortune.[44] The boys are fascinated by the car. Steinbeck intro-duces some satire in his portrayal of a Ford mechanic who speaks of studying "the literature" in the Ford manual. Lee quips, "So young to be so erudite." The young mechanic, who does not understand the word "erudite," displays further ignorance and prejudice when he asks Adam, "What did the Chink say?" Lee, who can speak with great clarity and intelligence, immediately slips back into pidgin Chinaman speech.[45] The mechanic, who now calls himself Joe although his name is Roy, rejects the idea of going to college and he spits on the ground. "What do them fellas know? Can they set a timer? Can they file a point?"[46] He went to automobile school. "The planetary system is rev-a-lush-shun-ary," he says. He will explain to them how the "do-hickey" works. His admonition to repeat "spark up—gas down" and other phrases begins to sound like they are at cheerleading practice, engaged in rote learning, or reciting the antiphon and response at a Catholic mass.[47] Modern mechanism is again placed alongside liberal education. The planetary system has shriveled and the cosmos has been reduced to the workings of a car engine presided over by a technically trained but limited individual. The word "literature" has been used to describe a Ford manual, which is devoid of aesthetic content. The self-educated Samuel Hamilton surely could set a timer and file a point as well as read the books that lined the shelves at the Delmar house. Lee dreams of a bookstore where he can have discussions and arguments and "see all the colors in the world."[48] However, here is Will Hamilton selling cars and a technician has been sent to educate Lee and Adam.

East of Eden is indeed sprawling but it is also filled with interesting characters and it is rich with ideas. While some of the more obvious symbolism is heavy-handed, the ethical reflection that is present in the novel and the experimental aspects of Steinbeck's approach to this story merit further new readings. *East of Eden* is a panoramic investigation of good and evil, a parable expressed within family histories. Its form may be compared with the romance, in Nathaniel Hawthorne's sense. The novel, with all of its range and the challenge Steinbeck faced in balancing the stories of the Hamiltons and the Trasks, certainly has its merits. Steinbeck incorporated allegorical materials and drew upon experience, imagination, family history, and newspaper accounts from Salinas. He had contemplated his fiction set in Salinas for a long time and spent several years at work on it. He makes use of lengthy expository passages and interjects a first-person narrative in which he appears to offer some of his own recollections. Three parts of *East of Eden* begin in the first-person narrative point of view. These are imaginative and self-reflexive passages, which may be viewed as features of romance, rather than intrusive narrative error as some critics have claimed. The voice is that of fictional narrator, author, and historian who is offering a mixture of materials.[49]

The characters in *East of Eden* represent opposing moral views. Samuel Hamilton reflects virtue ethics and classical elements of character, or arete, and moral self-improvement. He is a modern romantic and idealist with an aesthetic and moral sensibility. Will Hamilton, however, is more utilitarian and pragmatic in his work of selling Ford motorcars to consumers. We might note his name as a sign of human volition, or free will and choice. Cathy (Kate) Trask is described as an evil monster. From a feminist viewpoint, however, she may also be like the madwoman in the attic of Sandra Gilbert and Susan Gubar's well-known critical essay: a woman whose vital life is trapped by patriarchal codes and who insists upon breaking out, however violently. One may ask how assumptions revolving around gender affect Cathy Ames and contribute to her resistance and her morally problematic actions. Freudian psychoanalytical approaches may also be applied to a reading of Cathy/Kate within the family romance. Indeed, the sibling rivalry between Adam and Charles and Adam's attraction to his stepmother can all be read through a psychoanalytic lens.

American history is recalled in the wide narrative sweep of this novel. Steinbeck told his editor Pat Covici that it was "the story of my country and the story of me."[50] We are introduced to scenes that recall western settlement, the Civil War, the Indian Wars, politics in Washington, and the impact of modernization on town and country life. Within this broader frame we are given close-ups of the action between the characters. Part 2 begins to bring the families together as Samuel Hamilton begins to become familiar with the Trasks. Samuel is taken aback by Cathy's evil. He compels Adam to take more responsibility. Later, after Adam and Cathy move to Salinas Valley they have two sons. Cathy/Kate abandons the children and becomes a madam at a brothel.

Samuel and Lee meet with Adam to name the boys, Caleb and Aron. The Cain and Abel motif repeats in them and the discussion of this at the center of the novel makes this clear.[51] Lee assists in raising the boys and he offers moral advice. Samuel and Lee, who express the good, engage in discussions with Adam that probe the problem of good and evil. Lee discusses the Hebrew for *timshol*:

> The King James translation makes a promise in "Thou shalt" meaning that men will surely triumph over sin. But the Hebrew word *timshel*—"Thou mayest"—that gives a choice. It might be the most important word in the world.[52]

The boys attend school at West End, as opposed to East End, the other school in town. They ask each other questions about their missing mother. Cal feels that his father is cold toward him and he feels troubled that his father has more interest in his brother, Aron, who is representative of goodness. Cal Trask discovers that his mother, Kate, who his father, Adam, has said is dead, is working as a madam at a brothel. Cal follows her. "My name is Caleb," says Cal to his mother. "Caleb got to the Promised Land."[53] She exhibits no maternal care for him but provides him with some money. Adam loses money in a transportation business scheme and Cal gathers money to compensate for the lost investment. However, Adam rejects Cal's offer and Cal takes the rejection personally. Cal forces his brother, Aron, to face the truth of what their mother has become and Aron feels tortured by the facts and has a breakdown. Adam, upset by the loss of Aron, has a stroke. Adam's challenge is to move toward forgiveness of Cal, and Cal has to come to acknowledge his responsibility for his brother's death and how it affects his father. As the novel concludes, Adam Trask will repeat the word "timshel."[54]

Steinbeck carved that word onto a wooden box in which he presented the manuscript to Pat Covici. In a note that he enclosed he commented that *East of Eden* embodied "the pleasure of design and some despair and the indescribable joy of creation."[55] While completing *East of Eden* he had written to Covici that he believed that contemporary writers had "a tendency to celebrate the destruction of the spirit." However, writers have a social responsibility, he said. "It is the duty of the writer to lift up, to extend, to encourage. If the written word has contributed anything at all to our developing species and our half developed culture it is this—great writing has been a staff to lean on, a mother to consult, a wisdom to pick up stumbling folly, a strength in weakness to support weak cowardice."[56]

10

AMERICA AND AMERICANS

Steinbeck in the 1960s

Steinbeck's son, John IV, once described him as "a kind of American conscience figure."[1] This call to conscience appeared with great force in Steinbeck's work in the 1930s. However, there was an enduring quality of care in Steinbeck's work that brought him into war correspondence and government service in the 1940s. It entered his political support for Adlai Stevenson and his articles of the 1950s, and emerged in a strong, personal voice in the early 1960s. The decade began with a new president, John F. Kennedy. With him came the hope of a "new frontier" and the resolve to confront an array of social problems ranging from race and civil rights issues to the pressures of the Cold War. Steinbeck attended the inauguration on January 20, 1961. He included it in the last leg of his cross-country American journey with his poodle, Charley, which he wrote about in the national best-seller *Travels with Charley*.

Snow fell across Washington the day before the inauguration. It made the city peaceful, Steinbeck thought. From a house in Georgetown, he looked out on a scene of white. Steps were frost covered, parked cars lay under the snow blanket, and the motors of the cars that passed along the street were muffled. These were the quiet moments before his time under the rostrum of the Capitol as an honored guest struggling to warm his wife Elaine's frozen feet. Kennedy removed his overcoat. The sun was bright on his face and the air was bitter cold. Resolutely, he began: "We observe today not a victory of party but a celebration of freedom, symbolizing an end as well as a beginning, signifying renewal as well as change." His speech cast a forward-looking hope couched in an array of memorable phrases. He told his audience that a new age had emerged; humanity now had in its "mortal hands the power to abolish all forms of human poverty" and the ability to abolish "all forms of human life." Americans had a responsibility, a role to play, for they were heirs to a legacy of God-given human rights asserted by "that first revolution." The thirty-fifth president of the United States stood before them, his words pulsing, carried across to them under a clear blue sky: "Let the word go forth from this time and place, to friend and foe alike, that the torch has been passed to a new generation of Americans." He spoke boldly to the world, declaring American resolve: "We shall pay any price, bear any burden, meet any hardship, support any friend, oppose any foe to ensure the survival and the success of liberty." He spoke of science and discovery, of facing problems that unite rather than belaboring those that divide, and he famously urged his listeners to "ask not what your country can do for you; ask what you can do for your country." A "glittering time," David Halberstam called it, the beginning of an "Olympian age." It was the coming of a new Augustan age, Robert Frost said. Afterward, Steinbeck rejoiced that classical rhetoric had been revived in Kennedy's speech. He commented to a reporter that "syntax . . . has been restored."[2]

Words were always important to Steinbeck but decision making and action were more essential to the presidency. In October 1962 the president faced the Cuban missile crisis. Steinbeck was away in Europe a year later when he heard the news that Kennedy had been assassinated. Steinbeck had viewed Kennedy as representing a hope for the world and a sense of purpose for the American people. Yet he regarded Kennedy's famous phrase as a challenge to overcome selfishness and embrace civic contribution. Recalling the "ask not" phrase, Steinbeck wrote in July 1966: "And it is historically true that a nation whose people take out more than they put in will collapse and disappear."[3] He urged Americans to find a new path, a sense of duty, and a vision of purpose.

Steinbeck's works of the 1960s, *Travels with Charley*, *The Winter of Our Discontent*, and *America and Americans*, form what Jackson J. Benson has called a "moral trilogy." Benson and Susan Shillinglaw point out that Steinbeck "was constantly engaged with the manners, morals, and controversies of the world around him" and "had the moralist's urge" to comment on it all. They identify him as an "engaged artist" and a strong "advocate of democracy."[4] Into the 1960s he wrote opinion pieces in essay form. Whereas in his 1961 novel *The Winter of Our Discontent* he seems to have not quite found the tone and form to fully capture his sense of contemporary dissatisfaction or malaise, he did address issues directly in his essays. Shillinglaw and Benson call them "impassioned pleas from a man who cared deeply about his country."[5]

TRAVELS WITH CHARLEY

Steinbeck's American journey was one of back roads rather than major highways. He told Elizabeth Otis, his agent, that he wanted to see people "not in movement but at home in their own places."[6] On this idealistic journey, he brought his poodle Charley and he drove a vehicle he called Rocinante, after Don Quixote's horse. In the first pages of *Travels with Charley*, Steinbeck tells us how he prepared for his trip. He then sets out across Long Island and travels up through Connecticut and Massachusetts and up to the border of Canada. Northern Maine becomes a place of interest and he describes his visit of nearly a week there. Next, he has to deal with border patrol guards at Niagara who insist upon a vaccination for the poodle, Charley. Steinbeck soon sets out on a drive toward Chicago, where he meets with his wife. About seventeen days have gone by. From Chicago, Steinbeck rolls across the American landscape and we are treated to about a hundred pages of his narrative before he arrives in New Mexico. He will next have to revisit California, where he is remembered—and in some cases not with much welcome. Monterey has changed and so have the friends with whom he visits. He concludes that "Tom Wolfe was right. You can't go home again because home has ceased to exist except in the mothballs of memory."[7]

His journey through Texas is made more enjoyable by a visit with Elaine Steinbeck's relatives. This is Texas in the days before L.B.J. and the *Dallas* television series. It is Texas before the space center in Houston, high tech, and George W. Bush. "It is a mystique almost approaching a religion," Steinbeck wrote.[8] He enjoys Texan hospitality and then he drives off to the most distressing experience of his entire journey: his encounter with racism and the "spontaneous cry of anger, of insane rage" at a little black girl, Ruby Bridges, who was being ushered by federal marshals into the public school. Steinbeck recognizes that the women yelling at the girl are performing for their racist peers. He writes that they "hungered for attention, wanted to be admired."[9] Ruby Bridges passed under a barrage of verbal abuse that was too violent and vulgar for Steinbeck's publishers to reproduce on the page. Steinbeck wrote their words down. His publisher excised them, thinking that it would cause the book to be censored. Steinbeck had found some troubling aspects of America in 1960.

Travels with Charley was a best-seller. These recollections of a quixotic romp through America had moments of delight as well as ones of darkness. Yet Steinbeck critic John Ditsky called it "The Quest That Failed" in his essay in 1975. Steinbeck had met "the monster America that wins in the end," he wrote.[10] Why did such a book become so popular despite the wasteland vision that some Steinbeck critics have seen in it? The book was popular, even with its moments of melancholy and Steinbeck's musing over racist "cheerleaders," because it brought the broad American landscape to readers at a time of hope. The time of the Kennedy–Nixon election was a period during which there was a sense of promise. One of America's finest writers had gathered fragments of the diversity of America in his account of a personal journey. He had even traveled with his poodle, man's best friend. What could be more pop culture and hopeful than that?

The New Orleans experience, however, jolted Steinbeck, making him a witness of racism and increasing his concern about the problems of the Deep South. Had he seen the disaster of hurricane damage to New Orleans and the Gulf in 2005, that would likely have further prompted his concern about racial issues and poverty in America. Hurricane Katrina in 2005 brought a loss of life, ecological devastation, and national attention to the disparity between the well-off and the poor in the city and outlying areas. Given Steinbeck's scenes of flood, human struggle, and government camp organization in *The Grapes of Wrath*, he surely would have had something to say about the calamity and loss in New Orleans. Today the French Quarter is again bustling with crowds. The shops are open and you can get most anything: clothes, jewelry, food, and knickknacks, even a piece of pizza across the street from a place that advertises itself as a voodoo shop. Groups of musicians still play there: in clubs and on the streets. A riverboat, red and white, glides by in the early-morning sunlight and captures the view from the Marriott Hotel a few blocks away from the waterfront. Mardi Gras beads hang from the tree limbs on a main thoroughfare. Some of the streets are tight, narrow, and shadowed, as the airport taxi drives through picking up passengers. Ruby Bridges occasionally speaks to schoolchildren about her experience and hopes for America. The school where Steinbeck stood in 1960, empty for years and then damaged by the hurricane and flooding, has been restored as an educational institution.

THE WINTER OF OUR DISCONTENT

Steinbeck's essays and fiction of the 1960s embody the drive and moral tone of his earlier work. Yet something happens in a man as years go by and conditions change. Time passes, new concerns arise, and his perspective may shift. Culture also brings changes and a new era. The energy and concern of the 1930s, with its hard issues and revolutionary changes, had been absorbed in four difficult years of war. Postwar brought a degree of prosperity back to America, but Steinbeck also began to detect a kind of complacency and an emphasis on materialism that began to bother him. In the late 1950s Steinbeck increasingly began writing thoughtful opinion pieces about America and he contributed articles and an occasional piece of fiction to a wide variety of periodicals.

In 1952 and 1956 he fervently supported Adlai Stevenson's campaigns for the presidency. When he wrote "Adlai Stevenson and John Steinbeck Discuss the Past and the Present" for *Newsday*, his tone had shifted to that of a concerned moralist. America had to recognize its materialism, its need for civility, its racism, and its declining community. The way to a prosperous future of unity was to be found in embracing values: respect, courage, love of country. Steinbeck called for a kind of code of honor, a sense of trust and community that he saw expressed by the Arthurian knights. These principles, he believed, are enduring: the arete of the ancient Greeks, the law of the Hebrews, the virtue of Christian belief are grounded in these values. John Steinbeck continued to be an ethical writer in a new era. The jeremiad, or prophetic voice, he projected in the early 1960s aroused feelings, resistance, or misunderstanding. Steinbeck was shaking up the Leave-It-to-Beaver world of the 1950s, the complacency of the era of organization man. He would not stand for complacency. In a column for the *Louisville Courier-Journal* in 1956, he wrote on the Democratic National Convention. He affirmed: "I find to my consternation that I am basically, intrinsically and irresistibly Democrat."[11] Yet his emphasis was less on party than on the *demos*, the community of the *polis*. Politics for him was fundamentally a potential path to social justice, a means of participation, a way to declare and enact a moral stance. He took this stance into the Kennedy era and beyond.

For years, Steinbeck had written about outsiders, marginalized people. Now he was writing about the middle class, observing that there were problems in suburban enclaves like on Long Island, or in New England. Americans had moved after the war from Manhattan, Brooklyn, and Queens to places like the planned suburb of Levittown, Long Island. Steinbeck searched farther out on Long Island for a place that felt a bit like Monterey had felt on the West Coast. He settled in Sag Harbor, which is near the Hamptons, near the end of Long Island on its northeast coast. It was a peaceful former whaling town, which he described as one that still displayed some older houses built in "neo-Greek architecture with fluted columns."[12] Yet the new environment brought along a novel of disillusionment and questions about where America was going.

The Winter of Our Discontent (1961) is set in a fictional New England town, New Baytown, but Sag Harbor is a bit like Nantucket or Martha's Vineyard or Cape Cod. Steinbeck described his home at Sag Harbor as "a warm and cozy little fishing cottage" near the bay. Sag Harbor and Nantucket "lighted the lamps of the world until kerosene was developed and the whaling industry languished," he wrote.[13] The town was actually two-fifths in East Hampton. Steinbeck lived near Jesse Halsey Lane, named after a ship captain. From that name came the name of his story's main character, Ethan, whose last name was then changed to Hawley. The house Steinbeck lived in, once green, is now slate gray. He planted Japanese black pines and had a boat, the *Lillymaid*, named after his wife, and he could sail it out to Bluff Point. The land beyond the house was shaded by stately oak trees and he could walk across the broad lawn to the cove. He had a small writer's place built on the lawn, an octagon that looks like a small covered park gazebo.

The Winter of Our Discontent was Steinbeck's final novel. A short story from 1956, "How Mr. Hogan Robbed a Bank," served as the basis for this longer work. Ethan Hawley lives in his grandfather's house but the family fortunes have declined. He has lost his grocery store and has to work as a clerk for the man who purchased it: Marullo, an Italian immigrant who is a shrewd businessman. To try to make things better Ethan develops a plan to rob a bank but then gives up on that idea. His son wins an "I Love America" essay contest and then it is discovered that he plagiarized the content of his essay. Ethan reports the Italian immigrant to the immigration authorities. Ironically, he gets the grocery store back from Marullo because Marullo thinks that he is a good man. His son beats up his sister for telling on him for cheating on the essay. He insists that cheating is what everybody does. Steinbeck would not live to see the fraudulent future of Enron, hedge fund manipulation, or Ponzi schemes, but he recognized that the collapse of values in America may begin in small acts like a teenager cheating on an essay.

In an epigraph to *The Winter of Our Discontent*, Steinbeck wrote: "Readers seeking to identify the fictional people and places here described would do better to inspect their own communities and search their own hearts, for this book is about a large part of America today." The comment signals that this novel is a jeremiad: a prophetic call for reform. With a novel (*The Winter of Our Discontent*), a travel narrative (*Travels with Charley*), and an essay collection (*America and Americans*), Steinbeck offered a sometimes stinging critique of America in a "moral trilogy," as Jackson Benson has called these Steinbeck writings of the early to mid-1960s. In the 1960s, Steinbeck was engaged with the Arthurian tales and his sense of a chivalric code of virtue and honor met with his deep concern for America and the world. Steinbeck also experiments in this novel with point of view, dream sequences, wordplay, and the novel's self-reflexivity. His narrator, Ethan Hawley, reflects: "I've thought so often how telling changes with the listener."[14] He thinks of a speaker or writer's audience: "A man who tells secrets or stories must think of who is hearing or reading. . . . A story must have some point of contact with the reader to make him feel at home in it. Only then can he accept wonders."[15] Ethan has begun to ponder the uncertainty of his world: "I wonder how many people I've looked at all my life and never seen."[16]

The back cover of the Bantam Books paperback publication of *The Winter of Our Discontent* announces Steinbeck as a writer who has "revealed the hardscrabble morality of the thirties" and has interrogated ethical conduct and misconduct in American culture. In bold red letters, the back cover blurb begins with a reference to *The Grapes of Wrath* and then proceeds to *East of Eden*, of which we read:

> In 1952 Steinbeck bared to the pitiless, white light of day the conduct
> and ethics of three generations in EAST OF EDEN. Now Steinbeck
> scrutinizes with an unsparing eye our careless ways with decency,
> honesty, loyalty, the moral slackness that besets the men and women
> of our country today, in THE WINTER OF OUR DISCONTENT. [17]

Ethan Allen Hawley is a troubled man. The namesake of an American
hero, Ethan Allen, he has a wife he dearly cares for, Mary, and two
children, Ellen and Allan. He works at a grocery store that his family
once owned, but that he lost ownership of. The novel begins in the third-
person point of view. A shift to first-person narrative in chapter 3 gives us
Ethan's restless musing. His wife, Mary, rests easy with life. If she
dreams, her dreams are ones that she does not remember. Ethan, however,
is troubled by life and haunted with anxiety. He leaves his bed and wanders out into the night to streets named High Street and Porlock Street.
The latter street name recalls Samuel Taylor Coleridge's preface to his
imaginative poem "Kubla Kahn," in which he says that the man from
Porlock knocked at his door and disturbed his dreamlike poetic reverie.
Porlock Street is a figure of stifled imagination and broken poetry. Its
fancy houses are the remnants of a time that is gone. Ethan walks past a
street that corresponds to his disrupted sleep and inability to dream or to
ground himself in sure values any longer. Porlock is a street of memory,
the location of grand pleasure-dome houses that were built in the heyday
of village whaling enterprises. "The tall fluted columns of Porlock Street"
are part of a dream and part of the American dream. Yet, like Coleridge's
fantasy, those vanished days cannot be retrieved.

Ethan Allen Hawley is an American Adam figure who faces temptations on Good Friday and succumbs to bewilderment by the Fourth of
July. Hawley's conventional morality is disrupted and he is challenged to
reorient his life. The novel shows his decline into self-interest and selfishness. His self-esteem rests upon showing his wife and family that he is a
success who can provide for them and regain his family pride. Unnerved
by recent events, unable to find grounding, Ethan has become restless,
unable to sleep at night. He says, "In the dark . . . I inquired of myself
what they used to call matters of conscience." [18] During the daytime
hours, into the grocery store he once owned where he is now a clerk,
comes Margie Young-Hunt, a temptress and manipulator, an alleged
witch and fortune-teller. Ethan's wife, Mary, will have dinner with her
and she will make her play for Ethan. He is also tempted by Mr. Baker,

the local banker, who wants him to make use of his wife's inheritance money. For Mr. Baker, business is "a kind of war."[19] He is superstitious, for he will never step on the crack in a sidewalk, and his world view is soon contrasted with the church of St. Thomas (named after the doubting apostle) and religious values.[20] His creed is "let progress reign," and his notion of progress is whatever will be to his benefit.[21] Along with Baker's shrewdness comes his misogyny and ethnic prejudice. He insists that business is a male realm: "Business is dull to ladies," he asserts.[22] He later comments: "There's too much petticoat in business these days."[23] He insists that women are consumers, not producers: "The spending habit is like a dope with some women."[24] In his view, women can be vampires. He advises Ethan about his wife: "Just let her taste blood and she'll turn killer."[25] His ethnic prejudice is obvious: "I don't like to see these foreigners creeping in."[26]

Joey Morphy, a friendly soul who works at the bank next door to the grocery store, often drops by for coffee. In casual conversation, he tells Ethan how someone who wishes to rob a bank should go about it. Apprised of what to do and what not to do, Ethan invents an elaborate scheme to rob the bank, complete with a broom and a toilet chain that will make it look like he is still in the grocery store. Perhaps more ludicrous is his plan to hide behind a Mickey Mouse mask.[27]

The grocery store is owned by Alfio Marullo, a Sicilian immigrant. We learn about his business practices: "Marullo did not reward for things past; he bribed for things to come."[28] Baker suggests that Ethan can get the store back again and restore his family's honor. Ethan will place a call to Immigration Services that will get Marullo, an illegal immigrant, deported. Ironically, Ethan learns that Marullo would give the store to him because Marullo has always regarded him as trustworthy and honest. Ethan realizes his desired gain: his dream to own the store again. However, he has compromised himself by betraying Marullo to the immigration authorities.

Ethan earnestly wants to help his friend Danny, who lives in a lean-to, but he ends up betraying him. The family property of Ethan's lifelong friend Danny Taylor is necessary to Mr. Baker and his cronies' airport designs. Danny was cast out of the Naval Academy and across the years has dissolved into alcoholism. Ethan ponders loyalty and fairness, his relationship with Danny in "the old days." Baker has his eyes on Taylor's property, the only level area in town where an airport can be built. He persuades Ethan to betray his friend. Evidently, several officials in town are in on the plans for the airport. In his observations of the town council and the town manager, Ethan sees men who seek material advantages rather than public servants who practice social responsibility. They are engaged in deals, and favors are done for favors. If the town government of New Baytown were ever investigated, a hundred legal misdemeanors would be found and one would discover "a thousand moral rules broken."[29] Yet for these officials to resume their lives would be like changing their shirts. So, given that, what if he were to simply suspend the rules for a moment: "Suppose for a limited time I abolished all the rules," he muses.[30]

Ethan Hawley interrogates matters of money and social standing. He reflects: "Money not only has no heart but no honor nor any memory."[31] He concludes: "It does not matter how you get it, as long as you get it and use it to get more."[32] The ancestors he has esteemed may have had strong values but they were also mercenary whalers and to the British they were pirates. They were men with "commissions to raid commerce in the revolution."[33] We have inherited also that nineteenth-century science "that denied existence to anything it could not measure or explain," Ethan comments.[34] "What a frightening thing is the human," Ethan Hawley later says, "a mass of gauges and dials and we can read only a few and those perhaps not accurately."[35] When he reflects upon morality, he assumes that it is relative: "If the laws of thinking are the laws of things, then morals are relative too."[36]

Sleepless, Ethan drifts from his home into the night and toward the shore. At home, his daughter Ellen is a sleepwalker and they both wonder at a family heirloom, a talisman that is kept in the home. There is in this a Jungian sense of a collective dream. Ethan is caught between the moral figure of Aunt Deborah and the temptations of material society, and he wonders which is wakefulness and which is sleep. "This secret and sleepless area in me I have always thought of as black, deep, waveless water, a spawning place from which only a few forms ever rise to the surface." Or perhaps, he thinks, it is "a great library where is recorded everything that has ever happened to living matter back to the first moment when it began to live."[37] He has been pushed out of his normal direction by experience. He has been a man "caged by habits and attitudes I thought of as being moral, even virtuous."[38] A great challenge to his life has come from the forces and temptations around him and now he must sort this out and take new action.

Ethan Hawley is a man caught by the anxiety of the atomic age who is trying to adjust. He says: "We had maybe half a million years to get used to fire and less than fifteen to build thinking about this force so extravagantly more fierce than fire."[39] In our new age, we face the shifting of the foundations. "What are morals? Are they simply words?" Ethan asks.

Words must also be authentic. Margie uses witch words of enchantment.[40] Baker uses terms that are deceptive. Words from Old English appear in Ethan's memory. He conjures goofy terms of endearment for his wife. Ethan's son Allen steals the words of Henry Clay for his prizewinning essay and throws in a little Jefferson and some Lincoln for good measure without citing any of them. He is pleased that he will be on TV and tells his father that he cannot work in the family grocery store or work for a living because he expects to get offers from all the television talk shows. A concerned and possibly embarrassed representative of the contest arrives in a car one night to have a conversation with Ethan, who then confronts his son about the plagiarism. Young Allen's response is: "Everybody does it."[41]

The Winter of Our Discontent is a potent critique that calls for ethical reasoning and responsibility on both personal and societal levels. It highlights the problems that may arise from moral compromises by American citizens and the public officials who serve as their political representatives. It raises the question of how we might fairly treat immigrants like Marullo who enter the United States illegally, seeking a better life. Perhaps Steinbeck would ask for a solution other than investigating and deporting everyone, or building an impregnable wall between the southern border of the United States and Mexico as some public figures today urge. His novel asks how we might care for people who have been hurt, or made bad choices, fallen into addiction, or who are down on their luck like Danny Taylor. The moral or ethical aspect of Steinbeck's work merits reiteration within the post-1968 context of poststructuralism and postmodernism because a flexible consideration of values continues to be highly relevant for individuals and societies. Robert Coles writes that "morality not only defines how we get along with one another and the rules of life; it characterizes our very nature. Morality has to do with human connection. It has to do with the kind of connection that responds to others, and in turn earns the caring response of others."[42]

LIFE AT SAG HARBOR

Steinbeck now wrote from his home on Long Island, to which he had moved in the late 1950s. While living in Sag Harbor, from about 1956 through the 1960s, he contributed many short articles and essays to popular periodicals and newspapers. For the *Saturday Review* he was "editor-at-large." There were pieces for *Esquire*, *Sports Illustrated*, *Argosy*, *Photography*, and many other magazines, and a piece for a Ringling Brothers circus program. He wrote for *Le Figaro* in Paris and *Punch* in London.

In "Conversation at Sag Harbor," which appeared in *Holiday*, a conversation between his sons turns to popular music and payola. I don't know if it is against the law, says The Fly, "but it is said to be immoral." Tingler replies, "People buy what they hear. It's not [what's] good but what gets played."[43] The conversation seems to date from the time of disc jockey Alan Freed, many years before Billy Joel crossed Long Island with music that both was good and got played. A recording of the Benny Goodman Carnegie Hall concert is played loudly.

At Sag Harbor, writes Dan Rattiner, "most people left John Steinbeck alone. He'd get mail at the post office, eat at the Paradise Restaurant with Elaine or one of his friends, get the morning paper at the Ideal Stationery Store three doors down and walk home."[44] Rattiner offers his recollection of a plan to have Steinbeck as honorary chair of the Old Whaler's Festival scheduled for the end of August 1963. In the parade Steinbeck sat on the back of a convertible waving to the crowd.[45] The Old Whaler's Festival may have been a bit of an anomaly for Steinbeck, who kept a low profile in Sag Harbor. Rattiner's account begins with spring 1963, a time when, he says, the town of Sag Harbor was not in good shape. Some downtown businesses had closed and some houses were unoccupied. The Old Whaler's Festival emerged as an idea to try to revivify the town based upon its heritage. He describes a day on which American flags hung in some windows and pennants flew like those at a gas station opening. The town created "Old Whalers" T-shirts and people wandered around to hear concerts or to dance, to see the results of a beard-growing contest, to hear a reading from *Moby-Dick*, or to watch a re-creation of the nighttime Meigs' Raid by patriots from Connecticut who came to surprise the British camped at Sag Harbor. There was a chili-making contest and a costume party with pirates, whalers, and Indians, and there was John Steinbeck on the back of a convertible rolling down Main Street. The road curved from Long Wharf to the Presbyterian church and the parade came down the street led by the Pierson High School Marching Band and its baton twirlers.

AMERICA AND AMERICANS

John and Elaine Steinbeck were sitting at home in Sag Harbor, Long Island, on October 25, 1962, listening to news about the Cuban missile crisis, when Steinbeck learned that he had been awarded the Nobel Prize. His Nobel Prize acceptance speech on December 10, 1962, became an opportunity for him to voice his concern for the future and to express his creed as a writer. The award, he said, was for the increased "understanding and communication" among humanity that is literature's purpose. He spoke of the duty to seek perfection. Recalling Alfred Nobel's development of dynamite he contemplated the possibilities of "explosive forces capable of creative good or of destructive evil" and how humanity today faces the responsibility for how such "Godlike power" will be approached. He said that "the writer is delegated to declare and to celebrate man's proven capacity for greatness of heart and spirit—for gallantry in defeat, for courage, compassion and love." Yet the writer also exposes our faults, seeks improvement, and stands for our hope.[46]

John Steinbeck was in the midst of again applying this prophetic sense of purpose in his writing. In August 1964, Steinbeck was invited by Thomas H. Guinzburg to write an introduction for a book of photographs showing scenes from across America. Guinzburg brought photographs of America to Steinbeck, suggesting that he might write captions for them. Steinbeck began writing a series of essays that applauded the spirit of Americans and attempted to dissect and critique materialist greed, dishonesty, and other social problems. The essays would later become *America and Americans*.[47] Steinbeck presents his opinions and urges an appreciation of America's diversity while making some generalizations about it. "E Pluribus Unum" addresses this diversity, observing the many European immigrants who have become part of America. In "Paradox and Dream," he discusses the apparent contradictions of Americans. In "Created Equal," he launches into a discussion of civil rights. "Genus Americanus," which follows, rejects the idea of a classless society and opposes conformity. Steinbeck then expresses concern about the environment. In three more essays he looks at the world and the future.

In the essays of *America and Americans* (1966) Steinbeck spoke clearly, in his own voice, about the plurality and variety of images that made up America. He also voiced concern for preservation of the environment and "evils that can and must be overcome if America and Americans are to survive."[48] This jeremiad may be difficult to swallow for readers who are more accustomed to Steinbeck's fiction. Yet there is another difference from much of his other writing that is present in his text for *America and Americans*. In much of his work, Steinbeck strived for an objective tone. His work was largely about seeing things clearly and humanly, depicting common folks, and evoking a sense of place. Now he was writing passionate criticism with cranky idealism. He was interpreting America in opinion pieces that sometimes seem to have more guts than grace. He wrote, "This is a book of opinions, unashamed and individual."[49] As Shillinglaw and Benson point out, perhaps in his efforts "to locate the source of America malaise" he was unable to find the right tone or form to convey his ideas.[50] Overall, as they note, the essays lack humor, plot, and character. This is so despite occasional anecdotes that illustrate his points or lighten up our reading experience. His essay "Americans and the Future" is at times irritatingly blunt, alternating a griping and sour tone with a hopeful and determined one. He perceives trends through the lens of considerable concern but he often engages in generalities without providing demonstrable data or specific analysis. Indeed, these essays are "impassioned pleas from a man who cared deeply about his country."[51] Like the pronouncements of the Biblical prophets their urgency is surely intended to be disturbing. They are a wake-up call to America.

There is, perhaps unfortunately, a grain of truth to critiques like this. When sociologists such as Robert N. Bellah and his associates wrote of the loss of civic participation, when Robert Putnam argued that we are "bowling alone," when Christopher Lasch pointed to narcissism in the 1970s, or when M. Scott Peck argued for community or for greater civility in American life, they were on track with some features of America that warrant our attention.[52] Likewise, Steinbeck is not merely an angry pessimist; he remains hopeful about America's future. Steinbeck, who held ethical values of honor, duty, and courage that are consistent with those of the Knights of the Round Table, is decidedly concerned about retaining "gallantry" and honesty in American society. However, in these essays he is quite direct in his criticisms. "I strongly suspect that our moral and spiritual disintegration grows out of our lack of experience with plenty," he writes. To have our lives focused upon things promotes acquisitive behavior.[53] "We are poisoned with things. . . . We are trapped and entangled in things," he tells us. We cannot live fully with compromised values.[54]

The ethical call of Steinbeck in his essays in *America and Americans* John H. Timmerman sees as a criticism of "failure in regard to the environment" and "a failure in understanding and sympathy" that urges a new "positioning of the heart in regard to other living things."[55] People have "abandoned their knowledge of kindness to the land in order to maintain its usefulness."[56] Timmerman cites the land use ethic in interchapter 25 of *The Grapes of Wrath*: the fecundity of the green hills and the California valleys, the plentiful abundance that the Joads will not participate in.[57] Steinbeck's ethics, Timmerman points out, extends across *Travels with Charley*, in Steinbeck's descriptions of the Arizona desert and in his experience of civil strife in New Orleans.[58] Clearly, the essay "Americans and the Land" highlights his earth ethic.

The ecological criticism Steinbeck develops in *America and Americans* presents an urgent appeal for change. His argument is exactly like that of Thomas Berry in his numerous essays: the priorities of industrial economy are pillaging the earth's resources and undermining the sacredness of the human–earth relationship.[59] At present, Steinbeck writes, some Americans are still "stealing from the future for our clear and present profit."[60] The faults are named as thoughtlessness, lack of respect and reverence, and "the conviction that sky and water are unowned and that they are limitless."[61] He integrates history into his discussion, starting with East Coast settlements, efforts at protection, movements toward trade, suspicion of Native American Indians, and wonder at "an unknown land extending nobody knew how far."[62] He observes that Americans were travelers, "with little idea of permanence," who began to settle the West in a bountiful land. However, many were utilitarian, pragmatic, or "land hungry." They abandoned kindness and focused upon usefulness. He writes: "The merciless nineteenth century was like a hostile expedition for loot that seemed limitless."[63]

He tells the story of how he walked with "awe and humility" through an area of redwoods as a child—mighty, ancient trees in the midst of which "the light colored as though the great glass of the Cathedral at Chartres had strained and sanctified the sunlight."[64] A man bought up the land and cut down the trees. After that they "looked away" as he passed by because they "were ashamed for him."[65]

That dismay and shaking of his head at destruction extends to an obvious concern for preservation. "Conservation came to us slowly, and much of it hasn't arrived yet," he writes. America has set aside the great national and state park areas and preserved the "fantastic accidents of nature like the Grand Canyon and Yosemite and Yellowstone Park."[66] Yet, for all our appreciation of these natural wonders and our increased sense that what Steinbeck calls "this slow and sullen poisoning is no longer ignored or justified," we still are confronted with ecological concerns. Steinbeck writes: "All these evils can and must be overcome if America and Americans are to survive."[67] He affirms that Americans are "an exuberant people" but challenges Americans to not be "careless and destructive."[68] The man who cut down the redwoods is implicitly linked with those who made use of the atom bomb "under the pressure of war." The reasons for its use "seemed justifiable at the time" when it was unleashed on two Japanese cities, he writes. "I think we frightened ourselves." He adds that he knew nothing about the bomb and had nothing to do with it being used but that he feels "horrified and ashamed" and that those who justify its use on Hiroshima and Nagasaki "must be the most ashamed of all."[69]

Steinbeck was interested in science and he was fascinated by technology but he was concerned about nuclear arms and the arms race. He favored pure science and innovation but was thoroughly opposed to callous disregard for people or destruction of innocent human life or nature, under any circumstances. Steinbeck did believe firmly in fighting just wars strategically. While he rejected atomic warfare and a man's desecration of the redwood trees, he was not averse to a concerted bombing campaign in North Vietnam during the Vietnam War. He valued the soldier who was fighting for a cause and through much of the 1960s he believed that America's cause in Vietnam was a just one. It was only after his own visit there that he began to ask difficult questions about this.

He continued to believe that exploration would open new possibilities. In September 1966 in *Popular Science*, Steinbeck called for an underwater exploration program similar to NASA. To editor Ernest Heyn he wrote about the value of investigating the "inner space" of our own planet. His studies of marine biology and personal experience of Monterey and the Sea of Cortez lay behind his concern. "I know enough about the sea to know how pitifully little we know about it," he wrote. He assured readers that he was just as interested in space exploration. "There is something for everyone in the sea," he wrote: "food for the hungry . . . incalculable wealth . . . the excitement and danger of exploration."[70]

Purpose and direction are what America needs, Steinbeck asserts. "The roads of the past have come to an end and we have not yet discovered a path to the future," he writes. However, that path is possible, although "it may be unthinkable to us now."[71] Americans do not sit still and in an era of "perplexing" transition "we are running."[72] In the closing peroration of his book he affirms that hope for America's future lives in the "negation of these symptoms," the overcoming of simple "comfort, plenty, and security," which lead to cynicism, and in a reassertion of a sense of "poetry" and purpose. Finally, he implies that how America and Americans respond will have implications for the world. That response begins in the heart, mind, and ethical compass of an individual. "Here is a world or universe unknown, even un-conceived of, and perhaps at last open for exploration: the great and mysterious mind and soul of man, a land of marvels."[73]

"LETTERS TO ALICIA" AND WRITING FOR L.B.J.

Steinbeck's gaze into the future caused him to sharpen his pencils again. In *Newsday* he wrote two series of "Letters to Alicia," which ranged across a wide variety of issues, including the war in Vietnam. Steinbeck's columns were addressed to Alicia Patterson, Harry F. Guggenheim's wife, who had died three years before. This epistolary form enabled him to develop a voice that, in speaking to this founder of *Newsday*, spoke to his own readers. Indeed, one of Steinbeck's methods of writing across previous years was to imagine that he was writing to his friend Ed Ricketts. His "Letters to Alicia" built upon that familiar device. We see his photo over his column: he wears a suit and tie and looks off to our left.

The "Letters to Alicia" series began with Steinbeck's reflections on government support for the arts. The Johnson administration had recently founded the National Foundation for the Arts. Steinbeck concluded that having government strings attached to funding would not be helpful to

the arts in America. His second letter concerned an Eric Sevareid comment about Adlai Stevenson. In his third letter, he responded to Max
Lerner's question in the *New York Post*: Why was he writing a column in
Newsday? He recalled his pieces for *Le Figaro* in France. In his fourth
letter he said he had been an advisor to four presidents—Roosevelt, Truman, Kennedy, and Johnson—although this was a large claim. He offered
advice to them but noted that he "could find no evidence that they ever
took any of it." The record suggests that Roosevelt or Kennedy had not
paid much attention to him and there has been no published evidence to
date that he worked directly with Truman. He did become friendly with
President Johnson, whose wife had been in college in Texas with Elaine
Steinbeck.

Steinbeck's association with Lyndon Baines Johnson led to his involvement as an occasional speech writer, or political wordsmith. The
1964 Democratic platform was sent to Steinbeck for improvements to its
language and phrasing. On August 12, 1964, he wrote to Johnson aide
Jack Valenti that he had changed the beginning and the ending of the
document, for these were two places where emotion could be added.[74] In
a telephone call with President Johnson they discussed the subject of his
attendance at the Democratic Convention. The president requested Steinbeck's further assistance with speeches. Jack Valenti would make travel
arrangements for Steinbeck.[75] Steinbeck was flown to Washington for a
stay during which he could refine the documents.

For the inauguration of Lyndon Baines Johnson, staff member Eric
Goldman suggested "a prose poem on the theme of the meaning of
American experience written by John Steinbeck." Steinbeck sent his copy
from Dublin, where he was staying with Elaine. Goldman sent it by
courier to the Johnson ranch and says that Johnson replied to it: "It's too
good—it will upstage my speech." After the speech-writing team had set
aside a draft by Bill Moyers, Richard Goodwin, another Johnson speech
writer, wrote the inaugural address. Then Jack Valenti and Joseph Califano went over it further. A few of the lines from Steinbeck were incorporated into Johnson's address, which he presented from the front east end
of the Capitol on January 20, 1965. Goldman points to "an almost verba-
tim section, one of the more routine of Steinbeck's passages, which
proved to be the most quoted part of the President's speech": "I do not
believe that the Great Society is the ordered, changeless, and sterile battalion of the ants. It is the excitement of becoming—always becoming,

trying, probing, failing, resting, and trying again—but always trying and always gaining."[76]

What echoed as a vital hope within Steinbeck was Johnson's intention to respond to civil rights, to provide women their rightful share, and to assist the poor in America. Steinbeck supported the Johnson administration's domestic programs and overseas policy at a time when many Americans distrusted the president and had become opposed to American involvement in Vietnam. His allegiance to the president and the administration's goals did not always sit well with some Americans who opposed the president's policies. However, Steinbeck firmly maintained his personal support.

Johnson's inaugural address has been characterized as a jeremiad: a call to action and a sermon to "get right with God."[77] Americans had a destiny and a responsibility to reform society and to create change. This parallels Steinbeck's tone and stance at this time. Robert Bellah's essay on civil religion in 1967 quotes from Johnson's inaugural address and he cites Washington, Jefferson, Lincoln, and Kennedy. Johnson drew upon Steinbeck's words that "this generation" should be challenged to rely on "the unchanged character of our people and their faith. They came here— the exile and the stranger, brave but frightened—to find a place where a man could be his own man. They made a covenant with this land."[78]

On March 17, 1965, Steinbeck wrote to Lyndon Johnson following his March 15 message to Congress concerning the Voting Rights Act. This was during the period of the activist march from Selma to Montgomery. He called this a historic speech. He begins with the testament of a writer to the power of language: "Always there have been men who have had contempt for the word, although words have served better than any other man-made things. When you have finished using a weapon someone is dead or injured but the product of the word can be life and hope and survival. . . . In our history there have been not more than five or six moments when the word and the determination mapped the course of the future. Such a moment, Sir, was your speech to the Congress two nights ago. Our people will be living by phrases from that speech when all the concrete and steel have long been displaced or destroyed."[79]

STEINBECK IN VIETNAM

John Steinbeck was always a man who wanted to see things for himself and that was no less true when it came to the war in Vietnam. He had seen World War II as a correspondent in Europe. Now he made up his mind to go to Vietnam. President Johnson offered him that opportunity.

In a photo, we can see Steinbeck seated in a helicopter that flew above the central Vietnam highlands. The helicopter was a Bell UH-1 "Iroquois." He wears a headset and has a bit of squint in his eyes as he looks over the landscape. He has a watch on his wrist. Steinbeck was supportive of the American initiative in Vietnam before and throughout the time that he was there. In his final months he had begun to question the legitimacy of the war. However, he was always supportive of the men and women who had fought in Vietnam.

Steinbeck provides descriptions of the landscape, night combat, flares he sees and artillery he hears from the Caravelle Hotel in Saigon. He writes of the bravery of helicopter pilots and of problems with the water, with malaria, or with trip-wire explosives. He is critical of war protesters at home in the United States and he is supportive of the soldiers. His interest in the military goes back to his time as a war correspondent in World War II.

On January 7, 1967, he writes that the central highlands of Vietnam remind him of the Texas Panhandle. "Where do we get our impressions of the places we have never seen?" he writes. From Pleiku he writes about the incentive of local people who sell things to the soldiers and other customers. They have set up laundries, bars, and little stores and they wash cars and bicycles. At the makeshift laundries, army fatigues are draped over barbed wire. From Saigon on January 16, 1967, he writes of the complexity of the war. "This war in Vietnam is very confusing not only to old war watchers but to people at home who read and try to understand." Past wars, he says, were easier to report. There were clear troop lines and demarcations of battle. Big battles could be "reported like a bull fight." Vietnam could not be defined in the same way. Reporters there recognized this but their readers demanded clarity, so they tried to describe the war to them. "It's a feeling war with no front and no rear," Steinbeck writes. "It is everywhere like a thin ever-present gas."[80] Saigon, he writes, looks like a well-tailored suit that now is sagging. "And the war is here . . . always present," he says. His wife Elaine is as much in danger around the hotel in Saigon as he is when he goes to the country-side with the military. "This war is not like any other we have ever been involved in," he writes. [81]

There was political backlash against Steinbeck for his support of L.B.J. In his support of the Vietnam War he was also supporting his sons, who each served in the military. Their involvement "added to the complexity of the war for him," Mimi R. Gladstein and James Meredith point out. [82] His support of U.S. policy there seemed to some on the left to be inconsistent with his views in his earlier novels. Of course, this had much to do with their own interpretations. Steinbeck held traditional values and among these was a notion of honor and respect and support for America. Shillinglaw and Benson write that "he wanted to be involved, to offer advice, and to cultivate what was for him the highest calling of an artist—helping people understand one another." [83] Gladstein and Meredith say: "He believed in being actively engaged in the service of his country and democracy." [84]

In a letter to his son John IV, John Steinbeck recalled some of his first thoughts while in Europe as a World War II correspondent: "What the hell am I doing here?" He says that he developed "some kind of built-in anesthesia" to his surroundings and was glad that he had gone there. [85] He had earlier written: "No one, least of all themselves, knows what they will do when the terrible thing happens. No man there knows whether he can take it, knows whether he will run away or stick, or lose his nerve and go to pieces, or will be a good soldier." [86]

John IV wrote about his experiences in Vietnam. His father had been with the World War II military unit that landed in Italy on the island of Ventotene near Salerno. John IV was serving in the TV detachment Number 3. For him Vietnam was "a spiritual concussion grenade." [87] He had entered military service with high ideals, his "daring dreams." [88] He had also viewed his entry into the army as a way to get away from his family life and to explore something new. In retrospect he wrote: "I even became convinced that the war might help me where I couldn't help myself." [89]

The Steinbecks had become close to the Johnson family. Indeed, the Steinbecks are in two of Mrs. Johnson's home movies with friends at Camp David, in 1965 and 1967. John Steinbeck and his son met with President Johnson at the White House by invitation prior to John IV's deployment to Vietnam. President Johnson directed a memo to John

Steinbeck on June 21, 1966. It was mailed to Steinbeck in Sag Harbor, New York, by special delivery on June 24:

> Dear John, Your visits and your letters never fail to refresh me.
>
> I was delighted to meet your son and share your pride in him. He is a Steinbeck through and through, perhaps the greatest of the many gifts you have given this grateful nation. I shall pray for his safe and swift return.[90]

On December 4, 1966, Johnson called John Steinbeck to discuss his trip with Elaine Steinbeck to Vietnam. He mentioned Steinbeck's son, who was in military service. Steinbeck asked about signs of progress in Vietnam. Johnson asked him to be careful while he was there ("Don't be too adventuresome") and he asked to meet with him when he came back home.[91]

The World War II correspondence of John Steinbeck was collected enthusiastically by his editor Pat Covici in *Once There Was a War*. There has been less enthusiasm about collecting Steinbeck's Vietnam dispatches, although a book of them has recently been issued by the University of Virginia Press. Part of the reason for the low profile of the Vietnam dispatches was concern that they might affect Steinbeck's reputation. The war has often been a contentious topic and issue. Steinbeck supported the foreign policy of his friend the president, Lyndon Johnson, whose Great Society goals he admired. However, Steinbeck's position is understandable. As a parent he stood behind his sons who served in the military and he was always supportive of the soldiers who fought in Vietnam. The war was controversial and the reports from overseas were endlessly disturbing. Steinbeck's position was not aligned with the politics of the Left. He believed in responsibility and in accountability, in standing against Communism and for democracy and individuality, and he did not hesitate to express his views.

Steinbeck had seen and known the soldiers of World War II and he respected them. He continued to have the utmost respect for the soldier in Vietnam. He had a fascination with guns, weaponry, and military technology and with military history, but he did not like war in the least. What he did believe in was patriotism, honor, and standing up for what one believes in. Perhaps there was indeed that integrity in some protestors against the war. However, in protestors he sometimes saw something like

John Osborne's angry young man in the British theater: a James Dean figure of reaction rather than action. He told an interviewer that this angry young man is "against but not toward something. He's against things but not for things."[92] In one of his "Letters to Alicia" he wrote: "But would they enlist for medical service? . . . If they love people so much, why are they not willing to help save them?" A real protest against war might involve "carrying bedpans and cleaning infected wounds."[93]

The second series of "Letters to Alicia" included his letters about Vietnam. He describes his visit as a witness to the "drifting phantasm of war" (January 14, 1967). He flew on a helicopter with the Tenth Cavalry. He went down the Bassac River on Patrol Boat 37 and drew enemy fire on his way back from Tan An. He thoroughly rejected Communism and believed that China and the Soviet Union were supplying arms to North Vietnam. Only later, after his visit to Vietnam, did he come to question the war and wonder if the U.S. presence was not an intrusion upon a foreign people in their civil war. His reservations about the war grew during his last years, when he was too weakened by illness to write much about them. This is reflected in comments he made in private rather than in public forums. In a letter to Harry Guggenheim he argued that there had never been clarity about the war: "A lack of clarity has made people wonder exactly what our policy is."[94] He wrote to Jack Valenti: "There is no way to make the Vietnamese War decent. There is no way of justifying sending troops to another man's country."[95]

Steinbeck held traditional values, as Gladstein and Meredith point out: "a sensibility both romantic and realistic." He was a man who expressed "his sense of fairness and sympathy for oppressed people" and his "disdain for communism."[96] The war caused him anguish. He died at the end of 1968 and he did not see the further progress of the war and was never fully able to finish his thoughts about it.

President Johnson's final tribute to John Steinbeck came the day after Steinbeck's death:

> John Steinbeck was a man who had two abiding passions—a love of people and a hatred of injustice—and he fashioned these feelings into some of the most memorable books of our time. He was a uniquely American writer.[97]

WORLD CITIZEN

John Steinbeck was truly a world citizen and his writings help us to make better sense of the human condition. During his lifetime he visited places as far-flung as Norway, Germany, Ireland, Great Britain, Russia and Eastern Europe, Thailand, and Vietnam. His fiction, which is distributed widely, has had broad impact on readers throughout the world, from Europe to Latin America to East Asia. The presence of Steinbeck's novels in schools, in libraries, and in adaptation on the screen remains a valuable resource for us in the twenty-first century. "He was not a philosopher, but he was always a man of ideas," Jackson J. Benson has pointed out. Steinbeck was a rationalist with "mystical currents of feeling." The ethics we discover in Steinbeck's work are an interesting synthesis of virtue ethics and a Kantian sense of duty. To the end he held values rooted in the Western tradition and regarded the code of chivalry of King Arthur's knights as relevant for our own time. "Working on the Malory is a thing of great joy to me, like coming home," he wrote in January 1957.[98]

The stories of John Steinbeck and the human values that they convey continue to have an international presence and importance. Stories like his help us to see each other, to deepen our empathy. The stories of John Steinbeck challenge us to commitment, to care, and to integrity. For now we live virtually as well as geographically. We Google facts, send messages, and record our stories in photos and brief exchanges on the Internet. People continually are in contact with this diversity of expression and opinion in a social space that has fewer boundaries than in the past.[99] In this convergence of cultures, Steinbeck's stories of dreamers—paisanos like Danny and Pilon, farm workers like Lennie and George, strikers like Mac and Jim Nolan—offer us personalities, scenes, and issues that open our awareness to the hopes and needs of our common humanity. The global electronic world of e-books, television, and film allows us to see and identify with people who may be far from us, to empathize and respond with care. Steinbeck's stories provide scenes of human conflict and images of acts of compassion. They raise for us questions of social trust and tolerance. Reading fiction like his helps us to be open to others, to reject the actions of those who would damage our communities, and to identify through empathy with people whose lives may be quite different from our own. That is the quality of care that this tough yet gentle man, this committed artist, has left as his legacy: the work that contributes to "making people understand each other." [100]

NOTES

INTRODUCTION

1. John Steinbeck, *America and Americans and Selected Nonfiction*, ed. Susan Shillinglaw and Jackson J. Benson. New York: Viking, 2002, p. 142.

2. John Steinbeck, "The Pursuit of Happiness," *America and Americans and Selected Nonfiction*, p. 375.

3. John Steinbeck, *Working Days*, ed. Robert DeMott. New York: Viking, 1990, p. xl; Warren French, *John Steinbeck's Nonfiction Revisited*. New York: Twayne, 1996, p. 114. See Jackson J. Benson, *The True Adventures of John Steinbeck, Writer*. New York: Viking, 1984, p. 985.

4. Stephen K. George, "Steinbeck's Happy Hookers" (38–48), *Steinbeck's Women*, ed. Tetsamuro Hayashi. Muncie, IN: Steinbeck Society of America, 1979, p. 1. See also Stephen K. George, *The Moral Philosophy of John Steinbeck*. Lanham, MD: Scarecrow, 2005. Steinbeck sought community in America, observed playwright Arthur Miller. He hoped for a connection with people "toward which he could react in a feeling way." Quoted in French, *John Steinbeck's Nonfiction Revisited*, p. 80.

5. Susan Shillinglaw and Nancy Burnett (photographer), *A Journey into Steinbeck's California*. Berkeley, CA: Roaring Forties Press, 2011, p. 111.

6. Richard Corliss, "We're the People: John Ford's *The Grapes of Wrath* at 75," *New York Times* (January 24, 2015).

7. Robert Gottlieb (April 17, 2008) also wrote in the *New York Times* on the occasion of the fourth Steinbeck volume in the Library of America series.

8. John Steinbeck quoted in Robert DeMott, *Working Days*. New York: Viking, 1990, p. 320, caption.

9. Steinbeck quoted in DeMott, *Working Days*, p. 338.

10. Benson, *The True Adventures of John Steinbeck, Writer*, p. 107.

11. Susan Shillinglaw, introduction, *The Portable John Steinbeck*. New York: Penguin, 2012, p. 11.

12. Jackson J. Benson, "The Favorite Author We Love to Hate," *John Steinbeck, Critical Insights*, ed. Don Noble. Pasadena, CA: Salem Press, 2011, p. 95.

13. Benson, "The Favorite," p. 97.

14. Benson, "The Favorite," p. 98. Benson cites *The Literary History of the United States*, ed. Blair, Hornberger, Miller, and Stewart.

15. Michael J. Sandel, *Democracy's Discontent: America in Search of a Public Philosophy*. Cambridge, MA: Belknap Press of Harvard University Press, 1996.

16. Benson, "The Favorite," p. 102.

17. Jackson J. Benson refers us to Frank Kermode's distinction between two types of classic works of literature: "the work that encapsulates an era and thus allows us to reenter it mentally and the work that states our basic humanity so well as to triumph over time and space" (Kermode, *The Classic: Literary Images of Permanence and Change*. Cambridge: Harvard University Press, 1983, pp. 43–44, 130).

18. Terry Eagleton, *Literary Theory: An Introduction*. Minneapolis: University of Minnesota Press, 1983, p. 44.

19. John Ditsky has said that his generation did not assume that the late 1940s was a point of decline for Steinbeck's work. They had read *The Grapes of Wrath* and they worked backward from *The Winter of Our Discontent* and *East of Eden*. See *John Steinbeck and the Critics* (2000), p. 9. Ditsky says that earlier Steinbeck critics like Peter Lisca did not see that Steinbeck had forged a new path for his fiction with *East of Eden* and subsequent novels (Ditsky p. 10). However, he observes that with Lisca's *The Wide World of John Steinbeck* (1958) "the days when John Steinbeck was at the mercy of newspaper and magazine critics had ended" (p. 7). Lisca subtitled the introduction to his book "The Failure of Criticism" and opposed the views of Maxwell Geismar, Frederick J. Hoffman, and other critics who rejected Steinbeck for being a proletarian writer. Lisca's work was grounded in New Critical approaches and Ditsky regards both Lisca and Warren French as "pioneers" of Steinbeck criticism in the mid- to late twentieth century. Ditsky disagrees with French's "decline" thesis. Steinbeck, he says, did not so much decline as experiment with different modes of writing.

20. Harold Bloom excludes Steinbeck from the literary canon, although he is not hesitant to include Steinbeck repeatedly in his series of books for Chelsea House/Infobase: *John Steinbeck* (Bloom's Major Novelists), Bloom's Biocritiques, Modern Critical Views, Major Short Story Writers, *Bloom's How to Write about John Steinbeck*, *The Grapes of Wrath*, and *Of Mice and Men*. The result is collections of essays that are valuable for teachers and for students. However,

that does not change Professor Bloom's notions about Steinbeck, who, in his view, falls short of the benchmarks of literary quality.

21. Susan Shillinglaw, "Steinbeck and Ethnicity," *Critical Insights: John Steinbeck*, ed. Don Noble. Pasadena, CA: Salem Press, 2011, p. 255.

22. In his *Sea of Cortez*, Steinbeck reflects upon collective instincts, a "rhythm sense or memory which affects everything" (p. 34). See Peter Lisca, *John Steinbeck: Nature and Myth*, New York: Thomas Y. Crowell, 1978. As John Seelye points out in Noble's *Critical Insights*, "Chance is the factor that rules all his fictions" (p. 164).

23. These stories are viewed by Warren French as interrelated. See *John Steinbeck's Fiction Revisited*. New York: Twayne, 1994. See also French in "Steinbeck's 'Self Characters' as 1930s Underdogs," *Critical Insights: John Steinbeck* (Noble). The stories emerge from Steinbeck's work between 1935 and 1937 and immediately precede his attention to the migrants of *The Grapes of Wrath*.

24. Robert DeMott, *Steinbeck's Typewriter: Essays on His Art*. Troy, NY: Whitston, 1996.

25. John Steinbeck quoted in Benson, *The True Adventures of John Steinbeck, Writer*, p. 376.

26. Warren French, *John Steinbeck's Fiction Revisited*. Boston: Twayne, 1994, p. 198.

27. John Steinbeck, *A Russian Journal*. New York: Viking, 1948, p. 25.

28. Karl Beckson, ed., *Oscar Wilde: The Critical Heritage*. London: Routledge, 1974.

29. Ethical predicates change over time. History, culture, gender, race, class, and circumstances may all play a role in how we evaluate the good. The moral fiction of F. R. Leavis may be held to have issued from a white, male, middle-class or upper-class privileged perspective. However, the position taken here is that there can exist an ethical hermeneutics after postmodern literary theory.

30. For a thoughtful approach to this see Daniel R. Schwarz's essay "A Humanistic Ethics of Reading" in *Mapping the Ethical Turn: A Reader in Ethics, Culture, and Literary Theory*, ed. Todd F. Davis and Kenneth Womack. Charlottesville: University Press of Virginia, 2001, pp. 3–15.

31. Steve Brie and William T. Rossiter, eds., *Literature and Ethics: From the Green Knight to the Dark Knight*. Newcastle-on-Tyne: Cambridge Scholars Publishing, 2010, p. 12.

32. Wayne C. Booth, *The Company We Keep: An Ethics of Fiction*. Berkeley: University of California Press, 1989, pp. 131–132.

33. J. Hillis Miller, "How to Be 'in Tune with the Right' in *The Golden Bowl*," *Mapping the Ethical Turn* (Davis and Womack), p. 271.

34. Wayne C. Booth, "Why Ethical Criticism Can Never Be Simple," *Mapping the Ethical Turn* (Davis and Womack), pp. 20, 26.

35. Booth, "Why Ethical Criticism Can Never Be Simple," pp. 18–19.

36. Booth, "Why Ethical Criticism Can Never Be Simple," p. 20.

37. Aldo Leopold, *A Sand County Almanac and Sketches Here and There* (1949). New York and Oxford: Oxford University Press, 1989, pp. 224–225.

38. Richard A. Posner, "Against Ethical Criticism," *Ethics, Literature and Theory: An Introductory Reader*, ed. Stephen K. George. Lanham, MD: Rowman & Littlefield, 2005, p. 64

39. Oscar Wilde's comment appears in his preface to *The Picture of Dorian Gray* (London, 1891). John Gardner, *On Moral Fiction*. New York: Basic Books, 1978; Martha Nussbaum, *Poetic Justice: The Literary Imagination and Public Life*. Boston: Beacon Press, 1995; Richard Rorty, *Contingency, Irony and Solidarity*. Cambridge: Cambridge University Press, 1989.

40. Carol Gilligan, *In a Different Voice*. Harvard University Press, p. 170.

41. The ethics of care has been discussed by Nel Noddings, *Caring: A Feminine Approach to Moral Education*. Berkeley: University of California Press, 1984; Virginia Held, *Ethics of Care*. Oxford: Oxford University Press, 2006; Joan Tronto, "An Ethic of Care," *Feminist Theory: A Philosophical Anthology*, ed. Ann Cudd and Robin O. Andreasen. Oxford: Blackwell, 2005, pp. 251–263.

42. Booth, "Why Ethical Criticism Can Never Be Simple," p. 23.

43. Booth, "Why Ethical Criticism Can Never Be Simple," p. 25.

44. Booth, "Why Ethical Criticism Can Never Be Simple," p. 26.

45. Charles Altieri, "Lyrical Ethics and Literary Experience," *Mapping the Ethical Turn* (Davis and Womack), p. 31.

46. Gardner, *On Moral Fiction*, p. 18.

47. Gardner, *On Moral Fiction*, p. 17.

48. Gardner, *On Moral Fiction*, p. 27.

49. John Steinbeck, Nobel Prize acceptance speech, *America and Americans and Selected Nonfiction*, pp. 172–174.

50. Steinbeck, *America and Americans and Selected Nonfiction*, p. 15.

51. Susan Shillinglaw, "Steinbeck and Ethnicity," *Critical Insights: John Steinbeck* (Noble), p. 253.

52. Shillinglaw, "Steinbeck and Ethnicity," pp. 252–274.

53. Jackson J. Benson, ed., *The Short Novels of John Steinbeck: Critical Essays with a Checklist to Steinbeck Criticism*. Durham, NC: Duke University Press, 1990, p. 8.

54. Benson, *The Short Novels of John Steinbeck*, p. 7. See the introduction (pp. 6–8) for reflections like these. Benson argues that central to Steinbeck is a concept of "acceptance." One ought to accept others and look at what "is" and accept what "is."

55. Benson, *The Short Novels of John Steinbeck*, p. 8.
56. Benson, *The Short Novels of John Steinbeck*, p. 8.
57. French, *John Steinbeck's Fiction Revisited*, p. 31.
58. French, *John Steinbeck's Fiction Revisited*, pp. 31–32.
59. French, *John Steinbeck's Fiction Revisited*, p. 32.
60. French, *John Steinbeck's Fiction Revisited*, p. 34.

1. THE LIFE OF JOHN STEINBECK

1. John Steinbeck, *Steinbeck: A Life in Letters*, ed. Elaine Steinbeck and Robert Wallsten. New York: Viking Press, 1975, p. 71. For further details on Steinbeck's life consult Jackson J. Benson's superb biography, *The True Adventures of John Steinbeck, Writer*. New York: Viking, 1984.

2. See Jackson J. Benson, *The True Adventures of John Steinbeck. Writer*. New York: Penguin, 1990.

3. Steinbeck (December 1930), *Steinbeck: A Life in Letters*, p. 30.

4. John Steinbeck discusses his friend in "About Ed Ricketts," his preface to *The Log from the Sea of Cortez* in *John Steinbeck:* The Grapes of Wrath *and Other Writings 1936–1941*, ed. Robert DeMott and Elaine Steinbeck. New York: Library of America, 1996, pp. 697–750.

5. See Steinbeck, letter to Carlton Sheffield (June 21, 1933), *Steinbeck: A Life in Letters*, pp. 69–72.

6. See Steinbeck, *Steinbeck: A Life in Letters*, pp. 174–175, 181–182.

7. During the casting of *The Grapes of Wrath* film, Steinbeck recommended Henry Fonda for the role of Tom Joad.

8. Linda Wagner Martin, introduction to John Steinbeck, *The Pearl*. New York: Penguin, 2014.

2. A SENSE OF PLACE

1. John Steinbeck, *America and Americans and Selected Nonfiction*, ed. Susan Shillinglaw and Jackson J. Benson. New York: Viking, 2002.

2. Jackson J. Benson and Anne Loftis, "John Steinbeck and Farm Labor Unionization: The Background of *In Dubious Battle*," *American Literature* 52.2 (May 1980), pp. 195–196.

3. John Steinbeck, *To a God Unknown*. New York: Robert O. Ballou, 1933, p. 4.

4. Jackson J. Benson, *The True Adventures of John Steinbeck, Writer*. New York: Viking, 1984, pp. 114–115. The first issue of *Cup of Gold* sold a reported 1,533 copies.

5. John Steinbeck, *Cup of Gold.* New York: Robert McBride, 1929, p. 28.

6. Steinbeck, *Cup of Gold*, pp. 254–255.

7. See the reviews in the *Evening Post* and the *New York Herald Tribune* in Joseph McElrath, Jesse S. Crisler, and Susan Shillinglaw, eds., *Steinbeck: The Contemporary Reviews*. Cambridge: Cambridge University Press, 1996, pp. 3–4. To Kate Beswick, he wrote of his discontent with the novel and its "wretched structure" (Benson, *The True Adventures of John Steinbeck, Writer*, p. 125). To Carl Wilhelmson he mentioned "the failure of the Cup" (*Steinbeck: A Life in Letters*, ed. Elaine Steinbeck and Robert Wallsten. New York: Viking 1975, p. 27). Benson makes the point that for a reader of the later novels *Cup of Gold* may not even seem to have been written by the same person (Benson, *The True Adventures of John Steinbeck, Writer*, p. 116).

8. Steinbeck told his agents that the novel's imperfections bothered him (*Steinbeck: A Life in Letters*, p. 42). He told Ted Miller: "The story will be cut to pieces" (p. 47). *To a God Unknown*, the story about a large family in a valley community, began as a play by Toby Street at Stanford University, *The Green Lady*. In the play a man does not want his daughter to go back to college because he thinks that all of those books and professors will draw her interest away from the land. The play stalled somewhere in the first act and Steinbeck tried to take it over. He changed the plot and introduced a character named Joseph Wayne, who has left Vermont for new prospects in the West.

9. *Steinbeck: A Life in Letters*, p. 42. "*To a God Unknown* should have been a play," he wrote to Mavis McIntosh (*Steinbeck: A Life in Letters*, p. 39). For a discussion on Steinbeck's sense of organism, see Benson, *The True Adventures of John Steinbeck, Writer*, pp. 238–243.

10. James C. Kelley, "John Steinbeck and Ed Ricketts: Understanding Life in the Great Tide Tool," *Steinbeck and the Environment: Interdisciplinary Approaches*, ed. Susan F. Beegel, Susan Shillinglaw, and Wesley Tiffney Jr.. Tuscaloosa: University of Alabama Press, 1997, p. 210. See also Richard Astro, *John Steinbeck and Edward F. Ricketts: The Shaping of a Novelist*. Minneapolis: University of Minnesota Press, 1973; Benson, *The True Adventures of John Steinbeck, Writer*, pp. 238–239.

11. Kelley, "Steinbeck and Ed Ricketts," p. 210. One of Steinbeck's reflections on the action of men in groups is expressed in a June 21, 1933, letter to Dook Sheffield, in *Steinbeck: A Life in Letters*, pp. 69–72.

12. This observation and phrase is from Jackson J. Benson, *The True Adventures of John Steinbeck, Writer*, p. 245. For possible influences from Steinbeck's reading see Robert DeMott, *Steinbeck's Reading: Catalog of Books Owned and*

Borrowed. New York: Garland, 1984, pp. 69, 108; Joel Hedgpeth, *The Outer Shores: Ed Ricketts and John Steinbeck Explore the Pacific Coast.* Eureka, CA: Mad River Press, 1978, p. 23; Kelley, "Steinbeck and Ed Ricketts," p. 213. Ricketts referred to Lao Tze's text in his essay "The Philosophy of 'Breaking Through'." In 1975, Robert DeMott offered a Jungian archetypal analysis of "Toward a Redefinition of *To a God Unknown*," *University of Windsor Review* 8 (1975), p. x.

13. "John had a spiritual streak that never left," said Elaine Steinbeck in November 1999 in an interview with Susan Shillinglaw. See Susan Shillinglaw, "John Steinbeck's Spiritual Streak," *Literature and Belief* 21.1–2 (2001), pp. 76–90. Available online at http://literatureandbelief.byu.edu.

14. Steinbeck, *America and Americans*, p. 336.

15. Steinbeck, *America and Americans*, p. 337.

16. Steinbeck, *America and Americans*, p. 338.

17. Steinbeck, *America and Americans*, p. 338.

18. Steinbeck, *To a God Unknown*, p. 105.

19. Steinbeck, *To a God Unknown*, p. 23.

20. Steinbeck, *To a God Unknown*, p. 50. "We have been going through one identical with the one of 1880," Steinbeck observed in a January 25, 1932, letter to Mavis McIntosh (*Steinbeck: A Life in Letters*, p. 49). Californians experienced parched land and drought recently in 2015.

21. See Louis Owens's discussion of the theme of commitment. *John Steinbeck's Re-vision of America.* Athens: University of Georgia Press, 1985, pp. 27–28.

22. Steinbeck, *To a God Unknown*, pp. 312–313.

23. Steinbeck, *America and Americans*, p. 389.

24. Steinbeck, *America and Americans*, p. 390.

25. Steinbeck, *Steinbeck: A Life in Letters*, pp. 39–40.

26. John Steinbeck, *The Pastures of Heaven.* New York: Robert O. Ballou, 1932, p. 24.

27. Steinbeck, *The Pastures of Heaven*, p. 25.

28. Owens, *John Steinbeck's Re-vision of America*, p. 89.

29. Joseph Fontenrose, *A Study of the Pastures of Heaven.* New York: Berkeley, 1981, pp. 46–47.

30. Steinbeck is quoted on the back cover of Thomas Fensch, *Conversations with John Steinbeck.* Oxford: University Press of Mississippi, 1988. Steinbeck wrote to Carl Wilhelmson in 1933 that he believed that *Pastures* "seems to be getting a better break in England than it did in this country" (*Steinbeck: A Life in Letters*, p. 81).

31. John Steinbeck, *The Red Pony.* New York: Viking Press, 1937, p. 235.

32. Steinbeck, *The Red Pony*, p. 238.

33. Steinbeck, *The Red Pony*, p. 241.

34. Steinbeck, *The Red Pony*, p. 241.

35. Steinbeck, *The Red Pony*, p. 242.

36. Steinbeck, *The Red Pony*, p. 252.

37. Steinbeck, *The Red Pony*, p. 288.

38. Steinbeck, *The Red Pony*, p. 303.

39. John Steinbeck, "The Chrysanthemums," *The Long Valley*. New York, Viking, 1938, p. 9.

40. Steinbeck, "The Chrysanthemums," p. 18.

41. John Steinbeck, "The White Quail," *The Long Valley*, p. 32.

42. Steinbeck, "The White Quail," p. 20.

43. John Steinbeck, "Flight," *The Long Valley*, p. 45.

44. Steinbeck, "Flight," p. 53.

45. John Ditsky, "Steinbeck's 'Flight': The Ambiguity of Manhood," *Steinbeck Quarterly* 5.3–4 (Summer–Fall 1972), p. 83.

46. Owens, *Steinbeck's Re-vision of America*, p. 34.

47. Owens, *Steinbeck's Re-vision of America*, pp. 29, 35; Ditsky, "Steinbeck's 'Flight'," p. 84.

48. John Steinbeck, "The Harness," *The Long Valley*, pp. 111–112.

49. John Steinbeck, "Johnny Bear," *The Long Valley*, p. 163.

50. John Steinbeck, "The Murder," *The Long Valley*, p. 173. Steinbeck wrote to Robert Ballou, February 11, 1933, that "The Murder" "might be sold to a pulp if it were cut down" (*Steinbeck: A Life in Letters*, p. 65).

51. Peter Lisca, "'The Raid' and 'In Dubious Battle,'" *Study Guide to Steinbeck's* The Long Valley, ed. Tetsumaro Hayashi. Muncie, IN: Ball State University, 1976, p. 41.

52. John Steinbeck, "The Vigilante," *The Long Valley*, p. 134.

53. Owens, *Steinbeck's Re-vision of America*, p. 162.

54. Tetsumaro Hayashi, ed., *John Steinbeck: The Years of Greatness, 1936–1939*. Tuscaloosa: University of Alabama Press, 1993. For critical perspectives on the short stories in *The Long Valley* see Owens, *John Steinbeck's Re-vision of America*, pp. 29–34, 106–127, 161–163; Ditsky, "Steinbeck's Flight," p. 85; Tetsumaro Hayashi, *A Study Guide to Steinbeck's* The Long Valley, which includes Brian Barbour's "Steinbeck as a Short Story Writer," William V. Miller's "Sex and Spiritual Ambiguity in Steinbeck's 'Chrysanthemums,'" Reloy Garcia's "Steinbeck's 'The Snake': An Explication," Joseph Fontenrose's analysis of "The Harness," and Warren French's commentary on "Johnny Bear." Roy S. Simmonds investigates "Steinbeck's 'The Murder': A Critical and Biographical Study," *Steinbeck Quarterly* 9.2 (Spring 1976), p. 46. He suggests that this story may have been planned as one of the scenes of *The Pastures of Heaven*.

55. John Steinbeck, "Making of a New Yorker," *America and Americans*, p. 36. This comment reflects the Steinbeck comment that Thomas Fensch records in *Conversations with John Steinbeck*.

3. IN DUBIOUS BATTLE

1. Jackson J. Benson and Anne Loftis, "John Steinbeck and Farm Labor Unionization: The Background of *In Dubious Battle*," *American Literature* 52.2 (May 1980): 198. See David Wyatt, "Steinbeck's Light," *Southern Review* (Spring 2002). Wyatt discusses *In Dubious Battle* and light imagery.
2. Jackson J. Benson, *Looking for Steinbeck's Ghost*. Norman: University of Oklahoma Press, 1988, p. 226.
3. John Steinbeck (January 15, 1935), *Steinbeck: A Life in Letters*, ed. Elaine Steinbeck and Robert Wallsten. New York: Viking, 1975, p. 92.
4. Steinbeck (January 15, 1935), *Steinbeck: A Life in Letters*. "Argument of Phalanx" is recalled by Dick Albee and in a letter by Steinbeck to Dook Sheffield cited in Jackson J. Benson, *The True Adventures of John Steinbeck, Writer*. New York: Viking, 1984, pp. 268–270.
5. The story's protagonist, Jim Nolan, is a fictional creation but his efforts also reflect those of the young writer working amid "dubious prospects," as Warren French points out in *John Steinbeck's Fiction Revisited*. New York: Twayne, 1994, pp. 70–71.
6. John Steinbeck, *In Dubious Battle*. New York: Library of America, 1994, p. 640; *In Dubious Battle*, New York: Bantam Books, 1964, p. 103.
7. Steinbeck, *In Dubious Battle*, Library of America, p. 640; *In Dubious Battle*, Bantam Books, p. 103.
8. Steinbeck, *In Dubious Battle*, Library of America, p. 641; *In Dubious Battle*, Bantam Books, p. 104.
9. John Steinbeck, "Genus Americanus," *America and Americans and Selected Nonfiction*, ed. Susan Shillinglaw and Jackson J. Benson. New York: Viking, 2002, p. 357.
10. Alfred Kazin, *On Native Grounds: An Interpretation of Modern American Prose Literature*. New York: Doubleday, 1956.
11. Steinbeck, *Steinbeck: A Life in Letters*, p. 162.
12. Steinbeck, *Steinbeck: A Life in Letters*, p. 98.
13. Steinbeck, *Steinbeck: A Life in Letters*, p. 87.
14. Morris Dickstein, *Dancing in the Dark: A Cultural History of the Great Depression*. New York: Norton, 2010, p. 129.
15. Dickstein, *Dancing in the Dark*, p. 138.
16. Dickstein, *Dancing in the Dark*, p. 129.

17. John Steinbeck, "A Primer on the Thirties," *America and Americans and Selected Nonfiction*, p. 30.

18. Steinbeck, "A Primer on the Thirties," p. 24.

19. Steinbeck, "A Primer on the Thirties," p. 30.

20. Steinbeck, "A Primer on the Thirties," p. 20.

21. Steinbeck, "A Primer on the Thirties," p. 18.

22. Steinbeck, "A Primer on the Thirties," p. 17.

23. Steinbeck, "A Primer on the Thirties," p. 18.

24. Steinbeck, "A Primer on the Thirties," p. 20.

25. Steinbeck, "A Primer on the Thirties," p. 21.

26. Arthur Train, *The Strange Attacks on Herbert Hoover: A Current Example of What We Do to Our Presidents*. New York: John Day, 1932, p. 92.

27. David Burner, *Herbert Hoover: A Public Life*. New York: Alfred A. Knopf, 1979, p. 315.

28. Franklin Delano Roosevelt, inaugural address, March 4, 1933.

29. Steinbeck, "A Primer on the Thirties," p. 26; see also pp. 17–31.

30. Dickstein, *Dancing in the Dark*, p. 70.

31. Steinbeck, "Genus Americanus," p. 364.

32. Steinbeck, "Genus Americanus," p. 364.

33. Fred T. Marsh in *John Steinbeck: The Contemporary Reviews*, ed. Joseph McElrath, Jesse S. Crisler, and Susan Shillinglaw. Cambridge: Cambridge University Press, 1996, p. 7.

34. Steinbeck, "A Primer on the Thirties," pp. 17–18.

35. Herbert Hoover speech, June 16, 1931.

36. Franklin Delano Roosevelt, inaugural address, March 4, 1933.

37. Harry Thornton Moore, *The Novels of John Steinbeck: A First Study*. Chicago: Normandy House, 1939, p. 102.

38. John Steinbeck quoted in Benson and Loftis, "John Steinbeck and Farm Labor Unionization," p. 195.

39. The *New York Times* (October 18, 1933); "Strike Flares Up," *New York Times* (October 9, 1933); "California Clash Called 'Civil War,'" *New York Times* (October 22, 1933); "San Joaquin Valley News: Growers Move to Fight Strike," *Los Angeles Times* (October 7, 1933). Jackson J. Benson notes that *two* people— a man and a woman—died at Pixley on October 10 (*The True Adventures of John Steinbeck, Writer*, p. 308).

40. One could apply a neo-Marxist analysis or a Bakhtinian approach to the multiplicity of voices in a text to seek the voices of those silenced by the hegemony of a dominant culture. In *Cannery Row, Tortilla Flat, The Grapes of Wrath*, and other works Steinbeck sounds these voices and brings these people into full view.

41. Harold Bloom, *John Steinbeck*. New York: Chelsea House, 1987, p. 1; French, *John Steinbeck's Fiction Revisited*, p. 199. Frederick J. Hoffman, who wrote colorfully on *The Twenties*, called *In Dubious Battle* "the superior novel of its class," suggesting that it was also unlike the 1930s novels he viewed as period pieces ("Aesthetics of the Proletarian Novel," *Proletarian Writers of the Thirties*, ed. David Madden. Carbondale: Southern Illinois University Press, 1968, pp. 193–194).

42. Steinbeck, "Genus Americanus," p. 360.

43. Steinbeck, "Genus Americanus," p. 360.

44. Steinbeck, "Genus Americanus," p. 364.

45. Steinbeck, "Genus Americanus," p. 364.

46. Steinbeck, "Genus Americanus," p. 364.

47. Steinbeck, "A Primer on the Thirties," p. 17; *America and Americans and Selected Nonfiction*, p. 334.

48. Steinbeck, "A Primer on the Thirties," p. 20.

49. Steinbeck, "A Primer on the Thirties," p. 21.

50. Steinbeck, "Americans and the Future," *America and Americans and Selected Nonfiction*, p. 398.

51. Steinbeck, "A Primer on the Thirties," pp. 25–26.

52. Steinbeck, "A Primer on the Thirties," p. 35.

4. OF MICE AND MEN

1. The circular structure that Peter Lisca has discerned in this novel brings its readers from two lonely wanderers—George and Lennie—moving down from the highway to two men—George and Slim—returning up the hill to the highway. See Louis Owens, *"Of Mice and Men*: The Dream of Commitment," *Steinbeck's Re-vision of America*. Athens: University of Georgia Press, 1985, p. 150; Morris Dickstein, *Dancing in the Dark: A Cultural History of the Great Depression*. New York: Norton, 2010, p. 72; Steinbeck, letter to George Albee (January 11, 1937), *Steinbeck: A Life in Letters*, ed. Elaine Steinbeck and Robert Wallsten. New York: Viking, 1975; Jonathan Leaf, "Of Mice and Melodrama," *The New Criterion* 26.4 (December 2007).

2. John Steinbeck, *America and Americans and Selected Nonfiction*, ed. Susan Shillinglaw and Jackson J. Benson. New York: Viking, 2002, p. 157.

3. Steinbeck, *America and Americans*, p. 156.

4. Robert Coles, *Mindful* (interview, August 24, 2010), http://mindful.org. See also Robert Coles, *The Call of Service: A Witness to Idealism*. Rpt. New York: Mariner, 1994.

5. Coles, *Mindful*; see also Coles, *The Call of Service*.

6. Robert Coles, *The Call of Stories: Teaching and the Moral Imagination.* Boston: Houghton Mifflin, 1990, p. 203. As Adrian van Kaam and Kathleen Healy write, "The more deeply we penetrate the mystery of the great literary masterpieces, the closer we come to really knowing and being ourselves" (Adrian Van Kaam and Kathleen Healey, *The Demon and the Dove: Personality Growth Through Literature.* Pittsburgh, PA: Duquesne University Press, 1967, p. 37).

7. Warren French, *John Steinbeck.* Boston and New York: Twayne, 1975, p. 74; Edmund Wilson, "The Boys in the Back Room," *Notes on California Novelists.* San Francisco: Colt Press, 1941, p. 41; Peter Lisca, *John Steinbeck: Nature and Myth.* New York: Thomas Y. Crowell, 1978. Steinbeck wrote to George Albee in 1936: "I finished a little book sometime ago. As usual it is disliked by some and liked by some. It is always that way" (*Steinbeck: A Life in Letters*, p. 124).

8. Michael Meyer, ed., *The Essential Criticism of John Steinbeck's "Of Mice and Men."* Lanham, MD: Scarecrow Press, 2009; Lewis Gannett, "Books and Things," *New York Herald Tribune* (February 25, 1937); Wilbur Needham, "John Steinbeck Does Dramatic Novel," *Los Angeles Times* (February 28, 1937), pp. 13–14; Louis Paul, "Prose Made of Wind and Soil and Weather," *New York Herald Tribune* (February 28, 1937), Books, section 5, p. 15. See *John Steinbeck: The Contemporary Reviews*, ed. Joseph R. McElrath, Jesse S. Crisler, and Susan Shillinglaw. Cambridge: Cambridge University Press, 1996, pp. 75–130.

9. F. Scott Fitzgerald, letter to Edmund Wilson, cited by Gore Vidal, who calls Fitzgerald's charge that Steinbeck was cribbing one of Fitzgerald's "cries at midnight" (Gore Vidal, *United States: Essays 1952–1992.* New York: Random House, 1993, p. 292).

10. This *New York Times* article by Winnie Ho ("Split by Race and Wealth but Discovering Similarities as They Study Steinbeck") highlights different student readings. Michael J. Meyer's volume *The Essential Criticism of John Steinbeck's "Of Mice and Men"* is useful for students who want to read criticism on this short novel. Meyer's book offers "representative studies" that consider themes of the novel: land and property, American dreams, friendship, loneliness and isolation, class, gender, age, race, and social critique of haves and have-nots in America. The novel continues to reflect contemporary conditions, Meyer asserts in the preface to his book. Steinbeck offers us "identifiable" characters, and "readers empathize with the unlikely friendship and devotion to each other" between George and Lennie.

11. Steinbeck, *America and Americans and Selected Nonfiction*, p. 143. Steinbeck is quoted in Mimi R. Gladstein, "Steinbeck and the Woman Question: A Never Ending Puzzle," *Critical Insights: John Steinbeck*, ed. Don Noble. Pasadena, CA: Salem Press, 2011, p. 243. See Mimi Reisel Gladstein's many reflections

on Steinbeck and women, including *The Indestructible Woman in Faulkner, Hemingway, and Steinbeck*. Ann Arbor, MI: UMI Research Press, 1986; "Deletions from the Battle: Gaps in the Grapes," *San Jose Studies* 18.1 (Winter 1992), pp. 43–51; "*Of Mice and Men*: Creating and Recreating Curley's Wife," *Beyond Boundaries*, ed. Susan Shillinglaw and Kevin Hearle. Tuscaloosa: University of Alabama Press, 2002, pp. 205–220.

12. Steinbeck, *America and Americans and Selected Nonfiction*, p. 143.

13. Steinbeck, *America and Americans and Selected Nonfiction*, p. 143.

14. http://ncac.org/update/ncac-responds-to-of-mice-and-men-challenge-in-appomattox-high-school .

15. "Good Reads: Students Dive into *Of Mice and Men* during Banned Books Week," *Montana Standard* (September 25, 2014). Report on Union Press High School, Cameron, North Carolina, by Elaina Athans for ABC-11.com (December 9, 2014).

16. Richard Lea, "Idaho Parents Push for Schools to Ban *Of Mice and Men* for Its 'Profanities'," *Guardian* (May 7, 2015).

17. School board members and the town's librarian were quoted in the article by Richard Lea, *Guardian* (see above note). Early in board discussions, school board member Tom Hamilton pointed out that when his daughter read the novel in a seventh-grade class this led to thoughtful family discussions. Another board member, Christa Hazel, recalled reading the book in high school; she reread the novel and commented that she believed that teachers could approach "hard issues" like racism, classism, and euthanasia through work with the book. Ann Seddon suggested moving reading *Of Mice and Men* to a higher grade. See Daniel Walters's June 1, 2015, post ("The Fate of Both Mice and Men Hang on Tonight's CdA School Board Meeting") on http://www.inlander.com/Blogland-er/archives/2015/06/01/the-fate-of-both-mice-and-men-hang-on-tonights-cda-school-board-meeting.

18. The story is documented in J. Anthony Lukas in *Big Trouble*. New York: Simon & Schuster, 1997; and Beau Riffenburgh, *Pinkerton's Great Detective: The Amazing Life and Times of James McParland*. New York: Penguin, 2013.

19. Steinbeck, *America and Americans and Selected Nonfiction*, p. 362.

20. Steinbeck, *America and Americans and Selected Nonfiction*, p. 362.

21. Steinbeck, *America and Americans and Selected Nonfiction*, p. 362.

22. Steinbeck, *America and Americans and Selected Nonfiction*, pp. 371–372.

23. British Broadcasting Company Report (March 2011).

24. Martin Phillips, "Steinbeck Goes to High School," *Steinbeck Studies* 15.2 (Fall 2004), pp. 163–165.

25. Morris Dickstein, "Steinbeck and the Great Depression," *South Atlantic Quarterly* 103.1 (Winter 2004), p. 111.

26. "Should *Of Mice and Men* Be Taught to High School Teenagers?" http://www.enotes.com/homework-help; Debora Stonich, "Sharing Steinbeck with Students," *Steinbeck Studies* 15.2 (Winter 2004), p. 168, https://muse.jhu.edu/journals.steinbeck.

27. Jerry Heverly, "Of Mice and Men and Students Who Don't Read," http://www.sanleandropatch.com; Vincent Gibbs, "*Of Mice and Men* as Read by Vincent Gibbs—Peary High School," http://www.dedicationtechnologies.com and http://www.lastfm/music/John-Steinbeck; William Johnson, "Of Mice and Men and My Students," http://www.chalkbeat.org/posts/ny/2012/02/27/of-mice-and-men-and-my-students/#V0PCxJErK70; Deborah Solomon Baker, "Am I My Brother's Keeper?" *Teaching Tolerance* (November 18, 2010), http://www.tolerance.org/bloglam-am-i-my-brother-s-keeper.

28. Mark Miazga, "Epiphany in Baltimore," http://epiphanyinbmore.blogspot.com/2014/08.

29. http://www.learningfrommymistakes.blogspot.com/2012.

30. La Jolla High School Department of English, http://www.ljhs.sandi.net/departments/english/corelessons/of-mice-and-men.

31. Dickstein, "Steinbeck and the Great Depression," p. 125.

32. Dickstein,"Steinbeck and the Great Depression," p. 126.

33. Martha Nussbaum, *Love's Knowledge: Essays on Philosophy and Literature*. New York: Oxford University Press, 1982, p. 431. See also *Poetic Justice: The Literary Imagination and Public Life*. Boston: Beacon, 1997.

34. Nussbaum, *Love's Knowledge*, p. 426.

35. Nussbaum, *Love's Knowledge*, p. 433.

36. Lee Siegel, "Should Literature Be Useful?" *The New Yorker* (November 6, 2013). Sources are available online for *American National Biography*; National Steinbeck Center; eNotes; and *Of Mice and Men: Teacher's Deluxe Edition*, introduction by Susan Shillinglaw, Penguin (2013).

5. THE GRAPES OF WRATH

1. Otis Durant Duncan, "Oklahoma's Farm Population." Bulletin B-329. Stillwater: Oklahoma A&M College, 1952, p. 28.

2. James N. Gregory, *American Exodus: The Dust Bowl Migration and Okie Culture in California*. New York: Oxford University Press, 1989; Carey McWilliams, *Factories in the Fields: The Story of Migratory Farm Labor in California* (1939). Berkeley: University of California Press, 2000.

3. Robert T. McMillan, *Migration of Population in Five Oklahoma Townships*. Bulletin 271. Oklahoma A&M University, 1933, p. 30.

4. The Biblical allusion to *Exodus* suggests that this is God's people who are seeking freedom from oppression. The words "we're the people" conclude the film of *The Grapes of Wrath*. The term "people" occurs many times in the Book of Exodus.

5. John Steinbeck, *The Grapes of Wrath and Other Writings, 1936–1941*. New York: Library of America, 1996, p. 212.

6. National Weather Service documents. See http://www.srh.noaa.gov/oun/?n=events-19350414.

7. Robert E. Geiger, Associated Press (April 15, 1935). Report from Boise City, Oklahoma. Edward Stanley, an editor at the Kansas City Associated Press, is said to have coined the term "dust bowl" upon rewriting Geiger's report.

8. Donald Worster, *Nature's Economy: A History of Ecological Ideas*. Cambridge: Cambridge University Press, rpt. 1994, p. 223.

9. Worster, *Nature's Economy*, p. 223.

10. These articles appeared in the *M'Alester Guardian* in October and November 1929. The population of McAlester is derived from census figures.

11. Tom Cameron, "*The Grapes of Wrath* Author Guards Self from Threats at Moody Gulch," *Los Angeles Times* (July 9, 1939), p. 2.

12. Susan Shillinglaw, "California Answers *The Grapes of Wrath*," *Critical Insights: John Steinbeck*, ed. Don Noble. Pasadena, CA: Salem Press, 2011, p. 180.

13. Gregory, *American Exodus*, p. 88.

14. See Shillinglaw, "California Answers *The Grapes of Wrath*," p. 185; Frank J. Taylor, "The Merritt System," *Commentator* (November 1938), pp. 84–87, rpt. in *Reader's Digest* 35 (February 1939), pp. 104–106. The Frank J. Taylor Papers are in the Stanford University Libraries, Department of Special Collections.

15. Shillinglaw, "California Answers *The Grapes of Wrath*," pp. 189–190.

16. *Bakersfield Californian* (June 11, 1939), p. 1.

17. McWilliams, *Factories in the Fields*, p. 231.

18. McWilliams, *Factories in the Fields*, p. 231.

19. McWilliams, *Factories in the Fields*, p. 232.

20. McWilliams, *Factories in the Fields*, p. 231.

21. McWilliams, *Factories in the Fields*, p. 233.

22. McWilliams, *Factories in the Fields*, p. 333.

23. Steinbeck, *The Grapes of Wrath*, p. 160.

24. David N. Cassuto, "Turning Wine into Water: Water as a Privileged Signifier in *The Grapes of Wrath*," *Language and Literature* 69 (1993), p. 57.

25. Donald Worster, *Rivers of Empire*. New York: Oxford University Press, 1992, pp. 227–230.

26. Worster, *Rivers of Empire*, p. 229.

27. R. McLeman and B. Smit, "Migration as an Adaptation to Climate Change." Guelph, ON, Canada: University of Guelph, 2006, p. 33, http://www. uoguelph.ca .

28. McLeman and Smit, "Migration as an Adaptation to Climate Change," p. 32.

29. Shillinglaw, "California Answers *The Grapes of Wrath*," p. 196, n. 38.

30. Quoted in Shillinglaw, "California Answers *The Grapes of Wrath*," p. 196.

31. Robert DeMott, ed., *Working Days*. New York: Viking, 1990, p. 40. Steinbeck kept a series of journal entries while he was writing *The Grapes of Wrath*. These have been published in *Working Days*, a volume edited by Robert DeMott that shows some of Steinbeck's process and concerns as he wrote the novel. On August 22, 1939, he noted "nervous exhaustion" (p. 69). There was a lack of sleep, stomach distress. He had had his tonsils removed in July and he had to deal with a leg infection. On August 8, he wrote: "Well the work has pretty much gone to hell. Might as well take it in stride" (entry 48, August 8 [1938], 11:00 [Monday], p. 53).

32. John Seelye, "Come Back to the Boxcar: Steinbeck and Sentimentality," *Critical Insights: John Steinbeck* (Noble), p. 171. When Seelye discusses Steinbeck and sentimentality in *The Grapes of Wrath* in comparison with Harriet Beecher Stowe's *Uncle Tom's Cabin*, he refers to Leslie Fiedler's sharp criticism of Steinbeck. Fiedler observed that *The Grapes of Wrath* is in the twentieth century "the greatest of all novels of sentimental protest" (Fiedler, *Love and Death in the American Novel*. New York: Stein and Day, rev. 1966, p. 264). However, Fiedler also called *The Grapes of Wrath* "maudlin, sentimental, and overblown" ("Looking Back after 50 Years," *San Jose Studies* 16.1 [1990], p. 55). In Seelye's view, Fiedler's objections to Steinbeck's novel must be balanced by inquiry into aspects of the novel that are decidedly not sentimental. Steinbeck is "an anomalous realist," Seelye points out: a writer who uses symbolic narrative schemes arising from archetypes (p. 185). There is romanticism in Steinbeck's work, which may be correlated with the sentimental. However, there are naturalistic elements and realism as well.

33. Several critics have offered descriptions of Jim Casy as a Christ figure. See Theodore Ziolkowski, *Fictional Transfigurations of Jesus*. Princeton, NJ: Princeton University Press, 1978.

34. Seelye, "Come Back to the Boxcar," p. 161.

35. Seelye, "Come Back to the Boxcar," p. 158.

36. The distortions of social Darwinism and the Hobbesian war of all against all underscore the conflict in the novel. In the documentary *I Am* (Shady Acres Entertainment [US], 2010), director Tom Shadyac addresses our contemporary world with the question: Is not empathy as deep a human characteristic as the

social Darwinian notion of survival of the fittest through competition and aggression?

37. Steinbeck, *The Grapes of Wrath*, p. 572. The quotations that follow are drawn from the film adaptation of the novel, unless otherwise noted.

38. John Steinbeck quoted in Jackson J. Benson, *The True Adventures of John Steinbeck, Writer*. New York: Viking, 1984, p. 376. Steinbeck had tossed out his manuscript for "L'Affaire Lettuceberg," a precursor to *The Grapes of Wrath*. He realized that the story might alienate readers rather than assist them in understanding.

39. Hannah Arendt, *Eichmann in Jerusalem: A Report on the Banality of Evil (1963)*. New York: Penguin, 2010.

40. Warren G. French, "Steinbeck's Self-Characters as 1930s Underdogs," *Critical Insights: John Steinbeck* (Noble), p. 203.

41. Patrick Dooley, "John Steinbeck's Lower Case Utopia: Basic Human Needs, a Duty to Share, and the Good Life," *The Moral Philosophy of John Steinbeck*, ed. Stephen K. George. Lanham, MD: Scarecrow Press, 2005, pp. 3–4. Such thoughts do reflect a Franciscan manner that perceives such things as excessive and as unnecessary.

42. Dooley, "John Steinbeck's Lower Case Utopia," pp. 5–6.

43. Joseph Allegretti, "John Steinbeck and the Morality of Roles: Lessons for Business Ethics," *The Moral Philosophy of John Steinbeck* (George), p. 21. Allegretti's is the second essay that appears in the collection.

44. Allegretti, "John Steinbeck and the Morality of Roles," p. 21.

45. Allegretti, "John Steinbeck and the Morality of Roles," p. 22.

46. Allegretti, "John Steinbeck and the Morality of Roles," p. 23.

47. Rick Wartzman in *A Political Companion to John Steinbeck*, ed. Cyrus Ernesto Zirakzadeh and Simon Stow. Lexington: University Press of Kentucky, 2013, p. 2.

48. Shillinglaw, "California Answers *The Grapes of Wrath*," p. 184.

49. Rick Wartzman, *Obscene in the Extreme: The Burning and Banning of John Steinbeck's* The Grapes of Wrath. New York: Public Affairs, 2008, p. 70.

50. Thomas Fensch, *Conversations with John Steinbeck*. Oxford: University of Mississippi Press, 1988, pp. x–xi.

51. Wartzman, *Obscene in the Extreme*, pp. 73, 52. See John Steinbeck, letter to Chase Horton, in Steinbeck, *Steinbeck: A Life in Letters*, ed. Elaine Steinbeck and Robert Wallsten. New York: Viking, 1975, p. 175.

52. Wartzman, *Obscene in the Extreme*, p. 71; see also Steinbeck, *Steinbeck: A Life in Letters*, pp. 212–213, 214, 217–218.

53. Wartzman, *Obscene in the Extreme*, p. 72.

54. Wartzman, *Obscene in the Extreme*, p. 73.

55. Christine Pawley, *Reading Places: Literacy, Democracy and the Public Library in Cold War America*. Madison: University of Wisconsin Press, 2010, p. 122.

56. John Steinbeck, *American and Americans and Selected Nonfiction*, ed. Susan Shillinglaw and Jackson J. Benson. New York: Viking, 2002, p. 363.

57. Quoted in Benson, *The True Adventures of John Steinbeck, Writer*, p. 402.

58. In *The Grapes of Wrath* a preacher is given some serious flaws. Casy has lost faith, is troubled by doubts, and grows to see that he must defend human rights as a labor organizer. He remains a preacher in the sense that he becomes a voice for a social gospel. Labor organization as a theme in Steinbeck's *The Grapes of Wrath* is explored by Helen Lojek, "Jim Casy: Politico of the New Jerusalem," *Steinbeck Quarterly* 15.1–2 (Winter–Spring 1982), pp. 30–37; Richard S. Pressman, "'Them's Horses—We're Men': Social Tendency and Counter-Tendency in *The Grapes of Wrath*," *Steinbeck Quarterly* 19.3–4 (Summer–Fall 1985), pp. 71–79.

59. Dwight Ott, "Camden County Drive against Book Banns," *Philadelphia Inquirer* (September 24, 1986).

60. Parents may be rightfully concerned about such things. However, the censoring of a book may have a reverse effect. Mark Twain once noted that it was advantageous to his book's sales when the Boston Library banned his novel *Huckleberry Finn*. He wrote in a letter that he believed that a public announcement of such a ban on his book would sell more copies.

61. For example, a brief essay by Kay Quinn, "Of Dust and Steinbeck," appeared on September 4, 2014, in an "Off the Shelf" blog for Salinas Reads. This was posted by Lori Berezovsky on September 6. Quinn recalled her father, Sam Quinn, born in 1929, who lived through the Dust Bowl storms. His mother placed dampened sheets on screened windows. Kay Quinn, a marketing and development coordinator for Salinas Arts and Humanities, mentioned Timothy Egan's *The Worst Hard Time* and Ken Burns's PBS production *The Dust Bowl*. She then provided an overview of Steinbeck's novel.

62. Chris McGreal, "The Grapes of Wrath Revisited: From Dust to Bust," *Guardian* (August 27, 2009); Rachel Dry, "A Recession Only Steinbeck Could Love," *Washington Post* (March 22, 2009).

63. Simon Stow, *A Political Companion to John Steinbeck*, ed. Zirakzadeh and Stow. *The Grapes of Wrath* has been seen as rejecting industrialism and the concentration of capital in the hands of the few. The novel confronts the idea of the beneficent invisible hand of the free market economy, or that local government is always good, observes Zoe Trodd in her essay in *A Political Companion to Steinbeck*.

64. Mary M. Brown, "*The Grapes of Wrath* and the Literary Canon of American Universities in the Nineties," *The Critical Response to John Stein-*

beck's The Grapes of Wrath, ed. Barbara Heavilin. Westport, CT: Greenwood Press, 2000, pp. 285–298.

65. Katherine Schulten, "Teaching Steinbeck and *The Grapes of Wrath* with *The New York Times*," http://www.learning.blogs.nytimes.2010/08/19/teaching-the-grapes-of-wrath-with-the-new-york-times/comment-page-1/?_r=0.

66. Deborah Thorsen, "Schools Mark 75th Anniversary of *The Grapes of Wrath*," http://www.izabuzz.com//.../schools-mark-seventy-fifth-anniversary; Daniel Reynolds, Northgate High School, Walnut Creek, California, interview. Susan Shillinglaw suggests that while *The Grapes of Wrath* is often introduced in high school or college, it is a book to be reread after one has had further life experience (Meredith Hindley, "Impertinent Questions with Susan Shillinglaw," *Humanities* 35.5 [September–October 2014], p. 54).

67. Professor Stephen Ziliak of Roosevelt University in Chicago offers his syllabus for perusal for anyone who may be interested in exploring teaching Steinbeck's novel in a social sciences class: http://sites.roosevelt.edu/sziliak; http://stephenziliak.com; http://theeconomicsconversation.com .

68. Posted on September 15, 2015, at http://www.reddit.com. Teachers responding to queries offered suggestions for teaching *The Grapes of Wrath* that included emphasizing multimedia and using the John Ford film alongside the text, creating dramatic monologues by students, using Smart Board technology to acquaint students with the geography of the Oklahoma and California settings, utilizing Ken Burns's documentary on *The Dust Bowl*, and making use of the Library of Congress online collection *Voices from the Dust Bowl* with attention to "Migrant Experience."

69. Katherine Milsop, "Marathon Reading Session Honors Retiring Saddle Brook High School Teacher" (June 17, 2014), http://www.northjersey.com/news/education/marathon-reading-session-honors-retiring-teacher-1.1036428.

6. SEA OF CORTEZ

1. John Steinbeck, *The Log from the Sea of Cortez*, p. 751. (Robert DeMott and Elaine Steinbeck, eds. *John Steinbeck: The Grapes of Wrath and Other Writings, 1936–1941*.) *Sea of Cortez: A Leisurely Journey of Travel and Research* was published in December 1941. *The Log from the Sea of Cortez* was reprinted by Viking Press in 1951. For this edition, Steinbeck wrote a sixty-page tribute to his friend Ed Ricketts.

2. Steinbeck, *The Log from the Sea of Cortez*, pp. 751–752. While Steinbeck expected only moderate sales from this collaboration with Ed Ricketts, he believed that the Gulf book, as he at first called it, would appeal to a general audience as well as to scientists. This book provides "a key to Steinbeck's think-

ing," notes Jackson J. Benson in *The True Adventures of John Steinbeck, Writer*. New York: Viking, 1984, p. 482.

3. Steinbeck, *The Log from the Sea of Cortez*, p. 755.

4. Steinbeck, *The Log from the Sea of Cortez*, p. 751. "Ed Ricketts held that non-teleological ideas derive through 'is' thinking, associated with natural selection as Darwin seems to have understood it."

5. Steinbeck, *The Log from the Sea of Cortez*, p. 754.

6. Steinbeck, *The Log from the Sea of Cortez*, p. 756.

7. Steinbeck, *The Log from the Sea of Cortez*, p. 782.

8. Steinbeck, *The Log from the Sea of Cortez*, p. 783.

9. Steinbeck, *The Log from the Sea of Cortez*, p. 783.

10. Steinbeck, *The Log from the Sea of Cortez*, p. 760.

11. Steinbeck, *The Log from the Sea of Cortez*, p. 763.

12. Steinbeck, *The Log from the Sea of Cortez*, p. 775.

13. Steinbeck, *The Log from the Sea of Cortez*, p. 928.

14. Steinbeck, *The Log from the Sea of Cortez*, p. 928.

15. James C. Kelley, "John Steinbeck and Ed Ricketts: Understanding Life on the Great Tide Pool," *John Steinbeck, Critical Insights*, ed. Don Noble. Pasadena, CA: Salem Press, 2011, pp. 27, 33. Kelley sees "breaking through" as Zen-like. The perception of group cooperation among living creatures was an important insight that might be applied to international relations. To try to understand the application of this knowledge to these wider concerns and share this ecological insight involved a breaking through as well (Kelley, pp. 31–32). See also "John Steinbeck and Ed Ricketts: Understanding Life in the Great Tide Pool," *Critical Insights: John Steinbeck*, ed. Don Noble. Pasadena, CA: Salem Press, 2011, pp. 208–226.

16. Steinbeck, *The Log from the Sea of Cortez*, p. 777.

17. Steinbeck, *The Log from the Sea of Cortez*, p. 929.

18. Steinbeck, *The Log from the Sea of Cortez*, p. 929.

19. Steinbeck, *The Log from the Sea of Cortez*, p. 773.

20. Steinbeck, *The Log from the Sea of Cortez*, p. 773.

21. Richard Astro and Tetsumaro Hayashi, *Steinbeck: The Man and His Work*. University of Oregon Press, 1971, p. 96.

22. Brian E. Railsback, in *Parallel Expeditions: Charles Darwin and the Art of John Steinbeck* (University of Idaho Press, 1995), addresses how the expeditions and methods of Steinbeck and Ricketts correspond with the work of Charles Darwin. Railsback points out that for Steinbeck and Ricketts, the works of W. C. Allee (*Animal Aggregations*), J. E. Boodin (*Cosmic Evolution*), and Jan Smuts (*Holism and Evolution*) were crucial resources.

23. John Steinbeck, *Sweet Thursday*. New York: Viking, 1954, p. 130.

24. Steinbeck, *The Log from the Sea of Cortez*, p. 28. We engage in birthday parties, graduations, baptisms, reunions, awards shows, religious ceremonies, and a wide variety of other ritual activities. E. O. Wilson's sociobiology, while refraining from ascribing any theological explanations, recognizes this religious and collective orientation of humanity.

25. Joseph Fontenrose in John Ditsky, *John Steinbeck and the Critics*. Rochester, NY: Camden House, Boydell & Brewer, 2000, p. 140.

26. Kelley, "John Steinbeck and Ed Ricketts: Understanding Life in the Great Tide Pool" (Noble), p. 210. Kelley points out that Steinbeck and Ricketts owned books on Zen Buddhism, including D. T. Suzuki's *Essays in Zen Buddhism* and Lao Tzu's *Tao Te Ching*. This is referenced by Robert DeMott in *Steinbeck's Reading*. New York: Garland, 1984, pp. 69, 108; Joel Hedgpeth, *The Outer Shores: Ed Ricketts and John Steinbeck Explore the Pacific Coast*. Eureka, CA: Mad River Press, 1978, p. 23; and Kelley, p. 213. These works express the notion of enlightenment, process, and overcoming dualism. Ricketts referred to Lao Tzu's text in his essay "The Philosophy of Breaking Through."

27. John Steinbeck, "About Ed Ricketts," *The Log from the Sea of Cortez*, p. xli.

28. Attention to Steinbeck's technique of counterpoint appears in Michael J. Meyer and Henry Veggian, eds., *East of Eden: New and Recent Essays*. New York: Rodopi, 2013. Darwin's analogy between science, music, and aesthetics appears in Charles Darwin, *Voyage of the Beagle* (published 1839 as *Journals and Remarks*). New York: Penguin, 1990, p. 373.

29. Richard Astro, *John Steinbeck and Edward F. Ricketts: The Shaping of a Novelist*. Minneapolis: University of Minnesota, 1973, p. 73.

30. Richard E. Hart has called Steinbeck "a soft determinist." See "Steinbeck on Man and Nature: A Philosophical Reflection," *Steinbeck and the Environment: Interdisciplinary Approaches* (Beegel, Shillinglaw, and Tiffney). Tuscaloosa: University of Alabama Press, 1997, p. 43.

31. Steinbeck, *The Log from the Sea of Cortez*, p. lxii.

32. Railsback, *Parallel Expeditions*, p. 127.

33. Railsback, *Parallel Expeditions*, p. 10. When Brian Railsback points out this distinction between the views of Ricketts and Steinbeck he notes that a book by Robert Briffault, *The Making of Humanity* (1919), was in Steinbeck's library and it carried a thesis that included the "linking of evolution to human social improvement" (p. 141). *In Dubious Battle*, *Of Mice and Men*, and *The Grapes of Wrath* are like the struggle of life in the tide pools, Railsback points out. Railsback discusses the imaginative relationship that Steinbeck had with Darwin's ideas via the journal Darwin kept while sailing aboard the *Beagle* (pp. 138–139).

34. Steinbeck, *Sweet Thursday*, p. 28.

35. Steinbeck, *The Log from the Sea of Cortez*, p. 779.

36. Steinbeck, *The Log from the Sea of Cortez*, p. 781.

37. Steinbeck, *The Log from the Sea of Cortez*, p. 782.

38. Steinbeck, *The Log from the Sea of Cortez*, p. 818.

39. Steinbeck, *The Log from the Sea of Cortez*, p. 820.

40. Steinbeck, *The Log from the Sea of Cortez*, p. 963.

41. Steinbeck, *The Log from the Sea of Cortez*, p. 963.

42. This point is emphasized by Benson, *The True Adventures of John Steinbeck, Writer*, p. 456. See Astro, *John Steinbeck and Edward F. Ricketts*, p. 59.

43. Robert Morseberger, ed., *Steinbeck's Zapata!* New York: Penguin, 2001.

44. John Steinbeck, *Steinbeck: A Life in Letters*, ed. Elaine Steinbeck and Robert Wallsten. New York: Viking Press, 1975.

45. John Steinbeck, "I Am a Revolutionary," *America and Americans and Selected Nonfiction*, ed. Susan Shillinglaw and Jackson Benson. New York: Viking, 2002, p. 90.

46. John Steinbeck, "The Trial of Arthur Miller," *America and Americans and Selected Nonfiction*, p. 103.

47. John Steinbeck, letter to Jules Buck, *Steinbeck: A Life in Letters*.

48. Biologists who sailed the Sea of Cortez in 2004 documented differences between their findings and those of Steinbeck and Ricketts in 1940 and observed present-day ecological issues.

49. Evelyn Fox Keller, *A Feeling for the Organism: The Life and Work of Barbara McClintock*. New York: Freeman, 1983. See also Evelyn Fox Keller, *Reflections on Gender and Science*. New Haven, CT: Yale University Press, 1985.

50. Steinbeck, *America and Americans and Selected Nonfiction*, p. 120.

51. *Steinbeck and the Environment: Interdisciplinary Approaches*, ed. Susan F. Beegel, Susan Shillinglaw, and Wesley N. Tiffney Jr. Tuscaloosa: University of Alabama Press, 1997.

52. John Steinbeck, "My War with the Ospreys," *America and Americans and Selected Nonfiction* (Shillinglaw and Benson), p. 42.

53. Steinbeck, "My War with the Ospreys," p. 42.

54. Steinbeck, "My War with the Ospreys," p. 42.

55. Susan Shillinglaw and Jackson Benson, *America and Americans and Selected Nonfiction*, p. xv.

56. Shillinglaw and Benson, *America and Americans and Selected Nonfiction*, p. xv.

57. Barry Lopez is quoted by Benson and Shillinglaw in *America and Americans and Selected Nonfiction*, p. 1. Barry Lopez, *Crossing Open Ground*. New York: Random House, 1989, p. 71.

58. J. Baird Callicott, "The Conceptual Foundations of the Land Ethic," *In Defense of the Land Ethic*. Albany: State University of New York Press, 1989, p. 87.

59. John Steinbeck, "About Ed Ricketts," *America and Americans and Selected Nonfiction*, p. 200.

60. Steinbeck, "About Ed Ricketts," p. 200.

61. Steinbeck, "About Ed Ricketts," p. 209.

62. Steinbeck, *America and Americans and Selected Nonfiction*, p. 377.

63. Steinbeck, *America and Americans and Selected Nonfiction*, p. 377.

64. Steinbeck, *America and Americans and Selected Nonfiction*, p. 379.

65. Steinbeck, *America and Americans and Selected Nonfiction*, p. 371.

66. Steinbeck, *America and Americans and Selected Nonfiction*, p. 380.

67. Arne Naess, "The Shallow and the Deep, Long Range Ecology Movement," *Inquiry* 16.1–4 (1973), pp. 95–100.

68. Murray Bookchin, *The Ecology of Freedom*. Palo Alto, CA: Cheshire Books, 1982, p. 1.

7. STEINBECK AT WAR

1. John Steinbeck, "A Primer on the Thirties," *America and Americans and Selected Nonfiction*, ed. Susan Shillinglaw and Jackson J. Benson. New York: Viking, 2002, p. 30.

2. Actor Burgess Meredith had invited Steinbeck to spend some time at his residence. Steinbeck's 1943 essay "The Making of a New Yorker" was written during this period.

3. Donald V. Coers, *John Steinbeck Goes to War: "The Moon Is Down" as Propaganda*. Tuscaloosa: University of Alabama Press, 1991, rpt. 2006.

4. Clifton Fadiman ("Two Ways to Win the War") and James Thurber reviews. Fadiman had criticized *The Grapes of Wrath* for "the tawdriest kind of fake symbolism" (*The New Yorker* 15 [April 1939], p. 81). For James Thurber, see *John Steinbeck: The Contemporary Reviews*, ed. Joseph M. McElrath, Jesse Crisler, and Susan Shillinglaw. Cambridge: Cambridge University Press, 1996.

5. John Steinbeck, *The Moon Is Down*. New York: Viking Press, 1942, p. 20.

6. Steinbeck, *The Moon Is Down*, p. 20.

7. Steinbeck, *The Moon Is Down*, p. 21.

8. Steinbeck, *The Moon Is Down*, p. 21.

9. Steinbeck, *The Moon Is Down*, p. 22.

10. Steinbeck, *The Moon Is Down*, p. 22.

11. John Steinbeck, *Steinbeck: A Life in Letters*, ed. Elaine Steinbeck and Robert Wallsten. New York: Viking, 1975, p. 80.

12. Warren French, *John Steinbeck's Fiction Revisited*. New York: Twayne, 1994, p. 90.

13. Christopher Browning, *Ordinary Men: Reserve Police Battalion 101 and the Final Solution in Poland*. New York: Harper, 1992; Robert J. Lifton, *The Nazi Doctors: Medical Killing and the Psychology of Genocide*. New York: Basic Books, 2000.

14. Steinbeck, *The Moon Is Down*, pp. 108–109, 113.

15. Coers, *John Steinbeck Goes to War*, p. 34.

16. Frank G. Nelson, letter to the *New Republic* (April 13, 1942).

17. Mark D. Bradbury, review of "The Moon Is Down," *Public Integrity* 9.2 (Spring 2007), pp. 201–204. Bradbury, on page 201, points out that there is no substantive entry for *The Moon Is Down* in Stephen K. George's book on Steinbeck and ethics, although the moral and ethical challenges raised by the book "remain vital and compelling." See Stephen K. George, ed., *The Moral Philosophy of John Steinbeck*. Lanham, MD: Scarecrow Press, 2005.

18. Coers, *John Steinbeck Goes to War*, p. 6.

19. Coers, *John Steinbeck Goes to War*, pp. 5–6. Steinbeck wrote to Frank Knox, the secretary of the navy, May 5, 1942, about Japanese scientists as "pure" scientists who were part of the scientific community (*Steinbeck: A Life in Letters*, pp. 230–231).

20. Quoted in Coers, *John Steinbeck Goes to War*, p. 7. Steinbeck notes his appointment as a special consultant to the secretary of war in a letter of July 25, 1942. He describes Times Square in Manhattan, dimly lit in wartime, as "ghostly" (*Steinbeck: A Life in Letters*, p. 232).

21. French, *John Steinbeck's Fiction Revisited*, p. 91; Warren French, *John Steinbeck's Nonfiction Revisited*. New York: Twayne, 1996, p. 47.

22. John Steinbeck, *Bombs Away: The Story of a Bomber Team*. New York: Viking Press, 1942, p. 17.

23. See Mimi Reisel Gladstein's essay "Mr. Novelist Goes to War: Hemingway and Steinbeck as Front-line Correspondents," *War, Literature, & the Arts: An International Journal of the Humanities* 15.1–2 (March 2003), p. 258.

24. John Ditsky, *John Steinbeck and the Critics*. London: Camden House, 2000, p. 5.

25. Steinbeck, *Bombs Away*, p. 17.

26. Steinbeck, *Bombs Away*, p. 114.

27. Rodney P. Rice cites statistics from Walter J. Boyne, *Clash of Wings: World War II in the Air*. New York: Touchstone, 1994, p. 282. See Rodney P. Rice, "Group Man Goes to War: Elements of Propaganda in John Steinbeck's *Bombs Away*," *War, Literature & the Arts: An Interdisciplinary Journal of the Humanities* 15.1–2 (2002), pp. 178–193.

28. Boyne cited in Rice, "Group Man Goes to War," p. 178.

29. Note 1 in Rice, "Group Man Goes to War," p. 191.

30. Steinbeck, *Bombs Away*, pp. 123–124.

31. Rice, "Group Man Goes to War," p. 179.

32. Steinbeck, *Bombs Away*, pp. 16–17.

33. Rice, "Group Man Goes to War," p. 186.

34. Rice uses some of these terms in identifying the men, "Group Man Goes to War," p. 187.

35. Joseph McElrath Jr., Jesse S. Crisler, and Susan Shillinglaw, eds., *John Steinbeck: The Contemporary Reviews*. Cambridge: Cambridge University Press, 1996, p. 267.

36. McElrath, Crisler, and Shillinglaw, *John Steinbeck: The Contemporary Reviews*, p. 262. Rodney Rice examines what propaganda is through reference to rhetoric and "wholes" in Gestalt psychology. Peter Lisca has referred to Gestalt in *The Wide World of John Steinbeck*. New Brunswick, NJ: Rutgers University Press, 1958, pp. 183, 188.

37. Jackson J. Benson, *The True Adventures of John Steinbeck, Writer*. New York: Viking, 1984, p. 511. See Robert E. Morsberger, "Steinbeck's War," *Critical Insights: John Steinbeck*, ed. Don Noble. Pasadena, CA: Salem Press, 2011, p. 291.

38. John Steinbeck, *Once There Was a War*. New York: Viking Press, 1958, p. 43.

39. Steinbeck, *Once There Was a War*, p. 62.

40. Steinbeck, *Once There Was a War*, p. 115.

41. Steinbeck, *Once There Was a War*, p. 125.

42. Steinbeck, *Once There Was a War*, pp. 131–132.

43. Steinbeck, *Once There Was a War*, pp. 136–138. Warren French makes the point that the invasion was like a Fairbanks film (*John Steinbeck's Nonfiction Revisited*, p. 57).

44. Steinbeck, *Steinbeck: A Life in Letters*, p. 264.

45. Cliff Lewis, "Art for Politics: John Steinbeck and FDR," *After "The Grapes of Wrath": Essays on John Steinbeck in Honor of Tetsumaro Hayashi*, ed. Donald V. Coers, Paul D. Ruffin, and Robert J. DeMott. Athens: Ohio University Press, p. 24.

46. Bill Mauldin cartoon (April 8, 1946), Library of Congress, photos and prints, http://www.loc.gov. Steinbeck lived for a brief time in the same Rockland County, New York, neighborhood as Mauldin.

47. John Steinbeck quoted in Benson, *The True Adventures of John Steinbeck, Writer*, pp. 734–735. See Steinbeck's foreword to the speeches of Adlai Stevenson reprinted in *America and Americans and Selected Nonfiction*, ed. Susan Shillinglaw and Jackson J. Benson. New York: Viking, 2002, pp. 219–222. Steinbeck wrote to Adlai Stevenson on June 29, 1960, his prediction that Richard

Nixon, "close and secret, a deep dissembler," resembled Shakespeare's Richard III, and he added: "The theme of Richard III will prove prophetic." *Steinbeck: A Life in Letters*, p. 632.

48. Steinbeck, *America and Americans and Selected Nonfiction*, p. 354.

49. Steinbeck, *America and Americans and Selected Nonfiction*, p. 354.

50. Danica Cerce, "A New Reading of an Old Text in Eastern Europe: John Steinbeck's *In Dubious Battle*," *Journal of Language, Literature and Culture* 60.3 (December 2013), p. 179.

51. Cerce, "A New Reading of an Old Text in Eastern Europe," p. 178.

52. Cerce, "A New Reading of an Old Text in Eastern Europe," p. 179.

53. Cerce, "A New Reading of an Old Text in Eastern Europe," pp. 179–180.

54. Cerce, "A New Reading of an Old Text in Eastern Europe," p. 180; Petr Kopecky, "The Literary Front of the Cold War: John Steinbeck as an Ideological Object in the Eastern Bloc," *Comparative American Studies: An International Journal* 9.3 (September 2011), pp. 204–216.

55. There have been opera and musical adaptations of *The Grapes of Wrath*, a novel that was never intended for the stage.

56. John Steinbeck, "The Making of a New Yorker," *America and Americans and Selected Nonfiction*, p. 38.

57. Elia Kazan, *Elia Kazan: A Life*. New York: Alfred A. Knopf, 1988, p. 785. Playwright Arthur Miller made a similar comment, wondering why Steinbeck left California and if his work suffered for it. Steinbeck wrote to his friend Dook Sheffield: "I should have known long before that I don't belong anywhere." See Benson, *The True Adventures of John Steinbeck, Writer*, pp. 702–703.

58. French, *John Steinbeck's Fiction Revisited*, p. 111.

8. THE SHORTER NOVELS

1. John Steinbeck, *Tortilla Flat*. New York: Covici-Friede, 1935, p. 35.

2. Steinbeck, *Tortilla Flat*, pp. 37, 41.

3. Susan Shillinglaw, "Steinbeck and Ethnicity," *Critical Insights: John Steinbeck*, ed. Don Noble. Pasadena, CA: Salem Press, 2011, p. 262.

4. Shillinglaw, "Steinbeck and Ethnicity," p. 263.

5. Shillinglaw, "Steinbeck and Ethnicity," pp. 266, 267, 268–269.

6. Steinbeck, *Tortilla Flat*, p. 1.

7. Joseph Fontenrose, "Tortilla Flat and the Creation of a Legend," *Critical Insights: John Steinbeck* (Noble), p. 113.

8. Nicholas Coles, "Democratizing Literature: Issues in Teaching Working-Class Literature," *College English* 48.7 (November 1986), p. 665. See also

Thomas M. Tammaro, "Sharing Creation: Steinbeck, *In Dubious Battle*, and the Working-Class Novel in American Literature," *Critical Insights: John Steinbeck* (Noble), pp. 124–133.

9. Steinbeck, *Tortilla Flat*, p. 1.

10. John Steinbeck, *America and Americans*, ed. Susan Shillinglaw and Jackson J. Benson. New York: Viking, 2002, p. 159.

11. Jason Spangler points out that in both the 1930s and the 1950s, cultural consolidation and hegemony were sought at the expense of individualism ("We're on the Road to Nowhere: Steinbeck and Kerouac, and the Legacy of the Great Depression," *Studies in the Novel* 40.3 [Fall 2008], pp. 308–327).

12. Steinbeck, *Tortilla Flat*, p. 56.

13. Steinbeck, *Tortilla Flat*, p. 56.

14. The memory of buried treasure around Monterey once inspired Robert Louis Stevenson's *Treasure Island*.

15. William Rose Benét, *Saturday Review*, see Joseph McElrath, Jesse S. Crisler, and Susan Shillinglaw, eds., *John Steinbeck: The Contemporary Reviews*. Cambridge: Cambridge University Press, 1996.

16. Steinbeck, *America and Americans*, p. 325.

17. Steinbeck, *American and Americans*, pp. 328–329.

18. Steinbeck, *America and Americans*, p. 347.

19. Steinbeck, *America and Americans*, p. 348.

20. Steinbeck, *America and Americans*, p. 348.

21. Steinbeck, *America and Americans*, p. 352.

22. Steinbeck, *America and Americans*, p. 353.

23. Steinbeck, *Tortilla Flat*, p. 5.

24. Steinbeck, *Tortilla Flat*, p. 82.

25. John Steinbeck, *Steinbeck: A Life in Letters*, ed. Elaine Steinbeck and Robert Wallsten. New York: Viking, pp. 111–112, quoted in Morris Dickstein, "Steinbeck and the Great Depression," *South Atlantic Quarterly* 103.1 (Winter 2004), p. 116.

26. John Steinbeck, *Cannery Row*. New York: Viking Press, 1945, p. 26.

27. Steinbeck, *America and Americans*, p. 163.

28. Steinbeck, *America and Americans*, p. 165.

29. Steinbeck, *America and Americans*, p. 159.

30. Steinbeck, *America and Americans*, p. 160. Granville Hicks made a similar comment on Aldous Huxley's *Brave New World*, quipping that Huxley was writing on utopia rather than on serious social issues (*New Republic*, 1932). While Steinbeck's short comic novel was criticized by some reviewers, other critics responded favorably. The shorter novels have "a sensuous simplicity," observed Morris Dickstein, who had read *Cannery Row* when he was "quite young" (Dickstein, "Steinbeck and the Great Depression," p. 111).

31. W. L. Scofield, "California Fisheries Report California's Commercial Fish Catch." University of California Digital Library, p. 30, http://swfsc.noaa. gov.

32. The attempt to use canning waste for chicken feed was eventually prohibited by the California Department of Fish and Game, which instituted laws that were in place from 1920 on (Scofield, California Fisheries Report, p. 33).

33. W. L. Scofield, "California's Commercial Fish Catch." Calisphere, University of California Digital Library, p. 12; Edward Ueber and Alec MacCall, *The Rise and Fall of the California Sardine Empire*, Southwest Fisheries Science Center, 2013.

34. Mimi Reisel Gladstein, "Steinbeck and the Woman Question: A Never-Ending Puzzle," *Critical Insights: John Steinbeck*, pp. 242–252. Questions about Steinbeck's position toward women have been raised and ought to be raised, given the roles in which they appear in his texts. Gladstein's inquiries provide significant first-wave feminist approaches to these issues.

35. Steinbeck, *Cannery Row*, p. 53.

36. Steinbeck, *Cannery Row*, p. 52.

37. Steinbeck, *Cannery Row*, p. 88.

38. Steinbeck, *Cannery Row*, p. 88.

39. Steinbeck, *Cannery Row*, p. 90.

40. Steinbeck, *Cannery Row*, p. 89.

41. Steinbeck, *Cannery Row*, p. 123.

42. Steinbeck, *Cannery Row*, pp. 17, 36, 113–114.

43. Steinbeck, *Cannery Row*, p. 9.

44. Steinbeck, *Cannery Row*, p. 17; Michael J. Meyer, *Literature and Music*. New York: Rodopi, 2002, p. 186.

45. Steinbeck, *Cannery Row*, p. 36.

46. Steinbeck, *Cannery Row*, p. 37.

47. Steinbeck, *Cannery Row*, p. 68.

48. This is noted by Michael J. Meyer, who observes that "the event is shocking and tragic, yet appears to depict some sort of ecstatic beauty cloaked beneath the fearful signs of death and mortality" (*Literature and Music*, p. 186). Doc's experience also calls to mind Edmund Burke's essay on the Gothic: that such terror evokes the sublime. In a theological context, Rudolf Otto refers to awe and the idea of the holy.

49. Steinbeck, *Cannery Row*, p. 122.

50. Steinbeck, *Cannery Row*, p. 122.

51. John Steinbeck, *The Wayward Bus*. New York: Viking Press, 1947, p. 149.

52. Steinbeck, *The Wayward Bus*, p. 150.

53. Steinbeck, *The Wayward Bus*, p. 49.

54. Steinbeck, *The Wayward Bus*, p. 100.

55. Steinbeck, *The Wayward Bus*, p. 56.

56. Steinbeck, *The Wayward Bus*, p. 44.

57. Steinbeck, *The Wayward Bus*, p. 43.

58. Cathryn Halverson, "John Steinbeck's Sweetheart: The Cosmic American Bus," *College Literature* 35.1 (Winter 2008): 82–99

59. Halverson, "John Steinbeck's Sweetheart," p. 89.

60. John Steinbeck, prologue, *Sweet Thursday*. New York: Viking, 1954, p. 1.

61. Steinbeck, prologue, *Sweet Thursday*, p. 1.

62. Steinbeck, prologue, *Sweet Thursday*, p. 1.

63. Steinbeck, prologue, *Sweet Thursday*, p. 1.

64. Robert DeMott, "*Sweet Thursday* Revisited: An Excursion in Suggestiveness," *Critical Insights: John Steinbeck* (Noble), p. 341.

65. DeMott, "*Sweet Thursday* Revisited," p. 332.

66. Steinbeck, *Sweet Thursday*, pp. 1–3. These comments are on pages 1, 2, and 3 respectively.

67. Steinbeck, *Sweet Thursday*, pp. 14–15.

68. Steinbeck, *Sweet Thursday*, p. 16.

69. Steinbeck, *Sweet Thursday*, pp. 118, 107.

70. Steinbeck, *Sweet Thursday*, p. 18.

71. Steinbeck, *Sweet Thursday*, p. 21.

72. Steinbeck, *Sweet Thursday*, p. 50.

73. Steinbeck, *Sweet Thursday*, p. 55.

74. Steinbeck, *Sweet Thursday*, p. 57.

75. Steinbeck, *Sweet Thursday*, p. 58.

76. Steinbeck, *Sweet Thursday*, p. 61.

77. Steinbeck, *Sweet Thursday*, p. 61. In 2016, there is a trend toward countering cultural distraction with meditation and awareness. Anderson Cooper's report on "Mindfulness" on CBS News' *60 Minutes* (September 6, 2015) was one expression of this.

78. Steinbeck, *Sweet Thursday*, p. 68.

79. DeMott, "*Sweet Thursday* Revisited," p. 321.

80. DeMott, "*Sweet Thursday* Revisited," p. 323.

81. DeMott, "*Sweet Thursday* Revisited," p. 324.

82. DeMott, "*Sweet Thursday* Revisited," p. 324.

83. Roy S. Simmonds, *John Steinbeck: The War Years, 1939–1945*. Lewisburg, PA: Bucknell University Press, 1996, p. 141. Louis Owens objects to the novel, and Peter Lisca, Warren French, and Joseph Fontenrose also do not applaud it. Mimi Reisel Gladstein sees "time-worn sexist clichés" in it, although she also attempts to account for the novel's "enjoyable" mysteries. See Mimi R. Gladstein, "Straining for Profundity: Steinbeck's *Burning Bright* and *Sweet*

Thursday," *The Short Novels of John Steinbeck*, ed. Jackson J. Benson. Durham, NC: Duke University Press, 1990, pp. 234–248.

84. DeMott, "*Sweet Thursday* Revisited," p. 325.

85. John Steinbeck, galley 1, cited in DeMott, "*Sweet Thursday* Revisited," p. 327. DeMott's comment on Steinbeck's "incipient postmodernism" appears in this essay, p. 329.

86. DeMott, "*Sweet Thursday* Revisited," p. 331.

87. DeMott, "*Sweet Thursday* Revisited," p. 332.

88. DeMott, "*Sweet Thursday* Revisited," p. 342.

89. DeMott, "*Sweet Thursday* Revisited," p. 343.

90. Frank O'Malley, "More Books of the Week," *Commonweal* (April 25, 1947): 43–44.

91. John Steinbeck, *The Pearl*. New York: Viking Press, 1947, p. 2.

92. Steinbeck, *The Pearl*, p. 4.

93. Steinbeck, *The Pearl*, p. 4. See Roger Caswell, "A Musical Journey through the Pearl: Motion, Engagement, and Comprehension," *Journal of Adolescent and Adult Literacy* 49.1 (September 2005): 62–67.. The usual presentation of *The Pearl* in eighth- and ninth-grade classrooms as a folktale with a message overlooks the "multifaceted" construction of this story, Michael J. Meyer argues (*Literature and Music*, pp. 191–200; see pp. 193–194). Meyer focuses much of his close reading with the notion of harmonic contrast: Kino's experience of "harsh sounds" with Kino's hope for the return of "positive melodic lines" (pp. 196–197). However, this tonal tension also corresponds with the relation of the human with the natural world.

94. Steinbeck, *The Pearl*, pp. 6–7.

95. Steinbeck, *The Pearl*, p. 22.

96. Steinbeck, *The Pearl*, p. 22.

97. Steinbeck, *The Pearl*, p. 23.

98. Steinbeck, *The Pearl*, pp. 35–36.

99. Steinbeck, *The Pearl*, p. 51.

100. Steinbeck, *The Pearl*, p. 80.

101. John Steinbeck, "Critics, Critics Burning Bright," *Saturday Review* 33 (November 11, 1950): 20–21. Jackson J. Benson writes of Steinbeck's books that "each was different, each was experimental" (*The True Adventures of John Steinbeck, Writer*, p. 880).

9. EAST OF EDEN

1. John Steinbeck, *Steinbeck: A Life in Letters*, ed. Elaine Steinbeck and Robert Wallsten. New York: Viking, 1975, pp. 433–434. See letter to Carlton A.

Sheffield (December 1952): "I had never expected to make a living writing." Steinbeck called *East of Eden* "much the longest and most difficult work I have ever done" in a letter to Bo Beskow (November 16, 1952) (*Steinbeck: A Life in Letters*, p. 402; cited in Jackson J. Benson, *The True Adventures of John Steinbeck, Writer*. New York: Viking, 1984, p. 697).

2. In Genesis we read: "And Cain went out from the presence of the Lord, and dwelt in the land of Nod, on the east of Eden."

3. John Steinbeck, *East of Eden*. New York: Viking, 1952, p. 189.

4. John Steinbeck, letter to Pascal Covici (September 11, 1951), *John Steinbeck: A Life in Letters*, p. 400; Louis Owens, *Steinbeck's Re-vision of America*. Athens: University of Georgia Press, 1985, p. 45. See Owens's discussion of the novel, pp. 140–155.

5. Howard Levant suggests that reference to the doctrine of free will is used to unify the novel (*The Novels of John Steinbeck: A Critical Study*. Columbia: University of Missouri, 1974, p. 42).

6. Henry Veggian, "Bio-Politics and the Institution of Literature: An Essay on *East of Eden*, Its Critics, and Its Time," *East of Eden: New and Recent Essays*, ed. Michael J. Meyer and Henry Veggian. New York: Rodopi, 2013, p. 110.

7. Veggian, "Bio-Politics and the Institution of Literature," p. 110.

8. Elia Kazan, *Eliza Kazan: A Life*. New York: Alfred A. Knopf, 1988, p. 546.

9. *Zapata!* ed. Robert E. Morsberger, quoted in Warren French, *John Steinbeck's Nonfiction Revisited*. New York: Twayne, 1996, p. 68. Kazan's letter to Steinbeck appears in Elia Kazan, *Kazan on Directing*. New York: Alfred A. Knopf, 2009, pp. 183–184.

10. Although the film's director, Elia Kazan, was unimpressed with James Dean upon meeting him, he believed that the young actor fit the part well. "I saw that the story of the movie was his story—just as it was, in a way, my own," he wrote. He told screenwriter Paul Osborn that James Dean *was* Cal Trask. After Steinbeck met him, he also agreed (*Elia Kazan: A Life*, pp. 534–535). In 1981, an eight-hour television miniseries of *East of Eden* appeared, adapting the full novel. This novel sells about fifty thousand copies annually, a figure that is likely supported by the film versions.

11. Steinbeck, *East of Eden*, p. 320.

12. Steinbeck, *East of Eden*, p. 328.

13. Steinbeck, *East of Eden*, p. 328.

14. Steinbeck, *East of Eden*, pp. 331–332.

15. Steinbeck, *East of Eden*, p. 331.

16. Steinbeck, *East of Eden*, p. 335.

17. Steinbeck, *East of Eden*, pp. 332–333.

18. Steinbeck, *East of Eden*, p. 332.

19. Steinbeck, *East of Eden*, p. 333.

20. Steinbeck, *East of Eden*, pp. 343–344.

21. Steinbeck, *East of Eden*, pp. 385.

22. Steinbeck, *East of Eden*, p. 40. See John Steinbeck, *Journal of a Novel: The* East of Eden *Letters*. New York: Viking, 1969, for Steinbeck's comments to Covici. Steinbeck wrote to Pascal Covici about his method of counterpoint (*Steinbeck: A Life in Letters*, p. 409).

23. Steinbeck, *East of Eden*, p. 54.

24. Michael J. Meyer, "Harmonic Dissonance: Steinbeck's Implementation and Adaptation of Musical Techniques," *Literature and Music*, ed. Michael J. Meyer. New York: Rodopi, 2002, p. 188.

25. Steinbeck, *Journal of a Novel*, p. 53; Meyer, *Literature and Music*, p. 188. Meyer points to Steinbeck's references to music in *Journal of a Novel* that suggest attempts to reflect musical structure in his fiction. See Michael J. Meyer, "Steinbeck's Implementation and Adaptation of Musical Techniques," *Literature and Music*, 2002. Peter Lisca refers to Steinbeck's use of juxtaposition in *John Steinbeck: Nature and Myth*. New York: Thomas Y. Crowell, 1978, p. 94.

26. Steinbeck, *Journal of a Novel*, p. 155.

27. Steinbeck, *Journal of a Novel*, p. 166; Meyer, *Literature and Music*, p. 189. When we consider that the long novel is, in part, a development of earlier material we might wonder what devices and techniques were made use of in "Dissonant Symphony," the work Steinbeck discarded in 1931. Jackson Benson points out that the text suggests "the fact that sometimes the smallest event or circumstance can lead to profound changes in a person's course of action" (*The True Adventures of John Steinbeck, Writer*, p. 201).

28. Meyer, *Literature and Music*, p. 188.

29. Meyer, *Literature and Music*, p.151.

30. Steinbeck, *East of Eden*, p. 385.

31. Steinbeck, *East of Eden*, pp. 385, 387.

32. Carol L. Hansen, "Beyond Evil: Cathy and Cal in *East of Eden*," *Critical Insights: John Steinbeck*, ed. Don Noble. Pasadena, CA: Salem Press, 2011, p. 312.

33. Steinbeck, *East of Eden*, p. 503.

34. Robert DeMott writes that "Steinbeck reprised his tumultuous marriage to Gwyn" in *Burning Bright* and *East of Eden*. See his essay in Tetsumaro Hayashi, ed., *John Steinbeck: The Years of Greatness, 1936–1939*. Tuscaloosa: University of Alabama Press, 1993, pp. 44–45.

35. Steinbeck, *East of Eden*, p. 464.

36. Steinbeck, *East of Eden*, p. 464.

37. Steinbeck, *East of Eden*, p. 465.

38. Steinbeck, *East of Eden*, p. 467.

39. Steinbeck, *East of Eden*, pp. 469–471.
40. Steinbeck, *East of Eden*, p. 480.
41. Steinbeck, *East of Eden*, p. 480.
42. Steinbeck, *East of Eden*, p. 482.
43. Steinbeck, *East of Eden*, p. 483.
44. Steinbeck, *East of Eden*, p. 696.
45. Steinbeck, *East of Eden*, p. 698.
46. Steinbeck, *East of Eden*, p. 698.
47. Steinbeck, *East of Eden*, p. 701.
48. Steinbeck, *East of Eden*, p. 661.
49. See Paul McCarthy, *John Steinbeck*. New York: Frederick Ungar, 1980, p. 120.
50. John Steinbeck, *Journal of a Novel: The* East of Eden *Letters*. He tells his two sons that he will express "the greatest story of all—the story of good and evil, of strength and weakness, of love and hate, of beauty and ugliness . . . how these doubles are inseparable." See *Steinbeck: Novels 1942–1952*, ed. Robert DeMott. New York: Library of America, 2001, p. 963.
51. Steinbeck, *East of Eden*, p. 591.
52. Steinbeck, *East of Eden*, p. 629. The Hebrew word is *timshol*. Steinbeck spelled the word *timshel* in the text. The Judaic core ethics were approached from different standpoints in the twentieth century by the neo-Kantian Hermann Cohen and the existentialist Martin Buber, who focused upon I–Thou relationships.
53. Steinbeck, *East of Eden*, p. 800.
54. Steinbeck, *East of Eden*, p. 947. Kristin M. Swenson, in "Care and Keeping East of Eden," explores the derivation of Hebrew words and concepts regarding care and responsibility in Genesis. "Am I my brother's keeper?" is Cain's question. "Simiru", also "shamar," she notes, is Hebrew for to keep watch and preserve. Swenson argues that the other is not only brother but also the earth. Care for the earth is inseparable from care for other people (*Interpretation* 60.4 [October 2006], pp. 373–384).
55. Steinbeck, *Steinbeck: A Life in Letters*, p. 405.
56. Steinbeck, *Journal of a Novel* (1969).

10. AMERICA AND AMERICANS

1. John Steinbeck IV, *In Touch*. New York: Alfred A. Knopf, 1969, xii.
2. All quotations are from John F. Kenney's inaugural address, January 20, 1961. David Halberstam, *The Best and the Brightest*. New York: Random House, 1972; rpt. Norwalk: Easton Press, 2005, p. 38. Theodore Sorensen later noted the many drafts that the inaugural address went through (p. 241). The full text of the

speech appears in Theodore C. Sorensen, *Kennedy*. New York: Harper & Row, 1965, pp. 245–248. There was a parade under "brilliant sky, shining snow," Arthur Schlesinger recalled (p. 165). With Kennedy "there were sparks," Nigerian diplomat Samuel Ibe once said (Arthur M. Schlesinger Jr., *A Thousand Days: John F. Kennedy in the White House*. Boston: Houghton Mifflin, 1965, p. 560). There were sparks from the lectern—short-circuited wires—on inauguration day. Steinbeck's comment that syntax has been restored appears in Jackson J. Benson, *The True Adventures of John Steinbeck, Writer*. New York: Viking, 1984, p. 892.

3. John Steinbeck (*Saturday Evening Post*, July 2, 1966) in *America and Americans and Selected Nonfiction*, ed. Susan Shillinglaw and Jackson J. Benson. Viking, 2002, p. 397. Steinbeck evidently held the perspective of the Warren Commission findings that Kennedy was killed by a lone gunman. In his view he was assassinated "by a man who had failed in everything"—marriage, politics, and desire to be accepted—who was jealous of Kennedy's "beautiful and loving wife . . . high position . . . respect and admiration of his countrymen" (*America and Americans*, p. 361).

4. Susan Shillinglaw and Jackson J. Benson, "Engaged Artist," *America and Americans and Selected Nonfiction*, pp. 66–67. Benson points out that *The Winter of Our Discontent* and *Travels with Charley* adopt a personal point of view (*The True Adventures of John Steinbeck, Writer*, p. 729).

5. Shillinglaw and Benson, *America and Americans and Selected Nonfiction*, p. 314.

6. John Steinbeck, *Steinbeck: A Life in Letters*, ed. Elaine Steinbeck and Robert Wallsten. New York: Viking, 1975, pp. 668–669. The title emerged from a phone call to his wife Elaine, who suggested that she was reminded of Robert Louis Stevenson's "travels with a donkey" (*Steinbeck: A Life in Letters*, p. 643).

7. John Steinbeck, *Travels with Charley*. New York: Viking, 1962, p. 205.

8. Steinbeck, *Travels with Charley*, p. 227.

9. Steinbeck, *Travels with Charley*, p. 256.

10. John Ditsky, "Steinbeck's *Travels with Charley*: The Quest That Failed," *Steinbeck Quarterly* 8.2 (Spring 1975). Pertinent to the discussion that follows is a comparison that has been made between Steinbeck's study of "The Harvest Gypsies" and the diaspora from New Orleans following Hurricane Katrina (Nicolaus Mills, "John Steinbeck's Hurricane Katrina Lesson," *Dissent* 53.4 [Fall 2006], pp. 97–98).

11. John Steinbeck, *Louisville Courier-Journal* (August 25, 1956).

12. John Steinbeck, "My War with the Ospreys," *America and Americans and Selected Nonfiction*, p. 41.

13. Steinbeck, "My War with the Ospreys," p. 41.

14. John Steinbeck, *The Winter of Our Discontent*, p. 57. The page numbers correspond with the Bantam paperback edition of the novel (New York: Bantam Books, 1962).

15. Steinbeck, *The Winter of Our Discontent*, p. 75.

16. Steinbeck, *The Winter of Our Discontent*, p. 66.

17. This is the blurb on the back cover of the Bantam paperback edition of *The Winter of Our Discontent* (New York: Bantam Books, 1962).

18. Steinbeck, *The Winter of Our Discontent*, p. 131.

19. Steinbeck, *The Winter of Our Discontent*, p. 99.

20. Steinbeck, *The Winter of Our Discontent*, pp. 106–107.

21. Steinbeck, *The Winter of Our Discontent*, p. 118.

22. Steinbeck, *The Winter of Our Discontent*, p. 117.

23. Steinbeck, *The Winter of Our Discontent*, p. 199.

24. Steinbeck, *The Winter of Our Discontent*, p. 153.

25. Steinbeck, *The Winter of Our Discontent*, p. 153.

26. Steinbeck, *The Winter of Our Discontent*, p. 120.

27. Perhaps Steinbeck is implying something like what postmodernist thinkers later called the Disneyfication of America. Certainly, Allen Hawley's obsession with television celebrity and the role-playing of Margie Young-Hunt and Mr. Baker would lend credence to such a view. The mask comes from the back of a cereal box and is associated with a "ventriloquism gadget" (*The Winter of Our Discontent*, p. 61).

28. Steinbeck, *The Winter of Our Discontent*, p. 132.

29. Steinbeck, *The Winter of Our Discontent*, p. 98.

30. Steinbeck, *The Winter of Our Discontent*, pp. 98–99.

31. Steinbeck, *The Winter of Our Discontent*, p. 61.

32. Steinbeck, *The Winter of Our Discontent*, p. 62.

33. Steinbeck, *The Winter of Our Discontent*, p. 61.

34. Steinbeck, *The Winter of Our Discontent*, p. 75.

35. Steinbeck, *The Winter of Our Discontent*, p. 82.

36. Steinbeck, *The Winter of Our Discontent*, p. 61.

37. Steinbeck, *The Winter of Our Discontent*, p. 92.

38. Steinbeck, *The Winter of Our Discontent*, p. 94.

39. Steinbeck, *The Winter of Our Discontent*, p. 166.

40. Steinbeck, *The Winter of Our Discontent*, p. 285.

41. Steinbeck, *The Winter of Our Discontent*, p. 294.

42. Robert Coles, *The Call of Stories: Teaching and the Moral Imagination.* Boston: Houghton Mifflin, 1990.

43. John Steinbeck, "Conversation at Sag Harbor," *America and Americans and Selected Nonfiction*, p. 54.

44. Dan Rattiner, *In the Hamptons: My Fifty Years with Farmers, Fishermen, and Artists*. New York: Random House, 2010, p. 79. Rattiner published the *Montauk Pioneer*, 1960, and the *East Village Other* with Walter Bowart, Allan Katzman, and John Wilcock in 1965. He writes *Dan's Papers*, which is distributed in the Hamptons. He hosted the WQXR Radio Hamptons Report in the 1990s. *Time* magazine in 1975 said that he created myths and legends.

45. Rattiner, *In the Hamptons*, pp. 81–83.

46. John Steinbeck, "Nobel Prize Acceptance Speech," *America and Americans*, pp. 172–174. Critic Arthur Mizener launched an attack on Steinbeck in the *New York Times*, asking if a writer of 1930s vision should be given the Nobel Prize. Mizener, who absorbed the perspective of the New Critics, wrote the first major biography of F. Scott Fitzgerald, *The Far Side of Paradise* (1951), and works on Ford Maddox Ford and Joseph Conrad, but he never published fiction or personally experienced the practice of a fiction writer.

47. Steinbeck, *America and Americans*, 1966. The illustrations in the original edition are a bit distracting from his text. The later collection of *America and Americans* with other essays by Steinbeck that Susan Shillinglaw and Jackson Benson have assembled is a more user-friendly volume for those who wish to focus on Steinbeck's thoughts (*America and Americans and Selected Nonfiction* [New York: Viking, 2002]).

48. Steinbeck, *America and Americans*, p. 127.

49. Steinbeck, *America and Americans*, p. 317.

50. Shillinglaw and Benson, *America and Americans*, p. 313.

51. Shillinglaw and Benson, *America and Americans*, p. 314.

52. See Robert Bellah et al., *Habits of the Heart: Individualism and Commitment in American Life*. Berkeley: University of California Press, 2007; Robert D. Putnam, *Bowling Alone: The Collapse and Revival of American Community*. New York: Touchstone, Simon & Schuster, 2001; Christopher Lasch, *The Culture of Narcissism: Life in an Age of Diminishing Expectations*. New York: Norton, 1991; M. Scott Peck, *A World Waiting to Be Born: Civility Rediscovered*. New York: Bantam, 1994.

53. Shillinglaw and Benson, *America and Americans*, p. 316.

54. John Steinbeck, "Americans and the Future," *America and Americans*, p. 396.

55. John H. Timmerman, "Steinbeck's Environmental Ethic: Humanity in Harmony with the Land," *Critical Insights: John Steinbeck*, ed. Don Noble. Pasadena, CA: Salem Press, 2011, p. 228.

56. Steinbeck, "Americans and the Land," p. 379.

57. Timmerman, "Steinbeck's Environmental Ethic," p. 235.

58. Timmerman, "Steinbeck's Environmental Ethic," p. 232: Roy S. Simmonds has called *America and Americans* "in some ways a deeply pessimistic

work" (*Steinbeck's Travel Literature: Essays in Criticism*, ed. Tetsumaro Hayashi. Muncie, IN: Steinbeck Society of America, 1980, p. 26).

59. Thomas Berry, *The Dream of the Earth*. San Francisco: Sierra Club Books, 1988.

60. Steinbeck, "Americans and the Land," p. 377.

61. Steinbeck, "Americans and the Land," p. 377.

62. Steinbeck, "Americans and the Land," p. 378.

63. Steinbeck, "Americans and the Land," p. 379.

64. Steinbeck, "Americans and the Land," p. 381.

65. Steinbeck, "Americans and the Land," p. 381.

66. Steinbeck, "Americans and the Land," p. 381.

67. John Steinbeck, "Then My Arm Glassed Up," *America and Americans*, p. 127.

68. Steinbeck, "Americans and the Land," p. 382.

69. Steinbeck, "Americans and the Land," p. 382.

70. John Steinbeck, *Popular Science* (September 1966), http://www.popsi.com/article/technology/john-steinbecks-1966-plea-create-nasa-oceans.

71. Steinbeck, "Americans and the Future," p. 400.

72. Steinbeck, "Americans and the Future," p. 402.

73. Steinbeck, "Americans and the Future," p. 401.

74. John Steinbeck, letter to Jack Valenti (August 12, 1964).

75. August 21, 1964, telephone log call at 8:45 P.M. Steinbeck. LBJ Library Records. Ref. 5111. Miller Center, University of Virginia, Charlottesville, Virginia, Scripps, 5111 WH6408 32 WAV MP3.

76. Eric Goldman, *The Tragedy of Lyndon Baines Johnson*. New York: Knopf, 1969, pp. 276–277.

77. Halford Ross Ryan, *Twentieth Century Addresses of American Presidents*. Westport, CT: Greenwood Press, 1993, p. 197.

78. Robert Bellah, "Civil Religion in America," *Daedalus* 96.1 (Winter 1967).The line from Steinbeck was incorporated in the Lyndon B. Johnson inaugural speech, January 20, 1965.

79. John Steinbeck, letter to President Lyndon Baines Johnson, *Steinbeck: A Life in Letters*, p. 763.

80. John Steinbeck's entry in "Letters to Alicia" also appears in "Vietnam War: No Front, No Rear," *America and Americans and Selected Nonfiction*, p. 296.

81. Steinbeck, *America and Americans*, p. 296.

82. Mimi R. Gladstein and James Meredith, "John Steinbeck and the Tragedy of the Vietnam War," *Steinbeck Review* 8.1 (Spring 2011).

83. Shillinglaw and Benson, *America and Americans*, p. 274.

84. Gladstein and Meredith, "Steinbeck and the Tragedy of the Vietnam War," p. 42.

85. Steinbeck, *Steinbeck: A Life in Letters*, pp. 780–781.

86. John Steinbeck, *Once There Was a War*. New York: Viking Press, 1958, p. 111.

87. John Steinbeck IV and Nancy Steinbeck, *The Other Side of Eden: Life with John Steinbeck*. Amherst, NY: Prometheus, 2001, p. 120.

88. Steinbeck and Steinbeck, *The Other Side of Eden*, p. 98.

89. Steinbeck and Steinbeck, *The Other Side of Eden*, p. 96.

90. Lyndon Baines Johnson, letter to John Steinbeck (June 21, 1966). Lyndon Baines Johnson Library Archives.

91. Lyndon Baines Johnson, phone call to John Steinbeck, December 4, 1966, at 2:22 P.M. Lyndon Baines Johnson Library Archives. Ref. 11112. http://www.YouTube.watch?v.tS2hTiN9utQ.

92. John Steinbeck quoted in Thomas Fensch, *Conversations with John Steinbeck*. Oxford: University of Mississippi Press, 1988, p. 66.

93. John Steinbeck, "Letters to Alicia," *Newsday* (January 21, 1967). Steinbeck's comments also appear in *America and Americans and Selected Nonfiction*, p. 305.

94. John Steinbeck, letter to Harry F. Guggenheim (January 19, 1967). See January 4, 1967, *John Steinbeck: A Life in Letters*, pp. 785–786.

95. Letters to Jack Valenti, *Steinbeck: A Life in Letters* (see pp. 765–766, 772).

96. Gladstein and Meredith, "John Steinbeck and the Tragedy of the Vietnam War," p. 54.

97. Lyndon Baines Johnson, Public Papers of Lyndon Baines Johnson (December 21, 1968). Elia Kazan describes Steinbeck's last day in his autobiography, *Elia Kazan: A Life*. New York: Alfred A. Knopf, 1988, p. 784. He adds: "When John didn't sharpen twenty wooden pencils every morning and sit down to write on his yellow legal pad, he didn't know why he was living. He was constantly in turmoil, a violent man with tender sensibilities" (p. 784).

98. Steinbeck, *Steinbeck: A Life in Letters*, p. 514. Steinbeck, while not trained in philosophy, wrote novels of ideas, observes Jackson J. Benson (*The True Adventures of John Steinbeck, Writer*, p. 832). Steinbeck's translation of Malory, *The Acts of King Arthur and His Noble Knights*, was published in 1976.

99. The global context calls us to be increasingly cosmopolitan, as writers like Jeremy Rifkin have pointed out, recalling the roots of that word in which *kosmos*, or "world," meets with *polis*, or "community." See Jeremy Rifkin, *The Empathic Civilization*. New York: Jeremy Tarcher, 2009, p. 428. He cites John Tomlinson, who observes that to be cosmopolitan is to be a "citizen of the world" (John

Tomlinson, *Globalization and Culture*. Chicago: University of Chicago Press, 1999, p. 184).

100. John Steinbeck, *Working Days*, ed. Robert DeMott. New York: Viking, 1990, xl.

BIBLIOGRAPHY

PRIMARY SOURCES

Allee, W. C. *Animal Aggregations: A Study in General Sociology*. Chicago: University of Chicago Press, 1931.

Allegretti, Joseph. "John Steinbeck and the Morality of Roles: Lessons for Business Ethics." *The Moral Philosophy of John Steinbeck*, ed. Stephen K. George. Lanham, MD: Scarecrow Press, 2005.

Altieri, Charles. "Lyrical Ethics and Literary Experience" (30–58). *Mapping the Ethical Turn: A Reader in Ethics, Culture, and Literary Theory*, ed. Todd F. Davis and Kenneth Womack. Charlottesville: University Press of Virginia, 1994.

Ambrose, Stephen. *Citizen Soldiers: The U.S. Army from Normandy Beaches to the Bulge to the Surrender of Germany*. New York: Touchstone, 1997.

Ariki, Kyoko, Luchen Li, and Scott Pugh, eds. *John Steinbeck: Global Dimensions*. Lanham, MD: Scarecrow Press, 2008.

Arnold, Martin. "Making Books: Of Mice and Men and Novelists." *New York Times* (February 7, 2002): E3.

Arnold, Matthew. *Culture and Anarchy* (1869), ed. J. Dover Wilson. Cambridge: Cambridge University Press, 1932.

Astro, Richard. *John Steinbeck and Edward F. Ricketts: The Shaping of a Novelist*. Minneapolis: University of Minnesota Press, 1973.

Astro, Richard, and Joel Hedgepath. *Steinbeck and the Sea*. Proceedings of a Conference Held at the Marine Sciences Auditorium. Newport, Oregon, May 4, 1974.

Bakersfield Californian (June 11, 1939): 1.

Bayley, Elizabeth. "Mimesis, Desire, and Lack in John Steinbeck's *East of Eden*" (145–166). *East of Eden: New and Recent Essays*, ed. Michael J. Meyer and Henry Veggian. New York: Rodopi, 2013.

Beegel, Susan F., Susan Shillinglaw, and Wesley N. Tiffney Jr., eds. *Steinbeck and the Environment: Interdisciplinary Approaches*. Tuscaloosa: University of Alabama Press, 1997.

Bellah, Robert N. "Civil Religion in America." *Daedalus* 96.1 (Winter 1967): 1–21.

Bellamy, Brent. "Tear into the Guts: Whitman, Steinbeck, Springsteen and the Durability of Lost Souls on the Road." *Canadian Review of American Studies* 41.2 (2011): 223–243.

Benét, William Rose. "Affectionate Bravos." Review of *Tortilla Flat*. *Saturday Review* 12.5 (June 1, 1935): 12.

———. "Apple Pickers' Strike." Review of *In Dubious Battle*. *Saturday Review* 13.14 (February 1, 1936): 10.

Benson, Jackson J. "John Steinbeck: Novelist as Scientist" (103–123). *John Steinbeck*, ed. Harold Bloom. New York: Chelsea House, 1987.

———. "John Steinbeck: The Favorite Author We Love to Hate" (93–109). *Critical Insights: John Steinbeck*, ed. Don Noble. Pasadena, CA: Salem Press, 2011.

———. *Looking for Steinbeck's Ghost*. Norman: University of Oklahoma Press, 1988.

———. *The True Adventures of John Steinbeck, Writer*. New York: Viking, 1984, rpt. Penguin, 1990.

Benson, Jackson J., ed. *The Short Novels of John Steinbeck: Critical Essays with a Checklist to Steinbeck Criticism*. Durham, NC: Duke University Press, 1990.

Benson, Jackson J., and Anne Loftis. "John Steinbeck and Farm Labor Unionization: The Background of *In Dubious Battle*." *American Literature* 52.2 (May 1980): 194–223.

Bloom, Harold, ed. Introduction (4–5). *John Steinbeck's "The Grapes of Wrath."* New York: Chelsea House, 1988.

———. *John Steinbeck*. New York: Chelsea House, 1987.

Boodin, John Elof. *Outline of Cosmic Evolution*. New York: Macmillan, 1925.

Booth, Wayne C. *The Company We Keep: An Ethics of Fiction*. Berkeley: University of California Press, 1989.

———. "Why Ethical Criticism Can Never Be Simple" (16–29). *Mapping the Ethical Turn: A Reader in Ethics, Culture, and Literary Theory*, ed. Todd F. Davis and Kenneth Womack. Charlottesville: University Press of Virginia, 2001.

Brie, Steve, and William T. Rossiter, eds. *Literature and Ethics: From the Green Knight to the Dark Knight*. Newcastle-on-Tyne: Cambridge Scholars Publishing, 2010.

Brown, Mary M. "*The Grapes of Wrath* and the Literary Canon of American Universities in the Nineties" (285–298). *The Critical Response to John Steinbeck's* The Grapes of Wrath, ed. Barbara A. Heavlin. Westport, CT: Greenwood Press, 2000.

Buell, Lawrence. *The Environmental Imagination: Thoreau, Nature Writing, and the Foundations of American Culture*. Cambridge: Belknap, 1995.

Burkhead, Cynthia. *Student Companion to John Steinbeck*. Westport, CT: Greenwood Press, 2002.

Butcher, Fanny (F.B.). "Books." *Chicago Daily Tribune* (February 27, 1937): 11.

"California Agricultural Strike." *New York Times* (October 18, 1933).

"California Clash Called 'Civil War.'" *New York Times* (October 22, 1933).

Cameron, Tom. "*The Grapes of Wrath* Author Guards Self from Threats at Moody Gulch." *Los Angeles Times* (July 9, 1939): 1–2.

Canby, Henry Seidel. "Casuals of the Road." *Saturday Review* 15.7 (February 27, 1937): 7.

Cassuto, David N. "Turning Wine into Water: Water as a Privileged Signifier in *The Grapes of Wrath*." *Language and Literature* 69 (1993). http://www.digitalcommons.pace.edu.cgi.

Cerce, Danica. "A New Reading of an Old Text in Eastern Europe: John Steinbeck's *In Dubious Battle*." *Journal of Language, Literature and Culture* 60.3 (December 2013): 178–192.

———. *Reading Steinbeck in Eastern Europe*. Lanham, MD: Rowman & Littlefield, University Press of America, 2011.

"Clothing Salesmen Having Hard Going." *M'Alester Guardian* (McAlester, Oklahoma) 25.15 (Thursday, December 5, 1929).

Coers, Donald V. *John Steinbeck Goes to War: "The Moon Is Down" as Propaganda*. Tuscaloosa: University of Alabama Press, 1991, rpt. 2006.

Coles, Robert. *The Call of Service: A Witness to Idealism*. Boston: Houghton Mifflin, 1972.

———. *The Call of Stories: Teaching and the Moral Imagination*. Boston: Houghton Mifflin, 1990.

———. Interview. *Mindful* (August 24, 2010). http://www.mindful.org.

Darwin, Charles. *On the Origin of Species by Means of Natural Selection; or, The Preservation of Favored Races in the Struggle for Life* (1859). Norwalk, CT: Easton Press, 1993.

———. *The Voyage of the Beagle* (1839). New York: Penguin, 1990.

Davis, Robert Con, ed. *"The Grapes of Wrath": A Collection of Critical Essays*. Englewood Cliffs: Prentice-Hall, 1982.

Davis, Todd F., and Kenneth Womack, eds. *Mapping the Ethical Turn: A Reader in Ethics, Cultures, and Literary Theory.* Charlottesville: University Press of Virginia, 2001.

DeMott, Robert. *Steinbeck's Reading: Catalog of Books Owned and Borrowed.* New York: Garland, 1984.

———. *Steinbeck's Typewriter: Essays on His Art.* Troy, NY: Whitston, 1996, rpt. iUniverse, 2012.

———. "*Sweet Thursday* Revisited: An Excursion in Suggestiveness" (320–351). *Critical Insights: John Steinbeck,* ed. Don Noble. Pasadena, CA: Salem Press, 2011.

DeMott, Robert, and Elaine Steinbeck, eds. *John Steinbeck: The Grapes of Wrath and Other Writings 1936–1941.* New York: Library of America, 1996.

Dickstein, Morris. *Dancing in the Dark: A Cultural History of the Great Depression.* New York: W. W. Norton, 2010.

———. "Steinbeck and the Great Depression." *South Atlantic Quarterly* 103.1 (Winter 2004): 111–131.

Ditsky, John. *Critical Essays on John Steinbeck.* Boston: G. K. Hall, 1989.

———. John Ditsky Papers. Archive and Special Collections, Ball State University, Muncie, Indiana.

———. *John Steinbeck and the Critics.* Rochester, NY: Camden House, Boydell & Brewer, 2000.

———. "Steinbeck's *Travels with Charley*: The Quest That Failed." *Steinbeck Quarterly* 8.2 (Spring 1975), 45–50.

———. "Steinbeck's *Bombs Away*: The Group Man in the Wide Blue Yonder." *Steinbeck Quarterly* 12 (Winter–Spring 1979): 5–14.

———. "Steinbeck's 'Flight': The Ambiguity of Manhood." *Steinbeck Quarterly* 5.3–4 (Summer–Fall 1972): 83.

Dooley, Patrick K. "John Steinbeck's Lower Case Utopia: Basic Human Needs, a Duty to Share, and the Good Life." *The Moral Philosophy of John Steinbeck,* ed. Stephen K. George. Lanham, MD: Scarecrow Press, 2005.

Doyle, Robert P. *Banned Books: Challenging Our Freedom to Read.* Chicago: American Library Association, 2014.

Dry, Rachel. "A Recession Only Steinbeck Could Love." *Washington Post* (March 22, 2009).

Fadiman, Clifton. "Highway 66: A Tale of Five Cities." Review of *The Grapes of Wrath. The New Yorker* (1939).

———. "Mice, Men, Matadors, Miasmas." Review of *Of Mice and Men. The New Yorker* (February 27, 1937): 67.

———. "Steinbeck Again." Review of *The Moon Is Down. The New Yorker* (April 4, 1942).

———. "Two Ways to Win the War." Review of *The Moon Is Down. The New Yorker* (March 7, 1942): 52–53.

Fensch, Thomas, ed. *Conversations with John Steinbeck.* Oxford: University of Mississippi Press, 1988.

———. *Steinbeck and Covici: The Story of a Friendship.* Middlebury, VT: P. S. Eriksson, 1979.

Fiedler, Leslie. "Looking Back after 50 Years." *San Jose Studies* 16.1 (1990): 54–64.

———. *Love and Death in the American Novel.* New York: Stein and Day, rev. 1996.

Fontenrose, Joseph. *John Steinbeck: An Introduction and Interpretation.* New York: Holt, Rinehart and Winston, 1963.

———. "Sea of Cortez" (122–134). *John Steinbeck: Twentieth Century Views.* Englewood Cliffs: Prentice-Hall, 1972.

———. "*Tortilla Flat* and the Creation of a Legend" (19–30). *Critical Insights: John Steinbeck,* ed. Don Noble. Pasadena, CA: Salem Press, 2011.

French, Warren. *John Steinbeck.* Boston and New York: Twayne, 1975.

———. *John Steinbeck's Fiction Revisited.* New York: Twayne, 1994.

———. *John Steinbeck's Nonfiction Revisited.* New York: Twayne, 1996.

Gaither, Gloria. "The Postmodern Mind in the Modern Age." *Steinbeck Review* 7.1 (March 2006): 53–68.

Gannett, Lewis. "Books and Things." *New York Herald Tribune* (February 25, 1937).

Gardner, John. *On Moral Fiction*. New York: Basic Books, 1978.

Geiger, Robert. "Black Sunday Dust Storm." Associated Press (April 15, 1935).

George, Stephen K. "The Disintegration of a Man: Moral Integrity in *The Winter of Our Discontent*" (93–111). *The Moral Philosophy of John Steinbeck*, ed. Stephen K. George. Lanham, MD: Scarecrow Press, 2005.

———. "Of Vice and Men: A Virtue Ethics of *The Pearl, East of Eden* and *The Winter of Our Discontent.*" Ph.D. Dissertation.

———. Stephen K. George Papers. Archive and Special Collections, Ball State University, Muncie, Indiana.

George, Stephen K., ed. "Crossing the Oceans: The Future of Steinbeck Studies in America, Japan, and Beyond." *Steinbeck Review/Steinbeck Studies* 3.1 (Spring 2006): 97–107.

———. *The Moral Philosophy of John Steinbeck*. Lanham: Scarecrow Press, 2005.

George, Stephen K., and Barbara Heavilin. *John Steinbeck and His Contemporaries*. Lanham, MD: Scarecrow Press, 2007.

Gibbons, Michael T. "The Indifference of Nature and the Cruelty of Wealth." *A Political Companion to John Steinbeck*, ed. Cyrus Ernesto Zirakzadeh and Simon Stow. Lexington: University Press of Kentucky, 2013.

Gladstein, Mimi R., and James Meredith. "John Steinbeck and the Tragedy of the Vietnam War." *Steinbeck Review* 8.1 (Spring 2011): 39–56.

Gladstein, Mimi Reisel. "Missing Women: The Inexplicable Disparity between Women in Steinbeck's Life and Those in His Fiction" (84–98). *The Steinbeck Question: New Essays in Criticism*, ed. Donald Noble. Troy, NY: Whitston, 1993.

———. "*Of Mice and Men*: Creating and Recreating Curley's Wife." *Beyond Boundaries*, ed. Susan Shillinglaw and Kevin Hearle. Tuscaloosa: University of Alabama Press, 2002.

———. "Steinbeck and the Woman Question: A Never Ending Puzzle" (242–251). *Critical Insights: John Steinbeck*, ed. Don Noble. Pasadena, CA: Salem Press, 2011.

———. "Straining for Profundity: Steinbeck's *Burning Bright* and *Sweet Thursday*" (234–248). *The Short Novels of John Steinbeck: Critical Essays with a Checklist to Steinbeck Criticism*, ed. Jackson J. Benson. Durham, NC: Duke University Press, 1990.

Godwin, Jeff, James Jasper, and Francesca Polletta. *Passionate Politics: Emotions and Social Movements*. Chicago: University of Chicago Press, 2001.

Goldman, Eric F. *The Tragedy of Lyndon Baines Johnson*. New York: Alfred A. Knopf, 1969.

Good, Paul. "Meredith March: June–July 1966" (510). *Reporting Civil Rights*. Volume 2. New York: Library of America, 2003.

Gottlieb, Robert. "The Rescue of John Steinbeck." *New York Review of Books* (April 17, 2008).

Gregory, James N. *American Exodus: The Dust Bowl Migration and Okie Culture in California*. New York: Oxford University Press, 1989.

Griffith, Benjamin. "The Banishing of Caldwell and Steinbeck." *Sewanee Review* 103.2 (Spring 1995): 325–328.

Guignon, Charles. *On Being Authentic*. London: Routledge, 2004.

Guthrie, Woody. "So Long, It's Been Good to Know Yuh" (1940). Woody Guthrie Publications/TRO-Ludlow, 1951.

———. "Song of Tom Joad" (1960). Woody Guthrie Publications/TRO-Ludlow, 1963.

Halverson, Cathryn. "John Steinbeck's Sweetheart: The Cosmic American Bus." *College Literature* 35 (Winter 2008): 82–99.

Hart, Richard E. Foreword. *The Moral Philosophy of John Steinbeck*, ed. Stephen K. George. Lanham, MD: Scarecrow Press, 2005.

———. "Steinbeck on Man and Nature: A Philosophical Reflection." *Steinbeck and the Environment: Interdisciplinary Approaches*, ed. Susan F. Beegel, Susan Shillinglaw, and Wesley N. Tiffney Jr. Tuscaloosa: University of Alabama Press, 1997.

Hartranft, Marshall V. *Grapes of Gladness: California's Refreshing and Inspiring Answer to John Steinbeck's "Grapes of Wrath."* Los Angeles: De Vorss and Company, 1939.

Hayashi, Tetsumaro. "Emotion Recollected in Tranquility: A Context for Romanticism in *Of Mice and Men*" (276–289). *The Essential Criticism of* Of Mice and Men, ed. Michael J. Meyer. Lanham, MD: Scarecrow Press, 2009.

———. "John Steinbeck and Adlai E. Stevenson: The Moral and Political Vision." *Steinbeck Quarterly* 24 (Summer–Fall 1991): 94–107.

———. Tetsumaro Hayashi Papers. Archive and Special Collections, Ball State University, Muncie, Indiana.

Hayashi, Tetsumaro, ed. *John Steinbeck: The Years of Greatness, 1936–1939*. Tuscaloosa: University of Alabama Press, 1993.

———. *A New Study Guide to Steinbeck's Major Works*. Metuchen, NJ: Scarecrow Press, 1993.

———. *Steinbeck's Literary Dimension: A Guide to Comparative Studies*. Metuchen, NJ: Scarecrow Press, 1973.

Hayashi, Tetsumaro, Yasuo Hashiguchi, and Richard F. Peterson, eds. *John Steinbeck East and West*. Papers from the First International Steinbeck Congress, 1976.

Heavilin, Barbara A., ed. *The Critical Response to John Steinbeck's* The Grapes of Wrath. Westport, CT: Greenwood Press, 2000.

Hedgpeth, Joel W. "John Steinbeck: Late Blooming Environmentalist." *Steinbeck and the Environment*, ed. Susan Beegle, Susan Shillinglaw, and Wesley Tiffney Jr. Tuscaloosa: University of Alabama Press, 1997.

Ho, Winnie. "Split by Race and Wealth but Discovering Similarities as They Study Steinbeck." *New York Times* (March 5, 2012).

"House Bill No. 4 Knocked Out by Supreme Court: The People Still Rule in Oklahoma." *Tulsa Daily World* (April 7, 1929).

Jackson, Joseph Henry. "Steinbeck's Art Finds Powerful Expression in *Of Mice and Men*." *San Francisco Chronicle*, section D (February 28, 1937): 7

Johnson, Charles. "Reading the Character of Crooks in *Of Mice and Men*: A Black Writer's Perspective" (236–250). *Steinbeck Studies: The Essential Criticism on* Of Mice and Men, ed. Michael J. Meyer. Lanham, MD: Scarecrow, 2009.

Johnson Presidential Archives. "John Steinbeck Material for Reading at the Inauguration." Eric F. Goldman Teletype to Mrs. Johnson (January 16, 1965). Inaugural Address Folder, 1-20-65, Lyndon Baines Johnson Library.

———. Letter, John Steinbeck to Jack Valenti (July 22, 1965). John Steinbeck Speech Material, Jack Valenti Papers, AC-84-57, Lyndon Baines Johnson Library.

Kazin, Alfred. "The Unhappy Man from Unhappy Valley." *New York Times Book Review* (May 4, 1958): 1.

Kisor, Henry. "Disdained by the Literati." *Chicago Sun-Times* (February 24, 2002): 14.

Kopecky, Petr. "The Literary Front of the Cold War: John Steinbeck as an Ideological Object in the Eastern Bloc." *Comparative American Studies: An International Journal* 9.3 (September 2011): 204–216.

Kouta, Ashraf, and Engy Selah. "From Alienation to Connectedness: A Postmodern Ecocritical Reading of John Steinbeck's *The Winter of Our Discontent.*" *European Scientific Journal* 9.11 (2013).

Kozol, Jonathan. *Savage Inequalities: Children in America's Schools*. New York: Harper Perennial, 1991.

Lange, Dorothea, and Paul Taylor. *An American Exodus: A Record of Human Erosion*. New York: Reynal and Hitchcock, 1939.

Lawrence, D. H. *Studies in Classic American Literature*. London: Secker, 1923.

Lea, Richard. "Idaho Parents Push for Schools to Ban *Of Mice and Men* for Its 'Profanities'." *Guardian* (May 7, 2015).

Leaf, Jonathan. "Of Mice and Melodrama." *The New Criterion* 26.4 (December 2007).

Leopold, Aldo. *A Sand County Almanac and Sketches Here and There* (1949). New York: Oxford University Press, 1989.

Levant, Howard. *The Novels of John Steinbeck: A Critical Study*. Columbia: University of Missouri Press, 1974.

Lieber, Todd M. "Talismanic Patterns in the Novels of John Steinbeck." *American Literature* 44.2 (May 1972): 262–275.

Lisca, Peter. *John Steinbeck: Nature and Myth*. New York: Thomas Y. Crowell, 1978.

———. *The Wide World of John Steinbeck*. New Brunswick, NJ: Rutgers University Press, 1958.

Lojek, Helen. "Jim Casy: Politics of the New Jerusalem." *Steinbeck Quarterly* 15.1–2 (Winter–Spring 1982): 30–37.

M'Alester Guardian (McAlester, Oklahoma). Vol. 25, No. 10 (Thursday, October 31, 1929).

M'Alester Guardian. Vol. 25, No. 12 (Thursday, November 14, 1929).

M'Alester Guardian. Vol. 25, No. 13 (Thursday, November 21, 1929).

M'Alester Guardian. Vol. 28, No. 8 (Thursday, October 17, 1929).

Manley, Lorne. "Catching Broadway on Camera." *New York Times* (October 6, 2014).

Marsh, Fred T. "*In Dubious Battle*." *New York Times Book Review*, section 6 (February 2, 1936): 7.

———. "John Steinbeck's Tale of Drifting Men." *New York Times Book Review* 86 (February 28, 1937): 7.

Marx, Leo. *The Machine in the Garden*. Oxford: Oxford University Press, 1964, rpt. 1976.

McElrath, Joseph R., Jr., Jesse S. Crisler, and Susan Shillinglaw, eds. *John Steinbeck: The Contemporary Reviews*. Cambridge: Cambridge University Press, 1996.

McLeman, Robert. "Migration Out of 1930s Rural Eastern Oklahoma: Insights for Climate Change Research." Paper 151. *Great Plains Quarterly* 26.1 (Winter 2006): 27.

McWilliams, Carey. *Factories in the Field: The Story of Migratory Farm Labor in California* (1939). Berkeley: University of California Press, 2000.

"Measures Taken to Reclaim Denuded Land in Oklahoma." *Tulsa Daily World* (April 7, 1929).

Meyer, Michael J., ed. *The Essential Criticism of John Steinbeck's* Of Mice and Men. Lanham, MD: Scarecrow Press, 2009.

Meyer, Michael J., and Henry Veggian, eds. East of Eden*: New and Recent Essays*. New York: Rodopi, 2013.

———. *Literature and Music*. New York: Rodopi, 2002.

Miller, J. Hillis. "How to Be 'in Tune with the Right' in *The Golden Bowl*" (271–286). *Mapping the Ethical Turn: A Reader in Ethics, Culture, and Literary Theory*, ed. Todd F. Davis and Kenneth Womack. Charlottesville: University Press of Virginia, 2001.

Mills, Nicholaus. "John Steinbeck's Hurricane Katrina Lesson." *Dissent* 53.4 (Fall 2006): 97–98.

Milton, John. *John Milton: Complete Poems and Major Prose*, ed. Merritt Y. Hughes. Indianapolis, IN: Hackett Publishing, 2013.

Mitchell, Ruth Comfort. *Of Human Kindness*. New York: D. Appleton-Century Company, 1940.

Moore, Harry Thornton. *The Novels of John Steinbeck: A First Study*. Chicago: Normandy House, 1939.

Moore, Thomas, ed. *The Education of the Heart*. New York: HarperCollins, 1996.

Morsberger, Robert E. "Steinbeck's War" (275–309). *Critical Insights: John Steinbeck*, ed. Don Noble. Pasadena, CA: Salem Press, 2011.

Motley, Warem. "From Patriarchy to Matriarchy: Ma Joad's Role in *The Grapes of Wrath*." *American Literature* 54 (October 1982): 397–412.

Needham, Wilbur. "Steinbeck Refuses to Be Pigeonholed." *Los Angeles Times*, part 3 (February 28, 1937): 8.

Noble, Don, ed. *Critical Insights: John Steinbeck*. Pasadena, CA: Salem Press, 2011.

———. *The Steinbeck Question: New Essays in Criticism*. Troy, NY: Whitston, 1993.

Nussbaum, Martha C. "Perceptive Equilibrium: Literary Theory and Ethical Theory." *Love's Knowledge: Essays on Philosophy and Literature*. Oxford: Oxford University Press, 1990.

O'Brien, Kate. "Fiction." *Spectator* 163 (September 15, 1939): 386.

Oliver, James Ross. "Book News and Views." *Monterey Peninsula Herald* (February 25, 1937): 5.

Olson, John. *Down John's Road: Recreating Steinbeck's 1960 American Road Trip*. Create Space Independent Publishing Platform, 2009.

Ott, Dwight. "Camden County Drive against Book Banns." *Philadelphia Inquirer* (September 24, 1986).

Owens, Louis. *John Steinbeck's Re-vision of America*. Athens: University of Georgia Press, 1985.

———. "Writing 'In Costume': The Missing Voices in *In Dubious Battle*." *John Steinbeck: The Years of Greatness, 1936–1939*, ed. Tetsumaro Hayashi. Tuscaloosa: University of Alabama Press, 1993.

Owens, Louis, and Hector Torres. "Dialogic Structure and Levels of Discourse in Steinbeck's *The Grapes of Wrath*." *Arizona Quarterly* 45.4 (Winter 1989): 75–94.

Parini, Jay. *John Steinbeck*. New York: Henry Holt, 1995.

Paul, Louis. "Prose Made of Wind and Soil and Weather." *New York Herald Tribune* (February 28, 1937): 15.

Pawley, Christine. *Reading Places: Literacy, Democracy and the Public Library in Cold War America*. Madison: University of Wisconsin Press, 2010.

Phillips, Martin. "Steinbeck Goes to High School." *Steinbeck Studies* 15.2 (Winter 2004): 163–165.

Pizer, Donald. "John Steinbeck and American Naturalism." *Steinbeck Quarterly* 9 (Winter 1976): 12–15.

"Pro America Gives 'Other Side' of Story to Migrant Problems." *Los Gatos Times* (August 25, 1939): 1.

Rahv, Philip. "A Variety of Fiction." *Partisan Review* 6 (Spring 1939): 111–112.

Railsback, Brian, and Michael J. Meyer, eds. *A Steinbeck Encyclopedia*. Westport, CT: Greenwood Press, 2006.

Railsback, Brian E. "John Steinbeck Philosophy Unsettled: A Mind of the East and the West." *John Steinbeck: Global Dimensions*, ed. Kyoko Ariki, Luchen Li, and Scott Pugh. Lanham, MD: Scarecrow Press, 2008.

———. *Parallel Expeditions: Charles Darwin and the Art of John Steinbeck*. Moscow: University of Idaho Press, 1995.

Rascoe, Burton. "The Play Accentuates the Consummate Art of John Steinbeck." *English Journal* (March 1938): 205–216.

Rattiner, Dan. *In the Hamptons: My Fifty Years with Farmers, Fishermen, and Artists*. New York: Random House, 2010.

Rice, Rodney P. "Circles in the Forest: John Steinbeck and the Deep Ecology of *To a God Unknown*." *Steinbeck Review* 8.2 (Fall 2011): 31–52.

———. "Group Man Goes to War: Elements of Propaganda in John Steinbeck's *Bombs Away*." *War, Literature & the Arts: An Interdisciplinary Journal of the Humanities* 15.1–2 (March 2002): 178–193.

Ritter, William Emerson. *The Unity of the Organism; or, The Organizational Conception of Life*. Boston: R. G. Badger, 1912.

Ryan, Halford Ross. *Twentieth Century Inaugural Addresses of American Presidents*. Westport, CT: Greenwood, 1993.

"San Joaquin Valley News: Growers Move to Fight Strike." *Los Angeles Times* (October 7, 1933).

Schlesinger, Arthur M., Jr. *A Thousand Days: John F. Kennedy in the White House*. Boston: Houghton Mifflin, 1965.

Schlesinger, Robert. *White House Ghosts: Presidents and Their Speechwriters*. New York: Simon & Schuster, 2008.

Schultz, Jeffrey D., and Luchen Li. *A Critical Companion to John Steinbeck: A Literary Reference*. New York: Facts on File, 2005.

Schwarz, Daniel R. "A Humanistic Ethics of Reading" (3–15). *Mapping the Ethical Turn: A Reader in Ethics, Culture, and Literary Theory*, ed. Todd F. Davis and Kenneth Womack. Charlottesville: University Press of Virginia, 2001.

Seelye, John. "Come Back to the Boxcar, Leslie Honey; Or, Don't Cry for Me, Madonna, Just Pass the Milk: Steinbeck and Sentimentality" (152–176). *Critical Insights: John Steinbeck*, ed. Don Noble. Pasadena, CA: Salem Press, 2011.

Shillinglaw, Susan. "The Book That Brought Oprah's Book Club Back: *East of Eden*." *Steinbeck Studies* 15.1 (Spring 2004): 137–140.

————. "California Answers *The Grapes of Wrath*" (177–196). *Critical Insights: John Steinbeck*, ed. Don Noble. Pasadena, CA: Salem Press, 2011.

————. *Carol and John Steinbeck: Portrait of a Marriage*. Reno: University of Nevada Press, 2013.

————. "Introduction: A Steinbeck Scholar's Perspective." *Steinbeck and the Environment*, ed. Susan F. Beegel, Susan Shillinglaw, and Wesley Tiffney Jr. Tuscaloosa: University of Alabama Press, 1997.

————. "John Steinbeck's Spiritual Streak." *Literature and Belief* 21.1–2 (2001): 76–90.

————. *On Reading* The Grapes of Wrath. New York: Penguin, 2014.

————. "Steinbeck and Ethnicity" (252–274). *Critical Insights: John Steinbeck*, ed. Don Noble. Pasadena, CA: Salem Press, 2011.

Shillinglaw, Susan, and Kevin Hearle, eds. *Beyond Boundaries*: *Rereading John Steinbeck*. Tuscaloosa: University of Alabama Press, 2002.

Shillinglaw, Susan, and Nancy Burnett (photographer). *A Journey into Steinbeck's California*. Berkeley, CA: Roaring Forties Press, 2006, rpt. 2011.

Shockley, Martin Staples. "The Reception of *The Grapes of Wrath* in Oklahoma." *American Literature* 15.4 (January 1944): 351–361.

Simmonds, Roy S. "Composition, Publication, and Reception of John Steinbeck's *The Wayward Bus*." *Steinbeck Review* 10.1 (2013): 2–10.

————. *John Steinbeck: The War Years, 1939–1945*. Lewisburg, PA: Bucknell University Press, 1996.

Smuts, Jan Christian. *Holism and Evolution*. London: Macmillan, 1927.

Sorensen, Theodore C. *Kennedy*. New York: Harper & Row, 1965.

Spangler, Jason. "We're on the Road to Nowhere: Steinbeck and Kerouac and the Legacy of the Great Depression." *Studies in the Novel* 40.8 (2008): 308–327.

Springsteen, Bruce. *The Ghost of Tom Joad*. Columbia Records. Released November 21, 1995.

Steigerwald, Bill. *Dogging Steinbeck: Exposing the Truth about* Travels with Charley. Fifty Fifty Books, Amazon Digital, 2014.

Stein, Walter J. *California and the Dust Bowl Migration*. Westport, CT: Greenwood Press, 1973.

Steinbeck, John. "Adlai Stevenson and John Steinbeck Discuss the Past and the Present." *Newsweek* 20.92 (December 22, 1959): 34–35.

————. *America and Americans* (1966). *America and Americans and Selected Nonfiction*, ed. Susan Shillinglaw and Jackson J. Benson. New York: Viking, 2002.

————. *Bombs Away: The Story of a Bomber Team*. New York: Viking Press, 1942.

————. *Burning Bright*. New York: Viking, 1950.

————. *Cannery Row*. New York: Viking Press, 1945.

————. *Cup of Gold*. New York: Robert McBride, 1929.

————. "Dear Teachers, Sweet Teachers, I Beg You, Call Them Off!" *NEA Review* (September 1955): 359.

————. *East of Eden*. New York: Viking, 1952.

————. *The Forgotten Village*. New York: Viking Press, 1941.

————. "For Stevenson: Rivals Contrasted." Letter to the Editor. *New York Times*, section 4 (October 26, 1952): 9.

————. *The Grapes of Wrath*. New York: Viking Press, 1939.

————. *The Grapes of Wrath and Other Writings, 1936–1941*, ed. Robert DeMott and Elaine Steinbeck. New York: Library of America, 1996.

————. *In Dubious Battle*. New York: Viking Press, 1936.

————. Interview. *Voice of America*. February 11, 1952.

————. *Journal of a Novel: The* East of Eden *Letters*. New York: Viking Press, 1969.

————. "Letters to Alicia." *Newsday*, 1965.

————. *Lifeboat* (March 26, 1943). Unpublished Screenplay. 20th Century Fox Film Corporation.

————. *The Moon Is Down*. New York: Viking Press, 1942.

————. *Novels 1942–1952*, ed. Robert DeMott. New York: Library of America, 2002.

————. *Novels and Stories, 1932–1937*. New York: Library of America, 1994.

————. *Of Mice and Men*. New York: Viking Press, 1937.

————. *Once There Was a War*. New York: Viking Press, 1958.

————. *The Pastures of Heaven*. New York: Robert O. Ballou, 1932.

————. *The Pearl*. New York: Viking Press, 1947.

————. Personal Diary, 1946. J. Pierpont Morgan Library, New York.

————. Personal Diary, 1951. J. Pierpont Morgan Library, New York.

————. "A Plea to Teachers." *Saturday Review* 8.18 (April 30, 1955): 24.

————. "A Primer on the 1930s." *Esquire* 53 (June 1960): 85–93.

————. *The Red Pony*. New York: Viking Press, 1937.

————. *A Russian Journal*. New York: Viking Press, 1948.

————. *Sea of Cortez: A Leisurely Journal of Travel and Research*. New York: Viking Press, 1941. Coauthor Edward F. Ricketts.

————. *The Short Reign of Pippin IV*. New York: Viking, 1957.

————. *Steinbeck: A Life in Letters*, ed. Elaine Steinbeck and Robert Wallsten. New York: Viking Press, 1975.

————. Stevenson Letter. *New Republic* 128.1 (January 5, 1953): 14.

————. *Sweet Thursday*. New York: Viking, 1954.

————. *Their Blood Is Strong*. New York: Viking Press, 1939.

————. *To a God Unknown*. New York: Robert O. Ballou, 1933.

————. *Tortilla Flat*. New York: Covici-Friede, 1935.

————. *Travels with Charley*. New York: Viking, 1962.

————. *Travels with Charley and Later Novels, 1947–1962*. New York: Library of America, 2007.

————. *The Wayward Bus*. New York: Viking Press, 1947.

————. *The Winter of Our Discontent*. New York: Viking, 1961.

————. *Working Days: The Journals of* The Grapes of Wrath *1938–1941*, ed. Robert DeMott. New York: Viking, 1990.

Steinbeck, John, IV. *In Touch*. New York: Knopf, 1969.

Steinbeck, John, IV, and Nancy Steinbeck. *The Other Side of Eden: Life with John Steinbeck*. Amherst, NY: Prometheus Books, 2001.

Steinbeck, Thomas. "My Father, John Steinbeck" (3–12). *John Steinbeck: A Centennial Tribute*, ed. Stephen K. George. Westport, CT: Praeger, 2002.

"Stocks Collapse." *New York Times* (October 30, 1929): 1.

Stonich, Debora. "Sharing Steinbeck with Students." *Steinbeck Studies* 15.2 (Winter 2004): 166–168.

"Strike Flares Up." *New York Times* (October 9, 1933).

Swerling, Jo. *Lifeboat* (July 29, 1943). Revised Screenplay. 20th Century Fox Film Corporation.

Tammaro, Thomas M. "Sharing Creation: Steinbeck, *In Dubious Battle*, and the Working-Class Novel in American Literature" (124–133). *Critical Insights: John Steinbeck*, ed. Don Noble. Pasadena, CA: Salem Press, 2011.

Tanner, Stephen L. "Steinbeck's *The Winter of Our Discontent* and the American Ideal" (85–95). *A John Steinbeck Reader: Essays in Honor of Stephen K. George*, ed. Barbara A. Heavlin. Lanham, MD: Rowman & Littlefield, 2009.

Taylor, Charles. *The Ethics of Authenticity*. Cambridge, MA: Harvard University Press, 1992.

Taylor, Frank. "California's *Grapes of Wrath*." *Forum* 102 (November 1939): 232.

————. "The Merritt System." *Commentator* (November 1938): 84–87; rpt. in *Reader's Digest* 35 (February 1939): 104–106.

Tedlock, E. W., Jr., and C. V. Wicker. *Steinbeck and His Critics: A Record of Twenty-Five Years*. Albuquerque: University of New Mexico Press, 1957.

"This County Selected as One of Two for Detailed Soil Surveys." *M'Alester Guardian* (McAlester, Oklahoma) 25, 9 (Thursday, October 24, 1929).

Thompson, P. Ralph. "Review, *Of Mice and Men*." *New York Times* (February 27, 1937): 15.

Timmerman, John H. *The Aesthetics of the Road Taken*. Norman: University of Oklahoma Press, 1986.

————. *The Dramatic Landscape of John Steinbeck's Short Stories*. Norman: University of Oklahoma Press, 1990.

————. John H. Timmerman Papers. Archive and Special Collections, Ball State University, Muncie, Indiana.

————. *Searching for Eden: John Steinbeck's Ethical Career*. Macon, GA: Mercer University Press, 2014.

————. "Steinbeck's Environmental Ethic: Humanity in Harmony with the Land" (310–322). *Steinbeck and the Environment: Interdisciplinary Approaches*, ed. Susan F. Beegel, Susan Shillinglaw, and Wesley N. Tiffney Jr. Tuscaloosa: University of Alabama Press, 1997; rpt. in *Critical Insights: John Steinbeck*, ed. Don Noble. Pasadena, CA: Salem Press, 2011.

Trosaw, Esther. Online Self-Guided Driving Tour of Pacific Grove, California. The Martha Heasley Cox Center for Steinbeck Studies, Martin Luther King Library, San Jose, California.

Turner, Frederick Jackson. *The Significance of the Frontier in American History* (1892). New York: Henry Holt, 1921.

Veggian, Henry. "Bio-Politics and the Institution of Literature: An Essay on *East of Eden*, Its Critics, and Its Time." East of Eden: *New and Recent Essays*, ed. Michael J. Meyer and Henry Veggian. New York: Rodopi, 2013.

————. "Displacements and Encampments: John Steinbeck's *The Grapes of Wrath*—A Reconsideration." The Grapes of Wrath: *A Reconsideration*, ed. Michael J. Meyer and Henry Veggian. New York: Rodopi, 2009.

Vidal, Gore. *United States: Essays 1952–1992*. New York: Random House, 1993.

Wagner, Charles A. "Books." *New York Mirror* (February 24, 1937): 25.

Wald, Alan M. "Steinbeck and the Proletarian Novel" (677–685). *Cambridge History of the American Novel*, ed. Leonard Cassuto. Cambridge: Cambridge University Press, 2011.

Wartzman, Rick. *Obscene in the Extreme: The Burning and Banning of John Steinbeck's "The Grapes of Wrath."* New York: Public Affairs, 2008.

Weisiger, Marsha L. "The Reception of *The Grapes of Wrath* in Oklahoma: A Reappraisal." *Chronicles of Oklahoma* 70.4 (Winter 1992): 394–415.

Wilde, Oscar. *The Picture of Dorian Gray*. London: Folio, 2001.

Winter, Jessica. "The Ghost of John Steinbeck." *Village Voice* (April 17–23, 2002): 12.

Worster, Donald. *Nature's Economy: A History of Ecological Ideas*. Cambridge: Cambridge University Press, rpt. 1994.

————. *Rivers of Empire*. New York: Oxford University Press, 1992.

Wyatt, David. *Secret Histories: Reading Twentieth Century American Literature*. Baltimore: Johns Hopkins University Press, 2010.

Zirakzadeh, Cyrus Ernesto, and Simon Stow, eds. *A Political Companion to John Steinbeck*. Lexington: University Press of Kentucky, 2013.

WEBSITES

Baker, Debra Solomon. "Am I My Brother's Keeper?" Southern Poverty Law Center's *Teaching Tolerance*(November 18, 2010). http://www.tolerance.org/blog/am-i-my-brother-s-keeper.

Cannery Row, Monterey, California. http://www.canneryrow.com/the-canneries.

Harrington, Theresa. California Reads. Contra Costa County School (April 15, 2002). http://www.mercurynews.com.

Hughes, Elizabeth. Plymouth North High School Lesson Plans for *Of Mice and Men*. http://www.steinbeckinstitute.org.

Johnson, William. "Of Mice and Men and My Students." *Chalkbeat*. http://www.chalkbeat.org/posts/ny/02/27/2012/of-mice-and-men-and-my-students/#V0PCxJErk70.

National Weather Service Forest Office, Norman, Oklahoma. http://www.srh.noaa.gov/oun/?n=events-19350414.

Pennington, Daria. "The Best Laid Schemes for Teaching *Of Mice and Men*." http://www.mylearningspringboard.com.

Quinn, Kay. "Of Dust and Steinbeck." Salinas Reads (September 4, 2014). http://www.salinaspubliclibrary.org/blog/p=743.

Schulten, Katherine. "Teaching Steinbeck and *The Grapes of Wrath* with *The New York Times*." *New York Times* (August 19, 2010). http://www.learningblogs.nytimes.com/2010/08/19/teaching-the-grapes-of-wrath-with-the-new-york-times/comment-page-1/?_r=0.

Scofield, W. L. "California's Sardine Catch." Calisphere, University of California. University of California Digital Library.http://www.content.cclib.org .

Steinbeck Bibliography. Martha Heasley Cox Center for Steinbeck Studies. http://steinbeckbibliography.org.

Ueber, Edward, and Alec MacCall. "The Rise and Fall of the California Sardine Empire." http://www.swfsc.noaa.gov/publications/CR/1992/92104.PDF.

ARCHIVES

John Steinbeck Collection, Ransom Center, University of Texas, Austin, Texas. Pascal Covici Letters. Drafts of Steinbeck articles and stories. (Correspondence by mail.)

John Steinbeck Papers, Alfred M. and Clarisse B. Hellman Collection, Columbia University, New York, New York. Proofs of thirteen works by Steinbeck. Play production material for *Burning Bright*, Plymouth Theatre, 1950. Seymour B. Durst Papers, Columbia University. Louis Drophin Papers, radio adaptation for *Of Mice and Men*.

John Steinbeck Papers, 1939–1962. Library of Congress Manuscript Division, Washington, D.C.

J. Pierpont Morgan Library, Special Collections, Steinbeck Diaries, New York, New York.

Preston Breyer Collection, Firestone Library, Princeton University, Princeton, New Jersey (19 boxes).

Steinbeck Collection at Ball State University, Muncie, Indiana: John Ditsky Papers, Archives and Special Collections, Ball State University Libraries. John H. Timmerman Papers, Archives and Special Collections, Ball State University Libraries. "The Moral Philosophy of John Steinbeck." 2005. Box 1, Folder 14. Roy Simmonds Papers, Archives and Special Collections, Ball State University Libraries. Stephen K. George Papers, Archives and Special Collections, Ball State University Libraries. Tetsumaro Hayashi Papers, Archives and Special Collections, Ball State University Libraries.

THE WORKS OF JOHN STEINBECK

Cup of Gold (1929).

The Pastures of Heaven (1932).

To a God Unknown (1933).

Tortilla Flat (1935).

In Dubious Battle (1936).

The Red Pony (1937). Limited Edition. "The Gift," "The Great Mountains," *North American Review* (1933); "The Promise," *Harper's* (1937, written in 1934); "The Leader of the People," "Argosy" (1936). "The Red Pony" appeared in *The Long Valley*, 1938.

Of Mice and Men (1937).

The Long Valley (1938). All these stories had been completed by mid-1934. "The Chrysanthemums"; "Flight"; "The White Quail"; "The Vigilante"; "The Murder"; "The Harness"; "The Snake"; "The Raid"; "Johnny Bear."

The Grapes of Wrath (1939).

Sea of Cortez (1941). With Edward F. Ricketts.

The Forgotten Village (1941).
The Moon Is Down (1942).
Bombs Away (1942).
Lifeboat (1943).
A Medal for Benny (1945).
Cannery Row (1945).
The Pearl (1945–1947).
The Wayward Bus (1947).
A Russian Journal (1948). With photographer Robert Capa.
Burning Bright (1950).
East of Eden (1952).
Viva Zapata! (1952).
Sweet Thursday (1954).
The Short Reign of Pippin IV (1957).
Once There Was a War (1958).
The Winter of Our Discontent (1961).
Travels with Charley (1962).
"Letters to Alicia" (1965).
America and Americans (1966).
Journal of a Novel: The East of Eden *Letters* (1969).
The Acts of King Arthur and His Noble Knights (1976). Translation of Sir Thomas Malory.

INDEX

Abramson, Ben, 11
advertising (to children), 67
Agassiz, Louis, 102
Albee, George, 44, 60
Allee, Warder Clyde, 104, 105
Allegretti, Joseph, 94
Altieri, Charles, xxiv
America and Americans, 115, 116, 133, 136, 185–189
Ammon, Bette, 65
Ardrey, Bob, 161
Arendt, Hannah, 92
Argosy, 184
Aristotle, xix, 16, 93, 166
Arizona, 91
Arkansas, 14, 75, 78, 83
Arnold, Henry "Hap", 123
Arnold, Matthew, 151
Arthurian tales, ix, 24, 31, 41, 122, 135, 173, 179, 186, 196
Associated Farmers, 82
atomic age, 152, 183, 188
Austen, Jane, 68

Bach, Johann Sebastian (*Art of the Fugue*), 106
Bacon, Roger, 104
Baker, Deborah Solomon, 71
Bakersfield, California, 14, 58, 82
Bakersfield Californian (newspaper), 82
Bakhtin, Mikhail, 142

Ballou, Robert, 7, 8, 9, 10
Baltimore, Maryland, 71
Barthes, Roland, xix
Battle Hymn of the Republic, 16, 87
Beegel, Susan, 112
Bellah, Robert, 186
Benet, William Rose, 136
Bennett, Joseph, 152
Benson, Jackson J., ix, x, xi, xii, xiii, xiv, xv, xxv, 29, 30, 31, 33, 44, 101, 113, 174, 179, 186, 196
Bentham, Jeremy, xxiii
Bermuda, 23
Berry, Thomas, 187
Bible, xvi, 20, 25, 27, 30, 31, 32, 41, 77, 78, 80, 87, 89, 91
Big Sur, 30
Blair, William McCormick, 129
Blake, William, 45
Bloom, Harold, xv
Bombs Away, 19, 122–124
Bookchin, Murray, 116
Book-of-the-Month Club, 13, 60
Booth, Wayne, xix, xx, xxiii, xxiv
Boren, Lyle, 96
Brando, Marlon, 161
Bridges, Ruby, 62, 175, 176
British Broadcasting Company (BBC), 68
British educational testing, 68, 69
Broadway, xi, 12, 43, 61
Brontë sisters, 68

Brooklyn, New York, 71
Brown, Mary M., 99
Browning, Christopher, 120
Buck, Jules, 111
Buck, Pearl, 9
Buffalo, New York, 96
Burnett, Hugh Hammond, 77
Burning Bright, 149, 156–157
Burns, Ken (*The Dust Bowl*), 75
Bush, George W., xv, 175

Cabell, James Branch, 29
Califano, Joseph, 190
Callicott, J. Baird, 114
Cameron, Tom, 95
Campbell, Joseph, 2, 7, 30, 106
Canada, 68
Cannery Row, 5, 9, 21, 41, 45, 74, 106,
   128, 138–143, 144, 146, 154
Cannery Row (place), 24, 48, 56, 149, 150
Capa, Robert, 127, 128, 130, 149
Capra, Frank, 88, 125
Carson, Kit, 145
Cassuto, David N., 83
Caswell, Roger, 152
censorship, 65–71
Cerce, Danica, 130
Charley (Steinbeck's poodle), 25, 112,
   173, 175
Chicago, Illinois, 24, 53, 175
"Chrysanthemums", 38
Civil War (American), 23, 162, 170
Clay, Henry, 183
Clemons, Walter, xii
Coers, Donald V., 118, 121, 122
Coeur d'Alene, Idaho, 65–67
cognitive science, 166
Cold War, 130, 164, 173
Coleridge, Samuel Taylor ("Kublai
   Kahn"), 180
Coles, Nicholas, 134
Coles, Robert, 62, 183
collective behavior, xvi
Colletto, Tiny, 102
Collins, Tom, 14, 58, 96
Commonweal, 154
Conrad, Joseph, xxvi, 29
Cousteau, Jacques, 101

Covici, Pascal "Pat", 11, 12, 14, 19, 20, 21,
   22, 23, 24, 88, 89, 90, 96, 126, 152,
   159, 165, 171, 194
Crane, Stephen, xxv
Cranston, Bryan, 43
The Criterion, 60
Cuban missile crisis, 174, 185
Cup of Gold, 27, 29, 88, 106
Cupp, Ora M., 64
Curley, John, 48

Dante Allegieri (*Inferno*), 84
Darwin, Charles, 5, 6, 7, 30, 47, 102, 104,
   105, 106, 107, 136
de Tocqueville, Alexis, 56
Dean, James, 160, 161, 194
Dearborn, Michigan, 53
Dekker, William, 19
democracy, xii, 52, 56, 57, 123, 174
Democratic National Convention, 127,
   177, 190
Democratic Party, 52
DeMott, Robert, xv, xvii, 30, 149, 152, 153
Denmark, 121
Descartes, René, 114
Detroit, Michigan, 53, 96
Dickens, Charles, xxi, 68, 72, 73, 93
Dickstein, Morris, 47, 51, 59, 69, 73
Dissonant Symphony, 7
Ditsky, John, xv, 13, 25, 39
D'Onofrio, Vincent, 43
Dooley, Patrick, 93, 94
Dostoevsky, Fydor, 33, 166
Dreiser, Theodore, xi
drought, 78, 83
dualism, 30
Duncan, Otis Durant, 76
Durkheim, Emile, 46
Dust Bowl, 14, 54, 75, 76, 77, 78, 87, 88
Duvall, Robert, 43

East Hampton, New York, 173
East of Eden, 23, 41, 106, 111, 131,
   159–171, 179, 180
East St. Louis, Illinois, 96
ecology, 90, 103–105, 176, 188
education, xi, xiii, xv, xvii, xx, xxv, 13, 62,
   63–65, 67–72, 84, 85, 99–100, 121, 167
Einstein, Albert, 104, 105

Eisenhardt, Harry G., 78
Eisenhower, Dwight D., 129
Eliot, George, 68
Eliot, T. S., 151
empathy, xvii, xviii, 66, 73–74, 116
Empire State Building, 53
Enea, Sparky, 102, 108
Esquire, 184

Fadiman, Clifton, 118, 124
Fairbanks, Douglas, Jr., 127
Farrar and Rinehart, 4
Faulkner, William, xv, 25, 65
fishing industry, 140
Fitzgerald, F. Scott, 29, 63
"Flight", 39, 101
Floyd, Pretty Boy, 76
Fonda, Henry, xii, 18, 92
Fontenrose, Joseph, 36, 105, 134
Ford, Henry, 53
Ford, John, xv, xxv, 16, 17, 18, 88, 89, 90, 91, 92, 125
The Forgotten Village, 17, 18, 101, 109–110, 112
France, 118
Franco, James, 43
Frankel, Stanley, 129
Frazer, J. G., 30
French, Warren, xxvi, xxvii, 62, 93, 120, 131
Fresno, California, 55, 85
Freud, Sigmund, 162, 169
Frost, Robert, 173
Frye, Northrup, 29

Galbraith, John Kenneth, 25
Gannett, Louis, 12, 63
Gardner, John, xxii, xxiv
Garvey, James, 100
Gasset, Ortega y, 46
Geiger, Robert, 78
General Motors, 50
George, Stephen K., xxii, xxiii, 93
Germany, 50, 196
Gibbs, Vincent, 71
Gilligan, Carol, xxii, xxiii
Girard, Rene, xxvi
Gladstein, Mimi R., 123, 141, 193
Glendale, California, 2

global economy, 94
Goethe, Johann, 29
Goldman, Eric, 190
Gomez, Selena, 43
Goodman, Benny, 143, 184
Goodwin, Richard, 190
Gottlieb, Robert, x
Gove, Michael, 68, 69
The Grapes of Wrath, 13, 15, 16–17, 41, 45, 47, 55, 56, 58, 59, 71, 73, 75–100, 105, 110, 119, 120, 128, 130, 131, 141, 144, 146, 152, 159, 164, 176
Great Depression, 8, 12, 27, 46, 48–50, 52–53, 54, 55, 57, 77, 78, 79, 85, 138
Greece, 25
Gregory, James, 77
Greeks (ancient), 177, 179
The Guardian, 65, 98
Guggenheim, Harry F., 189
Guinzberg, Harold, 23, 185
Guthrie, Woody, xii, 75

Haggard, H. Rider, 29
Halberstam, David, 173
Halverson, Cathryn, 147
Hamilton, Joe, 17
Hamilton, Samuel, 23
Hannegan, Robert E., 127
Hardy, Thomas, 68
"The Harness", 40
Harper Brothers, 4
Hartranft, Marshall, 82
Harris, Ed, 43
The Harvest Gypsies, 14, 58, 71
Hawkins, Emma, 64
Hayashi, Tetsamuro, 41
Heavilin, Barbara, xv
Hemingway, Ernest, 25, 65
Hesse, Hermann, 152
Heverley, Jerry, 70
Hitchcock, Alfred, 19, 125
Hitler, Adolf, 50
Hollywood, California, 19, 80, 131, 148
Hopkins Marine Station, 1, 104, 105
Hoover, Herbert, 49, 53, 54
Houston, Texas, 175
"How Mr. Hogan Robbed a Bank", 178
Howe, Juila Ward, 16

HUAC (House Un-American Activities Committee), 111
Hurricane Katrina, 176

Ickes, Harold, 54
immigrants: Asian, 52; Mexican, xii, 52
In Dubious Battle, 10, 11, 12, 13, 14, 29, 41, 59, 67, 94, 105, 120, 144, 146, 154, 164

Jackson, Joseph Henry, xvi
Jeffersonian ideals, 84
Joel, Billy, 184
Johnson, Lady Bird, 26
Johnson, Lyndon Baines, 26, 175, 189, 190, 191, 192, 193–194, 195
Johnson, Nunally, 16, 86
Johnson, William, 71
Jonathan Cape Publishing, 7, 8
Journal of a Novel, 159, 165
Jung, Carl Gustav, xxvi, 30, 106

Kansas City, Missouri, 96
Kant, Immanuel, xxiii, 94, 196
Kaufmann, George S., 14
Kazan, Elia, xxv, 21, 22, 110, 111, 131, 160, 161
Kazin, Alfred, 47
Keller, Evelyn Fox, 112
Kelley, James C., 103, 106
Kennedy, John Fitzgerald, 25, 26, 129, 173, 176, 177, 189
Kern County, California, 82, 84, 85, 96, 97
King, Martin Luther, 89
Knief, Gretchen, 96
Kohlberg, Lawrence, xxiii
Krishnamurt, Jiddui, 151
Ku Klux Klan, 57

La Figaro, 184
La Jolla, California, 72
Lange, Dorothea, 96
Lao Tse, 30
Lasch, Christopher, 186
Lawrence, Jennifer, 161
Lea, Robin, 65
Lee, Harper, 68
Leopold, Aldo, xxi, 103, 114
Lepore, Amy, 70

Letters to Alicia, 189
Lewis, Cliff, 127
Lewis, Sinclair, 25
Levant, Howard, 165
Life (magazine), 58
Lifeboat, 19, 125
Lifton, Robert, 120
Lisca, Peter, 41, 62
Loesser, Frank, 24
Log from the Sea of Cortez, 17, 18, 101–116, 188
London, 19
London, Jack, xxv
Long Island, New York, 24, 25, 178
The Long Valley, 13, 14, 28, 38, 40, 41, 59
Lopez, Barry, 113
Los Angeles, California, 20, 146
Los Angeles Times, 63, 81, 95
Los Gatos, California, 14
Louisiana Purchase, 88
Louisville Courier, 177

Madison Square Garden (New York), 131
Maine, 175
M'Alester Guardian, 79
Malory, Sir Thomas (*L'Morte d'Arthur*), 24, 31, 41, 196
Marsh, Fred T., 52
Marx, Karl, 48
Maslow, Abraham, 5
Mauldin, Bill, 128
McAlester, J., 80
McBride Publishing, 3
McClintock, Barbara, 112
McIntosh, Mavis, 6, 7, 9, 11
McMillan, Robert, 77
McWilliams, Cary, 75, 77
Meredith, Burgess, 18, 123
Meyer, Michael J., 165
Mexican Americans, xxv, 2, 133–138
Mexico, 13, 17, 18, 20, 21, 57, 101–105, 108–109, 111, 112, 144, 146, 161
Miazga, Mark, 71
migrants, 83–84
Milestone, Lewis, 16, 96
Mill, John Stuart, xxiii
Miller, Arthur, ix, 67, 68, 111
Miller, J. Hillis, x
Miller, Ted, 3, 6, 29

Milton, John (*Paradise Lost*), 45, 150
Minow, Newton, 129
Mirrieles, Edith, 2
Montana Standard, 65
Monterey, California, xxv, 14, 113, 133, 134, 136, 139, 154, 178, 188
Montgomery, Alabama, 191
The Moon Is Down, 18, 19, 69, 97, 117–121
Moore, Harry Thornton, 55
Moore, Thomas, xxi
Morganthau, Henry, 122
Morrison, Toni, 65
Morseberger, Robert E., 125
Moses, 80, 91
Moyers, Bill, 190
"The Murder", 9, 40
"Murder at Full Moon", 64
Murphy, Dr., 1
Mussolini, Benito, 50

Naess, Arne, 103, 115
Nantucket, Massachusetts, 23
NASA, 188
Native American Indians, 108, 136, 187
Needham, Wilbur, 63
Nelson, Frank G., 121
New Criterion, 139
New Criticism, xiv, 164
New Deal, 12, 49, 54, 89
New Orleans, Louisiana, 57, 62, 176, 187
New Republic, 124
New School (New York), 74
New York Herald Tribune, 19, 63
New York Times, 53, 55, 63
The New Yorker, 74
Newsday, 26, 177, 189
Newton, Isaac, 105
Nixon, Richard, 129, 176
Noddings, Nel, xxiii
Norway, 117, 118, 121, 196
Norris, Frank, xxv, 63
North American Review, 9, 12
Nussbaum, Martha, xxi, 73

O. Henry Award, 10
The Odyssey, xii
Of Mice and Men, 13, 14, 16, 17, 29, 45, 56, 59–74, 93, 94, 97, 116, 156

Office of Strategic Services (OSS), 19, 122
O'Hara, John, 13
Oklahoma, xv, 14, 75, 77–80, 83–84, 96, 98
Once There Was a War, 126, 194
O'Neill, Eugene, 25
Osborn, Paul, 161
Osborne, John, 194
Otis, Elizabeth, 6, 7, 9, 11, 12
Owens, Louis, 35, 39

Pacific Biological Laboratory, 5, 17, 112
Pacific Grove, California, 1, 2, 4, 9, 18, 48
Paris, France, 24
Pastures of Heaven, 7, 8, 28, 34, 36, 59
Patterson, Alicia, 189
Paul, Louis, 63
Pawley, Christine, 96
The Pearl, 20, 21, 41, 64, 101, 106, 109, 110, 144, 149, 154–156, 165
Peck, M. Scott, 186
Phillips, Marty, 69
Photography (magazine), 184
Pipe Dream (Rodgers and Hammerstein), 24
Pixley, California, 55
Plainfield, New Jersey, 63
Plato, xix
Pomerantz, Kirsten, 65
Popular Science, 188
Putnam, Robert, 186

Rager, Matt, 43
"The Raid", 10, 41
Railsback, Brian, 105, 107
Rattiner, Dan, 184
reading, xii, xiii, xvii, 67, 69, 94
The Red Pony, 9, 11, 13, 14, 22, 36–38, 41, 45, 64, 69
"Red River Valley", 85, 88, 89
redwoods, 188
Reynolds, Daniel, 99
Rice, Rodney, 123
Ricketts, Ed, xxv, 4–7, 10, 11, 16–17, 20, 21, 22, 30, 41, 48, 101–104, 106–108, 114, 122, 151
Ritter, William Emerson, 104
ritual, xvi
Rockland County, New York, 18

Robinson, Edward G., 91
Rodgers (Richard) and Hammerstein (Oscar), 24, 130
Roosevelt, Eleanor, 18, 60, 96, 110
Roosevelt, Franklin Delano, 9, 12, 13, 17, 49, 53, 54, 77, 122, 127, 186
Roosevelt, Theodore, 49
Rorty, Richard, xxi
Ross, Brian, 161
Rushdie, Salman, 95
Russia, 21
The Russian Journal, 128, 130

Sabatini, Rafael, 29
Sacramento, California, 14
Sag Harbor, New York, 24, 25, 26, 178, 184–185
Saint Francis of Assisi, 104, 105, 133, 138
Salinas, California, ix, 1, 8, 28, 34, 40, 159, 162
Sallisaw, Oklahoma, 78
San Andreas Fault, 101
San Diego, California, 102
San Francisco, California, 14, 24, 40, 83, 168
San Francisco News, 58
San Joaquin, California, 15, 55, 81, 88
San Jose Mercury Herald, 83
Sandel, Michael, xii
Sander, William, xiv
Saturday Review, 136
Scott, Zachary, 22
Scribner's Magazine, 4
Seelye, John, 88
Selma, Alabama, 191
Serlin, Oscar, 19
Shakespeare, William, 29, 65
Shaw, George Bernard, 141
Sheffield, Dook, 2, 8, 16
Shelley, Percy Bysshe, 45
Shepard, Sam, 43
Sheridan, Mike, 100
Shillinglaw, Susan, xv, xvi, xxv, 69, 81, 112, 114, 133, 174, 186
The Short Reign of Pippin IV, 24
Shumlin, Harold, 12
Simon, Paul "America", 147
Simmonds, Roy, xv, 152
Spencer, Herbert, 30

Spokane Review, 65
Sports Illustrated, 184
Spreckles Sugar Company, xxv, 1, 167
Springsteen, Bruce, xii
Stalin, Josef, 50
Stanford University, 2
Stark, Peggy, 100
Steinbeck, Carol Henning, 2, 3, 4, 6, 7, 8, 9, 10, 14, 16, 17, 102
Steinbeck, Elaine, 22, 23, 24, 25, 26, 111, 113, 130, 131, 173, 175, 189, 192, 194
Steinbeck, Gwyn Conger, 16, 18, 19, 20, 21–22, 126, 127, 149
Steinbeck, John: allegory, xi, 9; censorship, xiii, 65–67, 95, 96, 97; ecology, xiii, xxvii, 112–116; education, xi, xiii, xv; fabulism, xi; folk tales, 31; music, 85, 87, 106, 142–143, 165; mythology, xi, 29, 30, 33, 105–106, 136; National Book Award, x; naturalism, xi, xviii, 9, 29, 107; Nobel Prize, x, xxiv, 25, 26, 59, 64; non-teleological method, 16, 107; O. Henry Award, 9; phalanx argument, xvi, 8, 41, 43, 44, 46, 105, 120; postmodern aspects, xv, 169; as proletarian writer, xi, 46; Pulitzer Prize, x, 17; race, 63, 136; sentiment, xii, 160; science, 101–116, 166; social realism, 73; speechwriting, 190, 191, 193; theater, 13, 24, 60, 61, 121, 130, 156; Vietnam, 26, 188, 191, 192; war correspondent, 19, 126–127, 188–192
Steinbeck, John Ernst (father), 1, 9, 12
Steinbeck, John IV (son), 21, 25, 173, 193, 194
Steinbeck, Olive (mother), 1, 9, 10
Steinbeck, Mary (sister), 1, 19, 105
Steinbeck, Thom (son), 20, 25
Steinbeck Center, 72
Steunenberg, Frank, 67
Stevenson, Adlai, 24, 127, 129, 173, 177
Stock Market crash, 48, 52, 79
Stonich, Deborah, 70
stories (importance of), xii, 94
Stow, Simon, 98
Strasberg, Lee, 19
Street, Toby, 2, 18
striking workers, xii, 44, 48, 53, 55, 56

Suzuki, D. T., 30
Sweden, 25, 50
Sweet Thursday, 24, 41, 105, 107, 148–154
Swerling, Jo, 125
Suffern, New York, 18, 117

Tagus Ranch, 55, 82, 97
Tao Te Ching, 30
Taylor, Charles Vincent, 105
Taylor, Frank J., 81, 82, 95
teachers, xvii, 68–72
teaching Steinbeck in the classroom, 68–72
Teaching Tolerance, 71
Their Blood Is Strong, 58
Thorsen, Deborah, 99
Thurber, James, 118
Tiffney, Wesley, Jr., 112
To a God Unknown, 2, 7, 8, 9, 27, 30, 31, 32, 41
Toffler, Alvin, ix
Toland, Gregg, 18
Tolstoy, Leo, xxiv, 33
Tortilla Flat, 9, 10, 11, 12, 14, 41, 46, 48, 74, 116, 121, 133–138, 146
Travels with Charley, 25, 62, 173–180, 186
Trenton, New Jersey, 96
Tronto, Joan, xxiii
Truman, Harry S., 189
Tulare County, California, 97
Turgenev, Ivan, 33
Twentieth Century-Fox, 16, 19, 125

United States Congress, 54, 78, 96, 111, 117, 191
United States Constitution, 88
University of Chicago, 105

Valenti, Jack, 190

Veggian, Henry, 160
Vendler, Helen, xxii
Viking Press, 19, 23
Viva Zapata!, 110–111, 131
Voice of America, 85
Voting Rights Act, 191

Wagner, Max, 16, 18
Wallace, Henry A., 54
Warren, Robert Penn, xv
Washington, D.C., 17, 173, 190
Washington Post, 98
The Wayward Bus, 101, 107, 128, 144–147, 165
"Weedpatch" (Arvin Camp), 14, 81
Welles, Orson, 117
Wells, H. G., 117
Welty, Eudora, xv
West, George, 58
Western Flyer, 102
Westfield, New Jersey, 63
Wheeler, Gregory A., 65
"The White Quail", 12, 39
Wilhelmson, Carl, 6
Winfrey, Oprah (book club), 160
Wilson, Edmund, 48, 63
The Winter of Our Discontent, 25, 62, 174, 177–178
Wolff, Nat, 43
Woolf, Virginia, xxiii, 141
World War II, 88, 104, 117–127, 139, 194
Worster, Donald, 78, 83

Zannuck, Darryl, 19, 111, 125
Zapata, Emiliano, xxv, 22, 110–111, 112, 161
Ziliak, Stephen, 99

ABOUT THE AUTHOR

Robert McParland is professor of English and associate dean at Felician College. He has published numerous book chapters and articles, including essays on Herman Melville, Ernest Hemingway, and Robert Penn Warren, among others. McParland is the editor of *Music and Literary Modernism* (2008) and *Film and Literary Modernism* (2013), as well as the author of *Charles Dickens's American Audience* (2010), *How to Write about Joseph Conrad* (2011), *Mark Twain's Audience: A Critical Analysis of Reader Responses to the Writings of Mark Twain* (2014), and *Beyond Gatsby: How Fitzgerald, Hemingway, and Writers of the 1920s Shaped American Culture* (2015).